# Embodied Reception

# The Study of Religion in a Global Context

**Series editors**

Satoko Fujiwara
Executive Editor
University of Tokyo

Katja Triplett
Series Editor
Leipzig University

Alexandra Grieser
Managing Editor
Trinity College Dublin

The series, published in collaboration with the International Association for the History of Religions, encourages work that is innovative in the study of religions, whether of an empirical, theoretical or methodological nature. This includes multi- or inter-disciplinary studies involving anthropology, philosophy, psychology, sociology and political studies. Volumes will examine the continuing influence of postcolonial, decolonial and intercultural dynamics, as well as contemporary responses from intersectional studies. They will also address the relevance and application of more recent approaches such as cognitivist, as well as ones concerned with aesthetic culture – art, architecture, media, performance and sound.

**Published**

***Global Phenomenologies of Religion***
*An Oral History in Interviews*
Edited by Satoko Fujiwara, David Thurfjel and Steven Engler

***Philosophy and the End of Sacrifice***
*Disengaging Ritual in Ancient India, Greece and Beyond*
Edited by Peter Jackson and Anna-Pya Sjödin

***Power and Agency in the Lives of Contemporary Tibetan Nuns***
*An Intersectional Study*
Mitra Härkönen

***Religion as Relation***
*Studying Religion in Context*
Edited by Peter Berger, Marjo Buitelaar and Kim Knibbe

***Researching Global Religious Landscapes***
*A Methodology between Universalism and Particularism*
Edited by Peter Nynäs, Ruth Illman, Nurit Novis-Deutsch and Rafael Fernández-Hart

***The Relational Dynamics of Enchantment and Sacralization***
*Changing the Terms of the Religion Versus Secularity Debate*
Edited by Peik Ingman, Terhi Utriainen, Tuija Hovi and Måns Broo

***Translocal Lives and Religion***
*Connections between Asia and Europe in the Late Modern World*
Edited by Philippe Bornet

# Embodied Reception

## South Asian Spiritualities in Contemporary Contexts

Edited by
Henriette Hanky, Knut A. Jacobsen,
and István Keul

equinox

SHEFFIELD UK BRISTOL CT

Published by Equinox Publishing Ltd.

UK: Office 415, The Workstation, 15 Paternoster Row, Sheffield, South Yorkshire S1 2BX

USA: ISD, 70 Enterprise Drive, Bristol, CT 06010

www.equinoxpub.com

First published 2024



British Library Cataloguing-in-Publication Data
A catalogue record for this book is available from the British Library.

ISBN-13 978 1 80050 353 3 (hardback)
978 1 80050 354 0 (paperback)
978 1 80050 355 7 (ePDF)
978 1 80050 614 5 (ePub)

Library of Congress Cataloging-in-Publication Data

Names: Hanky, Henriette, editor. | Jacobsen, Knut A., 1956- editor. | Keul, István, editor.
Title: Embodied reception : South Asian spiritualities in contemporary contexts / edited by Henriette Hanky, Knut A. Jacobsen, and István Keul.
Description: Sheffield, South Yorkshire ; Bristol, CT : Equinox Publishing Ltd., 2024. | Series: The study of religion in a global context | Includes bibliographical references and index. | Summary: "This volume investigates contemporary bodily practices as a mode of transmitting and receiving South Asian religious and spiritual traditions. The collection's essays explore processes of adoption and adaptation, and the ways in which somatic religious practices are transplanted into new contexts, acquiring new meanings and generating dynamics of their own"-- Provided by publisher.
Identifiers: LCCN 2024017380 (print) | LCCN 2024017381 (ebook) | ISBN 9781800503533 (hardback) | ISBN 9781800503540 (paperback) | ISBN 9781800503557 (ePDF) | ISBN 9781800506145 (ePub)
Subjects: LCSH: Human body--Religious aspects. | Identification (Religion) | Spirituality. | South Asia--Religion.
Classification: LCC BL65.B63 E43 2024 (print) | LCC BL65.B63 (ebook) | DDC 128/.60954—dc23/eng20240522
LC record available at https://lccn.loc.gov/2024017380
LC ebook record available at https://lccn.loc.gov/2024017381

Typeset by JS Typesetting Ltd, Porthcawl, Mid Glamorgan

# Contents

*List of Figures* vii
*Editors' Preface* viii

1 Introduction
*Henriette Hanky* 1

**Part I Theoretical and Methodological Considerations**

2 Training—Sensing—Predicting: Towards a Theory of the Reception of Practices as Embodied
*Anne Koch* 27

3 The Search for Rigor in Ethnographies of Bodily Practice
*Theo Wildcroft* 48

**Part II Performing Textual Traditions**

4 Transpersonal Therapy and a Tantric Temple: The *Parātrīśikā* in Western Practice
*István Keul* 71

5 Practicing the Yogasūtra? An Approach to the Analysis of Contemporary Yoga Philosophy's Somatic Aspects
*Laura von Ostrowski* 95

6 Lay Sāṃkhyayoga Practices in Contemporary India
*Knut A. Jacobsen* 118

**Part III Bodily Practices on the Move**

7 Embodied Receptions and the Creation of B.K.S. Iyengar's *Light on Prāṇāyāma*
*Suzanne Newcombe* 141

8 Between Patañjali and Psychology: Acem's "Classical, Meditative Yoga"
*Margrethe Løøv* 161

9 *Kaḷarippayaṟṟ*˘ in Performance: Adoptions and Adaptations of a South Indian Martial Art
*Lucy May Constantini* 181

**Part IV Embodied Meaning-Making**

10 Osho in a Nutshell? Dynamic Meditation and the Relationship between Bodily Performance and Meaning-Making
*Henriette Hanky* 201

11 "Being Here Fully": Autoethnographic Approaches to Mindfulness-Based Stress Reduction as an Embodied Group Interaction of an Authentic Self
*Alan Schink* 222

12 Moving Beyond the Mind through "Listening by Heart": The Role of Experience in Modern Advaitic Satsangs
*Elin Thorsén* 242

13 Aligning the Good and the Beautiful: Yogic Aesthetics in a Globalized World
*Amanda Lucia* 261

*Index* 281

# List of Figures


| | | |
|---|---|---|
| 1 | Statue of a human-like orange figure | 126 |
| 2 | The four sūtras painted on the wall in devanāgarī script underneath a human skull | 126 |
| 3 | Gathering of followers of Sāṃkhyayoga in Kāpil Maṭh, Madhupur | 129 |
| 4 | Annotated page of the draft manuscript of Light on Prāṇāyāma | 153 |
| 5 | Illustration of Dynamic Meditation’s five stages | 208 |

# Editors' Preface

This edited volume has grown from an online workshop hosted by the University of Bergen on 8–9 September 2021. We are grateful to Nicole Karapanagiotis and Michal Pagis who joined the workshop as respondents and gave insightful comments. We also thank Michael Stausberg for chairing one of the sessions and contributing to the discussions.

We are grateful to Katja Triplett and Alexandra Grieser, the editors of the IAHR series "The Study of Religion in a Global Context" at Equinox, for guiding the publication process and for valuable suggestions along the way. We thank Val Hall, Janet Joyce, and Sarah Lee at Equinox for their guidance during the publication process and Hamish Ironside for copy-editing the volume. We are also grateful to the anonymous reviewer for immensely helpful feedback and suggestions. Finally, we would like to thank our home institution, the Department of Archaeology, History, Cultural Studies and Religion at the University of Bergen, for providing such a conducive working environment for this project.

*Henriette Hanky, Knut A. Jacobsen, and István Keul*
*University of Bergen, Norway, June 2024*

-1-

# Introduction

HENRIETTE HANKY

Regarded as a source of self-knowledge, well-being, or spiritual insight, the body holds a central role in popular spiritual practices commonly labelled as "Eastern." Contemplative movement practices, particularly the myriad forms of modern postural yoga, meditation, and mindfulness techniques have become global trends. Scholars have observed an aestheticization (Da Silva Moreira 2018) or somatization of religion (Klinkhammer and Tolksdorf 2015) as well as a renewed interest in embodied practices in secular contexts such as the therapeutic sector (Pagis 2020). This spread correlates with an enormous diversification of how these practices are performed and which institutional frameworks and discourses they are embedded in.

This collection's chapters explore processes of adoption and adaptation and the ways in which somatic religious practices are transplanted into new contexts, acquiring new meanings, and generating dynamics of their own. The volume's contribution is twofold. First, the collection assembles a range of empirical cases: contemplative bodily techniques such as postural yoga, mindfulness, and meditation; ritual practices in modern advaitic satsang; South Indian martial arts; tantric goddess veneration; contemporary Sāṃkhyayoga practices. The empirical studies span devotional communities, yoga institutions, New Age milieus, and secularized contexts, providing a rich tapestry of contemporary embodied reception in and outside South Asia. Assembling research on embodied forms of reception both in South Asia and in Western countries, the volume advocates for paying close attention to entangled histories of knowledge.

Grounded in this empirical outlook, the volume secondly also speaks to theoretical and methodological debates on travelling bodily practices.

As Hauser (2018, 523) points out, "with regard to academic debates on global flows and interconnectedness, the human body and somatic processes as device in meaning production is heavily under-theorised." The contributions in this volume suggest theoretical and methodological frameworks ranging from the aesthetics of religion to the sociology of knowledge, from ethnographic to cognitive approaches.

Using the concept of "embodied reception" as a heuristic, we investigate contemporary bodily practices as a mode of receiving and adapting South Asian religious and spiritual traditions. The concept sensitizes for performative as well as discursive aspects of bodily practice. What traditions (if any) do people relate to when they move their bodies in particular ways? How do individual performance, shared forms and movement repertoires, and cultural contexts interrelate? The volume's contributions address the dialectic between a) incorporating (religious) knowledge by performing bodily practices and b) opening new avenues for (religious) meaning-making through bodily experiences.

This introductory chapter will first sketch out "embodied reception" as a heuristic concept by discussing some of the assumptions and challenges that its two terminological components—reception and embodiment—entail. It will then position the volume with regard to previous research on bodily practices in South Asia and their modern globalization. Two aspects of embodied reception that emerge from reading the contributions together will then receive closer attention. The first aspect is the *construction of lineages and origins* that appears to be crucial for turning bodily practices into a reception of something, be it a textual source, a guru, or a diffuse idea of Indian tradition. The second aspect concerns the *performativity and affectivity of bodily practices*. Here, the contributions show that while a bodily practice does not have a universal intrinsic meaning, it affects practitioners and interrelates with their meaning-making processes. Finally, the individual chapters that the four parts of the volume comprise will be presented.

## Embodied Reception: A Heuristic Approach to Travelling Bodily Practices

### Reception

The term "reception" is common in studies of modern, mostly Western adoptions of Asian religious thought and practice (see e.g., Cusack 2011) alongside concepts like transmission, appropriation, circulation, hybridization, or entanglement.[1] Referring to such processes as *reception* highlights an orientation toward, but also a certain deviation from an original: a creative adaptation or reinterpretation. This usage points to the term's conceptual background in disciplines concerned with the history and theory of text, literature, and other forms of art,[2] which is only partially transferable to the study of the global circulation of bodily practice.

In reception history, scholars look at how, for example, a religious text, the work of a certain author, genres or motifs are transmitted, interpreted, and adapted in new contexts. This interest has roots in hermeneutics and biblical exegesis (Roberts 2011) but is also connected to theoretical developments in literary studies from the 1960s onwards where scholars critically questioned the search for an author's intentions. Prominently, literary scholars Hans Robert Jauss and Wolfgang Iser put forward aesthetic reader-response theory (in German "Rezeptionsästhetik") and stressed the dialogical character of reading. Rather than assuming that meaning is inherent to a text, they proposed to look at how meaning is created in the act of reading (Iser 1976; Jauss 1982). While the literary work guides the act of reading through structure and stylistic devices, the reader plays an active part in realizing the text's potentialities by, for example, filling the gaps with their imagination. This thinking has also permeated the study of visual and performing arts, where scholars have studied art as an interconnected process between artwork and audience.[3] Not least fueled by the recent interest in new materialism and affect theory, these disciplines have paid particular attention to the role of corporeality in aesthetic experience (Manning 2012; Thomsen 2021).[4]

The notion of reception as it is used in the study of literature and art following Iser's and Jauss's influential work is useful in highlighting the dynamic reciprocal nature of engaging with cultural products. However, it needs to be adapted to fit the field of contemplative movement traditions and bodily religious practices. Bodily practices are fundamentally different from literary texts and other artworks. As I will unfold in the following section, bodies are not simply objects that can be read and decoded anew, but also the very medium through which humans act. Furthermore, the term reception presupposes an—at least relatively—stable and fixed object of reception. If contemporary practitioners are "doing reception," what is their practice a reception of? Are the different forms of yoga, meditation, or martial arts that we study in this volume,

3. Exemplarily for theatre see Bennett (1997).
4. The term "embodied reception" has been employed in sound (Ouzounian 2006) and film studies (Yamazaki 2018).

cultural products equivalent to Munch's "Scream" or Tchaikovsky's "Swan Lake"? Similarly, Beatrix Hauser asks in her study on travelling yoga: "What if the translocal circulation of bodily practices varies in its possibilities and dynamics of being appropriated, contextualized and modified from other cultural products that disseminate across national boundaries?" (Hauser 2018, 515).

As one component of global entangled histories of bodily practices, the concept of reception remains useful for highlighting the dynamics of turning these practices into cultural products, e.g., through branding, that will be discussed further on. Furthermore, investigating such processes as reception accentuates the receiver's side and the mediality of acquiring and adapting cultural knowledge. For investigating the specific modes of reception involved in performing South Asian bodily practices, adding the qualifier "embodied" acknowledges the central role that practitioners' bodies play and allows to make necessary theoretical and methodical adjustments.

## Embodiment

Addressed variously as "body turn," "corporeal turn," "somatic turn," or as part of the broader "material turn," a wave of attention to the body has swept through the humanities and social sciences since the 1990s. In the study of religions, Meredith McGuire asked programmatically: "What if people—the subjects of our research and theorizing—had material bodies?" (McGuire 1990, 283). McGuire and colleagues like anthropologist Thomas J. Csordas, argued for a paradigm shift in social and cultural analysis to bring attention to the body not only as a passive object of culture but as "the existential ground of culture" (Csordas 1993, 135).

While embodiment has become an axiomatic catchphrase in the humanities and social sciences, its consequences for research projects often remain unclear (see Koch, this volume). It is worthwhile for our purposes to revisit Csordas's paradigmatic work. At the core of Csordas's argument lies the differentiation of two perspectives on the body that he names "the semiotic/textual standpoint of representation" and "the phenomenological/embodiment standpoint as being-in-the-world" (Csordas 1993, 136). The first strand of theory ranges from symbolic and structuralist anthropology à la Mary Douglas and Claude Lévi-Strauss and the post-structuralist semiotics of Jacques Derrida to Michel Foucault. Despite their differences, these theorists share a sometimes explicit, sometimes implicit view of culture as text, and the body as a canvas. As the social is "inscribed in the body," researchers can "read the body" as a symbolic representation of culture (Csordas 1993, 136). The other strand of theory, that Csordas himself belongs to, is indebted to philosophical phenomenology, particularly the work of Maurice Merleau-Ponty and—notably for the social sciences—Alfred Schütz. Influenced by Edmund Husserl, these theorists argue that our perception of reality is conditioned by our corporeality. In this line of thinking, the body is not just a carrier of meaning but the point of departure for any meaning-making process. Following this latter understanding, Csordas argues that embodiment is more than the recognition that humans have bodies. Investigating embodiment requires a methodological shift.

Since the 1990s, embodiment approaches have proliferated,[5] and many scholars are on the task to develop adequate methodologies. Several of these are represented in this volume. Anne Koch presents her own and others' work in the interdisciplinary field of aesthetics of religion. Theo Wildcroft reflects on researchers' own embodied skillsets and their effect on data production in ethnographies of bodily practice. I will return to these recent advances in the last section of this introduction.

## Embodied Reception

With the concept of "embodied reception," this volume explores the body as a medium for receiving South Asian practices in various contemporary contexts. The authors investigate how practices change when they are embedded into different settings where they are not only shaped by specific discursive and material frameworks but also performed by different practitioner bodies.

Approaching reception processes as embodied can be connected to different lines of enquiry. Embodied reception can be studied in terms of diachronic historical processes of transfer and reception of bodily practices as well as the role that bodies and the senses play in the transmission of religious knowledge. This outlook builds on scholarship in the fields of material religion and aesthetics of religion that integrate the body and the senses into a history-of-religion framework (Morgan 2012; Plate 2014; Grieser and Johnston 2017a; Johannsen, Kirsch, and Kreinath 2020). The main argument here is that the history of religions does not amount to a history of ideas, but involves materiality and actors' living, breathing bodies. This reorientation towards bodies and materiality

5. See Koch (2012) for an overview and analysis of the "body boom" in humanities and social sciences from the 1980s onwards. For different approaches to the body and embodiment in sociology see Boero and Mason (2021) and Alkemeyer (2015), for anthropology see Mascia-Lees (2011).

makes visible historical dynamics related to gender, class, and ethnicity that had previously often been obscured. The call for a bodily or sensory history is also methodological as it requires moving past the textual paradigm that historically characterized the discipline.

In addition to and in conversation with historical approaches, embodied reception can also be investigated ethnographically and/or sociologically in studies on contemporary religious and spiritual practice. Here, embodied reception can be studied on a situational level, for example by analyzing how (religious) knowledge is received in bodily performance. Understanding reception as dynamic, this is not reduced to perception in a passive sense. In social constructivist terms, each performer partakes in the construction process (Berger and Luckmann 1966).[6] An empirical study of embodied reception sheds light on how a practitioner's individual and sociocultural embodiment as well as the specific social situation and context including spatial, temporal, and material aspects shape the way a certain practice is received—and possibly changed and re-interpreted.

These lines of enquiry connect well to work done in the study of religions around the term "body knowledge" or "embodied knowledge." This concept has been fruitfully introduced for studying bodily aspects of knowledge transfer in historical and contemporary settings (Koch 2007; Keller and Meuser 2011; Renger *et al.* 2016; Renger and Stellmacher 2018). Departing from an understanding of knowledge that includes not only "knowing that" but also "knowing how" (Ryle 1949), implicit or tacit dimensions (Polanyi 1966), Renger et al. address the challenges that lie in transmitting different forms of body knowledge. Knowledge *about* the body can be transmitted via textual and visual representations, as Newcombe shows regarding physiological knowledge in her chapter. Knowledge of the body, i.e., embodied knowledge, however, with its situatedness and subjective experiential side, is fleeting. As it evades complete fixation through language and is often approached through metaphors (Lakoff and Johnson 1980) or transmitted mimetically, the potential for creativity and change is particularly high (Renger *et al.* 2016, 18–19).

Embodied reception as a heuristic has been made fruitful in the contributions of this volume in at least three regards: First, for analyzing the specificities and challenges of transmitting bodily practices and embodied knowledge in religious and spiritual traditions. Second, for examining the body as a medium for relating to textual as well as material

6. For a refined theorization of this process that pays particular attention to the body see Knoblauch (2020).

sources from religious and spiritual traditions. And third, for reflecting the role of the researcher's body in ethnographies of bodily practice.

Theoretical and methodological development needs rich empirical material. One of the strengths of the study of religions is the attention to cultural nuance and detail, be it in the study of historical sources or ethnographic micro-contexts. This volume assembles a range of detailed empirical accounts of embodied reception. Some authors sharpen specific second-order theories of embodiment in light of their empirical cases, while others' contribution lies in carving out their research subjects' first-order conceptualizations of the body and bodily practice.

## Adoptions and Adaptations: South Asian Bodily Practices on the Move

The volume's contributions build on previous scholarship on South Asian religions, where the interest in the body and embodiment has brought about valuable research on images, theories, and categories of the body in different traditions. Examples include work on cosmological, physiological, and performative aspects of the devotional body in *bhakti* communities (Pechilis Prentiss 2000; Holdrege 2015; Dimitrova 2020), the yogic body (Singleton 2010), and the tantric body (Urban 2003; Keul 2012).

Scholars have pointed out "the limitations of applying Western theoretical models as the default epistemological framework for understanding notions of embodiment that derive from the 'Rest of the World,' and more specifically from premodern non-Western cultures," as Holdrege (2016, 2) phrases it. The question is if Western theories designed to overcome the Cartesian mind-body dualism are of much use when studying South Asian contexts that offer plenty of theories of the body of their own. In South Asian discourses, "ordinary modes of embodiment" coexist with "extraordinary forms of embodiment, which include divine bodies, absolute bodies, and transformed human bodies" (Holdrege 2016, 9). In many traditions, the material body is set up against a perfected form of embodiment that can be realized through transformational practice. Particularly the notion of "subtle bodies" has proved fruitful not only to understand body schemes in Hindu and Buddhist traditions (Pati and Zubko 2020; Johnston 2016, 2020) but also to "think with," as Jay Johnston (2020, 215) puts it. Subtle body concepts challenge established academic epistemologies and methodologies by calling for a "reconceptualization of a vast range of binaries, including the vexed issues of body–mind and matter–consciousness relations" (Johnston 2020, 215). Important work has also been done on how South Asian body concepts have been received and transformed in Theosophy (Johnston 2012, 2016), Western esotericism, and New Age thought (Leland 2016). The chapters by Suzanne Newcombe and Lucy May Constantini in this volume point not only to the challenges that lie in transmitting subtle body practices across cultures but also to the innovations that emerge when different cultural body maps are brought into conversation.

The performative aspects of body images and conceptualizations have particularly been addressed in the study of rituals (Hüsken 2011; Wenta 2018). While most studies focus on "how ritual shapes the body," the embodiment paradigm has increasingly led scholars to study "how the body shapes ritual" (Bell 2006, 538). Researchers have also applied the tools of the aesthetics of religion to South Asian religion (Wilke and Moebus 2011).

When it comes to the core interest of this volume, contemporary bodily techniques, the growing fields of yoga and contemplative studies stand for the bulk of previous research (Singleton 2010; Baier *et al.* 2018; Hauser 2013; Foxen and Kuberry 2021; Newcombe and O'Brien-Kop 2021b). Several of the authors in this volume have been part of building up this research field (Jacobsen, Newcombe, Wildcroft). Modern Yoga Studies scholars have been vital in historicizing modern yoga and showing that its current emphasis on *āsana*, postural practice, is a result of complex colonial and post-colonial developments in which South Asian contemplative traditions were blended with Western gymnastics and military culture (Singleton 2010).

An important task for scholarship is to investigate how these bodily practices are performed and understood in diverse and changing contemporary contexts (Hauser 2013; Prohl 2020). Rather than mapping expert discourses and textual traditions, one focus of this volume is on how everyday practitioners perform and interpret traditions, whether at home, in a temple, in a monastery, or in a gym.

This becomes even more acute given the changes that contemporary societies are undergoing. Not only academics have turned to the body in theoretical and methodical reformulations, but a new attention to the body has also characterized the religious field and late modern societies more broadly. Referred to as "somatization" (Klinkhammer and Tolksdorf 2015) or "aestheticization of religion" (Da Silva Moreira 2018), scholars observe a revival of sensual, experiential, and ecstatic forms of religion. The boom in yoga, meditation, alternative healing, and "embodied therapeutic culture" (Pagis 2020; Barcan and Johnston 2016) are as much examples of this process as the growth of Pentecostal congregations and their forms of worship all over the world. In addition to modern yoga communities (Wildcroft, Løøv, von Ostrowski), several of the authors look at popular experiential forms of practice such as satsang (Thorsén), Osho meditations (Hanky), and MBSR (Schink). While it is important to map broader trends and investigate them in small contexts, it is often communities and practices outside of mainstream trends that are particularly instructive research objects. Jacobsen's chapter on monastic Sāṃkhyayoga practices in Eastern India, for example, shows that modern yoga practice can also mean meditating on the frailty of the physical body rather than stretching it for longevity.

At the same time, societies are undergoing massive digitalization and mediatization that coincide with processes of "dematerialization" (Michaels and Wulf 2011, 5). Millions of practitioners turn to YouTube instead of their local yoga studio and imitate the shape of their yoga instructor's body reproduced on their screen. As Lucia discusses in her chapter, Instagrammers posting images of their "yoga bodies" are not only influential in popularizing yoga but also certain beauty and lifestyle ideals. Mediatization processes have transformed situations that formerly required co-presence into parasocial interaction or "synthetic situations" (Knorr Cetina 2014) such as Zoom sessions. By studying contemporary forms of practice in small contexts—face-to-face or online—researchers also gain insight into those larger processes of societal change and the shifting role of the body in these.

## Constructing Origins and Lineages

In Western societies, engaging with purportedly South Asian practices is often connected to holistic ideas of body and mind. The most popular practices tend to the body for therapeutic goals (healing, detox, stress relief), self-exploration, and growth. The labelling of practices such as yoga and meditation as South Asian is an important part of legitimizing these practices. However, as Newcombe and O'Brien-Kop point out, "[i]n many cases, a romanticised and highly selective skimming-off of South Asian cultures has been carried out by white yoga practitioners, to the detriment of engaging with these cultures as integral, living traditions" (Newcombe and O'Brien-Kop 2021a, 9). In her study on—mainly US-American—transformational festivals, Amanda Lucia argues that the predominantly white yogis, meditators, and psychonauts in these spaces "identify with alterity to forge personal solutions to the struggles of modernity," but "rarely engage with ethnically diverse populations" (Lucia 2020, 5). Despite their transformational orientation, such festivals remain "white utopias" (Lucia 2020).

While in the West contemplative practices are often appropriated in a language of universalism, Indian nationalist politicians are adamantly claiming them back in a form of "somatic nationalism" (Alter 1994). Not only have Bharatiya Janata Party (BJP) politicians declared them national property, but yoga and ayurveda have—in the guise of health intervention programs—also become tools for the Hinduization of India's multireligious population (Newcombe 2021; Longkumer 2018; Chakraborty 2006). These global dynamics between diffusion and universalization on the one hand, and the re-marking of national borders on the other (Knoblauch and Löw 2020), as well as debates around identity and cultural heritage, form the backdrop for most of the practices discussed in this volume. However, the empirical contexts investigated here differ strikingly in how topics of origin, heritage, and identity are addressed—or not addressed at all.

When a practitioner of modern postural yoga claims to practice an ancient Indian technique, scholars are aware of the practice's history of complex transcultural dynamics. Several researchers have mapped such transmission processes (Singleton 2010; Hauser 2013; Foxen and Kuberry 2021) and shown that in histories of spiritual practices, there is no single origin and no linear transmission. Instead, they demonstrate that knowledge travels in surprising ways and that transmission histories are complex and entangled. Still, in many of the cases presented in this volume, there are dynamics of institutionalization and canonization as well as attempts to stabilize and legitimize practices and ideas by constructing origins and authorities—thus making them a "reception of."

In South Asia, the transmission of knowledge—theoretical and practical—is often connected to guru-disciple relationships and passed down through guru lineages (*paramparā*). These lineage logics are still at play in many contemplative movement practices. However, the contemporary lineages studied in this volume are products of modernity. While they refer to pre-modern precursors, they are intimately connected to globalization and colonial and post-colonial dynamics as well as capitalist techniques of commodification and branding (Karapanagiotis 2021; Wildcroft 2020, 222; Sarbacker 2014, 108–110). Certified teacher training programs give legitimacy to instructors by connecting them to a tradition that is often traced back to a guru. Several such authoritative figures feature in the cases presented in this book: B.K.S. Iyengar, Maharishi Mahesh Yogi, Osho, or Jon Kabat-Zinn. However, as Suzanne Newcombe elaborates in her chapter, the construction of single authorship often conceals the many different contributors involved in cross-cultural processes of exchange and innovation. Today, many organizations in the field of contemplative movement practices exploit dynamics of neoliberal capitalism as well as intellectual property and corporate law to stabilize a technique or a system of movement and make it a product. But while a fixed repertoire of movements can be performed all over the world under the same name—say Iyengar yoga or OSHO Dynamic Meditation—, this does not mean that the practice will be the same in all regards (see Prohl 2020). Hauser argues: “Bodily practices from afar can be copied in mimetic and kinetic respects, yet they are likely to raise experiences configured by time and environment of the current practitioner rather than any intrinsic meaning” (2018, 516). Neither does it mean that the institutional marking as Iyengar or as Osho becomes meaningful to the practitioners.

The Osho meditation that I study in my chapter is made up of fragments from earlier traditions: a bit of *prāṇāyāma*, a bit of Sufi *dhikr*, and a bit of primal scream therapy. At the same time, it is trademarked and copyrighted, and Osho is stylized as the creator of a uniquely designed technique. It is this effort put into marking the technique as OSHO that makes performing the meditation a case of Osho reception. However, today, it is also performed in contexts where Osho as a person is of little or no importance. Referring to those meditators’ performance as a case of Osho reception would mean replicating the OSHO International Foundation’s claims of ownership and overriding practitioners’ own understandings.

As a countermovement to such constructions of authorship, new communities have emerged that explicitly reject positioning their practice in a guru lineage. Wildcroft (2020) investigated such forms of “post-lineage yoga” which gained currency not least following #MeToo debates and the disclosure of sexual and psychological abuse by yoga and meditation gurus. As Wildcroft shows, opposing lineages’ authority and orthopraxy often coincides with creatively configuring and adding to shared movement repertoires.

How the history of a practice, institutional, material, and discursive factors all play together in specific cases, is an empirical question. The contributions in this volume present different cases of how bodily practice becomes meaningful to practitioners. For example, in the case of secularized postural yoga (Løøv), practice is detached from religious notions and embedded into new frameworks, such as therapeutic discourses. In the case of the Indian monastic Sāṃkhyayoga community (Jacobsen), the daily ritual of meditative recitation of *stotras* that explicitly link them to premodern Sāṃkhya philosophy is the main form of yoga practice. In the German tantric temple (Keul), practitioners combine bodily performance with the thorough study of textual and material sources.

## Aisthesis, Affectivity, and Embodied Meaning-Making

In addition to varying institutional, material, and discursive frameworks of practice, it is also the practitioners' physical and social bodies that inform how a practice is made sense of (see Hauser 2018, 523). At the same time, as several authors in this volume show empirically, bodily practices themselves are affective and impact practitioners' meaning-making. While bodily practices do not determine how they are experienced, they *do* have effects, also beyond the practice situation (see Aschenbrenner and Ostrowski 2022).

Anne Koch notes in her chapter that "a special attractiveness, and notably, a specific effectiveness of the sensorial, comforting, or challenging embodiment of yoga as key for its reception is not commonly discussed, as the discourse lacks the respective theory" (Chapter 2, this volume, page 29). The interdisciplinary network developing the field of aesthetics of religion (Koch and Wilkens 2019; Grieser and Johnston 2017b; Johannsen *et al.* 2020) has been working to operationalize embodiment for research on religion. Aesthetics is understood in the sense of *aisthesis* defined as "the process of sentient sense perception that encompasses the entire sensoria, the actions that stimulate it, and how sensations are apprehended by subjects" (Baffelli *et al.* 2021, 423). Koch's and von Ostrowski's chapters demonstrate the productivity of an aesthetic approach, as it recognizes sensory perception and embodiment as efficacious factors in cultural reception.

In addition to, e.g., historical, philological, discourse theoretical, and ethnographic approaches, the aesthetics of religion also integrates cognitive and neuroscientific approaches. Contemplative practices such as Zen meditation had already been objects of interest in early work on "embodied cognition" (e.g., Varela *et al.* 1991), not least since many of these scholars were practitioners themselves (see Pagis 2020, 182). In the study of religions, such approaches have become institutionalized in some scholarly communities[7] and heavily debated in others.[8]

In phenomenologically informed sociology of religion, scholars also fruitfully analyze the role of the body in religious meaning-making and subjectivation processes. Daniel Winchester and Michal Pagis recently

7. For approaches in the cognitive science of religion (CSR) see McCorkle and Slone (2019) and the work of the Aarhus school, e.g., Geertz *et al.* (2022).
8. See McCutcheon's criticism of cognitive approaches (2010) and material religion (2013) as reintroducing *sui generis* religion through the back door. See also Smolka's metastudy on debates in the German aesthetics of religion working group (Smolka 2021).

examined the cultivation of specific sensory practices in religious communities as well as their role in constructing religious experiences (Winchester and Pagis 2022). In her micro-sociological study of Vipassana meditation, Pagis utilizes "a sociological framework for the study of the place of embodied awareness in processes of self-making" (Pagis 2019, 1). She shows how techniques of bodily based introspection make habitual parts of the self the subject of attention and in this way alter practitioners' subjectivity. Several chapters in this volume (Keul, Thorsén, Hanky, Schink) analyze such processes where bodily techniques facilitate experiences that are then interpreted in religious or spiritual language.

Taking seriously the affectivity of bodily practice while at the same time recognizing the contingency of bodily experience has consequences for methods of data production and analysis, as well as the role of the researcher. In Chapter 3, Theo Wildcroft raises important issues in this regard. While researching embodied practices calls for "doing religious studies with your whole body" (Orsi 2013), for "ethnography *from* the body" (Pagis 2019, 176; Csordas 1993) or "enactive ethnography" (Wacquant 2015), what data do we produce when we consider our own bodies as instruments? Wildcroft's suggestion to combine this type of immersive fieldwork with the tested tools of videography and post-practice interviews is a promising way to go.

Making researchers reflect on their own bodily socialization is crucial in such methodologies. Fruitful, if also challenging, debates arise from the fact that many scholars in the field of contemplative movement practices—represented also in this volume—are longstanding practitioners themselves (Singleton and Larios 2021). Wildcroft argues for yoga practitioners' embodied skillsets as a resource that allows them to see nuances in others' yoga practice that a non-practitioner would not. Many of the practices under scrutiny here involve not only easily observable movements but also subtle body practices that could easily be dismissed as invisible, and thus in the realm of imagination rather than action. However, as Constantini argues in her chapter, a practitioner might indeed be able to observe such subtle practices. It remains an important task for ethnographers to produce precise empirical accounts of such practices without reproducing field discourses while making transparent the embodied knowledge that allowed to generate them.

## The Contributions

Part I of this volume addresses theoretical and methodological questions regarding embodiment in empirical research on bodily practices in changing cultural contexts.

In Chapter 2, Anne Koch sets out to lay the ground for a reception theory that allows researchers to operationalize embodiment as a distinct factor in complex intercultural transmission processes. Koch advocates for the aesthetics of religion as a subdiscipline that bridges the natural and social sciences and cultural studies and grounds her approach epistemologically in a philosophy of mind informed by theories of predictive processing and embodied cognition. She presents "body knowledge" and "training knowledge" as connective concepts with subcategories such as body scheme and muscle tone. Koch demonstrates their application in empirical ethnographic research with case studies on bodily practices like dance and spirit incorporation. She shows that adding aesthetics to the study of historical subjectivities helps researchers to explain why certain movement practices travel more easily across cultures than others.

Theo Wildcroft (Chapter 3) reflects on her methodological choices while doing ethnographic work on post-lineage yoga. She presents a novel multi-method approach of co-practice, videography, post-practice interviews, and movement notation that allowed her to produce knowledge about individual yoga practice in intimate home settings. Wildcroft stresses the centrality of her own body as well as her respondents' bodies as sites and instruments of this methodological experimentation. Drawing on other forms of experiential research, she discusses the notion of the "expert mover" and her own embodied skillset as a yoga practitioner that proved crucial for her scholarly work. Wildcroft's work raises important questions on the effects of ethnographers' embodied positionalities when researching bodily practice.

In Part II, the authors explore how contemporary practitioners make sense of South Asian textual sources through their own bodily practice. István Keul (Chapter 4) introduces us to the life and work of the German therapist and tantric practitioner Ulrich Hennigs (1947–2010) that include a series of embodied reception processes. An unusually dedicated spiritual seeker, Hennigs not only translated the tantric text *Parātrīśikā* and its commentary by Abhinavagupta but used it as instruction for his own experiential practice. In a multi-layered narrative, Keul shows how Hennigs and his wife engaged the textual sources as well as the material spaces of ancient *yoginī* temples in India (and eventually in their own garden) through their bodily performances of meditation and ritualized sexuality. Following a further loop of transmission, Keul analyzes how Hennigs's tantric investigations were received and further psychologized by a group of German transpersonal therapy practitioners.

In Chapter 5, Laura von Ostrowski suggests approaching "contemporary yoga philosophy" (CYP) as a nexus of body practices and processes of worldview-building. Based on her own field research on Ashtanga yoga, she shows that the reception of the *Yogasūtra* is indeed embodied as it is fundamentally shaped by the exercises and experiences that form contemporary practitioners' "yoga bodies." For integrating biomedical and neurophysiological aspects of body–mind practices into cultural studies, von Ostrowski advocates for an aesthetics of religion approach and puts Anne Koch's body knowledge categories to work. Her analysis shows how bodily practice and late-modern readings of selected Indian sources become reciprocally effective. Von Ostrowski's findings point to how historical changes in yoga lineages and their interaction with other physical culture systems manifest in changing forms of body knowledge.

In Chapter 6, Knut A. Jacobsen presents a case of modern yoga that is utterly different from globalized postural yoga: the Bengali institution Kāpil Maṭh, founded by the Sāṃkhyayoga *saṃnyāsin* Hariharānanda Āraṇya (1869–1947). Jacobsen shows that Hariharānanda's teachings and practices derive from his reading of the *Yogasūtra/Pātañjalayogaśāstra,* which he understood in the historical framework of Sāṃkhya philosophy. As a result, the main lay practice at Kāpil Maṭh is not *āsanas*, but the recitation of *stotras* that repeat essential Sāṃkhyayoga teachings. Jacobsen contrasts Hariharānanda's revival of yoga, communicated in Bengali and Sanskrit for an educated Bengali audience, with early English-speaking global yoga. While the latter's entanglement with fitness and health culture led to an emphasis on *āsana* practice, practitioners at Kāpil Maṭh try to overcome the body by meditating on its eventual decay.

In Part III, the authors trace processes of transmission and adaptation when movement practices travel in and between South Asia and Europe. Suzanne Newcombe (Chapter 7) discusses embodied reception through a close reading of evidence connected to the publication of B.K.S. Iyengar's *Light on Prāṇāyāma* (1981). Newcombe's findings break with widespread assumptions of yoga teachings being transmitted in lineages of dyadic guru-disciple interaction. Far from being passed-on knowledge from Iyengar's guru Krishnamacharya, Newcombe shows that *Light on Prāṇāyāma* is an articulation of Iyengar's extensive embodied practice of interoception and self-study, legitimized through authoritative references to the Indic tradition. Newcombe's reading uncovers the dialogical process preceding publication that shows the constructedness of Iyengar's authorship. Not only does Iyengar's text bear traces of his dialogue with and observation of his famous students Krishnamurti and Yehudi Menuhin. It was also heavily revised in conversation with Iyengar's English editor Gerald Yorke and by the hidden labor of female student-practitioners of yoga. In the process, Iyengar's subtle body explorations were tested against Western practitioners' embodied knowledge and aligned with biomedical anatomy. Newcombe's study demonstrates the complications of transmitting embodied practice across cultures and the processes of adaptation, negotiation, and authorization that accompany it.

Margrethe Løøv (Chapter 8) investigates Acem School of Yoga's "classical, meditative yoga" both in terms of how Acem legitimizes the practice by linking it to Indian sources, and what their yoga looks like in performance. Acem originated as a Norwegian offshoot of Maharishi Mahesh Yogi's Transcendental Meditation movement and is best known for stripping TM off its Indian cultural as well as religious markers and embedding it instead in a secular, scientific framework. Løøv shows that while Acem similarly presents its yoga practice as devoid of unnecessary religious embellishment, they claim to transmit the essence of yoga in line with Patañjali's *Yogasūtra*. Examining early as well as contemporary Acem publications, Løøv shows that despite this attempt to anchor the practice in the Indian tradition, the organization's understanding of the body as a gateway to individual self-growth is mainly indebted to the counter-cultural currents of the 1970s, particularly humanistic psychology and existential philosophy.

In Chapter 9, Lucy May Constantini investigates the twentieth-century revival of the South Indian martial art *Kaḷarippayaṟṟ˘* and explores its imbrications with postmodern performing arts. Based on ethnographic and historical work, including performance and movement analysis, as well as her own long-term embodied experience as a dancer and *Kaḷarippayaṟṟ˘* practitioner, Constantini examines the challenges involved in translating a complex movement system rooted in tantric somatology and soteriology for contemporary contexts and bodies. Contemporary Indian artists have, on the one hand, adapted the movement repertoire as they moved it from the temple to the stage, favouring spectacular jumps over ritual details. But Constantini also shows that, on the other hand, it was precisely the subtle, internal qualities of the practice that accorded with postmodern artists' proclivity for somatic investigation.

Part IV of the volume assembles contributions that discuss how the bodily, performative aspects of practices are linked to religious as well as secular discourses and become meaningful to contemporary practitioners. Henriette Hanky (Chapter 10) looks at the case of OSHO Dynamic Meditation to investigate the relationship between contemporary meditation practice and the historical guru movement it has sprung out of. While OSHO Dynamic Meditation is a branded technique tied to the legacy of the controversial Indian guru Osho (Bhagwan Shree Rajneesh), she shows that the meditation is a mélange of different South Asian contemplative traditions as well as Western therapeutic practices. Drawing on ethnographic material from different Osho-related meditation centers, as well as sociological theory, Hanky demonstrates that practitioners' meaning-making is context-related and shaped by their interpretive communities. At the same time, Dynamic Meditation as a reflexively crafted technique has bodily effects that leave practitioners searching for meaning, and which Osho communities provide ample explanation for.

Based on his own experiences as a practitioner and trainer, Alan Schink (Chapter 11) explores the gradual process of inhabiting mindfulness concepts during 8-week Mindfulness-Based Stress Reduction (MBSR) programs. Schink analyzes how participants learn to embody the ideals of mindfulness practice through a combination of the disciplining course structure and behavioral rules as well as the interaction with the trainer and other group participants. He also demonstrates how he as an MBSR teacher has learnt to assess both the participants' progress as well as his own performance based on bodily cues. Reading his own and other people's bodies through the lens of the MBSR framework, specific bodily features such as facial muscle tone or vocal timbre become markers of an "authentic self." Schink's chapter shows how embodying mindfulness thus functions both as the communicative means of and the goal of MBSR practice.

Elin Thorsén (Chapter 12) ethnographically explores the transnational satsang scene that annually gathers in the North Indian town of Rishikesh. She analyzes how Modern Advaita teachings are transmitted during the satsang events where Western transnational guru figures come together with spiritual adepts. Her analysis starts from the observation that while these events evolve around verbal discourse, the goal is not for nondual tenets to be understood but to be realized and embodied. Thorsén shows how the interplay of physical proximity to the guru, communitas between participants, and the rhetoric structure of the discourses creates a social situation conducive to creating feelings of oneness and a nondual sense of self. She argues that the valorization of personal experience is both an expression of Advaita teachings and late-modern "self-spirituality."

Finally, in Chapter 13, Amanda Lucia analyzes the body ideals that permeate Western postural yoga both at physical gatherings and online. Based on her ethnographic fieldwork at transformational festivals and netnographic research on participants' social media presences, she carves out the dominant ideal of the yogic body as it is reproduced by celebrity yoga teachers and Instagram yogis: It conforms to Western beauty standards and is thin, lithe, female, and white. Lucia demonstrates that physical beauty is dealt with in the yoga scene as indexical of moral goodness. This interconnection disciplines yoga practitioners as they aspire to conform to the ideal and perfect their selves and bodies. Lucia shows how powerful this "economy of desire" is as she analyzes her own body dysphoria during fieldwork at yoga festivals. While supporting demands for inclusivity and body positivity in the yoga world, she questions the packaging of these initiatives as "decolonizing." Presenting sources from Hindu, Buddhist, and Jain traditions, Lucia shows that the good and the beautiful have been portrayed as mutually indexical in South Asia for the last 1000 years.

Together, the contributions in this collection underline the central role that embodiment plays in entangled global histories of knowledge. Analyzing the adaptations of bodily practices as they are performed by different practitioner bodies, we learn about histories of transmission as well as the conditions that shape late modern practitioners' embodied subjectivities.

## Acknowledgments

I am grateful to the other contributors, particularly the co-editors István Keul and Knut A. Jacobsen, for their insights and suggestions that helped this introduction take shape. The chapter benefited further from the anonymous reviewer's comments as well as conversations with Jan Ole Bangen, Anna Matter, Gerrit Lange, and Anne Koch.

**Henriette Hanky** is a doctoral candidate and university lecturer in the Study of Religions at the University of Bergen, Norway. Her doctoral research focused on contemporary forms of the Osho/Sannyas movement in Europe and India. She has published articles on Osho-related meditation retreats, new religious movements and mediatization as well as on religion and embodiment.

## References

Alkemeyer, Thomas. 2015. "Verkörperte Soziologie—Soziologie der Verkörperung: Ordnungsbildung als Körper-Praxis." *Soziologische Revue* 38(4): 470–502.

Alter, Joseph S. 1994. "Somatic Nationalism: Indian Wrestling and Militant Hinduism." *Modern Asian Studies* 28(3): 557–588.

Aschenbrenner, Lina and Laura von Ostrowski. 2022. "Embodied Neo-Spirituality as an Experience Filter: From Dance and Movement Practice to Contemporary Yoga." *Body and Religion* 5(2): 160–184. https://doi.org/10.1558/bar.20526.

Baffelli, Erica, Jane Caple, Levi McLaughlin and Frederik Schröer. 2021. "The Aesthetics and Emotions of Religious Belonging: Examples from the Buddhist World." *Numen* 68(5–6): 421–435. https://doi.org/10.1163/15685276-12341634.

Baier, Karl, Philipp André Maas and Karin Preisendanz, eds. 2018. *Yoga in Transformation: Historical and Contemporary Perspectives.* Göttingen: V&R Unipress.

Barcan, Ruth and Jay Johnston. 2016. "Fixing the Self: Alternative Therapies and Spiritual Logics." In *Mediating Faiths: Religion and Socio-Cultural Change in the Twenty-First Century*, edited by Guy Redden and Michael Bailey, 91–104. London: Routledge.

Bell, Catherine. 2006. "Embodiment." In *Theorizing Rituals: Issues, Topics, Approaches, Concepts*, edited by Jens Kreinath, Jan Snoek and Michael Stausberg, 533–543. Leiden: Brill.

Bennett, Susan. 1997. *Theatre Audiences: A Theory of Production and Reception.* Abingdon: Routledge.

Berger, Peter L. and Thomas Luckmann. 1966. *The Social Construction of Reality: A Treatise in the Sociology of Knowledge.* Garden City, NY: Anchor Books.

Boero, Natalie and Katherine Mason, eds. 2021. *The Oxford Handbook of the Sociology of Body and Embodiment.* New York: Oxford University Press.

Borkataky-Varma, Sravana. 2021. "The Yogic Body in Global Transmission." In *Routledge Handbook of Yoga and Meditation Studies*, edited by Suzanne Newcombe and Karen O'Brien-Kop, 366–379. Abingdon: Routledge.

Borup, Jørn and Marianne Qvortrup Fibiger, eds. 2017. *Eastspirit: Transnational Spirituality and Religious Circulation in East and West.* Leiden: Brill.

Chakraborty, Chandrima. 2006. "Ramdev and Somatic Nationalism: Embodying the Nation, Desiring the Global." *Economic and Political Weekly* 41(5): 387–390.

Csordas, Thomas J. 1993. "Somatic Modes of Attention." *Cultural Anthropology* 8(2): 135–156.

Cuffel, Alexandra, Licia Di Giacinto and Volkhard Krech. 2019. "Senses, Religion, and Religious Encounter." *Entangled Religions* 10. https://doi.org/10.13154/er.10.2019.8407.

Cusack, Carole M. 2011. "The Western Reception of Buddhism: Celebrity and Popular Cultural Media as Agents of Familiarisation." *Journal for the Academic Study of Religion* 24(3): 297–316. https://doi.org/10.1558/jasr.v24i3.297.

Da Silva Moreira, Alberto. 2018. "The Aestheticization of Religion in Brazil (and Probably Elsewhere)." *International Journal of Latin American Religions* 2(1): 125–141. https://doi.org/10.1007/s41603-018-0036-7.

Dimitrova, Diana. 2020. "Devotional Bodies and Embodied Devotion: Yoga, Bhakti, and Pilgrimage in the Radhasoami Tradition." In *Rethinking the Body in South Asian Traditions*, edited by Diana Dimitrova, 69–83. London: Routledge.

Foxen, Anya P. and Christa Kuberry. 2021. *Is This Yoga? Concepts, Histories, and the Complexities of Modern Practice.* Abingdon: Routledge.

Geertz, Armin W., Leonardo Ambasciano, Esther Eidinow, Luther H. Martin, Kristoffer L. Nielbo, Nickolas P. Roubekas, Valerie van Mulukom and Dimitris Xygalatas, eds. 2022. *Studying the Religious Mind: Methodology in the Cognitive Science of Religion.* Sheffield: Equinox.

Grieser, Alexandra K. and Jay Johnston. 2017a. "What Is an Aesthetics of Religion? From the Senses to Meaning—And Back Again." In *Aesthetics of Religion: A Connective Concept*, edited by Alexandra K. Grieser and Jay Johnston, 1–50. Berlin: De Gruyter.

Grieser, Alexandra K. and Jay Johnston, eds. 2017b. *Aesthetics of Religion: A Connective Concept.* Berlin: De Gruyter.

Hauser, Beatrix, ed. 2013. *Yoga Traveling: Bodily Practice in Transcultural Perspective.* Cham: Springer.

——. 2018. "Following the Transcultural Circulation of Bodily Practices: Modern Yoga and the Corporeality of Mantras." In *Yoga in Transformation: Historical and Contemporary Perspectives*, edited by Karl Baier, Philipp A. Maas and Karin Preisendanz, 507–528. Göttingen: V&R Unipress.

Holdrege, Barbara A. 2015. *Bhakti and Embodiment: Fashioning Divine Bodies and Devotional Bodies in Kṛṣṇa Bhakti.* London: Routledge.

——. 2016. "Introduction: Body Matters in South Asia." In *Refiguring the Body: Embodiment in South Asian Religions*, edited by Barbara A. Holdrege and Karen Pechilis, 1–13. Albany, NY: SUNY Press.

Hüsken, Ute. 2011. "Ritual Competence as Embodied Knowledge." In *Images of the Body in India: South Asian and European Perspectives on Rituals and Performativity*, edited by Axel Michaels and Christoph Wulf, 193–213. New Delhi: Routledge.

Iser, Wolfgang. 1976. *Der Akt des Lesens: Theorie ästhetischer Wirkung.* Munich: Fink.

Jauss, Hans Robert. 1982. *Toward an Aesthetic of Reception*. Minneapolis, MN: University of Minnesota Press.

Johannsen, Dirk, Anja Kirsch and Jens Kreinath. 2020. *Narrative Cultures and the Aesthetics of Religion*. Leiden: Brill.

Johnston, Jay. 2012. "Theosophical Bodies: Colour, Shape and Emotion from Modern Aesthetics to Healing Therapies." In *Handbook of New Religions and Cultural Production*, edited by Carole Cusack and Alex Norman, 153–170. Leiden: Brill.

——. 2016. *Angels of Desire: Esoteric Bodies, Aesthetics and Ethics*. Sheffield: Taylor & Francis.

——. 2020. "Frisky Methods: Subtle Bodies, Epistemological Pluralism and Creative Scholarship." In *Transformational Embodiment in Asian Religions: Subtle Bodies, Spatial Bodies*, edited by George Pati and Katherine C. Zubko, 206–218. Abingdon: Routledge.

Karapanagiotis, Nicole. 2021. *Branding Bhakti: Krishna Consciousness and the Make-over of a Movement*. Bloomington, IN: Indiana University Press.

Keller, Reiner and Michael Meuser, eds. 2011. *Körperwissen*. Wiesbaden: VS Verlag für Sozialwissenschaften.

Keul, István, ed. 2012. *Transformations and Transfer of Tantra in Asia and Beyond*. Berlin: De Gruyter.

Klinkhammer, Gritt and Eva Tolksdorf, eds. 2015. *Somatisierung des Religiösen: Empirische Studien zum rezenten religiösen Heilungs- und Therapiemarkt*. Bremen: Universität Bremen.

Knoblauch, Hubert. 2020. *The Communicative Construction of Reality*. London: Routledge.

Knoblauch, Hubert and Martina Löw. 2020. "The Re-Figuration of Spaces and Refigured Modernity: Concept and Diagnosis." Historical Social Research 45(2): 263–292. https://doi.org/10.12759/HSR.45.2020.2.263-292.

Knorr Cetina, Karin. 2014. "Scopic Media and Global Coordination: The Mediatization of Face-to-Face Encounters." In *Mediatization of Communication*, edited by Knut Lundby, 39–62. Berlin: De Gruyter.

Koch, Anne. 2007. "Körperwissen: Grundlegung einer Religionsaisthetik." Habilitationsschrift, Ludwig-Maximilians-Universität München.

——. 2012. "Reasons for the Boom of Body Discourses in the Humanities and the Social Sciences since the 1980s: A Chapter in European History of Religion." In *Menschenbilder und Körperkonzepte im Alten Israel, in Ägypten und im Alten Orient*, edited by Angelika Berlejung, Jan Dietrich and Joachim F. Quack, 3–42. Tübingen: Mohr Siebeck.

Koch, Anne and Katharina Wilkens, eds. 2019. *The Bloomsbury Handbook of the Cultural and Cognitive Aesthetics of Religion.* London: Bloomsbury.

Lakoff, George and Mark Johnson. 1980. *Metaphors We Live by.* Chicago, IL: University of Chicago Press.

Leland, Kurt. 2016. *Rainbow Body: A History of the Western Chakra System from Blavatsky to Brennan.* Lake Worth, FL: Ibis Press.

Longkumer, Arkotong. 2018. "'Nagas Can't Sit Lotus Style': Baba Ramdev, Patañjali, and Neo-Hindutva." *Contemporary South Asia* 26(4): 400–420. https://doi.org/10.1080/09584935.2018.1545008.

Lucia, Amanda J. 2020. *White Utopias: The Religious Exoticism of Transformational Festivals.* Oakland, CA: University of California Press.

Manning, Erin. 2012. *Relationscapes: Movement, Art, Philosophy.* Cambridge, MA: MIT Press.

Mascia-Lees, Frances E., ed. 2011. *A Companion to the Anthropology of the Body and Embodiment.* New York: John Wiley & Sons.

McCorkle, William W. and D. Jason Slone, eds. 2019. *The Cognitive Science of Religion: A Methodological Introduction to Key Empirical Studies.* London: Bloomsbury.

McCutcheon, Russell T. 2010. "Will Your Cognitive Anchor Hold in the Storms of Culture?" *Journal of the American Academy of Religion* 78(4): 1182–1193.

——. 2013. "A Modest Proposal on Method." *Method & Theory in the Study of Religion* 25(4/5): 339–349.

McGuire, Meredith B. 1990. "Religion and the Body: Rematerializing the Human Body in the Social Sciences of Religion." *Journal for the Scientific Study of Religion* 29(3): 283–296. https://doi.org/10.2307/1386459.

Michaels, Axel and Christoph Wulf. 2011. "Rethinking the Body: An Introduction." In *Images of the Body in India: South Asian and European Perspectives on Rituals and Performativity,* edited by Axel Michaels and Christoph Wulf, 1–16. New Delhi: Routledge.

Morgan, David. 2012. *The Embodied Eye: Religious Visual Culture and the Social Life of Feeling.* Berkeley, CA: University of California Press.

Nair-Venugopal, Shanta, ed. 2012. *The Gaze of the West and Framings of the East.* London: Palgrave Macmillan.

Newcombe, Suzanne. 2021. "Yoga and Meditation as a Health Intervention." In *Routledge Handbook of Yoga and Meditation Studies,* edited by Suzanne Newcombe and Karen O'Brien-Kop, 156–168. London: Routledge.

Newcombe, Suzanne and Karen O'Brien-Kop. 2021a. "Reframing Yoga and Meditation Studies." In *Routledge Handbook of Yoga and Meditation Studies,* edited by Suzanne Newcombe and Karen O'Brien-Kop, 3–12. London: Routledge.

——, eds. 2021b. *Routledge Handbook of Yoga and Meditation Studies.* London: Routledge.

Orsi, Robert A. 2013. "Doing Religious Studies with Your Whole Body." *Practical Matters Journal* Spring (2): 1–6. http://practicalmattersjournal.org/?p=908.

Ouzounian, Gascia. 2006. "Embodied Sound: Aural Architectures and the Body." *Contemporary Music Review* 25(1–2): 69–79. https://doi.org/10.1080/07494460600647469.

Pagis, Michal. 2019. *Inward: Vipassana Meditation and the Embodiment of the Self.* Chicago, IL: University of Chicago Press.

——. 2020. "Embodied Therapeutic Culture." In *The Routledge International Handbook of Global Therapeutic Cultures,* edited by Daniel Nehring, Ole J. Madsen, Edgar Cabanas, China Mills and Dylan Kerrigan, 177–190. Abingdon: Routledge.

Pati, George and Katherine C. Zubko, eds. 2020. *Transformational Embodiment in Asian Religions: Subtle Bodies, Spatial Bodies.* Abingdon: Routledge.

Pechilis Prentiss, Karen. 2000. *The Embodiment of Bhakti.* New York: Oxford University Press.

Plate, S. Brent. 2014. *A History of Religion in 5 1/2 Objects: Bringing the Spiritual to Its Senses.* Boston, MA: Beacon Press.

Polanyi, Michael. 1966. *The Tacit Dimension.* Chicago, IL: University of Chicago Press.

Prohl, Inken. 2017. "Same Forms, Same Sensations? The Practice of Sitting Still in Traditional Japanese and Contemporary Urban Settings." In *Eastspirit: Transnational Spirituality and Religious Circulation in East and West,* edited by Jørn Borup and Marianne Qvortrup Fibiger, 100–119. Leiden: Brill.

Renger, Almut-Barbara and Alexandra Stellmacher, eds. 2018. *Übungswissen in Religion und Philosophie: Produktion, Weitergabe, Wandel.* Berlin: Lit.

Renger, Almut-Barbara, Christoph Wulf, Jan Ole Bangen and Henriette Hanky. 2016. "Körperwissen: Transfer und Innovation." *Paragrana* 25(1): 13–19. https://doi.org/10.1515/para-2016-0022.

Roberts, Jonathan. 2011. "Introduction." In *The Oxford Handbook of the Reception History of the Bible,* edited by Michael Lieb, Emma Mason, Jonathan Roberts and Christopher Rowland. Oxford: Oxford University Press.

Ryle, Gilbert. 1949. *The Concept of Mind.* London: Hutchinson's University Library.

Sarbacker, Stuart Ray. 2014. "Reclaiming the Spirit Through the Body: The Nascent Spirituality of Modern Postural Yoga." *Entangled Religions* 1: 95–114. https://doi.org/10.46586/er.v1.2014.95-114.

Singleton, Mark. 2010. *Yoga Body: The Origins of Modern Posture Practice.* Oxford: Oxford University Press.

Singleton, Mark and Borayin Larios. 2021. "The Scholar-Practitioner of Yoga in the Western Academy." In *Routledge Handbook of Yoga and Meditation Studies*, edited by Suzanne Newcombe and Karen O'Brien-Kop, 37–50. London: Routledge.

Smolka, Mareike. 2021. "Why Does Controversy Persist? Paradigm Clash, Conflicting Visions, and Academic Productivity in the Aesthetics of Religion." *Science as Culture* 30(4): 465–490. https://doi.org/10.1080/09505431.2021.1918077.

Thomsen, Bodil M. S., Jette Kofoed and Jonas Fritsch, eds. 2021. *Affects, Interfaces, Events.* Lancaster: Imbricate! Press.

Urban, Hugh B. 2003. *Tantra: Sex, Secrecy, Politics, and Power in the Study of Religion.* Berkeley, CA: University of California Press.

Varela, Francisco J., Evan Thompson and Eleanor Rosch. 1991. *The Embodied Mind: Cognitive Science and Human Experience*. Cambridge, MA: MIT Press.

Wacquant, Loïc. 2015. "For a Sociology of Flesh and Blood." *Qualitative Sociology* 38: 1–11. https://doi.org/10.1007/s11133-014-9291-y.

Wenta, Aleksandra. 2018. "Becoming the Dancer: Dissolving the Boundaries Between Ritual, Cognition, and Theatrical Performance in Non-Dual Śaivism." *Cracow Indological Studies* 20(1): 259–295. https://doi.org/10.12797/CIS.20.2018.01.10.

Wildcroft, Theodora. 2020. *Post-Lineage Yoga: From Guru to #MeToo.* Sheffield: Equinox.

Wilke, Annette and Oliver Moebus. 2011. *Sound and Communication: An Aesthetic Cultural History of Sanskrit Hinduism.* Berlin: De Gruyter.

Willis, Ika. 2018. *Reception.* London: Routledge.

Winchester, Daniel and Michal Pagis. 2022. "Sensing the Sacred: Religious Experience, Somatic Inversions, and the Religious Education of Attention." *Sociology of Religion* 83(1): 12–35. https://doi.org/10.1093/socrel/srab004.

Yamazaki, Junko. 2018. "Embedded Film, Embodied Reception: Tsurumi Shunsuke's Autobiographical Film Criticism." *Journal of Japanese and Korean Cinema* 10(2): 130–146. https://doi.org/10.1080/17564905.2018.1517711.

# Part I

# THEORETICAL AND METHODOLOGICAL CONSIDERATIONS

-2-

# Training—Sensing—Predicting

## Towards a Theory of the Reception of Practices as Embodied

ANNE KOCH

Since the cultural turn, the embodiment of practices is an axiom. But what does "embodiment" mean? And how can embodied knowledge, embodied practices, and embodied reception be operationalized and related to specific contexts instead of just claiming embodiment as a matter of fact? What difference does an account of the embodiment of practices make regarding theoretical stances that take other dimensions into account, like semiotics or power structures? We will sketch the relevance of the philosophy of mind for embodiment because embodiment touches the very base of science: epistemology and the conception of the subject/agent. Against this backdrop, body knowledge and training knowledge will be introduced, which prepares us for a bundle of further subcategories appropriate for analyzing the dynamics of cultural reception, especially of embodied practices.

Keywords: embodiment, body knowledge, training knowledge, cultural transfer, predictive mind, aesthetics of religion

## Introduction: Synthesis of Parameters for Reception

Since the cultural turn, it is a fundamental axiom that practices are embodied. Most scholars are convinced that the embodiment of practices plays an important—if not crucial—role in their reception and in whether a belief and practice system is likely to successfully spread over societal subsystems, just as it does across cultures. But how can we be sure about this key role of the attractiveness of embodied practice within a specific historical context? And what are the multiple ways in which an embodied practice might appeal to recipients, especially given that recipients vary greatly in taste, social distinction, body conditions, cultural body socialization, and financial means to invest in a new body style? To answer these questions that are so vital for a theory of reception, we must be able to separate the parameters of this "reception." One challenge involved in such an approach is isolating the embodied quality in order to measure its impact as an autonomous factor. Even if this will often not be feasible in a strict sense, insofar as practices are always related within dense cultural communication, one might come to meaningful hypotheses and a sharpened awareness of and vocabulary for the sensorial and embodied aspects of practices. So, the question takes the direction of how embodied knowledge can be operationalized instead of just claiming it as a matter of fact.

Towards this aim, we start with broader cultural configurations since it is their entanglement with one another that makes practices significant. We know from countless examples of historical research[1] that cultural reception is a dense, multilayered, and interdependent process that sometimes resembles an invention more than a reception in the sense that elements are only "received" and moderately modified. A good example for such a multi-layered process is what modern yoga studies have to say about the reception of yoga. During this process of "reception" in the late nineteenth century until the 1920s, practices became enriched with bodily elements from North American culture. This took place following the World Parliament of Religions in Chicago in 1893 when Swami Vivekananda promoted *raja yoga* that lacks postural serial practice. Several elements of the then newly invented yoga were derived from so-called "relaxationism," with forerunners in esotericism, Mesmerism, and psychology. At this time, the physician Edmund Jacobson, with his progressive and differential muscle relaxation, and the therapist and protagonist of "harmonial relaxation," Annie Payson Call, were influential. Payson Call especially emphasized proprioceptive awareness and stretching coordinated with breathing (Singleton 2005).

This cultural configuration changes when compared with the cultural configuration of yoga reception in Britain from around 1900 until the 1980s. Suzanne Newcombe (2019) unfurls multiple contexts ranging

1. See e.g., *Entangled Religions. Interdisciplinary Journal for the Study of Religious Contact and Transfer* (https://er.ceres.rub.de/) with a special issue on "Senses, Religion, and Religious Encounter" (Cuffel *et al.* 2019). This work unfortunately ignores the aesthetics of religion, only citing older classics of the field.

from an already widespread physical culture movement in Britain to the state's interest in physical health prevention, occurring alongside the state's subsidization of the infrastructure of local adult education units. She also highlights the role of publishing houses with new book series on Buddhism and Hinduism, bookstores specialized in magic, occultism, and esotericism, and, finally, the charisma and life work of yoga personalities as part of the advent of this new moving style in Europe. Also, a new conceptual ordering of the subfields of the religious and the secular, exclusive to each other and then bridged by the spiritual, develops more intensely with the reception of what was regarded as Hindu practices (Vollmer 2021). Along those lines, a special attractiveness and, notably, a specific effectiveness of the sensorial, comforting, or challenging embodiment of yoga as key for its reception is not commonly discussed, as the discourse lacks the respective theory. All this is important historical work that touches on reasons why body practice changed so dramatically in the late nineteenth century in Europe and North America. This aesthetic theoretical analysis is aggravated by the fact that the body became so meaningful for healing and salvation with the arrival of new body therapies and holistic approaches in the history of religion and culture from the 1960s on.

Nevertheless, there is an urgent need to analyze embodied practices and to further singularize and separate the embodied factor from this entanglement to better evaluate its impact as an autonomous factor. This blank space confronts us with demanding theoretical and methodological challenges. For example: Can we say that the body of "Westerners" was an agent in the process in the sense that it was the body of stressed North American employees at early industrial plants who chose these new relaxationist techniques? Was it perhaps an implicit bodily experience that makes the coordination of moving and breathing more effective for relaxation, as Mark Singleton considers it? Or is it more the expression of thriving for intense feelings? Or is it mainly colonial or postcolonial power plays with sometimes orientalist, sometimes Western desires? What would count as an argument for answering these questions: subjective feelings, medical facts, or culturally dense descriptions? What makes it demanding is that all this must be considered. Cultural reasons and the intended and unintended effects of historical developments must be connected to accomplish the task.

My position here is very clear: I propose an epistemology for the aesthetics of religion to lay the groundwork for this subdiscipline, departing from epistemology (Koch 2019) in general and philosophy of mind to develop a respective intercultural reception theory. Part of this task is the proposal of categories as connective concepts between the natural and social sciences and cultural studies. One such concept is "body knowledge"; another one is "training knowledge". They will be introduced and detailed into subcategories that serve as analytical tools for embodied cognition. Following this, case studies in which several scholars took on these categories and elaborated new subcategories to describe the reception of embodied practices will be explored. The chapter will end with three conclusions.

## Philosophy of Mind: Predictive Processing and Embodied Cognition

I argued in the past for the need for the most advanced knowledge from the natural sciences on the body and on the processing of neural information and human perception as an essential dimension of understanding practices. We need "entangled interdisciplinary" work (Fitzgerald and Callard 2015)—not nice-to-have interdisciplinary work—as part of the groundwork for basic categories of embodiment. Note that it is not only the brain but also the body and behavior that I am talking about, with the central nervous system as well as the enteric nervous system enervating inner organs and afferent sensory information. Therefore, I have cooperated for years with colleagues from neurology and medical psychology at Munich University, with my colleague from medical psychology, specializing in placebo research—notably on spiritual healing, to gain empirical data for a better understanding of the involvement of bodies. Much of this work and contesting approaches are grouped together and discussed in the philosophy of mind, especially in theories of embodied cognition, the social mind, and, recently, popular predictive processing.

### Predictive Processing

Predictive processing (PP) is a computational theory of mind.[2] Nevertheless, there are many ideas on how these operations could also be expressed neurologically, that is how PP is congruent with neuroscientific findings and models. Essentially, PP regards the mind as a probability generator. The overall goal is action orientation and to minimize

2. A general problem arises from predictive mind theory about action theoretical explanations of motivations: Are actions to minimize social uncertainty, as in PP, or can people be driven by desire and value orientation (see Colombo 2017)?

errors in prediction, as these would eventually destabilize the organism or even endanger its life when it miscalculates a situation. This action orientation implicitly sets an environmental adaptation—the natural as well as social environment—as the task to be solved by organisms. Therefore, this theory is action-oriented and situational—converging in this way with early sociological theories. Put in a very basic way, mostly subconscious models are built from sensory inputs that serve, first, as predictive models for further comparable situations. So, from the beginning, evaluation and sensorial links are inseparable. On the base of these basic models, event models are formed in memory and consolidate or become corrected over the course of ongoing experiences. Event models limit awareness of features that support or saliently and overtly contradict the prediction. Based on this background, the philosophers Wanja Wiese and Thomas Metzinger suggest that we "hallucinate" our world insofar as it is according to our expectations (2017, 3).

In the context of the study of religion, PP is used within the cognitive study of religion at the Aarhus Interacting Minds Centre for topics such as charisma, ritual, magic, and social cognition, by Dirk Johannsen and Anja Kirsch (2019) for narrative cultures, and by Ann Taves (2015) and Egil Asprem (Taves and Asprem 2017) for a variant of event cognition and reverse engineering.

## Embodied Cognition

For sure, embodiment is part of the cultural turn in anthropology, sociology, and cultural studies. An often-named protagonist in the tradition of the phenomenology of the body, for example, is Thomas Csordas who, in his case studies of charismatic healing, investigated embodied modes of attention to unfold how they bring about mental states of absence in glossolalia. Also, the praxeological account of Pierre Bourdieu (2001, 185) fosters a closer look at embodiment, while he, nevertheless, stated that the task of really describing the body aspect in practices remains. Recently, Margret Wilson's repeatedly cited six cognitive studies' criteria for embodiment (2002) have been transposed to mostly consensual axioms of PP to bring precision to the debate (Hommel 2015).

Embodied cognition departs from the basic assumption that all cognition—also higher cognition and epistemic categories—still entails motor sensorial traits from their acquisition history in early childhood. A second important point is that understanding is much broader than ratio—a rule comprehension, as understanding involves, again, the whole psychic personality, with her feeling of "I," of integrity deeply connected with metabolic balance, with imaginary work, and learned affective patterns. In the study of religion, precise work has realized this approach, e.g., for ritual (Geertz and Klocová 2019), postures (Barsalou *et al.* 2005), and movement-based embodied contemplative practices (Schmalzl and Kerr 2016).

## The Need to Integrate Findings from Cognitive Studies into Cultural Studies

To understand the conceptual status of body knowledge, we need to start with a distinction from the beginning of the twentieth century between comprehension and explanation (Ger. "*verstehen und erklären*"), with the responsibility for comprehension and interpretation falling upon the humanities and the responsibility for explanation on the natural sciences. This distinction from philosophical hermeneutics and earlier theory of science does not hold any more for several reasons that have been amply discussed during recent decades in philosophy, literary theory, sociology, and beyond. In cultural studies, there is an urgent need for synthetic work if we consider, not least, our topic of the reception of embodied practices. Science and technology studies (STS) state that, for connecting the humanities and natural sciences, "it is no longer practicable to maintain a hygienic separation between sociocultural webs and neurobiological architecture" (Fitzgerald and Callard 2015). We also find, in this context, the metaphor of bridging concepts, for example in regard to the unifying theory of predictive processing that "may provide the means to build new conceptual bridges between theoretical and empirical work on cognition and consciousness" (Wiese and Metzinger 2017, 3).

In the study of religion, Armin W. Geertz developed a "biocultural approach" at Aarhus University at that time at the Cognition and Culture Research Unit and now Interacting Minds Centre (Geertz 2010).[3] The biocultural approach is "able to accommodate the methods and insights of recent hybrid cognitive sciences such as social neuroscience, cultural neuroscience, cognitive anthropology, cognitive archaeology, the cognitive science of religion and neuroanthropology" (Geertz 2010, 305).[4] Geertz holds cognition to be "embrained, embodied, encultured, extended and distributed," a theoretically demanding position insofar as it

3. See also Manuel Vasquez's "non-reductive materialism" from ecological perception theory (2011).
4. Geertz asks "for more precise 'conjunctive' theories and hypotheses" (2010, 314).

refers to several theories and methodologies.[5] And Alexandra K. Grieser and Jay Johnston (2017) lay out "aesthetics of religion" as a "connective concept" between, on the one hand, diverse knowledge cultures and, on the other hand, between the cultivation of senses and perception theories, artistic traditions, and aesthetic canonicity.

In relating several forerunners of enactive aesthetics, an aesthetics of human understanding or conceptual blending, a new research field emerges. The latter position is closely linked to the working group on aesthetics of religion within the German Association for the Study of Religion that was ethnographically examined by STS scholar Mareike Smolka. She notably emphasizes the paradigmatic clash between psychology, as natural science, and cultural studies, with their contested visions of causal relations versus subjective meaning-making and of universal versus contextual applications (Smolka 2021, 14, 30–32). Smolka comes to the result that, in this network of scholars, conflicting visions on cognition and culture led to high productivity, plural methodologies, and clarification of epistemological positions. The following paragraphs intend to lay out what a field of entangled disciplinarity may look like.

## "Body Knowledge" as a Connective Term

Embodiment has already been previously inferred from knowledge theory, as well as simulation as a central process for comprehension (Barsalou *et al.* 2005). We start from the heuristic of a particular type of body knowledge. Here, "body knowledge" functions as an umbrella term. There is no *one* body knowledge. It is a concept that aims at describing ways in which multisensorial information interacts with higher cognitive evaluations. Quite a lot of this interaction is preconscious or, put differently, executed within another register, that of partly non-propositional knowledge. Multisensorial representations are always intermodal anyway. This means that sensory systems—like vision, touch, the vestibular system, and pain reception—and where/in which body part the stimuli are felt are already weighed against one another in terms of intensity, the degree of threat for the organism, the urgency for action, and their role for subjectivity (see for example Garzorz and Deroy 2020). This processing and evaluation can be theorized according to predictive mind theory. Predictive mind details how cultural markers connect with the organism (psychophysiology, metabolism, hormonal

5. Extended mind, for example, is a position that gained popularity through an article by Clark and Chalmers (1998).

system, and more). The benefit of the meta concept of "body knowledge" will become clearer when spelled out through its subcategories. These subcategories are second-order concepts, including in the sense that there is no one body scheme or body zone as these are learned patterns.

A crucial aim of this theory building is to offer falsification criteria that are necessary for empirical work. The question of whether a subprocess did take place if a particular vegetative circuit was involved must be answered. It is by and large consensual that cognition is embodied and that this matters somehow for religion. But as regards specific meditations, rituals, or joint meals, we have yet to identify falsifiable criteria for determining which of the involved embodied dimensions are decisive and which are less important or even irrelevant insofar as they are not part of participants' perspective and perception. For example, which body posture is more intensive, which method of guiding attention is efficacious, or which differences of participants must be considered, such as degrees of suggestibility, attentiveness, or skillfulness? When embodiment is presented as an overly generalized theory of comprehension, it is not helpful for the development of an aesthetics of religion. And when those in cultural studies expect cognitive and medical psychology to test or verify their hypotheses, they are misdirected as well (Fitzgerald and Callard 2015, 12). The reason for this poor assessment is twofold. First, somatic parameters are so essential to symbolic, linguistic, and social parameters that this mutual involvement is only revealed at the behavioral or interpretive levels and does not substitute for cultural explanations. And second, the scope of cultural studies questions is the reconstruction of subjects' and institutions' interrelations with the world. These are culturally diverse, even if they fulfil a comparable function; their organizational configuration cannot sufficiently be explained by just one component, like psychosomatics.

The subcategories of body knowledge are, therefore, operationalizations as regards empirical, ethnographic, or laboratory settings. They are suggested as a tool kit that is elaborated by replicability. In the current phase of theory development, we need more testing.

## Categories of Body Knowledge

Several entangled categories from social, cognitive, and medical psychology and cultural studies have been propounded: somatic attention, the body scheme, body image, muscle tone, tattooing of body parts, embodied interface for mediation with entities, thermo control, peripersonal space, prosthetic perception, synchronized psychophysiology, joint speech, a moment of congruence between agents and presumed entity, and more (Koch 2017). Some will now be briefly discussed to give an idea of how they matter in cultural studies contexts.

The *body scheme* is the feeling of integrity, the feeling of "I," a meta-representation of feeling whole and complete (see Craig 2003, 501). Religions provide uncountable practices that effectuate the body scheme. All practices targeting autonomous circuits like heartbeat, body temperature, digestion, and respiration, influence the holistic feeling. The autonomous system activates the vegetative system, the sympathetic or parasympathetic nervous system. Aspects of the body scheme as the body figure have methodologically been raised by letting people draw their body shape. Patients, for example, lying on water beds to prevent bedsores, paint a shapeless, enlarged body figure. One might ask how huge head masks put over the head during rituals or imaginations of subtle bodies affect the body scheme.

The site of the body that functions to connect or communicate with the relevant counterpart is called the *interface*. This body site may be a body zone, an entryway of an energy channel in alternative medical conceptions (opened crown chakra or touched by the heart), an induced feeling, e.g., of warmth, a caught sound from some animal or phenomenon or the like. How and where in the body the counterpart interacts with a person is socio-culturally learned.

*Thermoregulation* is usually an autonomous homeostasis of bodies. Blood flow, muscle tension, inflammation, hormonal cycles, and cellular processes of inner organs (like digestion) can alter the temperature of the subjectively felt body or body parts.[6] An increase in body temperature (fever) serves as an important immune defense. Biofeedback experiments show how the feeling of warmth can also be intentionally influenced. The intentional manipulation of body temperature, like a felt warmth at specific body zones, has been employed in religious practices. For example, in both our studies on healing, in a theosophic as well as in an idiosyncratic-shamanic orientation, the healers explained to us that they work with light that they shine into energy channels or just into the body, but that they talk with those being healed about warmth, as it seems that made more sense and was more easily felt in the body.

The felt spatial embeddedness of a body, in the sense of a particular perceptive representation around the body's borders, expresses a non-arithmetic but rather *peripersonal* space. These perceived "near-body surroundings" alter reaction time to stimuli around the body parts. A needle in the hand of another person that comes into sight will for

6. And thermoception can aid orientation in space (Cheng *et al.* 2019).

example prompt an earlier reaction when approaching one's hand than when approaching one's shoulder or upper leg. For this peripersonal space, cross-modal correspondences of sensory organs or systems are decisive (Deroy *et al.* 2016).

## Training Knowledge: Reception through Training

Besides body knowledge, training knowledge (Ger. "*Übungswissen*") is a further relevant and connective term. Theories of learning and training are central to understanding religion (Luhrmann 2013). Training knowledge is an often-overlooked type of knowledge (Koch 2018), even when it is decisive for most religious actions in habituating of specific predictive models in imagination, body, and epistemic knowledge. Also, Bayesian inference[7] and intercultural embodied reception, within predictive mind theory, are both closely related to learning. The key insight of the two mentioned philosophies of mind is the ideomotor principle, stating that acquisition of knowledge is an interplay of ideas and sensorimotor input and observation drawn from one's own actions. Therefore, sensorial information is also an integral part of higher cognition. In this way, trained knowledge is sensorial and processual. Training knowledge does not denote knowledge as the outcome of training but rather the knowledge of how knowledge or skill acquisition performs and the way it is put into effect. Sports sciences have developed a whole subfield of exercise studies, and, from the perspective of evolutionary theory, training knowledge provides an "unprecedented degree of voluntary control over the body" (Wilson 2010, 180). In this way, people reach a differential degree of body mastery that may serve as a substrate for substantial symbolizations for communication (in arts, ritual, psychic manipulation, and symbolization).

The somatic training knowledge in focus here includes an awareness of the uncomfortable efforts of performance and the smoothness of habituation once acquired by repetitive action. These are already two types of knowledge. First, the experience of effort that occurs after a while within a practice sequence—e.g., when hunger arises, joints hurt, or the glycemic level decreases—is often accompanied by strong counter affects. This can be experienced as a temptation to interrupt or give up on it all or to go against the teacher. Experiential knowledge about the

7. Bayesian inference minimizes error predictions over time with the help of a hierarchical bottom-down prediction distributing probability values to sub-models to evaluate new information.

temporariness of these urges to interrupt or the specific time interval when they occur may help to mentally intervene and continue with the training. The second type is comparative knowledge: implicitly or explicitly, progress in muscle strength, flexibility, or resilience is experienced following the commencement of an exercise routine, and this comparison with the previous situation encourages advancement. Therefore, it is not only about specific virtues of training—like patience, withstanding temptation, and endurance—but also about bodily emotional states of euphoria, happiness, emptiness, and exhaustion that follow each other. They are effectuated by body postures, muscle tone, and metabolism (Schmalzl and Kerr 2016). The occurrence of embodied practice as somatic resistance is a salient psychic or political feature. It may indicate an inner unsolved conflict, the lack of conviction in the belief system of the practice, or denial that must be learned and governed.

From the sports and training sciences, we know that the rhythm of training phases of performance enhancement and periods of rest are decisive for progression. And overall, rewards increase training success, be it encouragement or the self-production of bodily substances that create euphoric, rewarding feelings. Training gives a central role to teachers, their instructions, adjustments, and alignments, and to sharing and evaluation that may also be accompanied by co-learners.

Further vital factors of training are psychoanalytic concepts to describe the processes, e.g., the above-mentioned resistance, symbolization, and externalization. Learning embodied practices can serve to externalize inner states and to materialize them into symbolic meaning that is ascribed to a body part, hair, skin, or a movement, for instance. The externalized state often takes the shape of a culturally significant symbol. In this way, one can become aware of a sensitivity, and that sensitivity can be made explicit and turned into an object for further therapeutic treatment. Training produces emotions that go beyond speech acts insofar as they are messages about the self and its emotional state. A problem that may arise with training knowledge is its idealization of feeling "free," "alive," and "authentic." A specific way of training becomes universalized and predominant over other practices, like critical reflection.

## Cultural Receptions of Embodied Practices and Their Transformation Due to Distinct Contexts

The following case studies are applications and elaborations of some body knowledge categories in specific contexts. All of them treat groups and their ritual and belief systems as transposed and adapted—that is, embodied—within different cultural contexts and, in that sense, distanced from their "origins."[8] That is why they are chosen over work that would lay out greater detail and the then necessary methods of the psychophysiological aspect.

### Spirit Incorporation Going European: The Terra Sagrada

The Terra Sagrada is a very small group in Switzerland, Austria, and Germany, organized in half a dozen local spiritual groups (*terreiro*) in the Afro-Brazilian tradition of Candomblé and Umbanda. It was founded by an Austrian woman who is still the spiritual leader. In her PhD research, Sarah F. Tran-Huu (2021), an educated intercultural psychologist, asks why the central ritual of spirit incorporation is attractive to Middle European people. Her field trips to group meetings and incorporation rituals and several guided interviews with members form the base of her examination of this group in the context of contemporary religion. Also, Tran-Huu raises the question of whether attractivity and verisimilitude can be understood as cult-need-congruence, as developed in research on conversion. For this aim, she also takes into account the somatic dimension of this congruence of cult and needs (Tran-Huu 2021, 208–223). The body must accustom itself to the ritual encounter with spirits and is trained, over years, to learn the ritual dynamics in correlation with altered body posture, body scheme, and the necessary psychomotor abilities to fall into a trance. During this observational learning, familiarity increases with time, variances and coping with disturbances are learned, and intimateness grows stronger. In the beginning, the aspirant participates as a guest and, later, in a ritual role. First, the embodied initiation moment creates the individual spirit whose facial expression and body language must be learned. Embodied *simulation* is an important means to acquire this aim. Simulation is a type of learning that takes synthetic and holistic information from each phase of ritual dynamics. Simulation of other bodies is realized via the empathy and observational skills of social cognition. The reason one is fascinated with body practices is an experienced truthfulness that the faculty of reason does not provide. These newly acquired perceptive patterns are transferred to everyday life.

8. I feel happy and honored that I could supervise these PhDs over the years, see also Laura von Ostrowski's research in this volume.

## An Israeli Movement Practice Going Global: Gaga

Gaga is a neoliberal well-being practice (Aschenbrenner and Koch 2022) that has now spread to many countries worldwide and is taught by certified Gaga teachers. Founded by the dancer and choreographer Ohad Naharin, born in 1952, Gaga is organized into professional and popular lines. Lina Aschenbrenner's PhD is based on her ethnographic fieldwork at the popular "Gaga people" line at a center in Tel Aviv and at Gaga workshops in Austria and Germany (Aschenbrenner 2023). Aschenbrenner, also an educated dancer herself, conducts participant observation, guides interviews, and analyzes diaries of participants about their practice that they produced specifically for her. As the practice is so dense and has not been analyzed academically before, she focuses on a cultural and cognitive aesthetics of religion perspective to reconstruct the movement style by "asking for the environment shaping enactment," the ritual enactment, for "Gaga's body topography" and the decisive "Gaga instructions and techniques" uttered and mediated by teachers during courses. She offers, for the first time, a glossary of the multiple verbal instructions and idiosyncratic, often metaphorical, requests of how to move and feel movement, that is the Gaga language. "Verbalizing the wow-effect" indicates that Gaga is a matter of holistic personal transformation.

Aschenbrenner seizes, for example, on the body knowledge subcategory of *muscle tone*. She uses it to decipher the bodily "default" mode of Gaga that is explicitly "floating" and can be observed with participants and is uttered by participants to relate their habitual movement style not only when practicing Gaga but also in everyday life. In that sense, floating becomes an "experience filter" that is "a body knowledge gained in practical experiences and applied to the experience of new situations, where the knowledge can again be updated by means of practicing" (Aschenbrenner and von Ostrowski 2022, 167). A precondition for the body to feel light, free, and effortless is a "balanced tone" (Payne and Crane-Godreau 2015). This recognizable body posture is taught with phrases like:

- Put your arms into water. Be the water.
- (Be) oil on water.
- Spread like bread in milk.
- Feel like you have a thousand balloons in your body lifting you up.
- Float your bone in soft flesh.

According to Aschenbrenner floating is introduced as a holistic mode of "being in one's body," referring to movement-based contemplative practices aiming at an experience of the self (Aschenbrenner 2023; referring to Schmalzl *et al.* 2014, 2)—here, called *body scheme*. The body tension links to the emotionality of what has been described as "flow" in literature on creativity and spiritual experiences during which hypnotic states are involved. With this background in mind, floating instructions unfold in multiple and demanding variations, for example, to keep the upper body floating and to engage in an opposite movement quality with the lower body.

## A Christian-Charismatic Aestheticscape

The categories also prove their explanative power with regard to global "evangelical," "Pentecostal," and "charismatic" practices and their production of trancelike states (Lifshitz *et al.* 2019, 3) and a specific configuration of emotions over a timespan. To reach this goal, persuasive aesthetic and fine-tuned "framing" is a prerequisite for what I call the "aestheticscape."

> Describing the [huge evangelical] conference gathering as heaven is not a designation that arises spontaneously from conference-goers' transcendent experiences: it also happens because conference organizers and leaders intentionally frame the conference gathering as a means of participating in the heavenly community.
>
> (Ingalls 2018, 73)

During the global expansion of the charismatic style, the intentional aestheticscape must be adopted to confessionally and culturally diverging contexts.

It is vastly aesthetic ways of performance that affect the somatosensory system and establish or transform a symbolic order to initiate the emotional habitus. At a Catholic youth event (Koch 2020), an emotional habitus of ideal piety within charismatic renewal is created as an alternative to and in competition with the common Catholic habitus. The soundscape of typical lulling music, the lightscape of professional illumination, and the *mise-en-scène* of blue and purple inner walls of the church building exert emotional effects. The affect economy consists of inward absorption and emotional turmoil, oscillating between a range of emotions from regret to relief and ease, also including informality and sociableness, a scene far from the quiet solemnity of usual Sunday services. Sharing well-introduced sensorial strategies of charismatic groups, the performance of the Evening of Mercy at the Pentecostal gathering employs soundscapes, lightscapes, touching, kinesthetics, and the visual multiplication of emotional icons via twelve huge screens in the Dome of Salzburg. These emotional icons are either the slowly moving bodies, faces, and closed eyes of band members or the light-radiating monstrance. To implement an emotional habitus via a specific aestheticscape, several performances overlap: the sacrament of penance at around twenty spots within the church, autosuggestions and touching at "pray stations" with two group members each dispersed in the church, the display and carrying around of the monstrance, and the typical tapestry of sound created by a live music band.

During transcultural reception, aestheticscapes are measured with regard to their ability to successfully adapt to different aesthetic surroundings and initiate the socialization of a respective affect economy.

## 5Rhythms: Energy as Rhythmic Body Movement

"Work" with immaterial or "fine" material "energies" is widely represented in contemporary religion of the so-called esoteric discourse, particularly in its manifestations as New Age and alternative healing or body therapies. A popular option that seems to work globally is to grasp this "energy" via body movement qualities that can be experienced and transformed in experience.[9] Several contemporary dance styles—like open floor, consciousness movement, ecstatic dance, therapy in motion, and somatic awareness dance—follow this body- and emotion-centered approach. Prototypical is 5Rhythms dance which dates to the time of the Gaia spirituality of founder Gabriele Roth at Californian Esalen Institute from 1965 onwards. We will only discuss the embodied aspect, leaving aside the fascinating blend of influences from different East Asian religious traditions, the wider context of Gestalt therapy, emerging humanistic (von Stuckrad 2022) and transpersonal psychology, psychoanalysis, and the mystical, Christian, and tantric understandings of an energy body.

According to Roth, dancers incorporate an underlying cosmic pattern in their rhythmic movement pattern. Kinetic qualities are associated with affects in a culturally learned and individually trained way (Nevrin 2008, 129). Tying in shamanism, Roth favors ecstatic dance states in which interoception and social cognition, i.e., intrapersonal perception, merge. In this way, the body image that has a perceptual, conceptual, and emotional dimension may change through performance. This is supported at the level of body tone, which typically changes with every phase of the dance and via the co-presence of other bodies in specific

9. Also observed for yoga (see Nevrin 2008, 123).

changing relations to the subjectively felt own body. Instructions that guide body awareness to specific body parts can enhance prosthetic perception, like haptically connecting with the solid floor in the first phase of flowing when the sole of the foot clomps down on the floor (Kunas 2013, 81). This anchoring works with the three-dimensionality of space, which spreads equally in all directions, and with unbalancing the body's center of gravity and following the movement impulse to recenter. Every phase of this "wave" of movement works with different movement qualities and accompanying affective patterns. Mostly, a holistic experience ensues with the completion of the performance, an experience that is envisaged in many contemporary (religious) practices.

## Conclusion

Let us draw three conclusions for a theory of the reception of embodied practices within the framework of an entangled history of religion and societies and evaluate their implications. Regarding the conclusions, first, received practices multiply in functional applications; second, received practices are related to specific embodied features and qualities; and third, the reception of embodied practices is related to specific historical subjectivities.

First, we were able to observe how body practices in the process of reception are dis-embedded from societal subsystems, transferred to other, transforming subsystems and freely floating between them, as Bourdieu already observed with his social field theory. Within these dynamics of de-differentiation, a straying body technique, like, for example, breathing, turns the secular/non-religion/religious discursive lines into nothing but lines. The questions of whether a neoliberal practice may be a neo-spiritual practice and whether the involvement of a cosmic self is sufficient to speak of a supernatural agency and to define it as religious are questions that only matter descriptively. Instead, it is more important to understand, from the viewpoint of the whole of society, which task the received practices fulfil, which problem they solve, and why they settle in which domain.

This trajectory opens up continuous historical observations. The thesis, for example, that especially the reception of body practices from South Asia has a transformative effect on recipients' selves deserves further consideration (Karstein and Benthaus-Apel 2012, 312). Their attractivity is explained by their role as an alternative to Christian ideas of salvation (doctrinal confession, sacramental mediation, and, especially in mainstream Protestantism and Catholicism, the mediation of salvation through the Church). For this alternative mode of well-being, the self and bodywork are central.

Second, as has been implied, embodied practices appear to be a new social form of religion and only matter as practices and not, any longer, as religious, artistic, or political practices and, therefore, must be dismantled in regard to the recipient culture. For this aim, we operationalize intercultural embodied reception through analytic (and explanative) categories of body and training knowledge. These categories enable us to determine which embodied element functions as the interface through which recipients link together on the body level.

Third, historical subjectivities, in the sense of Michel Foucault, determine the possibility space of reception. What is added here is that, with the aesthetical subject of embodied cognition, the aesthetics of historical subjectivities is in focus. The aesthetical subject substitutes for the hermeneutical subject and is less centered and determined than the former; it is instead open and fluid in the sense of changing in meaning with each repetition within a structure. As examples, one might think of aesthetically determined forms of historical subjectivities, like the theosophical subject (with meridians, subtle bodies, and energy centers), a subject of mindfulness (trained in detaching, non-evaluating, finely attuning to inner changes of state of mind as well as of body), traumatized subjects (caused by abuse, persecution, or forced displacement, characterized by uncontrolled or inaccessible fears, emotionlessness), the secular middle European subject (school medical image of a psychosomatic body, self-responsible, health preventive) overlapping with a fading Christian subjectivity that now experiences a growing proportion of a charismatic-ecstatic subjectivity (absorptive, trained into the collective). These and several more trainings of an aesthetic subjectivity will affect how we perceive phenomena. With regard to rational-instrumental subjectivity, Klas Nevrin states:

> [W]hen the body is habitually used as a neutral background to goal-oriented thoughts and actions, the body is not experienced as "alive" in itself. This may even produce an excessive disconnection of ourselves (i.e., our bodies) from the environment in which one might feel alienated and emotionally disconnected from "the world." [...] In these hyper-detached forms of experience, we might say, perceptual and imaginative skills are habitually set on producing an affectively neutral and nondynamic experience of ourselves and the world.
>
> (Nevrin 2008, 126)

In the past, sociological theories of subjectivity were either replaced by social structures or reintroduced the individual subject. The challenge for structuralism is its determinism. Ways to break up the structure, networks, or systems were suggested to enable space for action (like Derrida's *différance*, Butler's performance, and Laclau and Mouffe's subversive shine-out of indeterminacy). The attention towards aesthetic subjectivities establishes a middle position, as it points to reasons for receptive processes (like choices, easiness of linking together, success, elitism, popularity) on the basis of learned perceptive differentiations, body knowledge reflectivity, and evaluations of embodied states that are bundled in historical subjectivities. Diverse ways of the trans- and cross-cultural entanglements of embodied practices relate to the receptive culture's anthropological situation.

**Anne Koch** is Professor of the Study of Religion at the University of Freiburg/Germany. Her main areas of research are epistemology of cultural studies, economics of religion, and aesthetics of religion/embodied cognition with a focus on contemporary religion in Europe and global religious discourses of cosmopolitan spirituality. She co-edits *Zeitschrift für Religionswissenschaft*, co-edited the *Journal of Religion in Europe*, and is a board member of several book series and journals. Recent publication: with K. Wilkens (eds.), *The Bloomsbury Handbook of the Cultural and Cognitive Aesthetics of Religion* (2019).

## References

Aschenbrenner, Lina. 2023. *Neo-Spiritual Aesthetics: Embodied Transformation in the Israeli Movement Practice Gaga*. London: Bloomsbury.

Aschenbrenner, Lina and Anne Koch. 2022. "Do Gaga, Be Well? Well-Being as Intersectional Dispositif in the Neo-Spiritual Israeli Movement Practice Gaga." In *New Spiritualities and the Culture of Well-Being,* edited by Géraldine Mossière, 169–184. New York: Springer.

Aschenbrenner, Lina and Laura von Ostrowski. 2022. "Embodied Neo-Spirituality as an Experience Filter: From Dance to Movement Practice to Contemporary Yoga." *Body and Religion* 5(2): 160–184. https://doi.org/10.1558/bar.20526.

Barsalou, Lawrence, Aron K. Barbey, W. Kyle Simmons and Ava Santos. 2005. "Embodiment in Religious Knowledge." *Journal of Cognition and Culture* 5(1/2): 14–57.

Bourdieu, Pierre. 2001. "Connaissance par corps." In *Méditations pascaliennes,* 185–234. Paris: Éditions du Seuil. Translated by Achim Russer. With assistance by Hélène Albagnac and Bernd Schwibs, "Körperliche Erkenntnis." In *Meditationen. Zur Kritik der scholastischen Vernunft.* Berlin: Suhrkamp.

Cheng, Tony, Ophelia Deroy and Charles Spence, eds. 2019. *Spatial Senses: Philosophy of Perception in an Age of Science*. London: Routledge.

Clark, Andy and David J. Chalmers. 1998. "The Extended Mind." *Analysis* 58(1): 7–19.

Colombo, Matteo. 2017. "Social Motivation in Computational Neuroscience: Or, If Brains Are Prediction Machines, Then the Humean Theory of Motivation Is False." In *Routledge Handbook of Philosophy of the Social Mind*, edited by Julian Kieverstein, 336–356. Abingdon: Routledge. https://doi.org/10.4324/9781315530178-27.

Craig, AD. 2003. "Interoception: The Sense of the Physiological Condition of the Body." *Current Opinion in Neurobiology* 13(4): 500–505. https://doi.org/10.1016/S0959-4388(03)00090-4.

Cuffel, Alexandra, Licia di Giacinto and Volkhard Krech, eds. 2019. "Senses, Religion, and Religious Encounter. Literature Review and Research Perspectives." Special issue, *Entangled Religions. Interdisciplinary Journal for the Study of Religious Contact and Transfer* 10. https://doi.org/10.13154/er.10.2019.8407.

Deroy, Ophelia, Irène Fasiello, Vincent Hayward and Malika Auvray. 2016. "Differentiated Audio-Tactile Correspondences in Sighted and Blind Individuals." *Journal of Experimental Psychology: Human Perception and Performance* 42(8): 1204–1214.

Fitzgerald, Des and Felicity Callard. 2015. "Social Science and Neuroscience Beyond Interdisciplinarity: Experimental Entanglements." *Theory, Culture & Society* 32(1): 3–32. https://doi.org/10.1177/0263276414537319.

Garzorz, Isabelle and Ophelia Deroy. 2020. "Why There Is a Vestibular Sense, or How Metacognition Individuates the Senses." *Multisensory Research* 34(3): 261–280. https://doi.org/10.1163/22134808-bja10026.

Geertz, Armin W. 2010. "Brain, Body and Culture: A Biocultural Theory of Religion." *Method and Theory in the Study of Religion* 22(4): 304–321. https://doi.org/10.1163/157006810X531094.

Geertz, Armin W. and Eva Kundtová Klocová. 2019. "Ritual and Embodied Cognition." In *The Oxford Handbook of Early Christian Ritual*, edited by Risto Uro, Juliette J. Day, Richard E. Demaris and Rikard Roitto, 74–94. Oxford: Oxford University Press.

Grieser, Alexandra K. and Jay Johnston, eds. 2017. *Aesthetics of Religion: A Connective Concept*. Berlin: De Gruyter.

Hommel, Bernhard. 2015. "The Theory of Event Coding (TEC) as Embodied-Cognition Framework." *Frontiers in Psychology* 6: Article 1318. https://doi.org/10.3389/fpsyg.2015.01318.

Ingalls, Monique M. 2018. *Singing the Congregation: How Contemporary Worship Music Forms Evangelical Community*. Oxford: Oxford University Press.

Karstein, Uta and Friederike Benthaus-Apel. 2012. "Asien als Alternative oder Kompensation? Spirituelle Körperpraktiken und ihr transformatives

Potential (nicht nur) für das religiöse Feld." In *Körper, Sport und Religion. Zur Soziologie religiöser Verkörperungen*, edited by Robert Gugutzer and Moritz Böttcher, 311–339. Wiesbaden: Springer.

Koch, Anne. 2017. "The Governance of Aesthetic Subjects Through Body Knowledge and Affect Economies. A Cognitive-Aesthetic Approach." In *Aesthetics of Religion: A Connective Concept*, edited by Alexandra K. Grieser and Jay Johnston, 389–412. Berlin: De Gruyter. https://doi.org/10.1515/9783110461015-017.

——. 2018. "Übungswissen. Subjekttheoretische Bemerkungen zu somatischer Konditionierung, Widerständigkeit und Externalisierung." In *Übungswissen in Religion und Philosophie. Produktion, Weitergabe, Wandel*, edited by Almut-Barbara Renger and Alexandra Stellmacher, 1–18. Berlin: LIT.

——. 2019. "Epistemology." In *The Bloomsbury Handbook of the Cultural and Cognitive Aesthetics of Religion (HCCAR)*, edited by Anne Koch and Katharina Wilkens, 23–32. London: Bloomsbury. https://doi.org/10.5040/9781350066748.ch-003.

——. 2020. "Aestheticscapes und *joint speech* als ästhetische Strategie. Analyse eines katholischen Fürbittgebets mit 'Exorzismus.'" *Zeitschrift für Religionswissenschaft* 28(2): 259–275. https://doi.org/10.1515/zfr-2020-0002.

Kunas, Markus. 2013. "The Dancing Sangha. Die 5 Rhythmen als holistische Körpertechnik zwischen Tanz, Therapie und spätmoderner Spiritualität." Master thesis, University of Munich. Retrieved from https://epub.ub.uni-muenchen.de/21723/index.html.

Lifshitz, Michael, Michiel van Elk and Tanya M. Luhrmann. 2019. "Absorption and Spiritual Experience: A Review of Evidence and Potential Mechanisms." *Consciousness and Cognition* 73: Article 102760. https://doi.org/10.1016/j.concog.2019.05.008.

Luhrmann, Tanya M. 2013. "Building on William James. The Role of Learning in Religious Experience." In *Mental Culture. Classical Social Theory and the Cognitive Science of Religion*, edited by Dimitris Xygalatas and William W. McCorkle Jr, 145–163. Durham: Acumen.

Nevrin, Klas. 2008. "Empowerment and Using the Body in Modern Postural Yoga." In *Yoga in the Modern World. Contemporary Perspectives*, edited by Mark Singleton and Jean Byrne, 119–139. London: Routledge.

Newcombe, Suzanne. 2019. *Yoga in Britain: Stretching Spirituality and Educating Yogis*. London: Equinox.

Payne, Peter and Mardi A. Crane-Godreau. 2015. "The Preparatory Set: A Novel Approach to Understanding Stress, Trauma, and the Bodymind Therapies." *Frontiers in Human Neuroscience* 9: Article 178. https://doi.org/10.3389/fnhum.2015.00178.

Schmalzl, Laura, Mardi A. Crane-Godreau and Peter Payne. 2014. “Movement-Based Embodied Contemplative Practices: Definitions and Paradigms.” *Frontiers in Human Neuroscience* 8: Article 205. https://doi.org/10.3389/fnhum.2014.00205.

Schmalzl, Laura and Catherine E. Kerr. 2016. “Editorial: Neural Mechanisms Underlying Movement-Based Embodied Contemplative Practices.” *Frontiers in Human Neuroscience* 10: Article 169. https://doi.org/10.3389/fnhum.2016.00169.

Singleton, Mark. 2005. “Salvation through Relaxation: Proprioceptive Therapy and Its Relationship to Yoga.” *Journal of Contemporary Religion* 20(3): 289–304. https://doi.org/10.1080/13537900500249780.

Smolka, Mareike. 2021. “Why Does Controversy Persist? Paradigm Clash, Conflicting Visions, and Academic Productivity in the Aesthetics of Religion.” *Science as Culture* 30(4): 74–94. https://doi.org/10.1080/09505431.2021.1918077.

Taves, Ann. 2015. “Reverse Engineering Complex Cultural Concepts: Identifying Building Blocks of ‘Religion.’” *Journal of Cognition and Culture* 15: 191–216.

Taves, Ann and Egil Asprem. 2017. “Experience as Event: Event Cognition and the Study of (Religious) Experiences.” *Religion, Brain & Behavior* 7(1): 43–62. https://doi.org/10.1080/2153599X.2016.1150327.

Tran-Huu, Sarah Franziska 2021. *Faszination alternative Spiritualität. Zum Konversionsprozess in die neureligiöse Gruppierung “Terra Sagrada.”* Bielefeld: transcript.

Vasquez, Manuel. 2011. *More than Belief. A Materialist Theory of Religion.* Oxford: Oxford University Press.

Vollmer, Laura J. 2021. “The Role of ‘Spirituality’ in Religion-Secular Relational Discourse: The Case of Yoga in Britain.” *Journal of Religion in Europe* 13(3/4): 325–350.

von Stuckrad, Kocku. 2022. *A Cultural History of the Soul: Europe and North America from 1870 to the Present.* New York: Columbia University Press.

Wiese, Wanja and Thomas Metzinger. 2017. “Vanilla PP for Philosophers: A Primer on Predictive Processing.” In *Philosophy and Predictive Processing*, edited by Wanja Wiese and Thomas Metzinger. Frankfurt a. M.: MIND Group.

Wilson, Margret. 2002. “Six Views of Embodied Cognition.” *Psychonomic Bulletin & Review* 9(4): 625–636.

——. 2010. “The Re-tooled Mind: How Culture Re-Engineers Cognition.” *Social Cognitive and Affective Neuroscience* 5(2/3): 180–187. https://doi.org/10.1093/scan/nsp054.

– 3 –

# The Search for Rigor in Ethnographies of Bodily Practice

THEO WILDCROFT

The status of researcher as insider or outsider to the communities they study has long been of debate. Within long-term ethnographic research into cultural practices, a world of nuance arises in the possible relationships between researcher and researched. We are engaged in complex processes of reconciliation between the under-represented communities whose stories we aim to tell, and the power an academic position confers to "define reality for others." Besides the issue of positionality, the study of practices of movement and interoception confer distinct embodied skillsets. As a long-term practitioner of yoga who researches contemporary practice, my experience and analysis will be different from non-practicing scholars in the field. In this chapter I will build on insights from dance studies and yoga studies to discuss the methodological frameworks it was necessary to develop for my own doctoral research. I will describe co-practice as a method, notation as an analytic tool, and the concept of methodology as an experimental process, guided by the ideal of research as *seva*: research as a service freely dedicated to both academic rigor and the untold stories of our communities of practice. From this, I hope to offer space for an open and intellectually invigorating conversation about new methods and frameworks, so that we may break new ground together, in the ethnographic study of bodily practices.

Keywords: methodology, experiment, yoga, ethnography, positionality

The status of researcher as insider or outsider to the communities they study has long been of debate in the social sciences and religious studies in particular (McCutcheon 1999a). This debate has obvious relevance for the study of embodied practices such as yoga (Singleton and Larios 2021) and intersects with the increasing turn towards the material and lived aspects of cultural research more generally. For decades, theorists in the study of cultural practice, particularly in the study of religion, have declared the importance of the vernacular and the embodied, as a counterpoint to our long obsession with textual and semiotic analysis, as discussed in Dreyfus (1996), Orsi (2013), and Watts (2013), among others.

Indeed, as the introduction to this volume points out, to even talk about "embodied practices" or, more accurately here, embodied knowledge *transmission*, is to enter into a long-running debate as to what the term "embodiment" even means. In my own research, embodiment is theorized both as how meaning is made through bodily practice, and how a body of esoteric knowledge is transmitted through processes of bodily inscription. My participants' bodies are both the site of emergent knowledge about the meaning of practice, and also the repository for transmitted knowledge within a religious chain of memory (Hervieu-Léger 2000).

My own standpoint is largely phenomenological, which explains the methodological innovations I will go on to explore. I am persuaded by Maxine Sheets-Johnstone's argument (2009) that humans are animate bodies, rather than embodied minds. But in the course of my doctoral research, I found myself investigating processes of transmission and authority in a phenomenon I began to call "post-lineage yoga" (Wildcroft 2020). Seen from the perspective of this volume, one way to consider the "post-lineage" turn is as a move away from an understanding of modern yoga as a process of embodied knowledge transmission, and towards modern yoga as a site of emergent embodied meaning.

But whatever the aspect of embodiment in question, studying what we might call embodied ritual practices, particularly those embedded in long histories and private intimacies, often necessitates in-depth ethnographic research. To sit with, bow with, meditate with, and breathe side by side with a community of practice, day upon day and week upon week, is a very different process to examining archival texts, and thus involves new methodologies, and new research ethics to consider. A world of nuance arises in the possible relationships of researcher and researched as a result. We are inevitably implicated in complex processes of reconciliation between the communities whose less well-known stories we aim to tell (Shaw 1999, 108; Orsi 2013, 5), and the power an academic position confers to "define reality for others" (Hufford 1999, 298).

Besides the issue of positionality, the study of embodied practices involves distinct embodied skillsets. A scholar's own history of ritual movement and meditation becomes both an important tool for accessing the field, and an inescapable habitus to be considered. Both emic and etic histories of practice have useful perspectives to offer the role of researcher. More than that, whatever their history, each researcher and each practitioner holds a distinct and personalized repertoire of embodied experience, as unique to them. Embodied rituals and habits of embodiment are a universal feature of human culture, and academia is no exception. As Richard Carp writes: "The anybody of the Academic body corresponds to the nowhere of Academic space. Yet the universality of academic knowledge is premised on the universality of the academic body" (2001, 99).

As a long-term practitioner of yoga who researches contemporary practice, my experience and analysis will be different from that of non-practicing scholars in the field. But it is also distinct from those practicing scholars who trained with different schools, and different teachers. To develop one's research praxis in this way means becoming proficient at navigating, bracketing, and making use of one's positionality in numerous ways. Academic honesty and reflective praxis are essential, but arguably, even etic scholars should examine their own history of embodiment when studying embodied practice. As bell hooks reminds us, only "the person who is most powerful has the privilege of denying their body" (1994, 137), and only the traditional role power of the academic researcher has allowed the "academic" body to become a stand-in within scholarship for the universal and objective.

But while in the early stages of planning my doctoral fieldwork, I also found that there were no clear and obvious methodological tools available to me to gather the data under consideration. The *experiential* study of movement, and the *anthropological* study of religion, have rarely been combined in methodological debate. Like others in this relatively new research arena, many of them included in this volume, I extrapolated variously from performance studies, religious studies, and yoga studies to develop the methodological framework for my research. The research journey itself is therefore as interesting as the data and analysis it produces. In my own case, what emerges from reflecting on that doctoral research project and the years that immediately follow it, is a form of inquiry that is deliberately partial, self-referential, and productive of as many questions as answers.

To describe that research process here, I begin with the idea of methodology as an experimental process, guided by the ideal of research as *sevā*: research as a service freely dedicated to both academic rigor and the previously unheard stories of the communities that we study. I consider positionality and the notion of expert movement in the context of co-practice as a new methodological tool. I am choosing to refer only briefly to the notation processes that resulted from my data, which deserve their own reflective analysis elsewhere, in favor of staying close, in this chapter at least, to the productive tensions that arise from the interplay of positionality, history, and habitus: who we are and who we become being inseparable from what we have done. From this, I hope to offer space for an open and intellectually invigorating conversation about new methods and frameworks, so that we may break new ground together, in the ethnographic study of bodily practices.

## Method as Experiment

Existing studies of contemporary yoga cannot provide a significant benchmark of the most common practice forms correlated with practitioner experiences and associations, for future research to measure itself against. Modern postural yoga (like most embodied practices) is simply too diverse, its communities too fractured, and its epistemologies too contested for that to be possible. As a result, like others, I began my research journey not with a theory to be tested, but rather an unknown to be investigated.

Michael Stausberg and Steven Engler (2013, 4–5) remind us that "[m]ethods help us to analyse reality but, at the same time, they, in part, produce the data that are to be analysed." As such, my methodological considerations were also governed by an interdisciplinary search for the most appropriate lenses to bring the subject into sharpest focus (Knott 2009, 159).

No single method could provide sufficient data or analysis for comparing practice forms with the inner reality of any participant's prior intention, lived experience, nor how those combined to form an intimate and individualized process of meaning-making or semiogenesis. To include practice forms, some way of documenting the practice activity of my respondents was necessary. To investigate intent, meaning-making, and interoception, I would need to discuss that practice with my respondents. And as my overall focus was the relationship of individual practice to what I was starting to call "post-lineage yoga" culture, some form of immersive participation in that culture would be useful.

Participant observation can reveal a depth of visceral experience and fully embeds the research of lived religion within its ecologies (Harvey 2013, 219), but it privileges the voice and interpretation of the researcher over that of the researched. As explained by Anna Davidsson Bremborg (2013), qualitative interviewing enables a depth of analysis into motivation and personal and interpersonal narratives, but it also privileges the self-conscious, reflective thought processes of a participant in retrospect, over the pre-verbal experience of the practice in the moment. Video analysis could capture the detail of practice forms, but not the intent and experience inherent within them. Auto-ethnography that mimicked practice forms that I was observing, could deepen my understanding of what my participants were telling me. But to effectively address the focus of my research, I would need to engage all these methods and associated media, in careful overlap.

I decided upon a mixed methodology of linked processes: fieldwork and participation in both personal and taught practices, recordings of the same, and finally, interviews about both the individual practices and the camp environments. Some of my methods were less than totally successful. I explored the possibilities of mapping interpersonal connections on the basis of my fieldwork and interviews, employing analysis tools following Adams (2013, 326), in an attempt to map the broad flow of transmission: who was teaching which practice forms to whom. The results could only ever be indicative rather than exhaustive. There were simply too many connections I was unaware of, too many private or forgotten instances of informal transmission. Notation and comparison of practice forms, alongside the intentions and experiences of practitioners, was much more successful.

But as contemporary yoga, like most embodied practices, is still largely synchronously taught from teacher to student(s), one line of enquiry began to bear fruit above all: the transmission process itself. It could be argued that multiple media have served as complicating filters to the transmission of yoga in the modern era, which has been taught via everything from photographic manuals to YouTube tutorials. But in general, regardless of the technology that facilitates it, the most universal medium for modern yoga transmission is the body of the teacher, and the place of reception is the body of each student, in some form of mimesis modulated by additional instruction. Students are asked to mimic this bodily activity, in this way, for this amount of time. "Here," the teacher says, "let me show you, like my teacher showed me."

What began as an exploration of diverse methods developed into a multi-layered process in which the embodied understanding of both myself and participants was tested for its ability to produce useful and robust data on how practices were shared and narrated, how they were experienced and how they were integrated into each person's personal repertoire (Wacquant 2014, 4). In order to enable comparison between specific individual practices, professional identities and sub-cultural processes, these different methods involved the same community, and in many cases, the same respondents. But each medium is akin to a discrete lens that together produce diverse data with an overlapping but non-identical scope: different perspectives on different aspects of the process of transmission.

Those methodological lenses, each one designed to consider one aspect of transmission, be it practice forms, intention, or experience, was each one productive of its own discrete data, each one in imperfect relationship with every other methodological lens. This was reflected in the notation system I developed to map, analyze, and compare the data. Notation took shape as a series of parallel lines. Like the individual lines on a musical score for each section of an orchestra, the notations for intention or action, orientation to space or intensity of effort, were synchronous but not coterminous.

More interestingly, as the research progressed, the slippage between experience, observation, narration and transmission of practice, and the ongoing attempt to correlate my experiences and observations with that of my participants, became a way to understand some of the processes of practice evolution itself. The points of ease and tension, insight and flow, between my participants' perspectives and my own, echoed similar points in the transmission process between teacher and student(s). The lacunae formed from the partial correspondence of movement to experience, and movement to transmission, are key to understanding the incremental and individualized ways in which movement cultures both reproduce themselves and allow for those errors or echoes in reproduction that produce innovation and diversity (Holloway 2003, 1971).

Each member of the practice community is implicated in multiple chains of memory (Hervieu-Léger 2000, 106), attempting to both faithfully reproduce, and yet adapt and evolve, what has been taught to them in turn. Elements of practice are gathered into evolving repertoires of movement. Practices are shared in group mimesis and explored in the intimacy of personal practice. This is Thomas Tweed's (2006, 74) crossing and dwelling in microcosm, each person's repertoire forming part, not just of a chain of memory, but of a shared network and a personal palimpsest.

In the gap between the bodies of teacher and student, method, aim, and experience, transformation can occur. In the fault lines between the bodies of researcher and respondent, participant and target of observation, lie everyday fieldwork experiences such as fatigue, confusion, and misunderstanding, but also a deeper understanding of the crevasses of possible neurological and physical differences between one body and another, that the transmission structures of embodied practice aim to overcome.

## Guesthood and Service

The placing of my own, alongside participants' lived experience of yoga is an inevitable aspect of the research, but also a deliberate response to emic–etic debates involving prominent religious studies scholars from Clifford Geertz (1999) to Jonathan Z. Smith (1999).

Without some pre-existing knowledge of post-lineage yoga communities, I might never have been able to identify them as a productive site for research. This kind of practitioner-academic research involves the translation and contextualization of emic knowledge for the etic audience. But as that knowledge is ever-changing, and indeed changes both researcher and researched in the process of research, reliable representation of that emic reality is always to an extent also the active production of knowledge.

Before my thesis was even complete, yoga teachers that had not been part of the community of practice under investigation were starting to adopt the term I had coined for it: "post-lineage yoga." A term meant to accurately describe specific adaptations in transmission had been adopted as a rallying cry against abusive lineages (see as examples Dinsmore-Tuli and Robertson 2019; Zolotow 2020). Since the publication of my monograph, I have been increasingly involved in engagement activities, both paid and unpaid, and my intentions for the research have changed. Having begun with the idea of making visible an under-researched community of practice within academia, I am now most frequently asked by that practice community to share a synthesis of my respondents' most successful strategies of transmission. The more I spend time discussing pedagogical theory with communities of practice around the world, the deeper my understanding of post-lineage yoga becomes. When impact and engagement are a significant product of one's research, and become part of one's professional identity, one never quite leaves the field. I continue to be both insider and outsider.

Being honest about my ongoing relationship with both emic and etic realities continues to be the most ethical for my subject community, and the most intellectually honest stance within the academic environment. But honesty is not the only ethical value to consider. No research is morally neutral, especially when it aims to make visible the previously unseen. In bringing to light such subjective experiences as memory and identity, meaning-making and transcendence, any researcher has a difficult line to walk in faithfully representing the lived reality of one's respondents, while also subjecting it to critical analysis.

To be clear, a pretense of objectivity was never an option in my case. The communities of practice under consideration felt themselves to be unseen, misunderstood, and misrepresented by media and scholarship alike, who seemed to them only to be interested in the most visible, common, and superficial aspects of contemporary yoga. It became implicitly clear that my access to the field was contingent on my intention and ability to tell their story "fairly." Beyond that, after a few anxious enquiries, it became necessary to add a line in my thesis to clarify that my choice of case studies was not any stamp of approval (Wildcroft 2020, 39). These were not chosen as the most "ethical" or "gifted" or "popular" of teacher-practitioners, even if I could make such assessments. I chose them only according to the principles of my research, as those respondents that seemed most likely to produce interesting and illuminative data for the community of practice overall.

Nonetheless, these anxious enquiries were part of a larger pattern, in which my research began to matter perhaps most to those involved in it. It was essential to closely examine my ethical responsibilities to both them and to the production of academic knowledge. There was no neutral ground on which I could claim to be standing. Those of us (re) entering both the field and the academy in this way are among Ruth Behar's "vulnerable observers" (1997, 173), working despite "the risks in exposing oneself in an academy that continues to feel ambivalent about observers who forsake the mantle of omniscience" (Behar 1997, 12). While undertaking fieldwork, therefore, my role was most influenced by that which Graham Harvey describes as methodological guesthood.

For Harvey, as an anthropologist who researches and tells the unheard stories of many indigenous groups, the researcher engaged in fieldwork is akin to a trusted guest: one who understands the most important community values and experiences, and can be relied upon to behave ethically and respectfully (Harvey 2014, 94). In this role, one is never entirely emic nor etic, whatever one's prior history in the community.

The term "guesthood" neatly encapsulates a feeling prevalent during fieldwork: that of moving back and forth across the border between field and academy; that of never quite being at home but not quite being a stranger either. The researcher as guest benefits from privileged access to those who make the field their home, but this access is contingent on specific ethical responsibilities on the part of both guest and host, and can be rescinded at any time.

Methodological guesthood is by design and nature a less than comfortable position to hold. Again, it is vital to maintain the reflexive praxis necessary for "real world research," as described by Robson (2002). I was aiming for what Russell McCutcheon calls "methodological agnosticism" (1999c, 215–216). This entails making "the strange familiar" and "the familiar strange" (Muesse 1999, 291–292), and adopting what Amanda van

Eck Duymaer van Twist (2015, 30) refers to as the position of the "trusted stranger" who defers any judgment on the diverse and individual claims of metaphysical experience so as to focus on other categories of data. I could faithfully notate the shape of practice, and record the reflections of my respondents. I could even compare these to my own lived experience of the practice, and check my analysis with them. But I could not feel what they felt, be sure that I had understood what they were telling me. Furthermore, as I wrote above, the act of interpretation in this case surely changes the data on offer. My respondents were engaged in a highly reflexive practice. Their understanding of both self and practice inevitably changed in the light of what I reflected to them.

This is less precarious and less unusual than it might sound. Arguably no theorist of literature can truly know that they have understood what the author intended to write, and no artist's work remains unchanged by their most prominent critics. But in embodied practice, in the intimacy of the ethnographic field, side by side, researcher and researched, that process of communication, miscommunication, and transformation is magnified and accelerated. My position as a researcher therefore evolved, from one of guesthood to one of service.

Community service is one that holds practical, religious, and political significance for post-lineage yoga culture, and was a key theme in my doctoral data analysis. It is sometimes referred to as *karmayoga* (the yoga of action), or simply *sevā*, a word that has diverse and significant meanings across many modern yoga cultures (Beckerlegge 2015, 209). In post-lineage communities, among others, *sevā* is considered to be equally and at the same time: a practice of personal development and the freely offered currency that allows community events to thrive beyond commercial constraints. *Sevā* is part of the gift economy (Lucia 2014, 189) in that it is freely offered in a context of trust and reciprocity, but it is also an activity that signals one's adherence to a specific axiology and thus in-group status. Participants in many post-lineage yoga communities of practice perform *sevā* because they believe it to be essential to a thriving community, and particularly because they feel it to be sadly absent from what they consider to be the transactional nature of mainstream culture. Similar norms are present within many modern yoga communities that seek to separate themselves from what they consider to be more commercial forms of yoga teaching.

During my fieldwork I explored the field as a responsible guest would. Demonstrating my understanding of group norms meant not just eating, talking, resting, and practicing yoga with others, but serving the practical needs of this community in a number of capacities. In reality, that meant volunteering to lead the occasional yoga session, but more often helping in the kitchen or tidying up practice spaces. These activities provided a much greater diversity of experiences and facilitated a wider range of conversations with respondents. Including such acts of service that the community valued also signaled to respondents that I understood and respected what was important to them, as a guest who could be trusted. It reassured them that I was there to understand rather than expose them.

But with my prior experience of the community, at one and the same time, I was also entering the academy as an outsider, returning to scholarship a decade after my MA studies were complete, and in a new discipline entirely. Understandably, in the early stages of my research, other academics sought to ascertain if I had the requisite reflexivity to do the doctoral process justice. I needed to demonstrate that I could move beyond the purely auto-ethnographic and produce data analysis that contributed to the academic conversation. How intimate could I be to the community I was researching and still maintain the necessary scholarly rigor? I needed to understand and absorb the norms and responsibilities of the academy as much as those of the community I was researching.

Instead of showing a willingness to fold blankets and wash pots, that meant demonstrating my dedication to rigor and reflexivity, sampling validity and data analysis. After all, as one of Behar's "vulnerable observers" I am also ethically obliged to bring such critical skills to bear on the academy itself. I also needed to become skillful at managing those conflicts that arose between field and academy, between my respondents' self-image and its critical deconstruction. My research praxis was taking shape: the experiment as multi-lensed methodology. It needed to be continually tested for its ability to produce insights useful to the study of yoga as an academic discipline. I remain, like other researchers, part of a small and underfunded community of scholarly practice. My research contributes to illuminating an understudied phenomenon that is of importance to millions of practitioners. It is part of a vibrant and ongoing conversation.

Balancing my obligations to both the academic research process and the stories of my respondents was easier when I considered, at any given moment, the many ways in which I was serving both. Thus, my orientation as a researcher in the field evolved in its experimentation, from methodological guesthood to methodological *sevā*. I used this new term first in my thesis, but I continue to reflect on the ways in which research into embodied practices is a service freely dedicated to both academic rigor and the previously unheard stories of our respondents.

## Co-Practice

While my research activities began with fieldwork, as I have said, it was useful to record, and then discuss, specific practices with specific practitioners. I was already curious about the relationship between yoga as it is taught in the group situations of my fieldwork, and yoga as is experienced in the personal practices of participants. I was well aware that yoga teaching communities and trainings consider regular personal practice to be essential for any contemporary yoga teacher. It would be useful to compare those personal practices with the teaching practices of a few prominent teachers from the field. I approached a few such people to become case studies.

In an early experiment, I asked early respondents to choose a time and place where they could begin a practice of yoga according to the emergent needs and practice of their day, and I would attempt to follow them, and then interview them about it. My choices in this were largely intuitive. Simply watching them practice would have felt awkward, but practitioners are used to practicing side by side with others. My own history as a practitioner meant that I was used to trying out practice forms as a way of understanding them in the laboratory of the embodied self. Contemporary yoga teachers place a great deal of trust in their bodies as laboratories of practice (Wildcroft 2020, 115).

The early results of my experiment were very productive. Given my prior experience of yoga, in the interviews that followed respondents spoke of sharing their practice as with a peer, knowing that despite a wide diversity in our practice histories, a shared knowledge of the general scope and repertoire was implicit. Put simply, wherever the practice was headed, I could be expected to have some prior familiarity with the destination, even if the specific journey was unfamiliar to me.

Mimicking the respondent's practice also gave me some insight into how my body responded to the practice, if not theirs. Further reading of Taussig (1991) showed that physical mimesis can also be productive of an experience of high interpersonal attunement, which enhanced the interview process that followed it. This was an insight I would return to. The practice was recorded, with consent, but discretely, via a tiny Go Pro camera placed somewhere in the room. The interviews were similarly recorded, with a small MP3 recorder. When discussing methodology, it is unusual to credit the specific technologies involved. Yet it is clear to me that a different level of intimacy is possible when the recording technologies used in the field are so discrete. In co-practice, my respondents could not forget my presence, but such discrete recording equipment did allow them to relax further into the research process. And the smallness of my Go Pro camera in particular was such that in fieldwork, I frequently had to remind people of its presence, even if it was in my hand, or its most usual place, at the front of my yoga mat.

Between early experiments and the case studies that made it into my thesis, I made two key changes. The first was to my position in the space. I had begun facing and thus mirroring my respondents, and found that my presence dominated the data. My respondents were too distracted by making eye contact to settle into their usual practice. In subsequent sessions I placed myself instead just to one side and a little behind, copying rather than mirroring the respondent. My position there, as a literal shadow following them, was still intimate, but much less confronting.

My second change was to play back the recording of the practice in the background during the interview that followed it. This had one simple but useful effect of keeping a closer focus on the specific instance of practice under discussion. This was especially important given that the practice was not the naturally occurring data between multiple subjects that is common to much video analysis (Mondada 2012, 305), but a deliberate experiment in producing data with the researcher as participant, and the respondent as collaborator. The practice we were discussing could never be exactly the same as my respondent's regular practice. We had agreed to set the space together, enter and meet within it, move together and reflect on the experience together.

As later analysis showed, a regular practice of yoga is highly responsive to its setting. A practitioner's very identity is incrementally reshaped in each practice, their relationships to the human and more-than-human world redrawn in the practice space. For my own part, as the research evolved, unforeseeable challenges emerged when participants moved in ways that I could not follow, and each time I had to choose to adapt or abstain from the practice in some way.

Finally, my respondents were at one and the same time sharing this intimate and familiar practice, and performing their personal and professional identities for the research process. They had been chosen as case studies to represent themselves and their communities of practice. Although as I have said, I was clear that inclusion did not signal approval of them as teachers or practitioners, they wanted this one, special iteration of practice, to represent their best selves. Knowing this did not invalidate the data, it transformed it, provoking me to consider the nature and presentation of charisma in the practice space. In all these ways, the bodily presence of both researcher and researched became assets in the data to be investigated, rather than problems to be solved (Wacquant 2014, 10).

Despite a partially shared practice repertoire and scope of aims, the circumstances of what I had started to call the "co-practice" method were unique in many ways. Yoga teachers are often mimicked by yoga students in the normal process of teaching to a group, but this is at least ostensibly in the service of the evolving student and culture. The yoga teacher is not engaged in personal practice, but performing specific practice forms that they wish to transmit to the student, in ways that they will be most able to replicate. Gestures might be more expansive, variations chosen that are of an appropriate level of difficulty for the student body, and supine practices are rarely demonstrated at all, as it is difficult for a teacher to monitor how students are responding from a position on the floor.

Yoga practitioners, especially teachers, might share less formal co-practice sessions on occasion, blending individual need into shared aims and group practice. But in my experience and data, this is rare. Within yoga culture, while the experience of practicing side by side with other students is common, the experience of having one's individual practice shadowed by another practitioner is extremely unusual. Among others (Bubandt and Willerslev 2015; Sklar 1994), Maxine Sheets-Johnstone (2012, 2016) makes a strong case for mimesis as the basis of developing empathy itself, in infant, adult non-verbal, and even inter-species communication. Simply stated, we sit like others and move like others when we want to attune to their way of being. The fieldwork lens of my methodology entailed moving with over forty different yoga and movement teachers, while at the heart of the co-practice interviews I quietly mimicked individual practices in intimate depth.

Most of the respondents in my case study referred in their interviews to the unexpected and powerful sense of intimacy provoked by the co-practice method. Paraphrasing my respondent Sivani Mata: her usual practice involves her moving in deliberate relationship to, and honoring of, the altar in her room. This relationship of the practitioner to an altar of images and murtis (Wildcroft 2020, 30) is experienced by the practitioner as held within a wider circle of benevolent protection by the deities, divine beings, ancestors, or whoever was the focus of the practice as devotional act. Every one of my respondents spoke of their practice as a form of devotion, although individual ontologies varied. One respondent might be practicing to feel a connection with an animist earth, another in remembrance of a perfected inner self. But every practice was an act of relationship, even if that was to the diverse aspects of the experienced self.

When reflecting on the act of sharing her morning *pūjā* (ritual practice) with me, Sivani Mata spoke of an additional presence, in the form of myself as co-practitioner: researcher and interviewer. For her, it was as if my presence formed a shadow gaze to her own, a presence multiplied by the permanence of the camera's gaze in the corner. There was, as a result, a field containing the respondent and the altar and the intimate relationship therein, created by the gaze of the researcher as witness. This multiple gaze was itself held by the recording gaze of the camera. For my respondent, this was also all held within the circle of divine protection or presence. The result for her was both usual and unusual: an off-centering and an experience of being pulled slightly out of one's usual orbit, enhanced by the unexpected intimacy of being shadowed as well as witnessed.

None of my respondents experienced the intimacy of the co-practice event negatively, but it became essential to respect the emotional intimacy that emerged. There is some precedent for this way of working outside of the academy. A very effective but resource-intense therapeutic technique called Intensive Interaction, as introduced by Jefferies (2009) and reviewed by Hutchinson and Bodicoat (2015), uses physical mimesis to encourage non-speaking disabled people into social interaction, communication, and deeper relationship with care staff, social workers, teachers, and other professionals in their lives. Although the theory and practice of Intensive Interaction were, at best, tangential to the research, I had some familiarity with it, and my understanding of its effects also informed the co-practice lens of the research.

More widely, the issues of yoga in transmission are reflected in the method. Just as the choice of media generates certain forms of practice data, media choice privileges certain aspects of cultural transmission. And the presence of bodies in relationship to their histories, abilities, and tendencies, as well as who leads movement and who follows, is a vector for interpersonal power dynamics within the transmission of yoga culture, just as it is generative of power dynamics within the research relationship.

## Positionality and the Expert Mover

As I have said, my position in the research, whether in fieldwork or co-practice, was that of a trusted stranger. That trust was in part engendered by demonstrating my awareness of community norms through small acts of service. But it was also conferred by my existing familiarity with the practice.

Yoga, like any other physical discipline at any significant level of commitment, is an incremental learnt process. This applies to the physical competence not just to achieve the various acts of movement, posture, breath, and stillness, but also to the individualized knowledge of how to vary the practice according to one's embodied form, and the depth of awareness of sensations arising within the body. Long-term dedication to practice does not guarantee the most acrobatic results but does confer a certain grace, ease, and skillful negotiation of its lived experience (Lussier-Ley 2010, 203). That experience is thus commonly thought to be visible to other practitioners and is a mark, therefore, less of skill than of dedication: of one's history more than one's innate ability.

This process is largely intuitive. In interviews, my respondents sometimes struggled to describe how some aspects of another practitioner's experience are, for them, evident from observing their physical form in ways they are not for an observer without that embodied skillset. The same shape made by a body might be recognized by other practitioners as "authentically" yoga or not depending on subtle contextual clues. And in fact, any number of other activities within the cultural ecology, from walking the site to chopping vegetables, could be understood as somehow "yogic" depending on the intentionality and awareness brought to them, and this too is indefinably demonstrated by how the practitioner holds themselves during the activity. Put simply, it seems that practitioners both experience and observe yoga differently to non-practitioners: as a way of moving and holding oneself that is a result of embodied practice but observable both within and beyond the performance of the practice. It is arguable whether that difference is observable within my data, but its provability is irrelevant here, given that some difference, correlatable to experience within the practice, is real to practitioners, and shapes interpersonal relationships in the field in observable ways.

There is a useful concept within Dance and Performance Studies that can provide further illumination: that of the expert and non-expert mover, as discussed by Cole and Montero (2007, 303) and Ataria, Dor-Ziderman, and Berkovich-Ohana (2015, 134). Fiori *et al.* (2014) also highlight the difference between casual practitioners of an embodied form, and long-term practitioners whose history is foundational to their current practice.

My own long experience of various interoceptive and kinesthetic practices confers a clear difference between my own and many other academic bodies (McGuire 1990, 292). My own body, its flexibility, strength, and sensitivity, is heavily implicated in the research process. I cannot therefore claim that it is neutral within the field in the way that I might if my methodology was textual or material analysis. Despite the recent turn to the material and "embodied" in the study of religion, this and similar disciplines that rely on ethnography as a methodology, have rarely embraced the concept of embodied skillsets among *researchers* as well as respondents.

Besides this, much scholarly attention in the humanities and social sciences has been paid to the embodiment of abstract meaning, but much less to the creation and emergence of meaning as a product of bodies moving in proximity. Yet as I have demonstrated, this phenomenon has strong scientific backing and is of obvious relevance to any researcher engaged in long-term ethnography. Instead, as McCutcheon (1999b) describes, any emic status, whether it confers a practical advantage or not, has traditionally been considered an impediment to researcher clarity within the social sciences in particular, rather than a complication to be productively explored.

Beyond my research process, and the presentation of notation, co-practice, and methodological *sevā* as new tools for the ethnography of embodied practice, there remains much more work to be done in examining the effect of what might be called a yoga body (Singleton 2010) on the research of yoga in general. In my case, the body of the researcher is significantly implicated in the research. But in that, it is no different from the body of the researcher in any experiential research (Giardina and Newman 2011, 526). My research data thus emerged as a unique iteration of the phenomena it describes, negotiated in the relationship of multiple bodily presences, the ecology surrounding those bodies, and all our practice histories (Giardina and Newman 2011, 530). My body alongside the bodies of my respondents, and our shared and separate history, habits, and sensory fields, was a key site for my methodological experimentation.

The methodology that took shape throughout and beyond my doctoral research is productive of the partial truths and experimental conclusions familiar to qualitative research as a whole. I continue to design my research in order to provoke as many questions as answers and to explore and test new theories for the study of embodied practice. The question of how to research the performance of, and more specifically, the transmission of physical practice, survives the research process to become part of its conclusion.

**Theo Wildcroft**, PhD, is a teacher, trainer, writer, and scholar, whose research considers the democratization of yoga post-lineage, and the evolving practice of teaching yoga for community health. She is the author of *Post-Lineage Yoga: From Guru to #MeToo*, an Associate Lecturer at the Open University, and former Project Coordinator for the SOAS Centre of Yoga Studies.

## References

Adams, Jimi. 2013. "Network Analysis." In *The Routledge Handbook of Research Methods in the Study of Religion*, edited by Michael Stausberg and Steven Engler. Routledge Handbooks Online. London: Routledge. www.routledgehandbooks.com/doi/10.4324/9780203154281.ch2_14.

Ataria, Yochai, Yair Dor-Ziderman and Aviva Berkovich-Ohana. 2015. "How Does It Feel to Lack a Sense of Boundaries? A Case Study of a Long-Term Mindfulness Meditator." *Consciousness and Cognition* 37: 133–147.

Beckerlegge, Gwilym. 2015. "Seva: The Focus of a Fragmented but Gradually Coalescing Field of Study." *Religions of South Asia* 9: 208–239.

Behar, Ruth. 1997. *The Vulnerable Observer: Anthropology that Breaks Your Heart.* Boston, MA: Beacon Press.

Bubandt, Nils and Rane Willerslev. 2015. "The Dark Side of Empathy: Mimesis, Deception, and the Magic of Alterity." *Comparative Studies in Society and History* 57: 5–34.

Carp, Richard M. 2001. "Integrative Praxes: Learning from Multiple Knowledge Formations." *Issues in Integrative Studies* 19: 71–121.

Cole, Johnathan and Barbara Montero. 2007. "Affective Proprioception." *Janus Head* 9: 299–317.

Davidsson Bremborg, Anna. 2013. "Interviewing." In *The Routledge Handbook of Research Methods in the Study of Religion*, edited by Michael Stausberg and Steven Engler. Routledge Handbooks Online. London: Routledge. www.routledgehandbooks.com/doi/10.4324/9780203154281.ch2_13.

Dinsmore-Tuli, Uma and Laurie Hyland Robertson. 2019. "On Post-Lineage Yoga." *Yoga Therapy Today* Spring: 46–48.

Dreyfus, Hubert. 1996. "The Current Relevance of Merleau-Ponty's Phenomenology of Embodiment." *The Electronic Journal of Analytic Philosophy* 4.

Fiori, Francesca, Nicole David and Salvatore M. Aglioti. 2014. "Processing of Proprioceptive and Vestibular Body Signals and Self-Transcendence in Ashtanga Yoga Practitioners." *Frontiers in Human Neuroscience* 8: Article 734. https://doi.org/10.3389/fnhum.2014.00734.

Geertz, Clifford. 1999. "'From the Native's Point of View': On the Nature of Anthropological Understanding." In *The Insider/Outsider Problem in the Study of Religion: A Reader*, edited by Russell T. McCutcheon, 50–63. London: Cassell.

Giardina, Michael D. and Joshua I. Newman. 2011. "Physical Cultural Studies and Embodied Research Acts." *Cultural Studies ↔ Critical Methodologies* 11: 523–534.

Harvey, Graham. 2013. “Field Research: Participant Observation.” In *The Routledge Handbook of Research Methods in the Study of Religion*, edited by Michael Stausberg and Steven Engler. Routledge Handbooks Online. London: Routledge. www.routledgehandbooks.com/doi/10.4324/9780203154281.ch2_8.

——. 2014. *Food, Sex and Strangers: Understanding Religion as Everyday Life*. London: Routledge.

Hervieu-Léger, Danièle. 2000. *Religion as a Chain of Memory*. New Brunswick, NJ: Rutgers University Press.

Holloway, Julian. 2003. “Make-Believe: Spiritual Practice, Embodiment, and Sacred Space.” *Environment and Planning A* 35: 1961–1974.

hooks, bell. 1994. *Teaching to Transgress*. London: Routledge.

Hufford, David J. 1999. “The Scholarly Voice and the Personal Voice: Reflexivity in Belief Studies.” In *The Insider/Outsider Problem in the Study of Religion: A Reader*, edited by Russell T. McCutcheon, 294–311. London: Cassell.

Hutchinson, Nick and Anna Bodicoat. 2015. “The Effectiveness of Intensive Interaction, A Systematic Literature Review.” *Journal of Applied Research in Intellectual Disabilities* 28(6): 437–454. https://doi.org/10.1111/jar.12138.

Jefferies, Luke. 2009. “Introducing Intensive Interaction.” *Psychologist* 22(9): 756–758.

Knott, Kim. 2009. “From Locality to Location and Back Again: A Spatial Journey in the Study of Religion.” *Religion* 39: 154–160.

Lucia, Amanda J. 2014. “‘Give Me Sevā Overtime’: Selfless Service and Humanitarianism in Mata Amritanandamayi’s Transnational Guru Movement.” *History of Religions* 54: 188–207.

Lussier-Ley, Chantale. 2010. “Dialoguing with Body: A Self Study in Relational Pedagogy Through Embodiment and the Therapeutic Relationship.” *Qualitative Report* 15: 197–214.

McCutcheon, Russell T., ed. 1999a. *The Insider/Outsider Problem in the Study of Religion: A Reader.* London: Cassell.

——. 1999b. “Part 1: Theoretical Background: Insides, Outsides, and the Scholar of Religion—Introduction.” In *The Insider/Outsider Problem in the Study of Religion: A Reader*, edited by Russel T. McCutcheon, 15–11. London: Cassell.

——. 1999c. “Part 4: Neutrality and Methodological Agnosticism—Introduction.” In *The Insider/Outsider Problem in the Study of Religion: A Reader*, edited by Russel T. McCutcheon, 215–220. London: Cassell.

McGuire, Meredith B. 1990. “Religion and the Body: Rematerializing the Human Body in the Social Sciences of Religion.” *Journal for the Scientific Study of Religion* 29: 283–296.

Mondada, Lorenza. 2012. "Video analysis and the temporality of inscriptions within social interaction: the case of architects at work." *Qualitative Research* 12(3): 304–333. https://doi.org/10.1177/1468794112438149.

Muesse, Mark W. 1999. "Religious Studies and 'Heaven's Gate': Making the Strange Familiar and the Familiar Strange." In *The Insider/Outsider Problem in the Study of Religion: A Reader*, edited by Russel T. McCutcheon, 390–394. London: Cassell.

Orsi, Robert A. 2013. "Doing Religious Studies with Your Whole Body." *Practical Matters Journal* Spring (2): 1–6. http://practicalmattersjournal.org/?p=908.

Robson, Colin. 2002. *Real World Research: A Resource for Social Scientists and Practitioner-Researchers.* Oxford: Wiley-Blackwell.

Shaw, Rosalind. 1999. "Feminist Anthropology and the Gendering of Religious Studies." In *The Insider/Outsider Problem in the Study of Religion: A Reader*, edited by Russell T. McCutcheon, 104–113. London: Cassell.

Sheets-Johnstone, Maxine. 2009. "Animation: The Fundamental, Essential, and Properly Descriptive Concept." *Continental Philosophy Review* 42: 375–400.

——. 2012. "Movement and Mirror Neurons: A Challenging and Choice Conversation." *Phenomenology and the Cognitive Sciences* 11: 385–401.

——. 2018. "Why Kinesthesia, Tactility and Affectivity Matter. Critical and Constructive Perspectives." *Body & Society* 20(10): 1–29.

Singleton, Mark. 2010. *Yoga Body: The Origins of Modern Posture Practice.* Oxford: Oxford University Press.

Singleton, Mark and Borayin Larios. 2021. "The Scholar-Practitioner of Yoga in the Western Academy." In *Routledge Handbook of Yoga and Meditation Studies*, edited by Suzanne Newcombe and Karen O'Brien-Kop, 37–50. London: Routledge.

Sklar, Deidre. 1994. "Can Bodylore Be Brought to Its Senses." *Journal of American Folklore* 107: 9–22.

Smith, Jonathan Z. 1999. "The Devil in Mr. Jones." In *The Insider/Outsider Problem in the Study of Religion: A Reader*, edited by Russel T. McCutcheon, 370–389. London: Cassell.

Stausberg, Michael and Steven Engler. 2013. "Introduction: Research Methods in the Study of Religion." In *The Routledge Handbook of Research Methods in the Study of Religion*, edited by Michael Stausberg and Steven Engler. Routledge Handbooks Online. London: Routledge. www.routledgehandbooks.com/doi/10.4324/9780203154281.ch1_1.

Taussig, Michael T. 1991. *Mimesis and Alterity: A Particular History of the Senses.* New York: Routledge.

Tweed, Thomas A. 2006. *Crossing and Dwelling: A Theory of Religion.* Cambridge, MA: Harvard University Press.

van Eck Duymaer van Twist, Amanda. 2015. "On Being a Stranger in Their Midst." *Diskus* 17: 30–36.

Wacquant, Loïc. 2014. "Homines in Extremis: What Fighting Scholars Teach Us About Habitus." *Body & Society* 20: 3–17.

Watts, Fraser. 2013. "Embodied Cognition and Religion." *Zygon: Journal of Religion & Science* 48: 745–758.

Wildcroft, Theo. 2020. *Post-Lineage Yoga: From Guru to #MeToo.* Sheffield: Equinox.

Zolotow, Nina. 2020. "My Journey to Post-Lineage Yoga." Retrieved June 18, 2020, from https://accessibleyoga.blogspot.com/2020/04/my-journey-to-post-lineage-yoga.html.

# Part II

# PERFORMING TEXTUAL TRADITIONS

-4-

# Transpersonal Therapy and a Tantric Temple

## The *Parātrīśikā* in Western Practice

ISTVÁN KEUL

The chapter explores interconnected instances of cultural transfer from India to Europe of elements pertaining to the Trika school of Śaivism and tantric goddess traditions. The first instance concerns the translation and reception of a Trika text (the *Parātrīśikā*) and its commentary (Abhinavagupta's *Parātrīśikāvivaraṇa*) by a group of therapeutic practitioners based in Northern Germany, as well as its application in transpersonal psychotherapeutic and psychosomatic practice. The second case addresses the establishment of a *yoginī* temple by one of these therapists, after having visited sites dedicated to *yoginī* worship in Hirapur and Bheraghat. The chapter discusses the selective approach to Kashmirian Śaiva teachings in the process of their therapeutic application, as well as the transfer and reception of tantric traditions by Western practitioners.

Keywords: *yoginīs*, Tantric Śaivism, cultural transfer, transpersonal therapy

## Introduction

Two interconnected instances of cultural transfer from India to Europe of elements pertaining to the domain of tantric traditions constitute the main foci of the present text. The first instance concerns the translation and reception of a Trika text (the *Parātrīśikā*) and its commentary (Abhinavagupta's *Parātrīśikāvivaraṇa*) by German therapists. The second thread of cultural transfer is the construction and consecration of a *yoginī* temple near Hamburg, following visits to medieval temples in

Central India. The interconnecting link and central protagonist of our story is Ulrich Hennigs, translator of the text, tantric (and therapeutic) practitioner, and owner of the German *yoginī* sanctuary.

In 2005 Hennigs published a translation of the *Parātrīśikā* along with reflections on its potential relevance for transpersonal therapy. Hennigs's interpretation of the text was met with some interest by medical psychologists and psychotherapists, advocates of the transpersonal approach in their work. I introduce the *Parātrīśikā* and its context in the second section. The fifth section discusses selected aspects of Hennigs's book, connected to the claimed therapeutic relevance of the translated text. From 2006 onwards, Hennigs visited together with his wife Gabriele *yoginī* temples in Hirapur and Bheraghat, exploring the sites and performing rituals on their own or together with local religious specialists. They became attached to the *yoginī*s of Bheraghat, feeling connected "to certain elements of the old cult,"[1] so much so that they had copies made of several statues which were then shipped to Germany, established in a temple, and consecrated by one of the Bheraghat priests. I introduce the Indian *yoginī* temples in the third section, followed by a brief biographical segment on Hennigs's encounter with India and her religious traditions. The last (and sixth) section contains a brief presentation of the German *yoginī* temple and its consecration, and an epilogue.

## The Text

The *Parātrīśikā* (or *Parātriṃśikā*)[2] is one of the shorter texts in the vast scriptural corpus of Tantric Śaivism. Composed around the seventh century CE, this Tantra of 37 stanzas belongs to a subsystem of the Trika,

1. Hennigs, unpublished manuscript. Ulrich Hennigs wrote an autobiographical text in which he discussed his early interest in Indian religions, among other things. I am relying on this manuscript in the biographical parts of this chapter, along with material from personal communication. Hennigs and I met several times (both in India and Germany) and corresponded via e-mail over a period of more than three years (May 2007–August 2010). Our on-and-off conversation ended abruptly with his unexpected death in September 2010. I will remain grateful to Ulrich Hennigs for sharing his thoughts and experiences so generously, and to Gabriele, with whom I have stayed in touch over the years.
2. For example, Gnoli (1985), Muller-Ortega (1989), and Sanderson (2014). See Bäumer (2011, 2–3) for Abhinavagupta's discussion of the work's title. Abhinavagupta, the eminent Kashmirian Śaiva theologian and philosopher (main works between c. 975–1025), explains in his commentary *Parātrīśikāvivaraṇa* (192, II. 3–14)—philologically unconvincingly, according to Sanderson (2014, 69, n. 265)—that "Parātrīśikā" is the correct form.

a tradition within the Śaiva Mantramārga that has a decidedly Śākta character.[3] Common to the main Trika texts is a focus on the worship of the three goddesses Parā, Parāparā, and Aparā. As indicated in the title, translated by Bäumer (2011, 2) as "(The Tantra relating to) The Supreme (*parā*) Goddess (*īśikā*) of the Three (*tri*)," the *Parātrīśikā* teaches the propitiation of only one of the three female deities, Parā. The exegetical works connected to this text indicate its doctrinal importance for the non-dual Śākta-Śaiva traditions: In addition to the influential, extensive commentary written around the end of the first millennium by Abhinavagupta (*Parātrīśikāvivaraṇa*), another early exegetical text from South India initially attributed to that same author (*Parātrīśikālaghuvṛtti*) served as the basis for further commentaries and related texts over the centuries (Sanderson 2014, 68–69).[4] It was in connection with translations of these two major commentaries and of analyses of Abhinavagupta's exegetical oeuvre that the *Parātrīśikā* was translated into European languages, with Gnoli (1985), Singh (1989), and Bäumer (2011) working on the *Parātrīśikāvivaraṇa*, and Gnoli (1965), Padoux (1975) and Muller-Ortega (1989) on the *Parātrīśikālaghuvṛtti.*

The *Parātrīśikā* begins (as is usually the case in texts considered to be divine revelations) with questions addressed (this time) by the Goddess to Bhairava concerning the ways and means by which the "unsurpassable divine Consciousness (*anuttaram*) bring[s] about the achievement of the identity of the empirical I with the perfect I-Consciousness of Śiva" (verse 1, Singh 1989, 5–6), and about "the *kaulikī śakti* [...], the Śakti who is the chief source [...] and the presiding deity of the whole manifestation" (verse 2) (61). To this, Bhairava answers by calling the Goddess "*mahābhāge*," "most illustrious one," also interpretable as "the one of whom the god himself is only an aspect,"[5] and by saying that he will now expound on both the Absolute and its manifestation, the empirical reality, with which it is identical (verses 3 to 4, 65–66). Bhairava goes on to explain the various levels of reality (*tattvas*) in the order of their creation (*sṛṣṭi*), connecting them to elements of language, the phonemes of the Sanskrit alphabet (verses 5 to 9ab). The next part of the *Parātrīśikā* (9cd to 18) contains the introduction of the mantra *sauḥ*, described as "the heart of

3. The dating of the *Parātrīśikā* is somewhat uncertain. According to Bäumer (2011, 4), "[i]t may not be wrong to place the text in the seventh century or earlier." For extensive surveys of the scriptural and exegetical works of Tantric Śaivism, see Sanderson (1988, 2009, 2007a, 2014a, 2014b).
4. There are other early commentaries as well, that have not been preserved, such as the one by Somananda (ninth century).
5. This interpretation by Abhinavagupta implies that the Goddess is asking questions about the highest power that she is herself (see Bäumer 2011, 57–58).

the Self of Bhairava,"[6] and an explanation of its powers: By remembering this *hṛdayabīja* ("seed mantra of the heart") for various lengths of time, the tantric practitioner gradually attains a stage of absorption in which deities and other superhuman entities inhabit his body and grant his desires.[7] Verses 21 to 24 emphasize once again the importance of knowing the mantra and its all-embracing symbolism, introduce the triad of *śakti*s (*icchā*, *jñāna*, and *kriyā*) as the highest creative force, and identify Śiva with the supreme teacher of the seed mantra (Bäumer 2011, 234–235). This is followed by a description of central ritual elements and stages of an external ritual process to be performed by the male practitioner (*vīra*) together with his female companion, the *yoginī* (verses 25 to 33, Singh 1989, 245–246): placing mantras on parts of the body (*nyāsa*), tying the tuft of hair (*śikhā*) with 27 mantras, fettering the ten directions, consecrating and sprinkling water over the ritual implements and sexual organs (*liṅga* and *sthaṇḍila*), and preparing two seats (*āsana*s) made of flowers and consecrated with fourteen mantras. In the state of (sexual) union, the *vīra* and the *yoginī* worship the goddess Maheśānī and offer the fluids produced in the process as a sacrificial libation. Once again, the importance of the seed syllable is emphasized in verses 34 and 35: mentally dwelling on the *hṛdayabīja sauḥ*, the practitioner "attains complete perfection" (Bäumer 2011, 256), "attains to his goal, i.e., liberation, while alive" (Singh 1989, 259). This mantra "has neither beginning nor end," and "resides in the heart-lotus of Śiva" (262). The final two verses (36 and 37) of the *Parātrīśikā* state the fruit resulting from the mantra, which itself is seen as the union of Śiva and Śakti, namely, obtaining anything that is desired, and unmediated (perception-like) omniscience (*sarvajñatvam*).

The *Parātrīśikā* belongs to the subsystem of the Trika called Anuttara or Parākrama (Sanderson 2014, 53), with connections to the Kaula tradition. Historically, this subsystem "appears to have been the most enduring and influential" (Sanderson 1990, 80), spreading to the south of India and merging with the cult of Lalitā Tripurasundarī. Sanderson writes:

> This south Indian tradition is fully aware of its debt to Abhinavagupta and the other Kashmirian authorities of the ninth and tenth centuries. Their works were held in the highest esteem and continued to provide the

---

6. On *sauḥ*, see Padoux (1990, 417–418). On the meanings of the symbol of the heart in Tantric Śaivism see Muller-Ortega (1989). Bäumer (2011, 203, 207) translates *hṛdayaṃ bhairavātmanaḥ* as "the heart of the nature of Bhairava."
7. See Muller-Ortega (2002) for reflections on this section of the *Parātrīśikā* and its interpretation in the *Parātrīśikālaghuvṛtti*.

> theoretical basis of an āgamic, non-Upanishadic non-dualism among the devotees of the Goddess at least into the nineteenth century.
>
> (Sanderson 1990, 82)

In 2005 Ulrich Hennigs published a German translation of the text. The book includes short introductory chapters on Tantra, the philosophy of the Trika, and the *tattvas*, before offering a translation of and commentaries on the *Parātrīśikā* (31–80). In the third main section the author discusses topics such as spirituality and psychological development, spiritual practice (with a focus on the *upāyas*, the means of attaining liberation), and "transcendental states of consciousness." There are no notes or systematic references accompanying the translation and commentary, but there is an appendix with the transliterated Sanskrit text, notes on the Sanskrit alphabet, and a glossary of Sanskrit terms. Also, there is a bibliography with relevant literature (including works by Muller-Ortega, Padoux, Singh, and Dyczkowski) to which the author sporadically refers, as well as an index. From a brief biographical note at the end of the book we learn that Hennigs (nickname "Gandhi") was born in 1947 and has been interested in spirituality-related issues since his youth. His quest led him to India where he spent years of intensive study with spiritual teachers. The note ends stating: "His deep and continuous preoccupation with the nature of consciousness have marked not only his attitude towards life but have also led him to his profession. He lives in Hamburg and has been working there for more than 25 years running a private practice" (Hennigs 2005, 149).[8] From a photograph placed above these lines a man with a long, grey-white beard looks intently at the reader. We will return to this text and Hennigs's reflections on its usefulness for transpersonal psychotherapy in a later section.

## The *Yoginīs* and Their Temples

Complex developments within segments of Tantric Śaivism resulted in the emergence of sets of *yoginīs* as the focus of an elaborate cult in the last centuries of the first millennium C.E. With possible (and plausible) precursors both in the classical Hindu realm (*apsaras*, *grahīs*/*grahaṇīs*, *yakṣiṇīs*, *dākīṇis*, *mātṛs*/*mātṛkās*) (White 2003, 29) and in the worship of female deities in folk or tribal contexts (von Stietencron 2008), the *yoginīs* show clear continuities and overlaps with Mother-goddess conceptions from outside and inside the tantric fold, appearing first in texts of the

8. All translations from the German original are mine.

Vidyāpīṭha subsystem before gaining prominence in the Kaula traditions of Tantric Śaivism (Hatley 2012).

> These texts' ritual systems are for the most part highly antinomian, drawing on older traditions of cremation-ground asceticism augmented by mantra-based magical rites, ritualized sexuality, and impure offerings (such as alcohol and meat). The iconography of the cult deities is replete with images of violence, death, and eroticism. One of the paradigmatic aims of ritual is attainment of power-bestowing encounters with the goddesses, referred to as *yoginīmelaka* or *melāpa* (rendezvous with *yoginī*s).
> (Hatley 2019, 3)

The designation *yoginī* ("female practitioner of yoga") referred in the early medieval period to the female yogi, the female tantric adept (participant in rituals such as the one described in the *Parātrīśikā*), and to the tantric goddesses possessing (and bestowing upon the practitioner) not only the extraordinary powers of yoga (*siddhi*)[9] but also—as described in tantric literature—a wide range of other abilities such as the "six actions/rites" (*ṣaṭkarmāṇi*) that include the subjugation (*vaśīkaraṇa*), immobilization (*stambhana*), driving away (*uccāṭaṇa*) and killing (*māraṇa*) of enemies.[10] Based on textual and iconographic representations of *yoginī*s, Hatley (2013) proposed a definition[11] that includes factors such as multiplicity (*yoginī*s occur in groups of 6, 24, 64, or 81), the blurring of boundaries between goddesses and women,[12] organization into clans (*kula*, *gotra*), polymorphism,[13]

9. On this and the following, see Hatley (2013, 2019). On the extraordinary powers attained by yoga, see the contributions in Jacobsen (2012).
10. For a discussion (based on Mahīdhara's sixteenth-century *Mantramahodadhiḥ*), see Bühnemann (2000). A brief overview can be found in Padoux (2017, 124–125).
11. Vidya Dehejia provided a first important systematical attempt at defining *yoginī*s and their many aspects in her pioneering work *Yoginī Cult and Temples: A Tantric Tradition* (1986, 11–38).
12. "[T]hrough ritual perfection or other means, a tantric adept or another female may become a yoginī. Men, for their part, may seek to join the yoginīs and partake of their powers, aspiring to become like Bhairava in their midst. Taxonomies reflect this by positing yoginīs as a scale of beings, extending from powerful cult goddesses to the mortal yoginīs who emulate or even embody the deities" (Hatley 2013, 23–24).
13. In text and sculpture, they are often represented in therianthropic forms. Described as shapeshifters often transforming into female animals, classical Sanskrit tales (from the *Kathāsaritsāgara*) and tantric literature (f. ex. the *Kaulajñānanirṇaya*) highlight their ability to transform others into animals as well. For present-day accounts from rural Orissa regarding these forms and powers attributed to *yoginī*s, see Keul (2013, 6–7).

and ambivalence.[14] David White's definition includes a number of other features as well:

> The *yoginīs* ("female yokers," "female joiners") are a ravening horde of medieval tantric goddesses that granted supernatural powers to the male tantric virtuosi called *siddhas* (perfected beings), *vīras* (virile heroes), or Kāpālikas ("Skull Bearers"), who, in their quest for supernatural powers (*siddhis*), transacted with them in esoteric rituals on cremation grounds (*śmaśānas*, also called *pīṭhas*: mounds or power places). They possess the power of flight as well as the power to change their shape, both of which are fueled by their consumption of sacrificial victims or the sexual fluids of their male human consorts.
>
> (White 2018, n.p.)

> [T]heir power was intimately connected to the flow of blood, both their own menstrual and sexual emissions, and the blood of their animal (and human?) victims; [...] they were essential to Tantric initiation in which they initiated male practitioners through fluid transactions via their "mouths" [...].
>
> (White 2003, 27)

In both White's and Hatley's multilayered definitions the *yoginīs*' ability to fly plays an important role, a power that shaped the architecturally uncommon design of the medieval temples consecrated to them, which were often not only round (a reminder of the *maṇḍalas*' essential role in *yoginī*-related ritual interactions), with the goddesses' images placed in niches in the circular wall and oriented towards a central shrine, but also hypaethral (open to the sky), which would allow them to land and take off with ease.

Temples dedicated to the *yoginīs* were built from the ninth century onwards across central India as well as in the eastern and southern parts of the subcontinent, possibly involving royal patronage (Dehejia 1986, 85–86). The construction of these sites was an indication of the transformation gradually undergone by the *yoginī* cult, which became thus part of a more mainstream religious culture.[15] Most religious activities at these temples seem to have faded after the fourteenth century, and today they are in ruins or have disappeared altogether, with numerous *yoginī* images in museums. Among the surviving structures, the ones in Hirapur (Orissa) and in Bheraghat (Madhya Pradesh) are well-preserved,

14. They are dangerous to non-initiates, but sources of power to the tantric practitioner (*vīra*) participating in ritual encounters with them.
15. For texts that describe the consecration of and worship rituals for *yoginīs*, see also more recently Hatley (2020).

serving as historical monuments open to an interested public and as places of worship for the inhabitants of the surrounding settlements. In addition, in recent years the sites have attracted visitors from India and abroad fascinated by these temples' connection to tantric traditions, as well as—in the case of Hirapur—cultural performers, and the occasional company picnic (Keul 2004).

The Hirapur temple (ninth to tenth centuries), located not far from the old temple city of Bhubaneswar, is the considerably smaller one of the two. According to Dehejia (1986, 95–96) it has a diameter of thirty feet, with a roofless, circular sandstone structure not higher than eight feet. The sixty slabs with delicately carved *yoginī* images lining the interior wall are approximately two feet high and made of chlorite. In the center of the temple there is a quadrangular shrine that probably housed a (now lost) large image of Śiva/Bhairava, in the pillars of which there are more images of *yoginī*s, as well as four ithyphallic Bhairavas. Four other male figures are placed near the entrance, among them two gatekeepers (*dvārapālas*). Nine further images of female deities are to be found on the outer walls. To those intending to "experience the goddess" (Dupuis 2019), to modern-day practitioners of yoga and tantra, and to others looking to tap into an enigmatic source of power or aiming at reactivating practices of the *yoginī*s' "ancient cults" by means of choreography and performance (Lopez y Royo 2013), the Hirapur temple is a particularly special place with multiple valences.

The enclosure in Bheraghat (tenth to eleventh centuries) has a circular ground plan with a diameter of 125 feet. The images in its eighty-one niches are almost life-sized and form part of elaborately carved slabs. The enshrined deities—many of them substantially damaged—"are no slender, girlish damsels" like in Hirapur, but multiple-armed, "mature, voluptuous beauties," majestic and heavily ornamented (Dehejia 1986, 128–129). With the initial central shrine missing, a small temple dedicated to Śiva and Pārvatī (Gaurī-Śaṅkar) (late twelfth century), and positioned somewhat awkwardly off-center, is the focus of religious activities at the site. However, the local devotees who visit regularly, often circumambulate the entire enclosure, stopping at selected *yoginī* images. Perhaps also due to its location on top of a rather steep hill, this temple is not as integrated into the religious life of the surrounding localities as the easily approachable Hirapur temple. A large share of its visitors comes from outside the area and comprises mostly Indian tourists who include Bheraghat on their holiday circuits mainly because of the scenic beauty of the nearby gorge formed by the Narmada River (Marble Rocks). And then there are—here, too—those visitors from India and abroad who come with a different kind of agenda: To selectively (re)connect to an ancient *tantrapīṭha*, a seat of tantra, imagined as a place with extraordinary qualities.[16]

In 2006, Ulrich Hennigs and his wife Gabriele visited Hirapur and Bheraghat for the first time. The couple's names appear in my field notes even before having met them personally when, during one of our long conversations, one of the Bheraghat temple priests talked admiringly about their special connection with the site. He asked me to let them know on my return to Germany that he had received their letter, which I did in an e-mail. After having briefly introduced myself and my work, and duly delivered the priest's message, I inquired about the couple's plans regarding future trips to the site. Hennigs's reply came almost immediately:

> Yes, we are indeed going to return to Bheraghat. For us, this is a place we will most certainly visit quite often. [...] We had a wonderful time there, were even able to perform a ritual in the temple, worshipping the yoginis following the classical tradition. [...] I have been studying yoginis and matrikas, and mainly Kashmir Shaivism, for a long time. Everything started with my first trip to India in 1969. Overall, I must have spent six years in the country. My wife and I also visited the yogini temple in Hirapur, but Bheraghat is simply incomparable.
>
> (E-mail communication, 21 May 2007)

There were no more exchanges between us until—in the autumn of that same year—our stays in Bheraghat coincidentally overlapped and we ran into each other one morning at the temple on top of the hill. For a week or so we spent the greater part of each day in the wide circular enclosure, with little interaction and acknowledging each other's presence with a kind of reserved skepticism. While I was busy documenting as meticulously as possible the *yoginīs*' images in all their rich iconographical detail, trying at the same time to gather information on the rituals and motivations of the few regular visitors, the main interest of Hennigs and his wife lay clearly in absorbing the site's atmosphere, with the occasional round of meditation on the platform in front of the Gaurī-Śaṅkar shrine, followed by the contemplation of selected goddess statues. Then, towards the end of my stay, our conversations gradually became more frequent, both on and off site, and we kept in touch after leaving India.

Here is how Ulrich Hennigs describes the couple's first experiences in Bheraghat in his autobiographical text:

16. Some of the signification processes connected to the site are discussed in Keul (2012).

> Our first encounter with the yogini images in this temple made a deep and lasting impression. When we stepped inside, it became instantly clear that the temple had a tantric background. I recognized this based on the Padmas, the stylized vulvas on the walls of the shrine. [...] My wife and I instantly knew that we had found our temple. Of course, one should not forget that I had been studying the tantric traditions for decades, planning to visit Bheraghat for many years. I remember well our first walk around the place, along all the yogini statues. It was as if I was sensing vibrations, and much of it had an erotic component. But the strongest feeling was also a very encompassing one: It was about "being there," about having arrived. (Hennigs, n.d., 48; my translation)[17]

They returned three more times to this temple over the next two years, each time spending several weeks there. During their last visit in the fall of 2008, they commissioned a local sculptor to produce copies of three of the *yoginī* statues (Phaṇendrī, Sarvatomukhī, and Kāmadā), along with four other images of deities modeled after originals from the Vaital Deul temple in Bhubaneswar (Śiva, Pārvatī, and two *dvārapālas*) and a statue of Gaṇeśa, planning on establishing a *yoginī* sanctuary in their garden at home.

## Fragments of a Biography

Ulrich Hennigs's affinity with India and his subsequent preoccupation with tantric traditions has a prehistory that—according to Hennigs himself[18]—goes back as far as his early childhood. He was born in 1947 into a family of vegetarians. The mother, whom he describes as having a no-nonsense, rational attitude toward life, was a nurse, the father, esoterically interested, a classical musician. While his two brothers changed their diet at some point in their early youth, Ulrich remained resolutely lacto-vegetarian throughout his life. His grandmother started calling him "Gandhi" at the age of two or three: He had always been under-weight, writes Hennigs, and Mahatma Gandhi was a well-known figure in those days, short time after his assassination. The nickname stuck, and for good reasons, too, at least in that given context: He was the odd vegetarian in primary school, a supporter of non-violence in high school, and later a

17. See also Keul (2012, 209–210).
18. The following is based on a manuscript (44 pages, in German) authored by Ulrich Hennigs as part of a planned larger autobiographical work, which he sent me in November 2009. The fragment was work in progress, with some more carefully elaborated parts, and others that comprised many hurried sentences in need of reworking. All translations from the original are mine.

conscientious objector to military service. In the autobiographical fragment I rely on here, the narrative is less linear: Hennigs embeds these bits of information in meandering reflective passages, stressing repeatedly that he does not intend or imply any "esoteric explanations" when writing about these antecedents. Instead, the framework he proposes for looking back at his life is "seriality and synchronicity." Here is an example of what he sees as a seriality of biographical events: (1) When he was around fifteen, Hennigs found in the attic Indologist Heinrich Zimmer's 1944 biography of the Indian sage Ramana Maharshi (1879–1950). The book made a lasting impression on him, and (2) for a long time he carried it with him everywhere he went, even keeping it under his pillow at night. (3) Five years later (1967) in Paris, his first Indian teacher introduced him more thoroughly to the teachings of Ramana Maharshi and non-duality. (4) In 1969 Hennigs travelled to Tiruvannamalai, where Maharshi had spent the greater part of his life, (5) continuing in the years to come his studies of both experiential and doctrinal Advaita (Śaṅkara).

There are numerous other topics from the early 1960s that Hennigs writes about in the introductory part of his manuscript, such as the early fascination with sexuality and the first visual encounter with tantra;[19] feelings of loneliness and outbursts of poetic creativity; the search for meaning and "absolute freedom;" reading Ginsberg and experimenting with psychedelic drugs. In 1967 he embarked on what he calls his "years of peregrination." During a stay in Paris Hennigs meets Rammurti Mishra, who for the next two years becomes his Sanskrit and yoga teacher. Together they read a selection of Upaniṣads and work systematically through Mishra's book *Fundamentals of Yoga*.[20] As Mishra's assistant, he spends three months at the yoga school Schloss Aubach, where he meditates regularly and studies Sanskrit texts during daytime, and experiences ecstatic states during his nightly practice. Conversations with his teacher about yoga, *siddhis*, asceticism, and Vedānta had a major influence on his early formation, writes Hennigs. He then lives in Spain for some time, where he gives yoga and Sanskrit lessons and is introduced to the Ohsawa macrobiotic diet. There, in what he describes as a major spiritual experience, he transitions to a form of objectless meditation, "without support, without thoughts, without mantras."

19. A painting showing a severed-headed tantric goddess (probably Chinnamastā) standing on a copulating couple.
20. Rammurti Mishra, *Fundamentals of Yoga: A Handbook of Theory, Practice and Application*. New York: Julian Press, 1959. Mishra (1923–1993) founded—among other centers—The Yoga Society in New York and the Ananda Ashram in Monroe and was later known (and published several books) under the name of Brahmananda Sarasvati.

After a brief stint in Morocco, in the fall of 1969 Hennigs arrives in India, with little money and no clear goal, "except to explore and face up." He travels to South India, where he befriends an Ayurveda practitioner who takes him under his wings and sends him to an ashram in the Western Ghats. Hennigs spends a few months there, meditating and (re-) reading Sanskrit texts, instructed occasionally by the ashram's leader. In August 1970 Hennigs is back in Germany, three years after his unannounced departure. He spends some time in Switzerland, Morocco, and Spain before he returns to India in the fall of 1972. During this second stay he attends several private talks given by Jiddu Krishnamurti and is profoundly impressed. The encounter also results in intense self-reflection and self-doubt, and a prolonged state of apathy and depression. After this "transformative" encounter, Hennigs travels to North India and spends eight months in Almora, where he interacts with resident mystics Anagarika Govinda and Shunyata Baba and continues his intention- and support-free meditation practices.

A long section of Hennigs's manuscript (32–39) is dedicated to his study of Indian astrology under the guidance of T. S. Vasan[21] during another stay in India in 1975–1976, a preoccupation that eventually becomes one of the pillars of his professional work from the early 1980s onwards. Back in Germany, he rents a small cottage on the outskirts of Hamburg, marries (for the first time), and gradually establishes a name for himself as an astrologer and life counsellor.

The last part of the manuscript is titled "Tantra" (39–43). It contains a description of what Hennigs identifies as his first encounter with tantric sexuality during the months spent in the Himalayan foothills in 1973. One night, while doodling with colored pencils on a piece of paper in his sparsely lit cottage, the drawing suddenly begins to resemble a nude female body:

> I enhanced her contours and felt how my sexual energy awoke. And there it was, the control. I restrained my desire to relieve the tension and felt an insane overexcitement. I was torn. I stayed in this state of excitement, observing it merely, which was quite a challenge. That night was immensely tense. I experienced all kinds of phenomena: The roof beams started creaking, there were rustling sounds everywhere, and I was sensing the presence of something else. Because the suppressed excitement produced a strange tension, like an immersion into a kind of fullness, I tried the next

> night to build up that tension again, and not convert it into activity. The suppression was powerful and pushed me to my limits that night.
>
> (Hennigs, n.d., 40)

With the help of a visualization exercise found in Evans-Wentz's *Tibetan Yoga*, Hennigs intensifies his practice over the next two weeks. The energy flowing through his body gradually increases, the visualized entity appears more and more real, eventually morphing into a *yoginī*:

> I was in the presence of this yogini. And she was not just a mere product of my mind anymore but appeared to be very much real. She had a voice of her own. I knew how this voice felt: Not like a verbal utterance or vocal phenomenon [...], it was more of a nonverbal happening, in which her actions somehow also were her language. And her actions seemed to occur independently. [...] It is almost impossible to offer a full description of what happened in the weeks after that. I learned how to channel my energy, was able to let it circle in my body. The yogini made it clear how to do this, I could see it with her. She showed me how to restrain my energy, withdrawing briefly whenever I was close to orgasm. [...] And it happened several times that I fell into a deep trance during this practice, in the moments when the yogini and I became one.
>
> (Hennigs, n.d., 41)

Hennigs describes how the *yoginī* applied a drop of his semen onto her forehead, expressing thus to him that she regarded his sexual discharge as a sacrificial offering. Further such interactions (and transactions of bodily fluids) followed over a period of several days, culminating in a final experience:

> In the moment of orgasm, I perceived my death and was carried away into endless distances. She was with me in these distances, and then, at some point, I had a feeling of "that was about it." And so it was: I could still imagine her after that, but her dynamic, her being a distinct entity, was not there anymore.
>
> (Hennigs, n.d., 42)[22]

This experience, and similar later ones, Hennigs saw as his introduction to tantra and the *yoginī* cult, themes he continued pursuing more systematically from the 1990s onwards.

## Tantric Śaivism and Transpersonal Psychology

In the introductory chapter of his book on the *Parātrīśikā*, Hennigs describes tantric texts as different from other religious scriptures in that they are not prophetic revelations that followers need to believe in, but rather experiences which are both relatable and comprehensible. According to him, they ought to be understood primarily as the product of others' experiences and as instructions for how to confront "the facts of consciousness" (2005, 13). The tantric practitioner, Hennigs writes, explores reality, becomes aware of its presence and of the practitioner's own presence in this reality. It is this awareness that generates transformation and change, rather than the wish to elude or resist what is perceived as reality (16). Hennigs contrasts the psychology of what he calls "the tantric worldview," which he characterizes as one that integrates openness and unmediated experience, with the psychology of yoga. While the latter is a rather closed, rigorous system that assumes controllability of human life and emotion, having thus—according to Hennigs—certain similarities to behavioral therapy, the tantric view does not attempt to exert control by suppression, but allows for the possibility of experiencing totality. Hennigs concludes the introductory section by stating that the text he is about to discuss deals first and foremost with the issue of consciousness and is relevant to the field of transpersonal psychology (17).

A brief overview of some defining aspects of transpersonal psychology is probably useful at this point. This area of psychology has been described by Friedman (2018, 231) as a "heterodox approach to psychological science" resting on an "alternate worldview that contrasts with the dominant paradigm of mainstream contemporary psychology." It criticizes the narrow scientism of the latter, advocating for a broader understanding of psychology. On the other hand, as Friedman goes on to point out, it is itself susceptible to criticism based on its "culture of romanticism": "e.g., naively accepting beliefs that portray the world in 'enchanted' and 'magical' ways not in accord with contemporary scientific understandings" (231). In a retrospective article on the first three and a half decades of transpersonal psychology, Hartelius, Caplan and Rardin (2007) have identified three mutually reinforcing definitional themes of the field. The first is "beyond-ego psychology," with transpersonal *content* and including, among other theme strands, states of consciousness other than ordinary, as well as mystical/contemplative aspects. The second is integrative psychology, with transpersonal *context*, a broad framework characterized as "comprehensive, holistic, multicultural, integrative or integral" (Hartelius *et al.* 2007, 143). The third is transformative psychology, where the transpersonal perspective concerns *change* processes both on the level of the personal (development, psycho-spiritual growth, embodied knowledge) and social (application of the findings to fields such as education, therapy, ethics, social action, business) (Hartelius *et al.* 2007, 143). According to Hartelius and Ferrer

(2013), two main philosophical frameworks have defined transpersonal psychology since its beginnings in the late 1960s:[23] the perennialist and the participatory. The former, with a long line of precursors in philosophy and advocated in psychology from the 1970s onwards first by the transpersonal theorist Ken Wilber, claims that "spiritual traditions use culturally diverse language and symbols to represent what is essentially the journey to a single spiritual ultimate" (Hartelius and Ferrer 2013, 189). In the 1980s Wilber went on to develop a structuralist version in which the individual gradually evolves spiritually by passing through various levels of consciousness structures.[24] The perennialist paradigm was dominant until the early 2000s, when the participatory philosophy emerged, which not only "understands the world to be a dynamic and open-ended living system that is continually involved in co-creating itself" (Hartelius and Ferrer 2013, 194), but also holds that "the mind is made of the same stuff as the world: consciousness in some form goes all the way down to the basic materials of physicality. The mind can know the world because through the mind, the world knows itself" (Hartelius and Ferrer 2013, 195). In psychotherapies based on transpersonal psychology, consciousness plays an essential role, as it is assumed to constitute the core of being human.[25] An important aspect of consciousness, according to transpersonal psychotherapy, is spirituality, as "some experiential, notional, behavioral or intentional relationship with some transcendent reality, out of which arises meaning, solace or motivation for an individual" (Walach 2009, 2).

Reflections regarding the relevance of the *Parātrīśikā* for transpersonal therapy can be found throughout Hennigs's book, often when discussing central concepts from the stanzas themselves, or from Abhinavagupta's commentary. For instance, in connection with the very first verse, Hennigs discusses *āṇavamala*, the "impurity of/contamination by individuality," which is considered in non-dualistic Tantric Śaivism one of

23. In 1968, transpersonal psychology was proclaimed "an emerging force" (Sutich 1968). A year later, the first issue of the *Journal of Transpersonal Psychology* was published, introduced by Maslow's contribution titled "The Farther Reaches of Human Nature" (Maslow 1969).
24. Hennigs includes throughout his work references to transpersonal theorists and other thinkers whose work he appreciates, among them Ken Wilber. He also mentions in positive terms Jean Gebser, whose work *Ursprung und Gegenwart* (1986) is included in the reference list. Hennigs critiques, on the other hand, the approach of Stanislav Grof, another important founding figure of transpersonal psychology, whose regression theory he does not consider to be entirely transpersonal.
25. For a detailed introduction to transpersonal psychotherapy, including an overview of relevant research, see Rodrigues and Friedman (2013).

the reasons why the real nature of absolute consciousness (*anuttara*) has become obscured for the "empirical I." Hennigs (2005, 36) writes:

> We all know *āṇavamala* in our feelings and emotions, and we also know how deeply this separation can affect us. From a psychological point of view this could be compared to the existential aloneness of every human being. But we could also equate it with the birth process, which is a process of separation as well. From the perspective of the Kashmirian Tantras, the feeling of separation and disconnection is the root of the hardships of human existence. From here, further entanglements follow, due mainly to *māyīyamala* ["the impurity of illusion," I.K.], the wish for change and attainment of control, the avoidance of fear and guilt.

Reflections on the therapeutic usefulness of the *Parātrīśikā* follow, for example in connection with verse 9 that introduces the core mantra *sauḥ*, "the heart of the Self of Bhairava." According to Abhinavagupta, meditating (on) the all-encompassing *mantra*, understanding its meaning, entering the "divine heart," and realizing thus the core of reality, is (equal with) attaining liberation. Here's what Hennigs (2005, 45) has to say about this central part of the text:

> To me, there is a depth-psychological interpretation here: The entire phenomenal world of our experiences is nothing but a form of escape from the (apparently frightening) reality of Bhairava and his *śaktis*. [...] We are separating ourselves from our immediate experience giving names and meaning to objects and phenomena. We are making images for ourselves, living our lives according to them, thinking that this is how reality is. Reality, however, is in fact free of such pictures and imaginations. Instead, it integrates all differences on the level of meaning and dissolves them, rendering us speechless. The reality of Bhairava as the eruption of the primal consciousness leads to the questioning of the picture that we have of ourselves and to the suspension of all concepts. [...] Tantric texts are not mere philosophical speculation but offer a relevant psychological perspective. [...] Looking at the very moment when a "rupture" in the process of experiencing takes place, is essential to the spiritual seeker and should be given attention to, also in transpersonal psychology.

In a chapter titled "Spirituality and psychological development" (81–82), Hennigs systematizes some of his previous statements on the *Parātrīśikā* and transpersonal psychology. Reiterating that the text is primarily about consciousness, he sees in the concept of *khecarī* (verse 1) which he translates (like Singh 1989, 5, for that matter) as "the universal consciousness-power," a state of consciousness that is beyond the personal, and not a regression into pre-personal forms. As examples of the latter, he mentions trance, other forms of psychoactive techniques, as well as the pre-causal, pre-personal world of the shaman. Collective states of consciousness should not be mistaken for transpersonal states either. Hennigs goes on:

> Trance-like states and magical one-dimensionality do not alter given structures; a trans-mental state, however, does. It will not become entangled in these structures, even if such a person moves within them. This Tantra [the *Parātrīśikā*, I.K.] deals with the removal of the condition of separate(d)ness, but not by abandoning the ability to discriminate. It is simply not a "going back" but a "passing beyond."
>
> (Hennigs 2005, 81–82)

Hennigs emphasizes the importance of understanding the "real" motivations that lead to action, and not what an individual imagines them to be. The *Parātrīśikā* shows, he writes, that it is precisely this latter kind of "motivation" that generates the "empirical I" and with it the negative consequences of separation and illusion. Transpersonal psychology should therefore delve deeper into motivations, instead of just aligning itself with beliefs of Indian- or Tibetan-influenced modern spirituality (83). Several paragraphs take up the issue of psychological development and its relationship with a spiritual path. According to Hennigs, wanting to understand one's existence has a spiritual component only when it does *not* refer (mainly or exclusively) to something given or preconceived, but takes aim at "the paradoxal (rationally not comprehensible) nature of reality," without pursuing personal growth. On the other hand, "spirituality as a path of its own" (such as meditation or yoga) has the potential to influence psychological development, but not directly by changing its trajectory or by simply substituting certain developmental stages (85–86).

Various therapeutic specialists, advocates of a transpersonal approach in their work, found Hennigs's book inspiring enough to refer to him directly, either by mentioning his name and work on their webpages, or by incorporating certain aspects of his *Parātrīśikā*-interpretation in their own writings. In an article published online, in which he argues for the necessity of transpersonal therapy, Guido Peltzer,[26] a physician

26. Together with his wife Christiane, Guido Peltzer has run until recently a doctor's office for psychosomatic medicine and psychotherapy. On the office's website (peltzerundpeltzer.de), there is also a link to the second homepage of the couple, parasamvit.de (from the Sanskrit *parāsaṃvid*, "supreme/highest consciousness"). The text I refer to in this paragraph is titled "Über die Notwendigkeit von transpersonaler Psychotherapie" ("About the Necessity of Transpersonal Psychotherapy") and can be found there (www.parasamvit.de/wp-content/pdf/Notwendigkeit_von_TPPT, accessed July 22, 2021). A shorter version titled "Kashmirischer Shaivismus und transpersonale Psychotherapie" was published in a volume edited by Galuska and Pietzko (2005). Another text authored by G. Peltzer

with a specialization in psychosomatic medicine and psychiatry, refers to Hennigs's work to illustrate the ways in which "an ancient spiritual tradition can contribute to the handling of projections and to personality formation" (Peltzer n.d., 2). Without expressly connecting his reflections to the *Parātrīśikā* or its commentaries, but quoting from Hennigs's book, Peltzer introduces in the second part of his article the three means or methods (*upāyas*) described by Abhinavagupta by which the practitioner is gradually able to achieve higher stages of development on the way to attaining liberation-in-life (*jīvanmukti*),[27] and shows how they can be applied in therapy work. The first method is the individual way (*āṇavopāya*), which includes physical postures, breathing exercises, and elements of meditation known from Patañjali's *Yogasūtras*. This stage is a useful preparation for the next levels and can contribute to the development of patients' personality structures, according to Peltzer. He further states that even though states of consciousness characterized by emptiness can occur at this stage as well, it cannot be characterized as transpersonal, as it is the individual who is acting purposefully to achieve a goal, where subject and object are still differentiated (13). By eliminating the intentional factor, one then advances to the second way or method, the way of power (*śāktopāya*), which involves transitioning from outer to inner forms of spiritual discipline, developing an awareness of the everyday and confronting oneself in an all-encompassing way by asking existential questions. With the third means, the so-called divine method (*śāmbhavopāya*), the patient-practitioner transitions to a stage of pure awareness characterized by the cessation of any identification with "the projections of our world, consisting of the interpretations and ideas of our self, our person" (15).[28] However, the final goal is the stage "without method" (*anupāya*). Here, all differentiation between the pa-

has the title "Gebetsrituale in der transpersonalen Psychotherapie" ("Prayer Rituals in Transpersonal Psychotherapy") (https://www.parasamvit.de/wp-content/pdf/gebetsrituale.pdf).

27. Abhinavagupta dedicates in his *Tantrāloka* an entire chapter to each of these *upāyas*. In the *Parātrīśikāvivaraṇa* the description of the *upāyas* occurs in connection with the interpretation of (the rather cryptical) verse 35, in which the practitioner is invited to meditate on the seminal mantra and practice the "lunar part." For this and the following, see Bäumer (2011, 240–245) and Muller-Ortega (1989, 166–167). The *upāyas* are also discussed in Dyczkowski (1987, 170–171).

28. Muller-Ortega (1989, 167) describes *śāmbhavopāya* as the "releasing [...] into the inwardly-flowing, expansive current of consciousness." In Dyczkowski's interpretation, this stage implies "reconverting thought [...] back into the pure consciousness which is its source and essence. Practice here is centered on the flux of perception [...] through which the cyclic activity of the powers of the senses and mind merge with the cycle of universal consciousness" (1987, 173).

tient and everybody else ends, and the issue of relationality can now be addressed from an entirely new perspective. This state is, according to Peltzer, lastingly transpersonal and outside temporal boundaries: "It is a state beyond thinking [...], and also without place, a 'timeless no-place'" (16). Peltzer concludes his article with reflections on the position of the therapist, on the therapeutic, existential potential of non-dual thinking, and on the need for a transformed, transpersonal psychotherapy.

While Guido Peltzer has in the meantime retired, his wife Christiane continues working. Among her specializations listed on the website, Christiane Peltzer includes transpersonal psychotherapy. She has published several shorter online texts of her own on the topic and has co-authored others together with her husband.[29] Another therapist who mentions Hennigs as one of her teachers is Eugenie Delfs, a natural health therapist for thirty years. Listed on her website among her specializations we find "transpersonal energy-work," and under "Literature" the book on the *Parātrīśikā* and a reference to Ulrich Hennigs as her long-time teacher (1994–2010).[30]

## Consecration and Epilogue

The *yoginī*s and other deities arrived in Germany in the last days of October 2009. A month later Hennigs wrote that the images were in place in the newly erected, decagonal pavilion of metal and glass on a concrete foundation. The initial intention of building a round and hypaethral temple did not materialize, given the available building materials and the rather rough northern German climate. Inside, the images were arranged in a circle, with the gatekeeper deities on both sides of the entrance and the *yoginī* Kāmadā directly facing the visitor. To her left and right stood the images of Sarvatomukhī and Phaṇendrī. Pārvatī and Śiva faced each other in (approximately) nine o'clock and three o'clock positions respectively, and Gaṇeśa was positioned between Pārvatī and the gatekeeper.

Even before their consecration, regular worship rituals were conducted for all the deities. "Indeed," Hennigs replied in an e-mail in February 2010 to my question regarding *pūjā* or other types of rituals,

29. "Therapeutische Grundhaltung in der transpersonalen Psychotherapie" ("The Therapeutic Stance in Transpersonal Psychotherapy"), "Ein leerer Raum" ("An Empty Space"), "Nondualität" ("Non-duality," with G. Peltzer), and others. They can be accessed at www.parasamvit.de/projekte/.

30. See https://eugenie-delfs.de/hintergrund.html.

"our images are not only receiving flowers daily. They are also being clad and decorated, and their needs are taken care of in every way." As for their formal installation (*prāṇapratiṣṭhā*; see Keul 2017), he initially intended to perform the ritual himself, pointing out that he had been initiated into the brahmanical tradition by one of his teachers and had also learned how to consecrate various ritual objects, including statues. But he then added that he and his wife were planning to ask one of the priests from the Bheraghat *yoginī* temple whether he would be willing to travel to Germany and perform a thorough *pratiṣṭhā*.

The priest arrived on July 22, and four days later the formal consecration of the images was finalized. The ritual was quite detailed, with its various sequences conducted over three days, including a fire sacrifice (*homa*) on the last day. Further activating rituals were scheduled for the following three weeks, to be performed by the priest and/or by Ulrich Hennigs and Gabriele under the priest's direct supervision inside the temple. During this time, I paid a visit to the site, warmly welcomed by the two hosts and the priest, all generous enough with their time to engage in conversations on various temple- and ritual-related topics with me. Then, in an e-mail dated August 20, Hennigs wrote that the two of them were "on their own again," as the priest had returned to India after an intense period spent together. In that same e-mail he also asked me to send him titles of books on ritual theory. A few months earlier, I had invited him to participate in an academic conference on *yoginīs* (Keul 2013) to take place in October of that same year at NTNU Trondheim, where I was working at the time. I thought he would like to hear what other participants (specialists in the history of religions, Sanskrit, anthropology, art history) would have to say on a topic so central to him, and that he, as the practitioner that he was, would be an interesting conversation partner to some of them. Hennigs was hesitant but not uninterested in attending, and not sure whether he should also give a presentation. I assume that his request for theoretical literature had to do with him wanting to prepare for a potential participation.

* * *

Ulrich Hennigs did not live to attend the conference, passing away suddenly on September 7, 2010. He probably did not have the opportunity to look at Bell's or Grimes's volumes on ritual theory. He had gone, however, through another—less theoretical—relevant academic work a few years earlier, and his reaction was quite revealing when it comes to his interpretation of the ritual sections of the tantric literature he had been reading for decades:

> White's book [*Kiss of the Yoginī*, I.K.] echoes many of my own thoughts. His perspective casts a different light on many old texts. While I too have approached some of these issues in a very concrete, literal manner, I often tended to translate or interpret many contexts in a more abstract or philosophical way.
>
> (E-mail communication, December 15, 2007)

Ulrich Hennigs interpreted descriptions of rituals in tantric texts both metaphorically and literally. This is supported by his remarks on *Parātrīśikā* 31–33 (Hennigs 2005, 71–74), the retrospective treatment of some of his early tantric experiences, and occasional hints about ritual practices in the *yoginī* temples. He was, at the same time, fully aware of the position assigned to ritual in the scheme of the three methods (*upāyas*) or "modes of immersion in Śivahood (*samāveśaḥ*)" expounded on in Abhinavagupta's commentary: It was seen as part of the initial stage of immersion, to be followed (or to be replaced entirely) by "more subtle means, namely meditational practices, the gradual cultivation of liberating insight, or direct intuition" (Sanderson 2007b, 115).

**István Keul** is Professor in the Study of Religions at the University of Bergen, Norway. His areas of research include various aspects of the history and sociology of South Asian religions. He is the author of a monograph on the Hindu deity Hanumān and has edited volumes on tantra, *yoginīs*, Banaras and consecration rituals, and recently *Spaces of Religion in Urban South Asia* (2021, Routledge).

## References

Bäumer, Bettina. 2011. *Abhinavagupta's Hermeneutics of the Absolute. Anuttaraprakriyā: An Interpretation of his Parātrīśikā Vivaraṇa.* Shimla: Indian Institute of Advanced Study and New Delhi: D.K. Printworld.

Bühnemann, Gudrun. 2000. "The Six Rites of Magic." In *Tantra in Practice*, edited by David Gordon White, 447–462. Princeton, NJ: Princeton University Press.

Dupuis, Stella, ed. 2019. *Experiencing the Goddess: On the Trail of the Yoginīs.* New Delhi: Aryan Books International.

Dyczkowski, Mark S. G. 1987. *The Doctrine of Vibration: An Analysis of the Doctrines and Practices of Kashmir Shaivism.* Albany, NY: State University of New York Press.

Evans-Wentz, Walter. 1935. *Tibetan Yoga and Secret Doctrines.* London: Oxford University Press.

Friedman, Harris L. 2018. "Transpersonal Psychology as a Heterodox Approach to Psychological Science: Focus on the Construct of Self-Expansiveness and Its Measure." *Archives of Scientific Psychology* 6: 230–242.

Gnoli, Raniero. 1965. *La Trentina della Suprema* (Parātrīśikālaghuvṛtti). Torino: Boringhieri.

Hartelius, Glenn, Mariana Caplan and Mary Anne Rardin. 2007. "Transpersonal Psychology: Defining the Past, Divining the Future." *The Humanistic Psychologist* 35(2): 136–160.

Hartelius, Glenn and Jorge N. Ferrer. 2013. "Transpersonal Philosophy: The Participatory Turn." In *The Wiley-Blackwell Handbook of Transpersonal Psychology*, edited by Harris L. Friedman and Glenn Hartelius, 187–202. Chichester: John Wiley & Sons.

Hatley, Shaman. 2012. "From *Mātṛ* to *Yoginī*: Continuity and Transformation in the South Asian Cults of the Mother Goddesses." In *Transformations and Transfer of Tantra in Asia and Beyond*, edited by István Keul, 99–129. Berlin: De Gruyter.

——. 2013. "What is a Yoginī? Towards a Polythetic Definition." In *Yoginī in South Asia: Interdisciplinary Approaches*, edited by István Keul, 21–31. London: Routledge.

——. 2019. "*Yoginī*." In *Hinduism and Tribal Religions. Encyclopedia of Indian Religions*, edited by Pankaj Jain, Rita Sherma and Madhu Khanna, 1–6. Dordrecht: Springer.

——. 2020. "Yoginī Temples and Their Antecedents: Reassessing the Textual Evidence." Recording of an online presentation, October 21, SOAS Centre of Yoga Studies. Retrieved August 1, 2021, from www.youtube.com/watch?v=8PuLpZ3aylo.

Hennigs, Ulrich. 2005. *Parātriśikā—Die höchste Gottheit der Drei: Spiritualität und transzendente Bewusstseinszustände am Beispiel eines Tantras, mit Kommentaren und Erläuterungen von U. Hennigs.* Norderstedt: Books on Demand GmbH.

——. n.d. "Autobiographische Reflektionen; Der Yoginitempel in Bheraghat." Unpublished manuscript.

Jacobsen, Knut A., ed. 2012. *Yoga Powers: Extraordinary Capacities Attained Through Meditation and Concentration.* Leiden: Brill.

Keul, István. 2004. "Mahāmāyā und die Yoginīs: Tradition und Transformation in Hirapur." In *Gelebte Religionen: Untersuchungen zur sozialen Gestaltungskraft religiöser Vorstellungen und Praktiken in Geschichte und Gegenwart*, edited by Hildegard Piegeler, Inken Prohl and Stefan Rademacher, 151–163. Würzburg: Königshausen & Neumann.

——. 2012. "Reconnecting to What? Imagined Continuities and Discursive Overlaps at Tantrapīṭhas in Central and Eastern India." In *Transformations and Transfer of Tantra in Asia and Beyond*, edited by István Keul, 195–214. Berlin: De Gruyter.

——, ed. 2013. *"Yoginī" in South Asia: Interdisciplinary Approaches.* London: Routledge.

——, ed. 2017. *Consecration Rituals in South Asia.* Leiden: Brill.

Lopez y Royo, Alessandra. 2013. "Performing Hirapur: Dancing the Śakti Rūpa Yoginī." In *"Yoginī" in South Asia: Interdisciplinary Approaches*, edited by István Keul, 226–234. London: Routledge.

Maslow, Abraham H. 1969. "The Farther Reaches of Human Nature." *Journal of Transpersonal Psychology* 1(1): 1–9.

Muller-Ortega, Paul Eduardo. 1989. *The Triadic Heart of Śiva: Kaula Tantricism of Abhinavagupta in the Non-Dual Shaivism of Kashmir.* Albany, NY: State University of New York Press.

——. 2002. "Becoming Bhairava: Meditative Vision in Abhinavagupta's *Parātrīśikā-laghuvṛtti.*" In *The Roots of Tantra*, edited by Katherine Ann Harper and Robert L. Brown, 213–230. Albany, NY: State University of New York Press.

Padoux, André. 1975. *La Parātrīśikālaghuvṛtti d'Abhinavagupta.* Paris: Publications de l'Institut de Civilisation Indienne du Collège de France.

——. 1990. *Vāc: The Concept of the Word in Selected Hindu Tantras.* Albany, NY: State University of New York Press.

——. 2017. *The Hindu Tantric World: An Overview.* Chicago, IL: University of Chicago Press.

Peltzer, Guido. 2005. "Kashmirischer Shaivismus und transpersonale Psychotherapie." In *Psychotherapie und Bewusstsein: Spirituelle und transpersonale Dimensionen der Psychotherapie*, edited by Joachim Galuska and Albert Pietzko, 259–282. Bielefeld: J. Kamphausen Verlag.

——. n.d. "Über die Notwendigkeit von transpersonaler Psychotherapie." Unpublished manuscript, 1–25.

Rodrigues, Vitor and Harris L. Friedman. 2013. "Transpersonal Psychotherapies." In *The Wiley-Blackwell Handbook of Transpersonal Psychology*, edited by Harris L. Friedman and Glenn Hartelius, 580–594. Chichester: John Wiley & Sons.

Sanderson, Alexis. 1988. "Śaivism and the Tantric Traditions." In *The World's Religions*, edited by Stewart Sutherland, Leslie Houlden, Peter Clarke and Friedhelm Hardy, 660–704. London: Routledge and Kegan Paul.

——. 1990. "The Visualization of the Deities of the Trika." In *L'image divine: Culte et méditation dans l'hindouisme*, edited by André Padoux, 31–88. Paris: CNRS.

——. 2007a. "The Śaiva Exegesis of Kashmir." In *Mélanges tantriques à la mémoire d'Hélène Brunner / Tantric Studies in Memory of Hélène Brunner*, edited by Dominic Goodall and André Padoux, 231–442. Pondicherry: Institut français d'Indologie/École française d'Extrême Orient.

——. 2007b. "Swami Lakshman Joo and His Place in the Kashmirian Śaiva Tradition." In *Saṃvidullāsaḥ: Manifestation of Divine Consciousness. Swami Laksman Joo, Saint-Scholar of Kashmir Śaivism, A Centenary Tribute*, edited by Bettina Bäumer and Sarla Kumar, 93–126. New Delhi: D.K. Printworld.

——. 2009. "The Śaiva Age: The Rise and Dominance of Śaivism during the Early Medieval Period." In *Genesis and Development of Tantrism*, edited by Shingo Einoo, 41–349. Tokyo: Institute of Oriental Culture, University of Tokyo.

——. 2014. "The Śaiva Literature." *Journal of Indological Studies (Kyoto)* 24–25(2012–2013): 1–113.

Singh, Jaideva, transl. 1989. *Abhinavagupta: A Trident of Wisdom. Translation of Parātrīśikā-vivaraṇa by Jaideva Singh.* Albany, NY: State University of New York Press.

von Stietencron, Heinrich. 2008. "The Sixty-Four Yoginīs—A Secret Cult Still Unexplored." In *The Divine Play on Earth: Religious Aesthetics and Ritual in Orissa, India*, edited by Cornelia Mallebrein and Heinrich von Stietencron, 141–145. Heidelberg: Synchron Publishers.

Sutich, Anthony J. 1968. "Transpersonal Psychology: An Emerging Force." *Journal of Humanistic Psychology* 8: 77–78.

Walach, Harald, Niko Kohls, Nikolaus von Stillfried, Thilo Hinterberger and Stefan Schmidt. 2009. "Spirituality: The Legacy of Parapsychology." *Archive for the Psychology of Religion* 31(3): 277–308.

White, David Gordon. 2003. *Kiss of the Yoginī: "Tantric Sex" in Its South Asian Contexts.* Chicago, IL: University of Chicago Press.

——. 2018. "Yoginīs." In *Brill's Encyclopedia of Hinduism Online*, edited by Knut A. Jacobsen (ed. in chief), Helene Basu, Angelika Malinar and Vasudha Narayanan (associate eds.). Accessed August 10, 2021. https://doi.org/10.1163/2212-5019_BEH_COM_1030300.

Zimmer, Heinrich. 1944. *Der Weg zum Selbst. Lehre und Leben des Shri Ramana Maharshi.* Zürich: Rascher.

-5-

# Practicing the *Yogasūtra*?

## An Approach to the Analysis of Contemporary Yoga Philosophy's Somatic Aspects

LAURA VON OSTROWSKI

While historical, philological, and socio-cultural research on (modern) yoga saw an immense boom in the last two decades, the biomedical dimension of body practices associated with yoga has seldom been taken into account in cultural studies. This chapter proposes an approach to an interdisciplinary exchange between methods and theories in the social sciences combined with the insights of neuroscience and cognitive psychology on yoga. The chapter's topic itself, the contemporary reception of the *Yogasūtra*, an old Indian text, bridges textual exegesis and bodily practices: Combining fieldwork in an advanced Ashtanga Yoga teacher training in Germany with theories in aesthetics of religion, my research approach shows that the practitioner's understanding of the text is substantively related to the somatic techniques they practice and the experiential dimensions that emerge from their practices. In what I call "contemporary yoga philosophy," the exegesis of the *Yogasūtra* and modern body practices interact with one another and (re-)define each other. Therefore, I argue that such "philosophical" contemporary discourses cannot be adequately investigated without considering the physical practices and their effects with the help of an interdisciplinary approach. The chapter presents six aspects of contemporary yoga philosophy and introduces key body knowledge categories which enable a cultural-scientific analysis of body practices. It concludes with two examples, "touch" and "eutony," that show how contemporary religious practices that are intertwined with physical practices can be analyzed.

Keywords: yoga, *Yogasūtra*, contemporary yoga philosophy, embodiment, aesthetics, contemporary religion

## Introduction: Analyzing Contemporary Yoga Philosophy's Somatic Aspects

In her seminal book *A History of Modern Yoga* (2004), Elizabeth De Michelis investigated yoga as an entangled history of knowledge and based on that coined the popular term "Modern Postural Yoga" (MPY). She includes the style of yoga known as Ashtanga Yoga in this broad category which she defines as "generally shaped by the religio-philosophical assumptions characteristic of New Age" (De Michelis, 188–189), but as clearly more focused on body practices. In this respect, the term "MPY" has already been criticized by different scholars (see Hauser 2013; Wildcroft 2020). Hauser for example remarks: "De Michelis's ideal-typical categories thus have a weakness since they imply a vital difference in approaching yoga as belief system or as a set of physical exercises" (2013, 8). Indeed, in the twenty-first century the body practice called yoga is becoming increasingly associated with a particular worldview, often called "yoga philosophy," which has both a spiritual and body-practical orientation. My empirical research on late modern, globalized, and reformed Ashtanga Yoga has shown that the broader and more elaborate reception of ancient Indian texts, mainly Patañjali's *Yogasūtra*,[1] in the twenty-first century, is of great importance for this development. First, I will shortly introduce the term "contemporary yoga philosophy" (CYP), which describes a worldview that is based on ancient yoga scriptures but differs from them in significant ways. Among other things, exegetical deviations are caused by the influence of different transformative effects, reported by my research participants as well as shown in biomedical studies, that emerge from the sometimes-daily exercises contemporary "yoga bodies" perform on their mat. Meaning is thus also created in the act of doing, of practicing.[2] Accordingly, the second part of the chapter revolves around the question of how such a nexus of body practices and processes of worldview-building can be researched from a cultural studies perspective. Only recently, Suzanne Newcombe and Karen O'Brien-Kop highlighted the need for a better understanding of

1. While acknowledging the work of Indologist Philipp Maas, who points out that the *Yogasūtra* and its oldest commentary, Vyāsa's *Yogabhāṣya*, were likely a unified whole, together called the *Pātañjalayogaśāstra* (see Maas 2013), I use the name "*Yogasūtra*" and not "*Pātañjalayogaśāstra*" when referring to *Yogasūtra* receptions in my research field since the recipients did not include Vyāsa's commentary in their interpretations. Outside of this modern context, I speak of the *Pātañjalayogaśāstra* (PYŚ).
2. See Chapter 10 of this volume on meaning-making.

cultural scientists of likely neurophysiological effects of modern yoga practices in their Routledge Handbook of Yoga Studies:

> An important challenge for social science and humanities researchers going forward is to impress upon both biomedical researchers and the general public the importance of understanding health interventions in context—that their healing and meaning-giving potential cannot be reduced to, or fully understood by, biomedical measurements. Conversely, it can also be helpful for humanities and "soft" science scholars to have a better understanding of how the body is likely to react to certain psycho-physical techniques and what this might mean for the social construction of traditions and ontological understandings of reality.
> (Newcombe and O'Brien-Kop 2021, 5)

Paving one possible way for dealing with this "important challenge," the chapter proposes a methodological approach to the cultural study of yoga practices.[3] This cultural studies research approach is built upon the theorization of tacit body knowledge which has been developed in the academic field of aesthetics of religion (see Koch 2007, 2017; Grieser and Johnston 2017). It is insofar useful to apply a Western theory of body knowledge to modern and contemporary yoga, as it is partly shaped by Western culture. Ten body knowledge categories developed from biomedical, neurological, and psychological studies are introduced, which can serve as meta-categories for the analysis of body–mind practices and provide an analytical framework to examine body techniques alongside conventional ethnographic data compiled from interviews and other narrated data to give a multi-dimensional insight into practical contemporary yoga philosophy. To conclude, with "touch" and "eutony," the chapter provides two examples from the field research that show such a body-focused cultural analysis of CYP "in action."

## Research Field and Data Collection

The data that serves as a basis for the following analyses was mainly collected in an advanced Ashtanga Yoga teacher training course, led by Dr. Ronald Steiner, with students from all over Germany. Ashtanga Yoga is a global, dynamic, and strenuous style of yoga that was significantly shaped by South Indian Pattabhi Jois, a student of T. Kṛṣṇamācārya. Steiner, a former Jois student, reformulated Jois's Ashtanga Yoga to create a more therapeutic and individualized version of the practice that is

3. For other recent works that engage with this relevant task in their own specific ways see Wildcroft (2020) and Ciołkosz (2022).

open to different influences. The training had a duration of five weeks and was undertaken from 2015 to 2017. Over these two years, prospective yoga teachers went through daily yoga practice and were simultaneously introduced to a "philosophical" framework for their practice via nightly philosophy sessions held by Steiner. I joined the teacher training as an observing participant, collected experiential data related to the yoga practice and noted down my somatic experiences in a field diary. In terms of narrative data material, I conducted qualitative interviews with five global "*Yogasūtra* experts"[4] and four students in Steiner's formation. In addition, I generated 70 hours of audio recordings from Steiner's philosophy classes to gain insight into the teaching situation and to investigate the side of the *Yogasūtra* students thoroughly. This was supported by "philosophy homework" which nine of the training participants shared with me.

## Contemporary Yoga Philosophy (CYP)

While Indological or neo-Vedāntic readings of the *Yogasūtra*, at that time rarely read in conjunction with its accompanying Bhāṣya, shaped the early modern reception of the text, today's yoga philosophy has distanced itself from both Patañjali's metaphysics and the neo-Vedāntic interpretations of the influential Indian yoga teachers of the early twentieth century. As the PYŚ placed in its genuine philosophical (and cultural) context is not a text today's yoga practitioners can easily link to their āsana-based practices and experiences, the historical text is subject to contemporary exegetical changes.

I argue the textual exegesis by today's āsana-oriented practitioners has developed special characteristics (see von Ostrowski 2022, 25–38) which I subsume under the term "contemporary yoga philosophy." The origins of CYP are based on intercultural exchange but are inherently interwoven with the physical yoga practice and the daily life of contemporary yoga practitioners. In line with existing research on this phenomenon[5]

4. Next to Steiner (2015), I interviewed Dr. Ralph Skuban (2015/2016) who published a renowned German *Yogasūtra*-translation (see Skuban 2011) and the three global Ashtanga Yoga teachers John Scott (2015), Greg Nardi (2017), and Gregor Maehle (2018). It is important to note that none of these Ashtanga Yoga teachers were certified by the Jois family anymore and could thus design their physical as well as their philosophical teachings more creatively.
5. See for example Singleton (2008) who observed the first three aspects of CYP, White (2014, 235) who emphasizes in a short citation the points 2, 5, and 6 in

and based on my empirical data, I suggest that CYP is built upon the following six hermeneutic turns:

1. *Synthesis*, is centered in the observation that CYP relies on a blend of the worldviews of different Indian yoga texts like the *Yogasūtra*, the *Bhagavad Gītā, several Upaniṣads* and *Haṭhayoga* texts, but also of other (religious) traditions and worldviews, like Zen, positive psychology, or modern mindfulness. A syncretic approach lies at the heart of modernizing the *Yogasūtra*, a project initiated by influential Hindu reformers like Swāmi Vivekānanda or his contemporary Manilala N. Dvivedi. Their mission to frame the *Yogasūtra* as *Rājayoga*, the "royal yoga," in sharp distinction to the "lower" Haṭhayoga was accompanied by synthesizing it with Advaita Vedānta,[6] which continued in the teachings of all major gurus of modern yoga. Nevertheless, a synthetic way of approaching the text takes on new dimensions in the twenty-first century in the hands of Western interpreters.
2. *Breaking away from the textual tradition*, was famously brought forward by Vivekānanda, who mostly ignored the vast commentarial tradition of the *Yogasūtra* and wrote his own, modernized commentary. In a similar way, the ancient commentary literature of the *Yogasūtra* is largely not included in contemporary *Yogasūtra* treatises, which in most cases leads to a detachment of the text from its sociohistorical context.
3. *Selection and expansion*, consists of two seemingly contradictory aspects, which are however related. *Selection* refers to selecting from the *Yogasūtra* only such content which seems of direct relevance to the audience.[7] Additionally, a new trend towards *expansion* becomes evident. This is based on increased attention to previously neglected portions of the text, for example, the *vibhūti pāda*, the third chapter, on "supernormal powers." This differs from the eclectic teachings of Jois in particular, who did not teach the *Yogasūtra* to his Western students in any detail (see von Ostrowski 2022, 125–149).
4. *Focus on everyday life*, directly influences the contents of CYP. Since today "yoga philosophy" is generally expected to be applicable to "the here and now," interpretations suitable for everyday life were prevalent across all my empirical data. This is often accompanied

today's exegesis of the *Yogasūtra*, and Scholz (2017) whose brief analysis of a *Yogasūtra*-translation and other examples confirms all six enlisted aspects.

7. The most important part of the text for this purpose is, from Swami Vivekānanda until today, the section on the eight limbs (aṣṭāṅga-s) in the second chapter, which, for example, describes an ethical set of rules that many contemporary yoga practitioners try to respect (yama-s and niyama-s).

by a process of decontextualization—*Sūtras* are detached from their ontological, metaphysical, and sociohistorical context and placed in a new, worldly, and often Western context. In this context, a felt experience of "yoga philosophy" ranks higher than sharpening philosophical concepts or terminology.

5. *Reference to physical practice,* might be more or less important across different yoga schools and styles. Body practice is important for CYP in two different ways: First, the psychophysical experiences that emanate from the yoga practice on the mat become a crucial factor in understanding the content of yoga philosophy, an approach that Kṛṣṇamācārya and Jois, for example, did not teach directly (see von Ostrowski 2022, 107–149). My data nevertheless shows that much of CYP cannot be understood without additional consideration of the bodily practices. They are the main reason why most current interpretations are fundamentally different from the disembodied philosophy of the PYŚ. Second, CYP also narratively frames and influences the body practices called yoga, both quantitatively as well as qualitatively.[8]
6. *Sanskrit teaching and chanting*, refers to the observation that Sanskrit has a different connotation in the European or North American culture compared to the Indian one, and the new meaning first must be negotiated by the receiving culture in the course of the inevitable cultural transfer. The Indian yoga teachers of the twentieth century did not teach Sanskrit themselves, and yet it is usually part of yoga classes and yoga teacher trainings in some form or another, in which it is, like in my research field, taught by Germans and not by Indians. Emphasizing the meditative effect of Sanskrit chants, singing the *Yogasūtra* is increasingly developing into a distinct form of practice alongside bodily practice to experimentally approximate the experiences discovered in the *Yogasūtra.*[9]

The first three listed points form the historical basis that led to the development of today's expressions of yoga philosophy, the last three points provide experiential spaces that help generate new "philosophical" content and practices. How today's yoga philosophy is emically constructed must be elaborated in specific (experiential as well as narrative) analyses

8. For evidence of how CYP can qualitatively influence the physical yoga practice, see the two examples in this chapter. Quantitatively, the first *Sūtra* had an influence in my empirical data, as "atha yoga" was translated as "yoga is always now" and interpreted as a call to daily physical practice (see von Ostrowski, 2022, 293–297).
9. On the history of chanting the *Yogasūtra* in the Kṛṣṇamācārya-lineage see also White (2014, 208).

of the respective yoga style. In my research field, the deep interrelation between yoga philosophy and the physical practice was of particular importance, as Steiner expresses:

> The physical practice of Ashtanga Yoga is understood as a commentary on the philosophy it contains. Only with this is a direct access to the philosophical concepts, which at first seem abstract, made possible, based on one's own experience. For every single sentence of the *Sūtra* a counterpart exists in practice.[10]

Thus, in the following section, I will lay out a basic methodological framework for researching the somatic aspects of modern yoga practices with the help of an aesthetics of religion theorization of body knowledge. Acknowledging the difficulties of using the Sanskrit term "yoga" for such modern embodied practices (see Foxen 2020), performed mainly by Western women,[11] as opposed to the depiction of the male, Brahmanical "yogin" of the *Pātañjalayogaśāstra*,[12] this chapter argues that not taking into account the embodied effects of these modern practices, for example by displaying them merely as a preparation for meditation, ignores a large part of what modern yoga is grounded upon.

## Framing Body Knowledge for Yoga Studies

Following Anne Koch, "body knowledge" is used to demarcate implicit psycho-physical changes that emerge from regular (yoga) practice. The concept is of great importance in a framework building on embodied cognition, as both existing body knowledge and changes in body knowledge influence meaning-making. The framework of aesthetics of religion, which is based on the theory of embodied cognition, acknowledges that practices affect senses, change bodies, and, via bodies, cognition.[13] In

10. See https://de.ashtangayoga.info/philosophie/philosophie-und-tradition/120101-die-essenz-des-ashtanga-yoga (accessed May 23, 2022). Translation mine.
11. A study by the Federal Association of German Yoga Teachers from 2018 has shown the percentage of yoga practitioners among the total adult female population is still considerably higher, at 9%, whereas it is only 1% for the total adult male population in Germany (Berufsverband der Yogalehrenden in Deutschland 2018, 5).
12. Maas emphasizes: "Patañjali uses the Sanskrit term *brāhmaṇa* at four instances of his PYŚ to refer to a yogi. See PYŚ 2.30, 2.33, 3.51 and 4.29" (Maas 2018, 54). Written in Sanskrit, the text was the preserve of the male Brahmanical elite, sine qua non.
13. Grieser and Johnston define aesthetics of religion "as a framework for studying religion as a sensory and mediated practice. In close theoretical relation with approaches such as Sensory Studies, Material Religion, the Anthropology of the Senses and the Cognitive Science of Religion (CRS), an Aesthetics of Religion focuses

this theoretical framing, the body is not seen as a mere social construct, as is common in sociological body theories.[14] Consequently, it disagrees with Mark Singleton's claim in *Yoga Body*, where he writes that "corporal postures become "floating signifiers" whose meaning is determined according to context" (2010, 161). While there is no need to discuss the fact that the body, the senses, as well as physical activities are deeply shaped by context, historical circumstances, and culture, it is also true that practicing certain (cultural) techniques over a longer period of time inevitably leads to psychophysical and neurological changes. Taking both aspects equally into account, the applied religious-aesthetic methodology is based on a meta-language of cultural studies that facilitates a combined analysis of ethnographic data with the findings and insights of biomedical and neurological studies.

It needs to be stressed that an aesthetic approach does not seek to essentialize religious practices and understand them as "truth," because they are studied with methods drawn from natural sciences but provides an integrated perspective that considers different approaches from cultural studies and the natural sciences to understand religion or spirituality as an embodied practice. It allows the researcher to historize and contextualize the connection between body practices, their psychophysical effects, and religious discourses without ignoring the role of the body in such processes of worldview-building. Koch (2017) established a concept to talk about the aesthetic embodied effect in the context of cultural studies and anthropology of religion that builds upon a variety of interdisciplinary knowledge resources on embodiment. She provides seven body knowledge categories: "body scheme," "covert imitation," "tattooing," "muscle tone, posture and movement," "thermoregulation," "peripersonal space," and "prosthetic perception." For the analysis of yoga practices three more categories have proven to be helpful: "breath," "proprioception and nociception," and "extraordinary states of consciousness" (see von Ostrowski 2022, 46).[15]

The use of these categories is manifold: They help to examine the main "canonical" practices of the investigated yoga style, like *āsana*, *vinyāsa*, *bandha* or *dṛṣṭi* for Ashtanga Yoga. Moreover, their meta-character allows

---

on understanding the interplay between sensory, cognitive and socio-cultural aspects of world construction, and the role of religion within this dynamic" (2017, 1–2).

14. See for example Bourdieu's concept of the "habitus" (Bourdieu 2013), Marcel Mauss's "techniques of the body" (Mauss 1973), or Thomas Csordas's "somatic modes of attention" (Csordas 1993).

15. Based on those categories, other categories may be developed according to the focus of the investigated practices.

a focus on practices and effects that are not part of the emic discourse—like flow states, touch or eutony—and acknowledges their efficacy on various levels; biomedical, neurological, and socio-cultural.

## Body Scheme and Covert Imitation

The concept of body scheme frames the self-representation of the body (Koch 2017, 392). Its dimensions (i.e., where the body's limbs are in relation to each other and in space) are mediated by proprioception (Koch 2007, 171), thus the body scheme is actualized through movement and through somatic attention. Somatic and mental self-awareness emerge through the image of a homeostatic body state (Koch 2017, 395; my translation). Koch speaks of a "definition of the body scheme as a permanent image that conveys one's body as a perceptual whole that can be withdrawn from the action space" (2007, 190). Consequently, the body scheme is a holistically functioning process that is independent, mostly unconscious and relates to one's inherent sense of self and overall state of being, and yet it can be manipulated. Through somatic attention—to one's own and to other bodies—a specific body scheme is created, learned, and adapted, and cultural interactions can activate, change, or manipulate body schemes (Koch 2017, 393). Covert imitation is one factor through which body schemes can be shared intersubjectively because others imitate them (Schüler 2012, 97). Covert imitation is thus closely linked to the body scheme:

> According to neurological findings, imitable perceptions such as body postures, auditory noises, language sounds, and mimicry are copied and stored as isomorphic representations in brain modules. This copying, or covert imitation, happens routinely and automatically, and in fact the recognition of emotions is dependent on covert imitation.
>
> (Koch 2017, 395)

Covert imitation played a considerable part in how practices were taught and learned in my research field and one can assume, that regular practitioners of (Asthanga) yoga are connected through a shared body scheme.

## Tattooing

The category "tattooing" expresses the perceptual capacity of humans to experience the world and learn through the skin, "which at the same time provides a means of storage and expression" (Koch 2007, 211; my translation) Koch explains further:

> However, the skin is an organ that is permeated with receptors, and it is the source of a huge amount of information that is received through these neural receptors, such as humidity, pain, touch, temperature, tension, etc. [...] One might talk of a skin organ sense.
>
> (Koch 2017, 396)

Tattooing becomes relevant when looking at how touch is used in modern yoga, for example in the form of self-massage techniques or adjustments. The relation between touch and discourses that became evident in my research I call "deictic touch," a concept which designates a form of touch that indicates something specific and might be used to convey, share, and sediment explicit beliefs of a religious group in an implicit manner (see von Ostrowski 2022, 237–247).

## Muscle Tone, Posture, and Movement

In a more explicit manner than many other religious or spiritual practices, āsana-s and other techniques of modern yoga are actively influencing the muscle tone of the practitioner. Muscle tone refers to the state of tension of a muscle, maintained even at rest—individual tone is closely linked to posture, movement, and breathing (Payne and Crane-Godreau 2015, 56). Koch emphasizes the highly psychophysical aspect of muscle tone:

> Appropriate breathing may support posture. Imitation of postures and gestures has proven pivotal in psychological development. Posture influences a person's attitudes, affections and expectations. Studies have investigated this by relating expansive, involuntary or contractual postures, facial and vocal expressions with changes in endogenous substances.
>
> (Koch 2017, 397)

The dynamic and ritualistic vinyāsa principle of Ashtanga yoga combines breathing, posture, and movement directly, all of which are related to muscle tone.

## Proprioception and Nociception

Neurophysiological studies have shown that good interoception, the perception of internal bodily states and sensations, is of major importance for bodily self-location: "The processing of bodily sensations is also a key for our sense of bodily self, which originates through the integration of interoceptive, proprioceptive, kinesthetic, tactile and spatial information" (Schmalzl et al. 2015, 102). Proprioception is a form of interoception and refers to the body's own perception of position and movement in space that takes place via receptors. It is a feedback system of the body: "Proprioception refers to information coming to the brain about the position and movement of the body and is essential for coordinated movement" (Payne and Crane-Godreau 2015, 56), thus kinesthesia, the sense of movement, is part of proprioception. It involves depth sensitivity as well as the vestibular organ, and it is often referred to as the "sixth sense organ," which recent research has associated with fascia (connective tissue) as the primary proprioceptive sense organ (Schleip 2019, 41). The fascia tissue contains the most important receptors for proprioception, namely the Pacini, Ruffuni, and Golgi receptors as well as interstitial receptors, which signal pain and temperature in addition to pressure (Schleip 2019, 41–42) and are thus functionally also nociceptors, i.e., pain receptors. These receptors transmit information to the central nervous system and report on stretch, movement, and position of the muscle, organ, or body part. In the context of the "kinesthetic turn" of modern positional yoga, this category becomes relevant as it illustrates not only how yoga practices change towards a more proprioceptive approach, but it can trace back as well how—related to regular somatic experiences—worldview discourses change, too.

## Breath

"Breath" is a body knowledge category that is deeply related to other aspects of body knowledge like interoception, or more precisely, since the lungs are an organ, visceroception, muscle tone, posture, movement, autonomic functions as well as the emotional state. Breathing is considered to be part of the "preparatory set" humans use to respond or adapt to the environment (see Payne and Crane-Godreau 2015). Many therapeutic, but also religious or spiritual practices, use a wide variety of breathing techniques to produce an equally wide range of effects, from high arousal and hyperstimulation to deep relaxation. Studies show that a slow breathing rhythm, diaphragmatic breathing, as well as prolonged exhalation, influence the tone of the vagus nerve, the largest nerve of the parasympathetic nervous system, measurable in blood pressure, heart rate, and heart rate variability (Gerritsen and Band 2018, 6), resulting in a state of relaxation. It has also been noted that voluntary changes in breathing patterns can have a positive effect on emotional states (Schmalzl et al. 2015, 103). However, whether these factors are applicable to one's own object of study must be carefully examined on the basis of experiential as well as narrative data.

## Thermoregulation

Temperature—mainly heat in the context of Ashtanga Yoga—affects muscle tone, body scheme, body image, proprioception, and nociception among other factors. "Thermoregulation" is described by Koch as "[a] complex and mostly autonomous regulatory circuit. Blood flow, restricted blood flow and muscle tension are only some factors that take part in this organization" (2017, 395). Temperature shifts are automatically compensated by the body: Sweating is a thermoregulatory response that serves heat loss, while shivering leads to heat gain. Temperature perception is also directly linked to emotion; moderate warmth is usually experienced as relaxing and pleasant. Fascia researcher Robert Schleip argued, though, that heat can cause proprioception, or internal perception, to atrophy as the receptors become insensitive and no longer provide sufficient feedback (2019, 195). An aspect of thermoregulation that can become relevant when investigating yoga styles which are performed in hot rooms, like Ashtanga or Bikram Yoga, and that might for example explain their more collective and less individual scope of experiences, as individual sensation of the body ceases.

## Peripersonal Space

The peripersonal space (PPS) is "the perceptive sector around body parts that can be detected by its specific relation to visual and tactile stimuli" (Koch 2017, 398) and it reacts plastically to the environment (Serino 2019, 154). For example, it can expand to tools, fake limbs, and other people. It is the interface between the self and the environment. It also shows that the perception of the self is not limited to the boundaries of the body. In 1966, the anthropologist Edward T. Hall developed the concept of proxemics, i.e., different distance zones that people unconsciously define around themselves. The boundaries of one's own body are never only of an individual nature but always relate, whether it is a matter of proximity or distance, to the social counterpoint. Other people are people's most important stimuli. The peripersonal space can extend to other persons so that they are included in it—provided that they behave cooperatively and fairly: "[I]n presence of an unknown individual, our PPS shrinks, as to leave space to the other, whereas after a positive exchange, even if abstract, PPS expands as to create a common space of interaction" (Serino 2019, 149). This can serve as an analytical category to show processes of group building and interaction in yoga communities, for example when looking at consensual adjustments as a ritual transgression of personal bodily boundaries that can be interpreted as a ritual enhancement of everyday experience that results in a (potentially pleasurable) expansion of the intimate as well as the peripersonal space, which can pleasantly blur a certain sense of self (see Serino 2019).

## Prosthetic Perception

This category describes the integration of objects and the environment into the body scheme and thus the enlargement of sensory perception—a process based on neural plasticity. Koch mentions prostheses, transplanted organs, tools, but also the environment can be integrated into one's own body scheme which is constantly adapting to the surrounding. One popular example is the sensation of a walking stick (Polanyi 1966):

> We do not feel the cane in the palm of our hand, where the pressure is objectively located, but we feel the uneven, soft, or solid ground through it, as if we had a sensorium at the end of the stick. In other words, the stick is an extension, and enlargement of our sensory organ of touch. This distance perception through tool use means that tools can be integrated into the body scheme.
>
> (Koch 2017, 398; referring to Làdavas and Farné 2006)

Also other human agents or only imagined entities can be integrated into the body scheme through prosthetic perception, for example in a yoga context the "guru" or the collective (see Ostrowski 2022, 241).

## Extraordinary States of Consciousness

This last category gathers various states of concentration or absorption in the context of movement practices, "focused attention" (FA) (see von Ostrowski 2022, 206–207) "open monitoring" (OM) (von Ostrowski 2022, 217–218) and states of "flow" (von Ostrowski 2022, 202–204). FA is based on the release of noradrenaline and is defined as attention to a specific object, for example, to different areas of the body or body processes (see Russell and Arcuri 2014). In contrast, OM is defined as a state of concentration that is geared towards various focal points. As Schmalzl et al. emphasize, yoga-based practices "may primarily employ an OM type of attention, with a constant interplay of MW [mind wandering (L. v. O.)] and metacognitive awareness." (2015, 108) As "mind wandering" is defined by "TUTs," "task-unrelated thoughts" (Russell and Arcuri 2014, 16), OM is only a partly concentrated state. With these two categories, it has been shown that consciously performed movements are the basis for the development of self-awareness. Thus, they are relevant for self-development (Payne and Crane-Godreau 2015, 56). The flow state is defined as "a period during which a highly practiced skill that is represented in the implicit system's knowledge base is implemented without interference from the explicit system" (Dietrich 2004, 746). It is a condition which occurs when performing activities that are basically mastered but not boring. Practitioners have the impression of being completely focused and of having blanked out everything other than the current activity which is accompanied by a feeling of timelessness and the dissolution of the ego (Dietrich 2004, 758).

To conclude, it must be emphasized again that this theorization does not "medicalize" the body according to allopathic medicine, as is often the case in contemporary postural yoga but establishes new categories that acknowledge both cultural as well as biological aspects of embodiment.

## Examples: (Deictic) Touch and Eutony

### Touch

Touch is traditionally not understood as a main aspect of the Ashtanga Yoga practice, which makes it even more interesting from an aesthetics of religion point of view. My historical and ethnographic research highlighted the use of touch mainly in so-called "adjustments" or "assists," where the teacher touches a student for the sake of influencing his or her body in the practice, mainly to correct the posture but also to change the movement quality. These intersubjective interventions involve not only the skin sense but also fascia and muscles. Thus, the two body knowledge categories that can be employed to analyze the use and effect of "touch" in the field are mainly "tattooing" and "proprioception and nociception."

When it comes to Jois's Asthanga Yoga, it is now common knowledge that Jois caused lasting physical and psychological harm to many people—both women and men—with his abusive adjustments, since in 2017 the former Jois-student Karen Rain publicly exposed Jois's abuses in her #MeToo statement.[16] Remski's analysis of *Guruji* (Donahaye and Stern 2010), a nearly hagiographic book on Jois, highlights that not only his adjustments but the whole practice experience of Ashtanga Yoga was

16. See Remski's article in *The Walrus* at https://thewalrus.ca/yogas-culture-of-sexual-abuse-nine-women-tell-their-stories (accessed May 29, 2022).

deeply connected with the experience of pain.[17] Jois's student Tim Miller remembered: "We were all practicing to the best of our ability. We were all really nervous, afraid of being adjusted but really more afraid of being ignored" (Crooks 2003). Touch was connected to pain sensations in skin and tissues, thus evoked nociception. When it comes to the Ashtanga Yoga practice itself, on the one hand, the regular practice of āsana, vinyāsa, bandha, or the deep ujjāyī-breath inevitably enhanced proprioception and visceroception. On the other hand, not only the abusive adjustments but also the demand for an almost daily, extremely intensive practice evoked dissociation from the body through painful experiences, as the former Jois student Diane Bruni summarizes:

> [P]racticing asana made us very aware of our bodies. But it also taught us to dissociate with our bodies. It teaches us how to be okay with pain. You're stretching out, you're tearing connective tissues that are meant to be stable structures. The postures hurt! But we keep doing them.
>
> (Remski 2019, 144)

Intensifying the sense of bodily self collapsed with a turning away from one's own embodied self through pain experiences while maintaining focus on the "Guru," whose adjustments got a spiritualized connotation, as Nick Evans remembers:

> He says, "All is God." [...] Because when he puts his hands on you, when he smiles at you, when he is with you, that's what's with you. [...] when he touches us, it is like light flowing from him into us. Healing love, knowledge, power, forgiveness, kindness ... you are already perfect. He knows it, we don't know it. He knows it, he touches us, and with absolute certainty he knows that to be the case.
>
> (Donahaye and Stern 2010, 410)

Jois's touches were portrayed as an interface between the student and God and interpreted as sacraments. His adjustments can thus be analyzed as deictic touches that indicated something specific, in this example a spiritual discourse which was also transmitted through touch and nociception. In this context, "spirituality" did not equal wellness but surrendering to a higher power and, in the end, turning away from the embodied self.

17. Remski summarizes: "The interviews in Guruji seem obsessed with pain. The word appears 118 times over 460 pages. Guy Donahaye asked almost every one of his interviewees about how they dealt with pain in practice. Many gave voluminous answers about therapeutic and spiritual necessity, setting the stage for a new generation of readers to surge towards the 'edge'" (Remski 2019, 143).

This dissociation dissolves in late modern, Western adaptions of the practices which lead to positive associations with the body through a kinesthetic turn: Empirical evidence from my research shows that the Ashtanga Yoga practice is modified to suit the individual body and in accordance with this amendment, the culture of touch informing yoga practice transforms towards well-being, for example through therapeutic, anatomically informed adjustments based on consent. These "reformed" adjustments were experienced as enjoyable and helpful for many students (von Ostrowski 2022, 243).

While completely different to how Jois's adjustments have been interpreted, teachers in my field of research were nevertheless actively intending to transmit (often spiritual) discourses with their hands, sometimes inspired by their *Yogasūtra* readings. The discourse changes in late modern settings, but the deictic character remains, as Jois student Greg Nardi expresses:

> So, when I'm in the classroom I don't feel like I'm just trying to put people into shapes. [...] I feel like I try to move the students but not just to change their body but also maybe if they're practicing too aggressively, I encourage them to be more calm, if they're being apathetic or distracted I encourage them to be more focused. So, understanding Patañjali's use of Asana as freedom from the pairs of opposites.
>
> (von Ostrowski 2022, 247)

Nardi's interpretation of *Sūtra* II/48, to which he refers with his reference to the "pairs of opposites," leads him to establish an inner, psychophysical balance via his own hands in the body of his students. Thus, his adjustments "tattoo" his modern interpretation of the *Sūtra* into the body of the practitioner, into skin and tissues, via pleasant, therapy-like, and, at the same time, deictic touches. Turning away from pain sensations and the dependency on an omniscient guru and turning toward one's own bodily awareness and well-being reveals a shift in Ashtanga Yoga to a modernized, embodied, and Western understanding of spirituality, for example through selected *Yogasūtra* contents. The body becomes a place of performed and enacted contemporary yoga philosophy, in which "balance" is an important topic which is also employed via the reference to other Sūtras, as the next example will show.

## Eutony

CYP is thus influencing the physical yoga practice, and on a somatic level, the aforementioned search for a balanced state impacts not only the quality of movements, but also muscle tone and breath, and likely has an impact on thermoregulation and other forms of body knowledge. The

Sūtra most commonly associated with the topic of "balance" is probably II/46, sthira-sukham-āsanam, translated by Edwin Bryant as "Posture should be steady and comfortable." He clarifies that it originally solely referred to a seated meditation posture (Bryant 2009, 238). Furthermore, according to Philipp Maas it is to be read in conjunction with the following sentence II/47, prayatna-śaithilya-ānantya-samāpattibhyām. Maas concludes accordingly: "In this case, the two sūtra-s 2.46 and 2.47 can be translated in the following way: 'A steady and comfortable posture (YS 2.46) [arises] from a slackening of effort or from merging meditatively into infinity (YS 2.47).'" Such philological reflections, that steer *Sūtra* II/46 in a certain interpretative direction have not yet made their way to the practice-based contemporary text interpretations. Related to *Sūtra* II/46, David, already trained as a yoga teacher in a more static yoga style and trainee in Ashtanga Yoga, accounted:

> And I think I try to hold every asana in such a way that it is as stable as possible, and if it is not joyful, then it is an asana that I am doing incorrectly or an asana that is still too much for me. That's why I always take a step back very quickly, and I think that's how I never go beyond my own limits, even in Ashtanga Yoga. [...] And this is how I have also learned to respect my own limits in life.
>
> (von Ostrowski 2022, 335; my translation)

"Stable" is David's translation for "sthira" and "joyful" for "sukha." His attempt to align his dynamic practice with these two principles can be analyzed as the establishment of a balanced muscle tone, which then also affected him mentally and emotionally, as he was able to transfer the ability to respect his physical limits (and possibly maintain a balanced muscle tone as a result) to his everyday life. In this way, postural yoga is often understood as a holistic practice, because a well-balanced state created in the body also affects the mental and emotional state. The example of Steiner's student and yoga teacher Hanna shows how this important content of contemporary yoga philosophy is passed on from teacher to students, as she included *Sūtra* II/46 in her yoga lessons, interpreted in a similar way as David:

> I say it at the beginning, for example "sthira-sukham-asana," which fits quite well and then I let them practice, bring them into the practice, with everything that belongs to Ashtanga, and then I say again and again: "Look, where is the sthira for you, where is sukham, do you find some lightness in yourself, or do you move towards hardness."
>
> (von Ostrowski 2022, 334; my translation)

A study on the effects of yoga refers to such a balanced physical state as a state of "eutony." Although the Sanskrit terms sthira and sukha are not explicitly mentioned, how the study describes the desired state ("stable and well rooted, yet light and effortless") coincides with David's and Hanna's interpretations of *Sūtra* II/46 and their ways of framing its content:

> Lastly, yoga-based movement is practiced with the intent of obtaining a balanced muscle tone that allows the movement to feel stable and well rooted, yet light and effortless. While individual postures or parts of the practice may be characterized by a hypertonic (e.g., arm balances that require a high level of muscle tension) or hypotonic (e.g., a supine relaxation pose) state, the overall aim of the practice is to create a state of eutony or "well-balanced tension."
>
> (Schmalzl et al. 2015, 102)

The recent interpretation of this *Sūtra* can thus have a tangible effect on the muscle tone of the practitioners, since it encourages them to seek the said state of eutony[18] in their āsana-practice, i.e., of balanced tension, and to establish it, for example, by means of breath and concentration control (cf. Schmalzl et al. 2015).[19] Here, bodywork explicitly interlinks with a late-modern textual exegesis, and sensuality and textuality become reciprocally effective. Using *Sūtra* II/46 as a class theme, as Hanna accounted, initiates the search for a certain somatic state, and the bodily state attained has in turn an effect on the understanding of the Sūtra.[20]

## Conclusion

This chapter presented six different components of "contemporary yoga philosophy" and focused on one of them, which clearly distinguishes it from classical yoga philosophy, namely its relation to the physical practice. In today's yoga, text reception is inherently connected to embodied reception. Based on this insight, the chapter introduced a body-focused methodology to research those modern, somatic aspects of CYP by

18. Significantly, the concept of eutony referred to by Schmalzl *et al.* was founded by Gerda Alexander, who can be linked to the lineage of the well-known representative of physical culture, François Delsarte. With this direct reference, the search for a balanced physical state, as well as internal state through movement can be associated rather with the gymnastic traditions of the early twentieth century than with the contents of the PYŚ (see von Ostrowski 2022, 340–341).
19. In another article, I call this "the balance filter" (Aschenbrenner and von Ostrowski 2022, 176–177).
20. Steiner himself established "balance" via alignment principles, taught as a somatic, but also mental and emotional fine-tuning of oneself in the practice via stabilizing spiral movements in body structures (see von Ostrowski 2022, 227–236).

establishing body knowledge categories of a religious-aesthetic theory that can enrich similar future research. The suggested meta-categories can serve empirical researchers as firm tools to frame the practices they observe with terms that in themselves interrelate the cultural and the biological sphere.

The categories could show that in reformed Ashtanga Yoga, CYP becomes effective through various somatic interventions, for example, the āsana practice, which becomes geared towards "eutony," a term that denominates a balanced muscle tone, through the interpretation of *Sūtra* II/46. Many other somatic interventions of contemporary postural yoga can be investigated in a similar manner. The analysis of the somatic category "(deictic) touch" could show that the applied body knowledge categories "tattooing" and "proprioception" or "nociception" respectively help to break down changes in yoga lineages over time to the body level. In addition, on another historical level, both presented examples can relate modern yoga to the methods and forms of body knowledge of the physical culture movement by showing their similar aesthetic profiles. Indeed, many physical culture and gymnastic systems had a strong focus on skin or fascia stimulation like J. P. Müllers "My System" (1904) or on creating a balanced muscle tone like Gerda Alexanders "Eutony" (1985). The aesthetic analysis and profile of contemporary yoga practices and the associated "philosophy" adds a contemporary Western historical context to the history of Indian yoga. Such results from cultural studies research with a focus on the embodied effects of (yoga) practices and their history might be one way "to impress upon both biomedical researchers and the general public the importance of understanding health interventions in context," to return to the introductory quotation from Newcombe and O'Brien-Kop (2021, 5).

## Acknowledgments

I wish to thank Nick Lawler for his helpful edits and comments and Dr. Agi Wittich and Dr. Ruth Westoby for their thoughts on a first draft of this chapter.

**Laura von Ostrowski** studied Indology, Religious Studies, and Romance Studies at LMU Munich. From 2015 to 2018 she was a fellow of the DFG Research Training Group "Presence and Implicit Knowledge" at FAU Erlangen-Nuremberg and received her PhD in Religious Studies from LMU in 2021. For the Open Access publication of the book on her thesis *A Text in Motion* she was funded by Open Publishing in the Humanities. Her areas of research include modern and contemporary yoga, the reception of the *Yogasūtra*, the history of German yoga and of the physical culture movement, contemporary religion, aesthetics, and embodiment.

## References

Alexander, Gerda. 1985. *Eutony: The Holistic Discovery of the Total Person*. New York: Felix Morrow.

Aschenbrenner, Lina and Laura von Ostrowski. 2022. "Embodied Neo-Spirituality as an Experience Filter: From Dance and Movement Practice to Contemporary Yoga." *Body and Religion* 5(2): 160–184. https://doi.org/10.1558/bar.20526.

Berufsverband der Yogalehrenden in Deutschland. 2018. "Yoga in Zahlen." Retrieved September 9, 2020, from www.yoga.de/site/assets/files/2433/bdy_yoga_in_zahlen_2018-02-09.pdf.

Bourdieu, Pierre. 2013. *Outline of a Theory of Practice*. Translated by Richard Nice. Cambridge: Cambridge University Press, 2013.

Bryant, Edwin F. 2009. *The Yoga Sutras of Patañjali: A New Edition, Translation and Commentary*. New York: North Point Press.

Ciołkosz, Matylda. 2022. *Thinking in Āsana: Movement and Philosophy in Viniyoga, Iyengar Yoga, and Ashtanga Yoga*. Sheffield: Equinox.

Crooks, Deborah. 2003. "Tim Miller Interview." Retrieved May 29, 2022, from www.ashtanga.com/html/article_miller_tim.html.

Csordas, Thomas J. 1993. "Somatic Modes of Attention." *Cultural Anthropology* 8(2): 135–156.

Dietrich, Arne. 2004. "Neurocognitive Mechanisms Underlying the Experience of Flow." *Consciousness and Cognition* 13: 746–761.

Donahaye, Guy, and Eddie Stern. 2010. *Guruji. A Portrait of Sri K. Pattabhi Jois Through the Eyes of His Students*. New York: Northpoint Press.

Dvivedi, Manilal Nabhubhai. 1890. *The Yoga-Sutra of Patañjali*. Mumbai: Bombay Theosophical Publication Fund.

Foxen, Anya P. 2020. *Inhaling Spirit. Harmonialism, Orientalism, and the Western Roots of Modern Yoga*. New York: Oxford University Press.

Gerritsen, Roderik J. S. and Guido P. H. Band. 2018. "Breath of Life: The Respiratory Vagal Stimulation Model of Contemplative Activity." *Frontiers in Human Neuroscience* 12. Article 397. https://doi.org/10.3389/fnhum.2018.00397.

Grieser, Alexandra and Jay Johnston. 2017. "What Is an Aesthetics of Religion? From the Senses to Meaning—and Back Again." In *Aesthetics of Religion: A*

*Connective Concept*, edited by Alexandra Grieser and Jay Johnston, 1–49. Berlin: De Gruyter.

Hall, Edward T. 1966. *The Hidden Dimension*. Anchor Books.

Hariharānanda Āraṇya, Swāmi. 1983 [1963]. *Yoga Philosophy of Patañjali*. Translated by P. N. Mukerji. Albany, NY: State University of New York Press.

Hauser, Beatrix, ed. 2013. *Yoga Traveling: Bodily Practice in Transcultural Perspective*. Heidelberg: Springer.

Koch, Anne. 2007. "Körperwissen. Grundlegung einer Religionsaisthetik." Habilitation treatise, Ludwig-Maximilians-Universität München.

——. 2017. "The Governance of Aesthetic Subjects Through Body Knowledge and Affect Economies. A Cognitive-Aesthetic Approach." In *Aesthetics of Religion: A Connective Concept*, edited by Alexandra Grieser and Jay Johnston, 389–412. Berlin: De Gruyter.

Làvadas, Elisabetta and Alessandro Farné. 2006. "Multisensory Representation of Peripersonal Space." In *The Human Body Perception from the Inside Out*, edited by Günther Knoblich, Ian M. Thornton, Marc Grosjean and Maggie Shiffrar. Oxford: Oxford University Press.

Maas, Philipp A. 2013. "A Concise Historiography of Classical Yoga Philosophy." In *Periodization and Historiography of Indian Philosophy*, edited by Eli Franco, 53–90. Vienna: Sammlung De Nobili.

Maas, Philipp A. 2018. "'Sthirasukham Āsanam': Posture and Performance in Classical Yoga and Beyond." In *Yoga in Transformation. Historical and Contemporary Perspectives*, edited by Karl Baier, Philipp A. Maas and Karin Preisendanz, 49–100. Vienna: V&R unipress.

Mauss, Marcel. 1935. "Les techniques du corps." *Journal de psychologie normale et pathologique* 22: 271–239. Translated by Ben Brewster, "Techniques of the Body." *Economy and Society* 2(1): 70–88, 1973.

Müller, J. P. 1904. *My System. 15 Minutes of Exercise a Day for Health's Sake*. London: Athletic Publications.

Newcombe, Suzanne, and Karen O'Brien-Kop. 2021. "Reframing Yoga and Meditation Studies." In *Routledge Handbook of Yoga and Meditation Studies*, edited by Suzanne Newcombe and Karen O'Brien-Kop, 3–12. London: Routledge.

von Ostrowski, Laura. 2022. *Ein Text in Bewegung. Das Yogasūtra als Praxiselement im Ashtanga Yoga—eine historische, religionsästhetische und ethnographische Studie*. Open Publishing in the Humanities. Munich: Georg Olms Verlag. Universitätsbibliothek der LMU München.

Payne, Peter, and Mardi A. Crane-Godreau. 2015. "The Preparatory Set: A Novel Approach to Understanding Stress, Trauma, and the Bodymind Therapies."

In *Neural Mechanisms Underlying Movement-Based Embodied Contemplative Practices*, edited by Laura Schmalzl and Catherine E. Kerr, 54–75. Lausanne: Frontiers Media.

Polanyi, Michael. 1966. *The Tacit Dimension.* Chicago, IL: University of Chicago Press.

Remski, Matthew. 2019. *Practice and All Is Coming. Abuse, Cult Dynamics, and Healing in Yoga and Beyond.* Rangiora: Embodied Wisdom Publishing.

Russell, Tamara A. and Silvia M. Arcuri. 2014. "A Neurophysiological and Neuropsychological Consideration of Mindful Movement. Clinical and Research Implications." In *Neural Mechanisms Underlying Movement-Based Embodied Contemplative Practices*, edited by Laura Schmalzl and Catherine E. Kerr, 14–30. Lausanne: Frontiers Media.

Schleip, Robert. 2019. *Faszien Fitness*. Munich: Riva.

Schmalzl, Laura, Chivon Powers and Eva Henje Blom. 2015. "Neurophysiological and Neurocognitive Mechanisms Underlying the Effects of Yoga-Based Practices: Towards a Comprehensive Theoretical Framework." In *Neural Mechanisms Underlying Movement-Based Embodied Contemplative Practices*, edited by Laura Schmalzl and Catherine E. Kerr, 96–114. Lausanne: Frontiers Media.

Scholz, Susanne. 2017. "Reading Patañjali's Yoga Sutra Like the Bible in Sunday School: About Orientalist and Western Protestant Hermeneutical Assumptions in Contemporary English Translations of Patañjali's Yoga Sutra." In *Shifting Locations—Reshaping Methods: How New Fields of Research in Intercultural Theology and Interreligious Studies Elicit Methodological Extensions*, edited by Stanislav Grodz and Ulrich Winkler, 127–146. Berlin: Brill.

Schüler, Sebastian. 2012. "Synchronized Ritual Behavior. Religion, Cognition and the Dynamics of Embodiment." In *Religion and the Body. Modern Science and the Construction of Religious Meaning*, edited by Davin Cave and Rebecca Sachs Norris, 81–101. Leiden: Brill.

Serino, Andrea. 2019. "Peripersonal Space (PPS) as a Multisensory Interface Between the Individual and the Environment, Defining the Space of the Self." *Neuroscience and Biobehavioral Reviews* 99: 138–159.

Singleton, Mark. 2008. "The Classical Reveries of Modern Yoga: Patañjali and Constructive Orientalism." In *Yoga in the Modern World: Contemporary Perspectives*, edited by Mark Singleton, 77–99. London: Routledge.

——. 2010. *Yoga Body: The Origins of Modern Posture Practice.* Oxford: Oxford University Press.

Skuban, Ralph. 2011. *Patañjalis Yogasutra*. Munich: Arkana.

White, David G. 2014. *The Yoga Sutra of Patañjali.* Princeton, NJ: Princeton University Press.

Wildcroft, Theodora. 2020. *Post-Lineage Yoga. From Guru to #MeToo.* Sheffield: Equinox.

–6–

# Lay Sāṃkhyayoga Practices in Contemporary India

KNUT A. JACOBSEN

This chapter presents some of the practices of the Kāpil Maṭh monastic institution founded in the early twentieth century that subscribes to the teaching of the Yoga and Sāṃkhya systems of religious thought with *Pātañjalayogaśāstra* and *Sāṃkhyakārikā* as the foundational texts. The chapter argues that their practices are based on an understanding that all is suffering, which is stated prominently not only in the *Yogasūtra* but also in the *Sāṃkhyakārikā*. Suffering is caused by a basic disharmony at the foundation of the material creation (*prakṛti*) and the avoidance of pain means the avoidance of the uniting of the subject (*puruṣa*) and the object (*prakṛti*) (*Yogasūtra* 2.17) and when this union ends, the cycle of rebirth also ends. The followers of the Kāpil Maṭh realize that it will take many lifetimes to attain this. What is attainable in this life is the improvement of their *karmāśaya* and *vāsanās*. In the Kāpil Maṭh one important way of influencing the *vāsanās* is repeating the teaching of Sāṃkhya*yoga* every day in ritual recitation of *stotras* that state the teaching and goals of Sāṃkhyayoga. This recitation creates a state of mind and an embodied experience that leaves an impression, a *saṃskāra,* and forms a behavioral tendency, a *vāsanā,* and prepares for a Sāṃkhyayoga practice that will continue over many lives. This understanding that no practice of Sāṃkhyayoga is lost but shapes tendencies over many lives is an essential aspect of the yoga tradition of the Kāpil Maṭh. The teaching of Sāṃkhyayoga is here closely connected to conceptions of rebirth and does not make sense without the doctrine of repeated embodiment.

Keywords: Sāṃkhya, yoga, Kāpil Maṭh, Hariharānanda Āraṇya, *vāsanā*, *stotra*

Research on historical and modern traditions of yoga and the current global yoga phenomenon has become an important academic field. Findings from this academic research field have provided important knowledge about the roots of historical and modern yoga and the current global yoga phenomenon and furnished important correctives to conclusions of previous research as well as to assumptions made by many modern and new traditions of yoga (Alter 2004; De Michelis 2004; Jacobsen 2018; Mallinson and Singleton 2017; Newcombe 2009; Singleton 2010; Singleton and Byrne 2008). The term "modern yoga" refers to traditions and transformations of yoga caused by the early revival of yoga in India in the last decades of the nineteenth century and in the twentieth century, to new traditions of yoga created by multiple global influences as part of, and following its revival, and to the subsequent global dispersion and pluralization of these yoga traditions, which characterizes the current global yoga phenomenon. The revival of older yoga traditions in India and the creation of new ones resulted from the global circulation of ideas and practices (Jacobsen 2018; Singleton 2010). By the late twentieth century yoga had attained an immense global success and had become a global phenomenon. This "global yoga phenomenon" of the twenty-first century can be considered a later development of modern yoga. The "global yoga phenomenon" has been dominated by *āsana* or posture practice and has blended modern Western systems of physical fitness training such as traditions of gymnastics, ballet training, bodybuilding, etc. (Foxen and Kuberry 2021; Singleton 2010), and often with ideas of Hindu spirituality. The "global yoga phenomenon" has been dominated to such a degree by *āsana* practice that the term "yoga" in the English language has become mostly synonymous with this posture practice.

Another dominant feature of the current "global yoga phenomenon" is the setting in which it is performed, in which a teacher gives instructions in body postures (*āsanas*) to a large group in a classroom-like situation and the group performs body postures one after the other, often in a fixed sequence. There is no background for this way of instruction in *āsanas* or the performance of *āsanas* in pre-modern Indian yoga. The method seems to be derived from Western traditions of teaching and training. Vivekānanda is the most important figure of early modern yoga, in terms of global influence, and he developed his text *Rāja Yoga* (published in 1896 and is by many considered the origin of modern yoga) in dialogue with a Western audience in the United States. Notable, the audience was seated in chairs and quietly listening during his lectures. There were no *āsanas*. Vivekānanda travelled extensively in North America and also in Europe and he presented the lectures that *Rāja Yoga* is based on to an American audience (in winter 1895–1896) and his instructions, examples and interpretations were adapted to, and influenced by, the knowledge and interests of his American audience, probably also in order to be understood by, and engage in dialogue with the audience, a number of whom had background from Theosophy. Vivekānanda was especially influenced by American religious movements focusing on harmony and health such as American New Thought, Christian Science, Swedenborgianism, and Mesmerism. His use of the main concept *prāṇa* in the book *Rāja Yoga* was influenced by Mesmerism (Williamson 2016, 186). Vivekānanda's commentary on the *Yogasūtra* is therefore non-traditional and strongly influenced by the American religious environment of his audience.

The subject of this chapter is some of the practices of a yoga institution in Bengal that was one of the earliest to revive the yoga of the *Yogasūtra/Pātañjalayogaśāstra*. The Kāpil Maṭh was founded by Hariharānanda Āraṇya (1869–1947), who can be considered an early figure of modern yoga, but his revived yoga is quite different from modern posture yoga as well as the global yoga phenomenon. His earliest writings on yoga are from the same period as Vivekanānda's *Rāja Yoga*. Hariharānanda was probably the first person in modern India to establish a monastic institution based on the *Pātañjalayogaśāstra* (the combined *Yogasūtra* and *Yogabhāṣya/Vyāsabhāṣya*). Āraṇya's audience, unlike Vivekānanda's, was not Westerners but educated Bengalis. He communicated in Bengali and Sanskrit to his followers. In contrast, many of those who became world famous in the modern revival of yoga wrote and taught in English and it was mostly their texts and their teachings in English that became the basis for the global yoga movement. Many were international travellers. Hariharānanda Āraṇya on the other hand withdrew from the world. He had travelled in India as a *saṃnyāsin* but had stayed for several years in a cave outside of Gaya in Bihar, and he enclosed himself permanently in an artificial cave in 1926 in Madhupur, now in Jharkhand. He remained there until he passed away in 1947. Hariharānanda was from a wealthy zamindar family and belonged to the *kayastha* caste. A significant point for the development of modern yoga was probably that yoga was available as a practice and as a source of spiritual authority and leadership to non-Brahmans and also not controlled by Brahmans, in contrast to Hindu ritual worship and Sanskrit traditional scholarship. This feature of yoga gave non-Brahman upper-caste males opportunities for pursuing a profession as religious specialists claiming authority in a traditional textual and spiritual practice. It is probably not a coincidence that a significant number of early modern yogis and spiritual teachers of Bengal were from the *kayastha* caste such as Vivekānanda, Paramahansa Yogananda (the first major yoga teacher to settle permanently in the US), Bishnu Charan Ghosh, A. C. Bhaktivedanta Prabhupada, and many others.

## Hariharānanda Āraṇya and Sāṃkhyayoga

Hariharānanda Āraṇya was in his time probably the only Sāṃkhyayoga *saṃnyāsin* in India (Jacobsen 2018). His teaching was founded on the *Pātañjalayogaśāstra*. In modern yoga, the *Yogasūtra* (most often without the *Yogabhāṣya)* became a symbol of yoga as such and it attained the status of a fetish, that is an object of obsessive reverence. But Hariharānanda was interested in the textual tradition of the whole *Pātañjalayogaśāstra* and the Yoga *darśana* tradition, especially its Sāṃkhyayoga philosophical content and basis. What distinguished Hariharānanda and his teaching from many figures of modern and global yoga was first, that he understood the Sāṃkhya foundation of the Yoga philosophy of Patañjali (Pātañjala Sāṃkhya or Sāṃkhyayoga), and second, he tried to practice this Sāṃkhya teaching of yoga. Third, in contrast to many of the other individuals who can be considered part of the yoga revival, Hariharānanda had excellent Sanskrit reading and writing skills and he had full access to and studied the Sanskrit technical philosophical texts of the Yoga *darśana* tradition (especially important was Vācaspatimiśra's *Tattvavaiśāradī*, a technical philosophical commentary text on the *Pātañjalayogaśāstra*) as well as of the Sāṃkhya *darśana* tradition such as the philosophical texts *Sāṃkhyakārikā* and so on. His most important writing was the *Kāpilāśramīya Pātañjal Jogdarśan* (H. Āraṇya 1988 [1911]), a Bengali translation of the *Pātañjalayogaśāstra* with an elaborate scholarly commentary in Bengali. Fourth, Hariharānanda's fondness for solitude differed from many teachers of modern and global yoga. Many of those teachers did not cultivate solitude but were missionaries who had travelled widely and engaged in yoga instructions of larger groups of students. Fifth, Hariharānanda read Pali and he used also the Pali and Sanskrit texts of Buddhism for understanding the *Pātañjalayogaśāstra*. He understood the interdependence of Sāṃkhyayoga and Buddhism. He was influenced by Buddhism in his interpretations of Yoga (see Maharaj 2013), and he was occupied with understanding the relationship between Buddhism, Sāṃkhya and the *Pātañjalayogaśāstra*. Hariharānanda understood that the Buddha was an exponent of yoga. Academic scholarship has confirmed the importance of Buddhism for understanding the roots and early history of Yoga and the significant Buddhist influence on the *Pātañjalayogaśāstra* (Bronkhorst 1985; Maas 2017; O'Brien-Kop 2021; Poussin 1936). The exact relationship between Sāṃkhya, Yoga, and Buddhism is a subject of important current research. Hariharānanda understood the importance of this relationship. Sixth, Hariharānanda differed from many of the teachers of early modern yoga as well as the later yoga *āsana* teachers in his insistence on the Sāṃkhya philosophy as the basis of yoga philosophy and he did not teach or emphasize yoga *āsanas*. The type of gymnastic yoga that came to characterize the global yoga phenomenon is quite remote from the Sāṃkhyayoga philosophy of *Pātañjalayogaśāstra* and the practice of Hariharānanda. Sāṃkhyayoga is not postural yoga, in spite of the fetishization of the *Yogasūtra* in modern postural yoga. According to Sāṃkhyayoga, the term *āsana* in *Pātañjalayogaśāstra* mainly means being comfortable seated. Many founders of the institutions and teachings that have dominated the global yoga movement were interested in physical health, sports and gymnastics and developed yoga for that purpose, but Hariharānanda had apparently little interest in such matters. He seems to have neglected the body.[1] In contrast, worship of the body itself seems indeed increasingly to characterize the global yoga phenomenon, which is visible not least in the visual presentations of yoga in yoga magazines and on social media, which is quite contrary to Sāṃkhyayoga.[2] Seventh, Hariharānanda had some familiarity with Orientalist scholarship and seems to have been influenced by the Orientalist romantic views of ancient India. However, access to printed texts based on book printing as well as Indological research also gave Hariharānanda a scholarly foundation (see Jacobsen 2018).

Hariharānanda's fame beyond Bengal happened several decades after his death and is mainly due to the English translation of his *Kāpilāśramīya Pātañjal Jogdarśan* published as *Yoga Philosophy of Patañjali* by the University of Calcutta in 1963 (H. Āraṇya 1981 [1963]) and especially its publication in the United States in 1983 by SUNY Press, and also because *Yogasūtra* attained unprecedented prominence in the global yoga phenomenon. Hariharānanda re-established the extinct philosophical school of Sāṃkhyayoga as a living *saṃnyāsin* tradition. One

1. One photo displayed at Kāpil Maṭh of the young ascetic Hariharānanda is of him in *padmāsana* with emphasis, it seems, on strength, health, and correct posture. But Hariharānanda seems in his solitary Sāṃkhyayoga practice living in caves to have disregarded the body and none of his writings elaborates on *āsana* practice. Hariharānanda mostly wrote on philosophy and Sāṃkhyayoga meditation and control of the mind. Sāṃkhyayoga was for those who had already perfected *āsana* in a previous life and had moved beyond attachment to the body, according to Hariharānanda.
2. The emergence of this type of yoga as a cultural phenomenon seems to be not unrelated to the birth of the modern sports movement. The first modern Olympics were organized in 1896, the same year some researchers have claimed as the beginning of modern yoga, with the publication of Vivekānanda's *Rāja Yoga* (De Michelis 2004). That yoga posture competition most probably will become part of the competition program in the Olympics in the future seems to confirm this identity of modern yoga as related to the modern sports movement.

reason for this re-establishment was that Hariharānanda understood the importance of the *Yogabhāṣya* (*Vyāsabhāṣya*) and *Tattvavaiśāradī* for the developments of the philosophy of the *Yogasūtra*. *Vyāsabhāṣya* had been neglected and misjudged by some other early interpreters (Mitra 1883), but Hariharānanda attempted to revive the Yoga philosophy in its original Sāṃkhyayoga form and made Sāṃkhyayoga the basis for his ascetic practice. Ram Shankar Bhattacharya, a Sāṃkhyayoga scholar who was a follower of Kāpil Maṭh, the monastic institution of Hariharānanda, noted:

> Prior to the advent of Ācārya Swāmījī [Hariharānanda] the texts of the Sāṃkhya-yoga system had become quite distorted. The study and teaching of the Sāṃkhya system was done in a cursory manner. Nobody knew what spiritual practice was associated with the system. There were no Sāṃkhya organizations or living Sāṃkhya practitioners known in India in Ācārya Swāmījī's time. The extraordinary achievement of Ācārya Swāmījī was that he revived the knowledge of the Sāṃkhya texts and the practice of Sāṃkhya-yoga with his sole efforts.
>
> (Bhattacharya 2003, 152)

Although several scholars, from J. N. Farquhar in *An Outline of the Religious Literature of India* (Farquhar 1920) to David Gordon White in *The Yoga Sutra of Patañjali: A Biography* (White 2015) mistakenly interpreted Hariharānanda as a late representative of the classical Sāṃkhya and Yoga traditions instead of as an early representative of the modern yoga revival, there can be no doubt that Hariharānanda revived an ancient tradition and that he recreated a perceived Sāṃkhyayoga orthodoxy based on access to texts and not a living Sāṃkhyayoga tradition, and that he was part of the modern revival of yoga (Jacobsen 2018). The mention of Hariharānanda in Farquhar 1920 was quoted in Bhattacharya in his preface to the second edition of University of Calcutta edition of *Yoga Philosophy of Patañjali* (Bhattacharya 1981) and was subsequently quoted by other followers of the Maṭh (Chatterjee 2000). But Bhattacharya had changed some words in the quotation, unintentionally perhaps, or to correct Farquhar's misinterpretation of Hariharānanda as a leftover of an old lineage instead of an early representative of the revival of yoga. Farquhar had used the word "as late as" when mentioning Hariharānanda implying he was the last remaining of an ancient school of Sāṃkhya, but in Bhattacharya's quote it was changed to "as early as" to indicate that Hariharānanda was one of the earliest representatives of modern Sāṃkhyayoga, not a leftover of an old lineage (see Jacobsen 2018 for a discussion of this).

## Practices of Kāpil Maṭh

I have presented the background of Kāpil Maṭh in Madhupur and its followers and Hariharānanda's teachings on yoga and his yoga practices in my monograph *Yoga in Modern Hinduism: Hariharānanda Āraṇya and Sāṃkhyayoga* (Jacobsen 2018), and there is no space here to retell this history. I will mention only that the town of Madhupur emerged as a vacation spot for wealthy and educated Bengalis in the early twentieth century with a number of large mansions being built, and many of the followers of Hariharānanda have had or have some connection to this feature of Madhupur. Visitors from Kolkata went to Madhupur during their vacation times at which time the town became alive with leisure activities. In the 1970s, however, Madhupur lost this role due to political developments in Kolkata and Bengal and the mansions went into decay for several decades. Some mansions have been renovated in recent years with new owners who belong to different social categories. The followers of Kāpil Maṭh mostly belonged to the educated or upper caste in Bengal. The number of followers is however small. Publication of the texts by Hariharānanda and the second *ācārya* Dharmamegha (1892–1985), and translations of them into English, has been an important part of the work of the Maṭh the last decades under the current *ācārya,* Bhāskara.

Since little attention is paid to *āsana* in this yoga tradition, except to *padmāsana* and emphasis on the ability to be comfortably seated, what does it mean to be a lay follower of the Sāṃkhyayoga of Kāpil Maṭh? What is their yoga? I will draw attention here only to some aspects which I suggest are most relevant for lay followers.[3]

## Duḥkha

One of the main aspects of the teachings of the Sāṃkhyayoga of Kāpil Maṭh is the statement of the *Yogasūtra* 2.15 that, for the wise person, all is suffering (*duḥkham eva sarvaṃ vivekinaḥ*). That all is suffering is stated prominently not only in the *Yogasūtra* but also in the *Sāṃkhyakārikā*. Followers of Kāpil Maṭh are quite aware of this aspect of the teaching of yoga. Suffering is caused by a basic disharmony at the foundation of the material creation (the imbalance of the three material constituents [*guṇas*] of *prakṛti*), and this means that there is some element of suffering in everything, however small. An elderly member of the *maṭh* who

3. For an analysis of Hariharānanda's and Dharmamegha's Sāṃkhyayoga meditation instructions, see Jacobsen (2018).

had become blind due to diabetes since I met him last time expressed this to me when he said it was hard to lose eyesight, but such things were "what Kāpil Maṭh had taught all along." The Sāṃkhyayoga teaching had prepared him for it, i.e., the focus on the decay of the body was in accordance with the teaching, so he was well prepared and should not complain (interview, Kāpil Maṭh, Madhupur, October 2017). The truth about the real nature of the body is displayed in a written statement in the main building, the Kāpil Mandir, and at the outside next to the *samādhis*. The statement has a prominent place inside the Kāpil Mandir, where the *ācārya* meets the followers through an opening in the artificial cave, as well as on a statue next to the *samādhis* of the *ācāryas*. In the Kāpil Mandir a human skull is on display and underneath the statement is written in Sanskrit in Bengali letters and with Bengali translation underneath. The Sanskrit reads:

*Āsam sukomala suvarṇarucā tvacāhaṃ,*
*Prāgāvṛto vyavasitaṃ na kim etad artham.*
*Dṛṣṭvā 'dhunā pariṇatiṃ mama ghorarūpāṃ,*
*Bhrātar vicintaya sanātana-vastutattvam.*

For the followers of the *maṭh*, the text means: "I was once covered with a lovely skin and what have I not done to preserve it! Look at this hard reality and concentrate instead on the eternal realities." The same message is written on a statue of a human-like orange figure in the garden next to the *samādhis* of the two *ācāryas* for the devotees to contemplate when they have paid homage to them (see Figure 1).

The teaching of *duḥkha* is summarized in four terms from four *sūtras* in the *Pātañjalayogaśāstra*: *heya*, *heyahetu*, *hana* and *hanopāya*. In the Kāpil Sāṃkhyayogāśram in Sarnath founded by Om Prakāś Āraṇya, who was a disciple of Dharmamegha Āraṇya, and which belongs to the Kāpil Maṭh tradition, these four *sūtras* in Sanskrit are painted on the wall in devanāgarī script underneath the human skull and dominate the room where the followers meet (see Figure 2).

*heya—duḥkha heyaṃ duḥkham anāgatam*
(*Yogasūtra* 2.16)

*heyahetu—duḥkha kā kārṇa draṣṭṛ-dṛśyayoḥ saṃyogo heyahetuḥ*
(*Yogasūtra* 2.17)

*hana—duḥkha nāś tad abhāvāt saṃyogābhāvo hānaṃ taddṛśoḥ kaivalya*
(*Yogasūtra* 2.25)

*hanopāya—duḥkha nāśopāya vivekakhyātir aviplavā hānopāya*
(*Yogasūtra* 2.26)

**Figure 1.** The statue of a human-like orange figure with a text for the devotees to contemplate the inevitability of old age and death.

**Figure 2.** The four sūtras in Sanskrit are painted on the wall in devanāgarī script underneath the human skull in the Kāpil Sāṃkhyayogāśram in Sarnath founded by Om Prakāś Āraṇya and belonging to the Kāpil Maṭh tradition.

In English translation it means:

> Future pain can be avoided
>
> (*Yogasūtra* 2.16)
>
> The contact between the seer (*draṣṭṛ* i.e., *puruṣa*) and the seen (*dṛśya*, i.e., *citta* or *prakṛti*) is the cause of the pain that is to be avoided
>
> (*Yogasūtra* 2.17)
>
> When there is absence of ignorance, there is absence of contact which means abandonment i.e., the realization of salvific liberation
>
> (*Yogasūtra* 2.25)
>
> The means to abandonment is unshaking discriminative knowledge
>
> (*Yogasūtra* 2.26)

Some of the main teachings of the *Pātañjalayogaśāstra* are summed up in these four *sūtras* which treat *duḥkha*: the causes of *duḥkha*, *kaivalya* as the liberation from *duḥkha*, and the means for the escape from *duḥkha*. The cycle of birth is *heya*, to be discarded. The association of *puruṣa* and *prakṛti* is *heyahetu* (the cause of *heya*), stoppage of this association is *hāna* or liberation, and right knowledge is the means of liberation (*hānahetu*). Hariharānanda comments on *Yogasūtra* 2.15 that "[e]nlightened Yogins of pure character finding the cycle of rebirth to be full of sorrow, try to bring about its cessation" (H. Āraṇya 1981, 147; trans. P. N. Mukerji). Āraṇya explains that "Cessation of misery and dissolution of the mind are the same thing. [...] we practice for liberation with the resolution 'Let me be free from misery by suspending the activities of the mind'" (H. Āraṇya 1981, 149; trans. P. N. Mukerji). Hariharānanda argues that this practice is rational and proves the existence of the *puruṣa* principle:

> It is rational to think that "I shall be free from misery when the activities of the mind are stopped," i.e. there will then remain a pure "I" free from the pangs of misery. The Self beyond the mind is the real nature of the agent. If the existence of that agent is not admitted, then the question "for whose sake is liberation being sought" cannot be answered.
>
> (H. Āraṇya 1981, 149; trans. P. N. Mukerji)

The current *ācārya* Bhāskara told me once that the dissolution of the mind caused extraordinary happiness and added: "You should try it!" Bhāskara probably here referred to the attainment of a pure "I" free from the pangs of misery.

## The Yoga of Cessation

The avoidance of pain means the avoidance of the uniting of the subject and the object (*Yogasūtra* 2.17), which means the dissolution of the mind. The goal of Sāṃkhyayoga is the avoidance of this union, and when this union ends, the cycle of rebirth also ends. The Sāṃkhyayoga *ācārya*s have dedicated their life to the attainment of this goal. Laypeople on the other hand believe that their devotion to the Kāpil Maṭh tradition can improve their understanding of Sāṃkhyayoga and bring them closer to the goal, but they realize that it may take many lifetimes to attain *kaivalya*. Laypeople can improve their understanding of Sāṃkhyayoga and improve their *karmāśaya* and *vāsanā*s, but do not think they can attain *samādhi* and *kaivalya*, which are the stated ultimate goals of Sāṃkhyayoga. It is not something lay followers of Kapil Maṭh try to attain, and there is nothing wrong in being a lay person. Only the *ācārya* and a few *brahmacari*s have talked about it to me as goal. Lay persons on the other hand have often commented to me on the complexity of the Sāṃkhyayoga teaching and that most of it is beyond their grasp. Lay followers of Kāpil Maṭh use the Sāṃkhyayoga teaching to relate to life in this world. Most of the conversations between the *ācārya* and lay followers I have witnessed are about worldly matters.

The emergence of modern yoga, with posture (*āsana*) yoga considered the dominant form of yoga, meant that the Kāpil Maṭh definition of yoga understood as the peaceful state of mind, in which all its modifications have been stopped (*Yogasūtra* 1.2), had to be defended from these other meanings of yoga:

> The tranquil state of the mind is attainable only through Yoga. Yoga is the stopping of the modifications of the mind (Yoga-sūtra 1.2). The word Yoga has no other meaning though sometimes it has been used for denoting control of breath, particular postures of the body for purposes of exercise, etc. Yoga mainly denotes efforts to make the mind still, ultimately stopping all its activities.
>
> (Dharmamegha 1989, 72; trans. Adinath Chatterjee)

Hariharānanda recommended to lay followers that they as a start could imagine a luminous figure inside the heart. The luminous figure in the heart should be imagined as calm and peaceful, similar to the liberated person. When Dharmamegha initiated lay disciples, he gave them a small print of a drawing of Yogeśvara (*īśvara* of the *Pātañjalayogaśāstra*) and told the lay disciples to look at the print when they meditate, then close their eyes and imagine Yogeśvara inside. Hariharānanda further recommended that when one's own mind becomes calm and able to rest in the feeling of godliness, then one should imagine a transparent white limitless luminous sky within the heart. Next, knowing that god pervades that space, the devotee should know that his whole self is in god who is present in his heart. Finally, the mind should be merged with the mind of *Īśvara* residing in the void-like space within his heart. When this is practiced it leads, according to Hariharānanda, to the realization of the self (H. Āraṇya 1981, 56). Brahmacaris and *saṃnyāsins* of this tradition have devoted their life to pursuing this goal. But for many lay disciples Sāṃkhyayoga means especially honouring the Sāṃkhyayoga *ācāryas* and the melodious recitation of Sāṃkhyayoga *stotras*.

## Honoring the Ācāryas

Practicing Sāṃkhyayoga in the Kāpil Maṭh tradition as a layperson means maintaining some type of relationship with the Kāpil Maṭh either physically or mentally. Maintaining this relationship includes paying homage to the current *ācārya* as well as honouring the two *ācāryas* who have passed (see Figure 3). When present at the Kāpil Maṭh they pay respect to the *ācāryas* by circumambulation of their *samādhis* every day in the early morning, usually around 6.45 a.m. The ritual is mostly silent, but a few devotees may pronounce a short mantra or a greeting.

**Figure 3.** Gathering of followers of Sāṃkhyayoga in Kāpil Maṭh, Madhupur.

Some light sticks of incense but all circumambulate the *samādhis*. When that is done, they enter the main worship room of the Kāpil Maṭh, called Kāpil Mandir. Here there is an opening in the artificial cave, in which the *ācārya* is locked up, and all sit facing that opening. There is also a clock in the room which strikes every whole and half hour. After the clock has struck 7 (7.30 in the cold season), the recitation of the *stotras* begins.

## Melodious Recitation of Stotras

The main spiritual activity and bodily practice of the followers of Kāpil Maṭh is melodious reciting twice a day of Sāṃkhyayoga *stotras* (verses, devotional composition meant to be sung or recited) composed by Hariharānanda, in the morning for around 40 minutes and in the evening, a shorter program for around 30 minutes. They sit in *padmāsana* while they recite in a melodious meditative manner *stotras* that contain the teaching of Sāṃkhyayoga. This can be considered a form of embodied Sāṃkhyayoga practice and is the dominant embodied practice of the Kāpil Maṭh. They recite the same *stotras* in the same order every day. Most know the *stotras* by heart, but some new members bring a copy of the *Stotrasaṃgraha,* which is the text of *stotras* published by the Kāpil Maṭh tradition (either in Bengali [H. Āraṇya n.d.] or Devanāgarī script [H. Āraṇya 1997]). At home they supposedly recite the *stotras* alone. It is considered as a preparation for meditation, and even wife and husband are supposed to recite them separately, I have been told. When present at Kāpil Maṭh recitation is communal and participation in the recitation is considered mostly obligatory, and since the recitation happens in public it is to some degree socially controlled. The most important practice of Sāṃkhyayoga laypersons for maintaining a relationship with the living Sāṃkhyayoga tradition seems to be the memorization and recitation of the *stotras* composed by Hariharānanda and the ability to sit in *padmāsana* for the full duration of the recitation and the following few minutes of meditation. The recitation is melodious but restrained and monotonous and is not beautiful or aesthetically pleasing. It is without musical instruments and is different from both Vedic recitation and from *bhajan* and *kīrtan* singing, which are the most widely practiced forms of Hindu devotional music in India. The Kāpil Maṭh way of reciting these *stotras* seems unique to this tradition. It was perhaps introduced both as a form of laypeople meditation and to create coherence and a sense of community. Followers are present at Kāpil Maṭh only a few times a year and only during the five first days of the Bengali month in those months when the *ācārya* is available at the opening of the Kāpil Guhā. Usually, between 10 and 20 people are present, during special days and festivals some more, but mostly less than 100. In the early days, visitors would come mainly only during the holidays, the main festival of the Maṭh, Kāpil *utsav* is celebrated on December 21 instead of January 14, which is the date of the annual Kapila festival at Gaṅgā Sāgar.[4]

The recitation of *stotras* was started by Hariharānanda but it was the second *ācārya*, Dharmamegha, who introduced the melodious recitation of the *stotras*. On the function of *stotra* recitation Dharmamegha writes:

> As long as we are unable to establish ourselves steadily at a particular level of spiritual experience, we need the support of symbols as aids in our meditation. The chanting of the hymns or their aphoristic essence in the form of a *mantra* serves as an aid in concentration. By chanting the mantra we awaken the consciousness of our desired goal in the mind, which is the awareness of the Self within us.
>
> (Dharmamegha Āraṇya 2003, 54)

Dharmamegha noted that repeating the mantra and chanting the hymns are part of the path of yoga called *svādhyāya* (Dharmamegha Āraṇya 2003, 70).

Two themes dominate the Sāṃkhyayoga *stotras* of Kāpil Maṭh. First, the veneration of *īśvara,* also called Yogeśvara, Mahāyogeśa, and Mahāyogeśvara, a divinity praised in the *Pātañjalayogaśāstra*, and of the masters of yoga such as Kapila, Āsuri, Pañcāśikha, Patañjali, and the two deceased gurus of Kāpil Maṭh; and second, the veneration of the teachings of Sāṃkhya and the goals of *samādhi* and *kaivalya*, and the aspiration to attain this goal. The *stotras* thus function to communicate to the devotees the essentials of the Sāṃkhyayoga teachings.

In the daily *stotra* recitation program, the first *stotra* is about Sāṃkhyayoga holy figures, the next group of *stotras* is about the desire to attain the salvific goal of Sāṃkhyayoga, and the final *stotras* are about the deceased gurus of Kāpil Maṭh. That they recite *stotras* about *samādhi* and *kaivalya* shows that the *stotras* function to keep the focus on the yoga of Kāpil Maṭh, i.e., the bodily practice of the tradition. Yoga according to the *Yogasūtra* is meditation, and the bodily practice of melodious recitation of the teaching of Sāṃkhyayoga while sitting in *padmāsana* prepares for silent meditation. The melodious recitation of the teaching of Sāṃkhyayoga can be understood as a form of intellectual mantra meditation that functions to make the teaching a bodily knowledge, an inherent part of one's being. I have discussed the *stotras* elsewhere (Jacobsen 2012, 2018) and one example will suffice here. The *stotra* "Collection

4. For Kapila and the Gaṅgā Sāgar festival see Jacobsen (2008, 2013, 106–109).

of Four Verses Describing the Desire for Attaining Salvific Liberation" (*Mumukṣācatuṣkam*) is illustrative of the way the *stotras* contrast the Sāṃkhyayoga philosophy of life as suffering with the gradual gaining control of the mind.

1. *Om kadā bhaviṣyāmi viśuddhasattvo vitarkaśūnyo gatarāgamanyuḥ,*
*Mānuṣyadivyair vasubhiś ca yo 'rtha stenāpi hīnaḥ sumanā bhavāmi.*

(H. Āraṇya 2007, 16)

Om.
When shall I get my mind completely purified?
When shall I be free from confusion?
When shall I be free from attachment and anger?
When shall I be free even from that purpose which is served by human and divine birth and by wealth,
so that I can get my mind completely pacified?

(Jacobsen 2018, 169)

2. *saṃgṛhyā ceto viṣaye nipāti sadaikatānasmṛtisādhanena,*
*svāntaṃ prasannañca sadekṣamāṇaḥ kadā sudhīraḥ sumanā bhavāmi.*

(H. Āraṇya 2007, 16)

Oh god.
When shall I be full of patience
with the mind completely peaceful
by having withdrawn my mind
which naturally runs towards worldly objects
by means of remembering you
always, without diversions
and realize my mind is completely happy?

(Jacobsen 2018, 169)

3. *arthānnivṛtte karaṇe samaste ānandabhāvaḥ paramo vibhāti,*
*tatrāvadhānena sukhī kadāham aduḥkhaśokaḥ sumanā bhavāmi.*

(H. Āraṇya 2007, 17)

When shall I be happy
by means of concentration,
because the highest bliss shines when all the sense organs
have been withdrawn from external objects,
and thus shall with a completely peaceful mind,
be totally free from suffering and greed?

(Jacobsen 2018, 169)

4. *vivekadṛṣṭyā nihate vimohe nihatya rāgañca samūlaghātam,*
*nirudhya cittaṃ hyajaniṣyamāṇaṃ tritāpaśūnyaḥ puruṣo bhāvami.*

(H. Āraṇya 2007, 18)

After ignorance is destroyed by discriminative wisdom,
and thereafter having destroyed attachment
including its root cause
and having controlled my mind,
  not transforming any more into the form of any worldly objects,
I shall be a person devoid of the threefold suffering.
(Jacobsen 2018, 170)

A notable verse from *Samādhiṣaṭkam* is a description of the person who practices *samādhi* (for translation see Jacobsen 2012, 335–336) and states that only a *saṃnyāsin* is able to attain *samādhi,* because they only have given up completely any hope of worldly success:

*yena tyaktā na lābhāśā samyagekāntatastathā,*
*divā vā na sa rātrau vā samādhim adhigacchati.* (H. Āraṇya 2007, 19)

Such a person
who has not given up hope
of worldly success
properly and completely,
cannot attain *samādhi,*
whether in the day or by night.
(Jacobsen 2018, 170)

## Karma, Saṃskāra and Vāsanā

Finally, a topic of utmost importance in Sāṃkhyayoga is the topic of rebirth, karma, *karmāśaya* (karmic trace), *saṃskāras* (latent impression), *vāsanā* (imprint), and *smṛti* (memory), that is, understanding the rebirth process and human identity as based on this process. A large number of pages of *Pātañjalayogaśāstra* is about this, and Hariharānanda wrote elaborate commentaries, essays, and also a book on this topic. The last book of Hariharānanda was on karma, *Karmatattva* (English translation: *The Doctrine of Karma*, H. Āraṇya 2008). According to Sāṃkhya and Yoga, everything, except *puruṣa*, is material, also the mind, and all material is analyzed in terms of cause and effect. The yoga teaching of the *Pātañjalayogaśāstra* that is most important to people at Kāpil maṭh, according to my fieldwork experiences in the *maṭh* in Madhupur, is the idea of *puruṣa* (contentless consciousness) *samādhi* (concentration) and *kaivalya* (salvific liberation), which is about the ultimate goal, and the related ideas of rebirth, *karmāśaya*, *saṃskāra*, *vāsanā*, *smṛti*, and *duḥkha*. One's present life is part of a trajectory of many lives, and our experiences are shaped by our thoughts, feelings, and acts over many lives. When I had first written to Kāpil Maṭh and asked to be allowed to visit, it had caused a puzzle, I learned when I first visited in 1999. How is it that I was schooled in Sāṃkhyayoga and how is it that I knew about Kāpil Maṭh and had developed a wish to visit? The explanation was that I must have had an interest in Sāṃkhyayoga in some previous life (in India?) and that these *saṃskāras* now had become actualized. That one is drawn towards Sāṃkhyayoga is proof of earlier encounters, but it also shows that no practice of Sāṃkhyayoga is lost. Sāṃkhyayoga practice will secure that the person also in the next life or later will be drawn towards Sāṃkhyayoga. While karma mostly determines only the next life, *saṃskāras* remain for many lives.[5] When the current *ācārya,* Bhāskara some years ago was informed by the librarian of Kāpil Maṭh that I had learned to read Bengali, his immediate response was that this meant that I next time would be born in Bengal! According to Hariharānanda, "[a]ny manifest state of the mind leaves a like impression, saṃskāra" (H. Āraṇya 1981, 132). By learning Bengali, I was simply preparing myself for the next rebirth by shaping my *vāsanās* and *saṃskāras*. I was preparing for a next life as a Bengali![6]

The bodily practice of repeating the teaching of Sāṃkhyayoga every day in the ritual recitation of *stotras* that state the teaching and goals of Sāṃkhyayoga while sitting in *padmāsana* in the Kāpil Maṭh shapes the *saṃskāras* and *vāsanās*. This is a yoga practice based on the *Pātañjalayogaśāstra*. Reciting these *stotras* in Sanskrit with Sāṃkhyayoga content can be considered the basic yoga practice of Kāpil Maṭh. Yoga means sitting in *padmāsana* while reciting and pondering the Sāṃkhyayoga view of life and the world. The recitation of Sāṃkhyayoga hymns creates a state of mind that leaves an impression, a *saṃskāra,* and forms a behavioural tendency, a *vāsanā*. The daily chanting of Sāṃkhyayoga teaching in the form of hymns thus shapes the *saṃskāras* and *vāsanās* and motivates a Sāṃkhyayoga practice that will continue over many lives. The concepts of *saṃskāra* and *vāsanā* represent attempts

---

5. Karmāśaya brings about three consequences: birth, span of life, and experience of pleasure and pain. *Pātañjalayogaśāstra* explains that *vāsanā* is derived from many previous rebirths, while Karmāśaya is derived from one birth or life (Hariharānanda 1981, 137).

6. *Saṃskāras* are latent impressions of mental as well as physical actions. *Karmāśaya* is latent impressions of actions that will eventually fructify. *Vāsanā* is the subliminal imprint of an experience which does not produce direct results like *karmāśaya*. *Vāsanā* is treated in a number of places in the *Pātañjalayogaśāstra* such as 2.12, 2.13, 2.15, 2.24, 4.8, 4.10, 4.11, and 4.24. This means that it is a dominant theme in the *Pātañjalayogaśāstra*, unlike the theme of *āsana* which is almost absent in the *Pātañjalayogaśāstra*. *Saṃskāra, vāsanā,* and *karmāśaya* are at the core of the *Pātañjalayogaśāstra*, the tradition which was revived as a living philosophy by Hariharānanda.

to understand how the body learns, transforms, and remembers. This understanding that no practice of Sāṃkhyayoga is lost but shapes tendencies over many lives is an essential aspect of the yoga tradition of the Kāpil Maṭh. The teaching of Sāṃkhyayoga is here closely connected to conceptions of rebirth and does not make sense without the doctrine of repeated embodiment.

Hariharānanda revived an ancient tradition based on knowledge of Sanskrit texts of the Sāṃkhya and Sāṃkhyayoga philosophical traditions. He was a learned *ācārya* with a *sāṃnyāsa* lifestyle. He promoted Sāṃkhyayoga as theory and practice. Anyone familiar with Westernized modern postural (*āsana*) yoga may be surprised to learn about Kāpil Maṭh and this early revival of the *Pātañjalayogaśāstra* and its Sāṃkhyayoga foundation. *Āsana* teaching and practice are mostly absent in Kāpil Maṭh and the Westernized globalized meaning of yoga as bodily exercises is considered a mistaken view having little to do with the yoga of *Pātañjalayogaśāstra* and the real meaning of yoga. *Āsana* in *Pātañjalayogaśāstra* means mostly only *padmāsana*, and yoga is an embodied practice of repeating the teaching of Sāṃkhyayoga every day in ritual recitation and pondering the Sāṃkhyayoga view of life and the world while seated in *padmāsana* in order to shape the *saṃskāra*s and *vāsanā*s, i.e., make knowledge embodied.

**Knut A. Jacobsen** is Professor in the Study of Religions at the University of Bergen. His most recent publications include *Hindu Diasporas* (2023), *Routledge Handbook of South Asian Religions* (2021), *Handbook of Hinduism in Europe* (2020), and *Yoga in Modern Hinduism* (2018). He is the founding Editor-in-Chief of the seven-volume *Brill's Encyclopedia of Hinduism* (Brill, 2009–2023).

## References

### Primary Sources

Āraṇya, Dharmamegha. 1989. *Epistles of a Sāṃkhya-Yogin*. Different parts translated from Bengali by Adinath Chatterjee, Shiba Prasad Mustafi and Viveka Prakāśa Brahmacārī. Revised by Tarit Kumar Mukherji. Madhupur: Kāpil Maṭh.

——. 1992. *Iti Śuśruma*. Translated from Bengali by Indirā Guptā, *So We Have Heard (Iti Śuśruma)*. Madhupur: Kāpil Maṭh, 2003.

Āraṇya, Hariharānanda. 1988 [1911]. *Kāpilāśramīya Pātañjal Jogdarśan*. Kolkata: Praścimabai Rājya Puṣtak Parṣad.

——. 1911. *Kāpilāśramīya Pātañjal Jogdarśan.* Translated from Bengali by P. N. Mukerji, *Yoga Philosophy of Patañjali.*, 3rd ed., revised and enlarged. Calcutta: Calcutta University Press, 1981.

——. 1931. *Karmatattva. The Doctrine of Karma (Karmatattva): A Philosophical and Scientific Analysis of the Theory of Karma.* Madhupur: Kāpil Maṭh, 2008.

——. 2007. *Divine Hymns with Supreme Devotional Aphorisms.* Translated from Sanskrit and Bengali by Hariharānanda Āraṇya and Avijit Dutt. Madhupur: Kāpil Maṭh.

——. N.d. *Stotrasaṃgraha.* [In Bengali]

——. N.d. *Stotrasaṃgraha.* Translated from Bengali to Hindi by Om Prakāś Āraṇya, *Stotrasaṃgraha.* 2nd ed. Sarnath: Kāpil Sāṃkhyayogāśram, 1997.

Bhattacharya, Ram Shankar. 1981 [1977]. "Preface to the Second Edition." In Hariharānanda Āraṇya, *Yoga Philosophy of Patañjali*, 3rd ed., xvii–xviii. Calcutta: Calcutta University Press.

——. 2003. "In remembrance of Reverend Swāmī Dharmamegha Āraṇya." In Dharmamegha Āraṇya, *So We Have Heard (Iti Śuśruma)*, 139–153. Madhupur: Kāpil Maṭh.

Chatterjee, Adinath. 2000. "Preface to the Fourth Edition." In Hariharānanda Āraṇya, *Yoga Philosophy of Patañjali with Bhāsvatī*, vii–x. Calcutta: University of Calcutta.

## Secondary Sources

Alter, Joseph S. 2004. *Yoga in Modern India: The Body between Science and Philosophy.* Princeton, NJ: Princeton University Press.

Bronkhorst, Johannes. 1985. "Patañjali and the Yoga Sūtras." *Studien zur Indologie und Iranistik* 10: 191–212.

De Michelis, E. 2004. *A History of Modern Yoga.* London: Continuum.

Farquhar, J. N. 1920. *An Outline of the Religious Literature of India.* London: Humphrey Milford/Oxford University Press.

Foxen, Anya and Christa Kuberry. 2021. *Is This Yoga? Concepts, Histories, and the Complexities of Modern Practice.* London: Routledge.

Jacobsen, Knut A. 2008. *Kapila: Founder of Sāṃkhya and Avatāra of Viṣṇu.* New Delhi: Munshiram Manoharlal.

——. 2012. "Songs to the Highest God (Īśvara) in Sāṃkhya-Yoga." In *Yoga in Practice*, edited by David Gordon White, 325–336. Princeton, NJ: Princeton University Press.

——. 2013. *Pilgrimage in the Hindu Tradition: Salvific Space*. London: Routledge.

——. 2018. *Yoga in Modern Hinduism: Hariharānanda Āraṇya and Sāṃkhyayoga*. London: Routledge.

Maas, Philipp A. 2013. "A Concise Historiography of Classical Yoga Philosophy." In *Periodization and Historiography of Indian Philosophy*, edited by Eli Franco, 53–90. Vienna: Sammlung de Nobili, Institut für Südasien-, Tibet-, und Buddhismuskunde der Universität Wien.

——. 2017 "From Theory to Poetry: The Reuse of Patañjali's *Yogaśāstra* in Māgha's *Śiśupālavadha*," in *Adaptive Reuse: Aspects of Creativity in South Asian Cultural History*, edited by Elisa Freschi and Philipp A. Maas, 29–62. Wiesbaden: Harrassowitz.

Maharaj, Ayon. 2013. "Yogic Mindfulness: Hariharānanda Āraṇya's Quasi-Buddhistic Interpretation of Smṛti in Patañjali's Yogasūtra I.20." *Journal of Indian Philosophy* 41(1): 57–78.

Mallinson, James and Mark Singleton, trans. and ed. 2017. *Roots of Yoga*. London: Penguin.

Mitra, Rājendralāla. 1883. *The Yoga Aphorisms of Patañjali with the Commentary by Bhoja Rājā*. Kolkata: Asiatic Society of Bengal.

Newcombe, Suzanne. 2009. "The Development of Modern Yoga: A Survey of the Field." *Religion Compass* 3(6): 986–1002.

O'Brien-Kop, Karen. 2021. *Rethinking "Classical Yoga" and Buddhism: Meditation, Metaphors and Materiality*. London: Bloomsbury.

Poussin, Louis de la Vallée. 1936. "Le Bouddhisme et le yoga de Patañjali." *Mélanges chinois et bouddhiques* 5(1936–37): 223–242.

Singleton, Mark. 2010. *Yoga Body: The Origins of Modern Posture Practice*. Oxford: Oxford University Press.

Singleton, Mark and Jean Byrne, eds. 2008. *Yoga in the Modern World: Contemporary Perspectives*. Abingdon: Routledge.

White, David Gordon. 2014. *The Yoga Sutra of Patañjali: A Biography*. Princeton, NJ: Princeton University Press.

Williamson, Lola. 2016. "Modern Yoga and Tantra." In *Hinduism in the World*, edited by Brian A. Hatcher, 180–195. New York: Routledge.

# Part III

# BODILY PRACTICES ON THE MOVE

– 7 –

# Embodied Receptions and the Creation of B.K.S. Iyengar's *Light on Prāṇāyāma*

SUZANNE NEWCOMBE

Using the creation of B.K.S. Iyengar's *Light on Prāṇāyāma* (1981) as a case study, this chapter challenges two common assumptions about how embodied traditions are transmitted, suggesting that embodied traditions should be understood as dialogical processes in *both* creation and transmission. In contrast to the often-assumed "legitimate" transmission of a South Asian tradition within a *guru-śiṣya paramparā* (student-teacher transmission lineage), Iyengar's development of *prāṇāyāma* demonstrates that his practice developed primarily from an ideomotor exploration of his own embodied experiences. Records around the publication of *Light on Prāṇāyāma* show that Iyengar drew upon surreptitious observation of Krishnamacharya's practice, as well as ideas introduced by Krishnamācārya, Krishnamurti and Yehudi Menuhin filtered through his own rigorous, interoceptive sensory explorations. *Light on Prāṇāyāma* can be understood as a roadmap for the reader's own inner ideomotor explorations, an intense and psychologically demanding interoceptive process. Secondly, in transmitting the results of his embodied knowledge in the text of *Light on Prāṇāyāma*, it becomes clear that effective transmission on the part of the guru is a complex dialogical process at the point of transmission, as well as being an interpretive experience in reception. To make the later point, this chapter explores the hidden labor of Iyengar's editor Gerald Yorke, as well as several (uncredited) women, especially Mary Stewart and Beatrice Harthan, as being essential to the eventual publication of *Light on Prāṇāyāma*. *Light on Prāṇāyāma* was only published after Iyengar's articulations were tested against others' experiences and a process of clarifying his written instructions with experienced practitioners as well as non-practitioners and experts in other fields.

Keywords: yoga, B.K.S. Iyengar, *prāṇāyāma,* ideomotor, transmission, women, embodiment

There is a common assumption that South Asian traditions of yoga are more legitimate if transmitted through close teacher–student relationships (i.e. *guru-śiṣya paramparā*). As Mark Singleton and Ellen Goldberg noted in their introduction to *Gurus of Modern Yoga*, it is often assumed that "Indian students had to undergo initiation and extensive training under a qualified guru before they could learn the techniques and practices of yoga" and that there is still "an ongoing preoccupation with and respect for lineage (*paramparā, sampradāya, saṅgh parivār*)" even as the concept of guru and its importance for the transition of yoga in modern times is being scrutinised and re-evaluated (Singleton and Goldberg 2014, 4). This chapter will continue to unpack this assumption as it explores the nature of the transmission of the embodied tradition of *prāṇāyāma* (purposefully controlled breathing) to and from the seminal teacher of physical yoga practices of the twentieth century, B.K.S. Iyengar (1918–2014).

B.K.S. Iyengar is perhaps "the most paradigmatic yoga guru of the last seventy-five years" (Smith and White 2014, 136). Iyengar's "trilogy" of *Light on Yoga* (1966), *Light on Prāṇāyāma* (1981) and *Light on the Yoga Sūtras of Patañjali* (1996) holds a unique place for the comprehensive detail they offer on techniques and practices of *āsana* and *prāṇāyāma* and their technical embodied framing with reference to the Patañjali *Yogaśāstra*.[1] This "Light on" series was concluded by the publications of *Light on Life* (2005) which offered more of Iyengar's personal reflections on his journey and teaching and *Light on Holistic Health* (2014). However, these later two books do not have the same canonical status either within the Iyengar yoga tradition or the wider yoga milieu. Undoubtably, it is the first of these volumes which has achieved the widest influence, the clear encyclopedic, photographic *Light on Yoga* being heralded as a "Bible" of yoga posture work soon after its publication.[2] B.K.S. Iyengar's precise presentations of *āsana* and its global spread through systematized syllabus focusing on principles of *āsana* technique, mark Iyengar as a key influence on the modern yoga revival. At the time of its publication, Iyengar was confident that *Light on Prāṇāyāma* might surpass the importance of his first publication. Although this now seems unlikely, *Light on Prāṇāyāma* will likely hold a significant place within the canonical transmission of yoga for generations.

1. For the complex role Patañjali's *Yoga Sūtra* has played in the revival of yoga in the modern period see Singleton (2008) and White (2014). Elizabeth De Michelis (2004) relied heavily on Iyengar's "trilogy" in identifying the distinctive features of yoga in the modern period.
2. For example, see Tuft (1971) as well as Smith and White (2014, 136).

An exploration of B.K.S. Iyengar's autobiographical reflections and the extant documents surrounding the publication of *Light on Prāṇāyāma* (1981) demonstrate that Iyengar's development of *prāṇāyāma* only marginally relied upon a *guru-śiṣya paramparā*. Rather, Iyengar's masterly embodiment, and eventual teaching of *prāṇāyāma* was developed primarily from what Koch explains in Chapter 2 as the "ideomotor principle, stating that acquisition of knowledge is an interplay of ideas and sensorimotor input and observation drawn from one's own actions" (Koch, this volume, page 36). Iyengar's development of skill in *prāṇāyāma* demonstrates a processual and sensorial refinement primarily created by reflecting upon sensory experiences in light of other ideas and observations. *Light on Prāṇāyāma* articulates the results of this personal, interoceptive and experiential exploration and attempts to guide others towards their own explorations of purposely controlled breathing. A teacher or *guru* might assist in this process of personal sensory exploration, but equally a teacher might act as an obstacle to this transmission, as was arguably the case with T. Krishnamācārya for B.K.S. Iyengar's development of *prāṇāyāma* practice.

As Hanky explains in the introduction to this volume, reception theory traditionally focused on the "dialogical character of reading," exploring interpretation on the part of the recipients of an artefact (such as a text or artwork). However, the archival evidence surrounding the creation and publication of *Light on Prāṇāyāma* emphasizes that the dialogical process of interpretation began prior to publication—and led to reformulations in the means of expression. The eventual publication of this book only came about after extensive dialogue with Gerald Yorke, a reader and editor associated with the publisher, and several English "test readers" who ensured that the instructions were coherent and understandable. This chapter will argue that *Light on Prāṇāyāma* is a powerful and rich document; it is a collaborative creation as well as a record of Iyengar's own process of self-study. This analysis relies heavily upon correspondence and draft manuscripts of *Light on Prāṇāyāma* donated by the Yorke family to Archives and Special Collections at the University of Reading.[3]

3. *Light on Yoga* (1966) went through a similar collaborative process which I have discussed elsewhere (Newcombe 2019, 28–39), but the extant evidence on the process leading up to publication is less substantial than for *Light on Prāṇāyāma*.

## *Light on Prāṇāyāma*

*Light on Prāṇāyāma* is a carefully organized book, a thoroughly practical manual on the performance of *prāṇāyāma*. *Prāṇāyāma* is the fourth limb of Patañjali's delineation of *aṣṭangayoga* and could be broadly understood as the practice of purposefully controlled breathing. In *Light on Prāṇāyāma*, Iyengar defines *prāṇāyāma* as "the prolongation of breath and its restraint" and in the glossary as: "Rhythmic control (āyama) of breath. The fourth stage of Yoga. It is the hub around which the wheel of Yoga revolves" (Iyengar 1981, 13, 227).

*Prāṇā* has a long history in Indic thought, being associated with both breath and a "vital principle." Within the medieval *haṭhayoga* tradition, some authors make the control of *prāṇa* the central mechanism to achieving the liberatory goals of yoga (Mallinson and Singleton 2017, 32). In the seventh century Śaivite text, the *Dharmaputrikā Saṃhitā, prāṇa* is understood as a principal bodily wind through which one can control bodily processes; it also noted in this text that "unconquered wind" can instigate disease. In this early text, *prāṇāyāma* techniques can both cause as well as correct problems caused by the derangement of the winds (Barois 2020, 52–53).

Iyengar was very conscious that *prāṇāyāma* has the potential to negatively affect mental and physical health which is one of the reasons why *prāṇāyāma* is not more widely practiced among contemporary Iyengar yoga practitioners. Iyengar related that in his personal experience, wrong practice can cause disturbance in the mind, body, and "nerves"; he explains that forceful breathing practices "can derange the nerves which can cause emotional and mental imbalance" (Iyengar 2004b [1982], 105). Although Iyengar repeats the traditional advice that these techniques are best learnt at the feet of a guru, Iyengar hopes that through his detailed explorations "Even the uninitiated sādhaka can practise independently without fear of ill-effects" (Iyengar 1981, xxi).

*Light on Prāṇāyāma* runs over 300 pages and contains 190 illustrations. It is laid out in two parts of unequal length. The first part of the book consists of 222 pages and is divided into three sections: (1) "The Theory of Prāṇāyāma" (52 pages) contextualizes the practice within yoga, contemporary understandings of physiology, traditional Indian teaching and discusses the general effects of the practice; (2) "The Art of Prāṇāyāma" (69 pages) details general points about sitting, *mudrās* and *bandhās* (ways of making energetic "seals" within the body), basic principles of inhalations (*pūraka*), exhalations (*rechaka*) and retentions (*kumbhaka*); and (3) "The Techniques of Prāṇāyāma" (99 pages) goes into detail of fourteen specific *prāṇāyāma* techniques and the "art of placing the fingers on the nose." Iyengar recommends his reader to "[r]ead, re-read and digest Part I of this book before starting to practice" (Iyengar 1981, xxi).

The second part of the book, entitled "Freedom and Beatitude" is only thirty-one pages long. It discusses *dhyana* (meditation) and gives detailed instructions for *śavāsana* ("the art of relaxation"). These two parts are followed by an appendix with a schedule of five courses of progressive *prāṇāyāma* practice intended to make the *sādhaka* "cautious and bold" as well as give "some idea of the infinite number of permutations and combinations possible in this noble art and science" (Iyengar 1981, xxi). The book is concluded with a glossary and an index.

## Learning *Prāṇāyāma*: Iyengar and His Guru

B.K.S. Iyengar began his practice of yoga in response to physical illness and a lack of other opportunities. At various times, Iyengar drafted autobiographies which contain some elements common to most modern yoga hagiographies (e.g., the sickly child transformed through the practice of yoga to a healthy and vibrant man), but also contain less flattering details of Iyengar's experience (e.g., an admission that he stole money to buy food while living with his guru and that he failed to secure good enough marks in English to continue his education to college level) (Iyengar 1978, 7, 9). Iyengar learned yoga, particularly the performance of *āsana*, during a short period of intense training with his brother-in-law Tirumalai Krishnamāchārya (1888–1989) at the Mysore Palace in the late 1930s. Iyengar credits his excellence in *āsana* teaching largely to his single-minded practice and the economic necessity for him to eke out a living teaching yoga after Krishnamāchārya arranged a short-term teaching position for him in Pune (Iyengar 2000). Despite documenting several occasions of being physically harmed by Krishnamāchārya, Iyengar continued to refer to Krishnamāchārya as guru throughout his life.[4] It is clear from the publishing correspondence that securing Krishnamāchārya's good opinion was extremely important to Iyengar. Iyengar gives formal gratitude for Krishnamāchārya's teachings at every appropriate opportunity.

4. Iyengar's own teaching of yoga has at times caused injury or public humiliation. This critique of Iyengar's methods was part of the discourse in 1970s Britain (e.g., Newcombe 2019, 170 and 242) as well as being part of a more recent reevaluation of power dynamics and yoga teaching (e.g., Remski 2019, 187, 221–222; Shaw 2016). Iyengar yoga teacher Hong Gwi-Seok has reflected on the need to expand critical colonial analysis within contemporary discussions of harm and discipline when considering modern transmissions of yoga (Hong 2020).

While Iyengar was living with Krishnamāchārya in Mysore, Iyengar reports seeing his guru perform *prāṇāyāma* at home and famously "stop" his heartbeat under the observation of visiting French doctors visiting the Mysore yogashala (Iyengar 1978, 11). However, Iyengar claims he was never directly taught any techniques of *prāṇāyāma* by Krishnamāchārya.

Iyengar recalls that when directly requested (around 1940), his guru gave him an "outline" of the breathing practice and advised him to do "deep breathing." Iyengar found this physically impossible. When Iyengar asked his guru why he was failing, he recalls being told: "Continue. It will come"; but in Iyengar's experience "it never came" (Iyengar 2000 [1985]). Again in 1941, Iyengar recalls explicitly requesting that his guru teach him *prāṇāyāma* and recalls that Krishnamāchārya dismissed him as "not fit for *prāṇāyāma*" (Iyengar 2000, 33). Not one to be deterred, on a 1943 visit staying at Krishnamāchārya's home, Iyengar recalls surreptitiously observing his guru:

> I stealthily peeped through the window and observed his movements very carefully. I wanted to learn to sit, to stretch the spinal column and relax the facial muscles. Each morning I watched his adjustments and movements, the dropping of the eyeballs, the closing of the eyes, movements of the eyelids, lift of the chest, movement of the abdominal organs, maintenance of the waist, the sound and flow of his breath. Having observed his practice minutely, I was tempted, approached him with humility and pleaded him to teach me *prāṇāyāma*. He said that it might not be possible for me to do *prāṇāyāma* in this life. His refusal to teach me was the seed for me to start the *prāṇāyāma* practices myself.
>
> (Iyengar 2000, 34)

According to his autobiographical reflections, Iyengar struggled with the practice of *prāṇāyāma* for many years, feeling frustrated and dejected in his attempts. For many years, Iyengar describes his body shaking, straining to hold his breath and keep any rhythm (Iyengar 1981, xix–xx), as well as being terrified by regular visions of a hissing cobra ready to strike when he commenced the practice (Iyengar 2000, 35).

Iyengar's autobiographical account of *prāṇāyāma* instruction by his guru diverges greatly from the idealized account of the yoga traditions being transmitted by detailed instruction from a master to student. Krishnamāchārya is always reported by Iyengar as the source of his inspiration and connection to yogic practice, but the actual relationship was complex and the direct teaching itself not always particularly instructive (Smith and White 2014).

## Learning *Prāṇāyāma*: Practice and Observation

So, if not from instructions given by a personal guru, how did the *prāṇāyāma* practice become embodied in B.K.S. Iyengar? According to his autobiographical writings, Iyengar primarily relied on a dogged commitment to practice, openness to external inspiration and intense self-observation.

Initially, Iyengar describes trying to force a practice that he believed that he should do. He describes awaking early, having a coffee, and then sitting in *padmāsana* (lotus position). He would try either the techniques of *ujjāyī* (deep inhalation, deep exhalation) or *nāḍi śodhana* (using the fingers against the nostrils). However, he recalls that "the inner carpets of the nostrils used to rebel" and within one minute "my mind would say, 'No *prāṇāyāma* today'" (Iyengar 2000 [1985], 62).

Perhaps what defined Iyengar's development within the yoga tradition more than anything else was his exceptional persistence in observation and exploration of techniques. Iyengar noticed that he could not sit straight and was very restless. To address this, he developed a technique of "oscillating between sitting *āsanas* and *śavāsana*" (Iyengar 2000 [1985], 63). Iyengar also noticed that his spine was not stable in a sitting position and discovered that while he could hold extreme backbends for long periods of time, he found forward bending very difficult. As he balanced out his *āsana* practice, he found stability in his sitting position (Iyengar 2000 [1985], 64–65).

Iyengar also carefully observed and learned from his students. With regards to the development of his *prāṇāyāma* technique, Iyengar specifically credits two of his internationally famous students, the philosopher-teacher Jiddhu Krishnamurti (1895–1986) and the virtuoso violinist Yehudi Menuhin (1916–1999).

Iyengar and Krishnamurti had an on-off association between 1948 and the mid-1960s, with Iyengar instructing Krishnamurti in *āsana* when the two men were in the same location. Iyengar's official biographer reflects that while "to Iyengar, this was one of the relationships that leveraged him into the realm of the wealthy and well known. On an emotional level, however, he [Iyengar] was left embittered by Krishnamrthy's [sic] treatment of him" (Palkhivala 2017, 92). While Krishnamurti did not deny the association with Iyengar (and later with Krishnamāchārya's son T.K.V. Desikachar (1938–2016)), Krishnamurti's official biography is careful to note that he "practised yoga as a form of physical exercise only" (Lutyens 2003, 137).

As a child in Madras, Krishnamurti was "discovered" by the Theosophical Society and adopted by its leader at that time, Annie Besant. Krishnamurti was believed to be the bodily host of the future "world teacher" which the Theosophical Society prophesized would guide the evolution of humanity. Krishnamurti was tutored for this role in England and began giving public talks to the Theosophical Society and the Order of the Star in the East which was built up around the expectation of his assuming a messianic teacher's mantle. However, in 1929, Krishnamurti dissolved the Order and declared that: "Truth, being limitless, unconditioned, unapproachable by any path whatsoever, cannot be organized; nor should any organization be formed to lead or to coerce people along any particular path" (Krishnamurti 1929). This declaration led to a rapid decline of the Theosophical Society. But Krishnamurti himself emerged as a kind of independent "world teacher" and achieved widespread influence.

Krishnamurti returned to India after independence, conducting a successful speaking tour and meeting with prominent figures including Prime Minister Nehru. It was during a lecture-tour visit to Pune in 1948 that Iyengar began teaching Krishnamurti yoga (Palkhivala 2017, 90).[5] Iyengar is reported to have attended Krishnamurti's public lectures in Pune from September 1948 in addition to teaching Krishnamurti daily at 4 am during his stay in the city after being introduced by a mutual acquaintance, the Parsi merchant F. P. Pocha whose health complaints Iyengar had helped resolve with *āsana* practice (Jayakar 1986, 96; Iyengar 1988, 44–51).

Iyengar claims during this period, he was introduced to Krishnamurti's theory of "passive alertness" and that this idea transformed his experience of inhalation during *prāṇāyāma* (Iyengar 2000, 64). The phrase "passive alertness" comes up occasionally in Krishnamurti's lectures. Jayakar explains that during this first teaching tour in independent India, Krishnamurti was emphasizing the necessity of experiencing "what is" with a "total, nonfragmented perception [that] can negate both the observer and the observed" (Jayakar 1986, 115–116). In April of 1948, Krishnamurti explained in Madras:

> See what happens when we are voluntarily or spontaneously giving our attention to something, without seeking a result—examining a human problem. The mind is then in an extraordinary state, passive, pliable and capable of seeing clearly. Such a state is not possible when there is contradiction. You know for yourself inwardly when you are not living in a state

5. For more reflections on Krishnamurti's likely influence on Iyengar's thinking see De Michelis (2004, 202–204).

> of contradiction, when you are in a state of integration. [...] Only when there is passive alertness there is openness.
>
> (Krishnamurti 1948a)

Iyengar used the idea of "passive alertness" to begin to soften his inhalation, exploring and creating sensations of openness, quietness, and exhilaration rather than experiencing sensations of heaviness and tension (Iyengar 2000, 64). Recall that his guru first advised the practice of "deep breathing," and that Iyengar found this practice impossible. Decades after writing *Light on Prāṇāyāma*, Iyengar reflected on the difference between *prāṇāyāma* and "deep breathing" in a way that suggests "passive alertness" as described by Krishnamurti:

> *Prāṇāyāma* is not just deep breathing ... In deep breathing the facial muscles and the brain cells are hardened. The chest walls (the intercostal muscles and ribs) are dynamically lifted with forceful sucking of air in inhalation and with heavy expulsion of air in exhalation. If the water gushes in, very forcefully, it splashes out, damaging the container. Forceful breathing does the same.
>
> In *prāṇāyāmic* breathing the brain cells and facial muscles are kept passive and receptive. As a passive spectator, each and every fibre of the chest wall is watched and kept receptive and mobile and the breath is taken with least force. As the breath is drawn in, room is created within the chest gradually to absorb the drawn-in breath so that it is moistened and soaked to reach the remotest parts of the lungs and to feed them. The art of balancing, the effort of drawing the breath in or out should be synchronised with the receptivity of the cells of the lungs so that they respond to receive the breath.
>
> (Iyengar 2001, 102)

We could see Iyengar's first attempts to apply his guru's injunction of "deep breathing" as part of his remarkable capacity for self-discipline and focus on a particular object. However, by adopting Krishnamurti's idea of "passive attention" Iyengar was able to look at his morning *prāṇāyāma* practice with a new conceptual tool, shifting Iyengar's embodied understanding of *prāṇāyāma*. This exemplifies embodied knowledge as ideomotor training, where "acquisition of knowledge is an interplay of ideas and sensorimotor input and observation drawn from one's own actions" (Koch, this volume, page 36).

From this new experience of "passive alertness," Iyengar began to create variations of sensory experience through "manipulating the intercostal muscles of the chest, the fingers on the nose and so forth" (Iyengar 2000 [1985], 64). In this way he extended his already intense practice of proprioception (a sense of bodily position and movement) internally into a focus on interoception (a felt sense of the internal body). The play between specific *prāṇāyāma* techniques, proprioception and interoception was intended to create a state of "effortless effort" in which the "intelligence and consciousness may spread to each and every cell" (Iyengar 2012 [1993], 59). Matylda Ciołkosz argues that this focus on promoting the development of proprioception and interoception is the central facet of B.K.S. Iyengar's understanding of yoga (see Ciołkosz 2018, 218, 222–226).

Iyengar was able to refine his *prāṇāyāma* technique further through observing his famous violinist student Yehudi Menuhin. Iyengar describes observing Menuhin's fingerwork on the violin:

> [T]he mobility of the knuckles on the violin strings and the placement of the tip of the thumb on the bow and fingers on the strings. This gave me the clue of placing the thumb and fingers on the nose to control the inner carpet of the membrane and to trace the exact air passage for my *prāṇāyāma*.
>
> (Iyengar 2000 [1985], 64)

Iyengar's intense observations led to somewhat idiosyncratic practice explorations which were articulated in *Light on Prāṇāyāma*. Iyengar's detailed and precise instructions for "digital *prāṇāyāma*" are significantly more comprehensive and in-depth than *prāṇāyāma* instructions found elsewhere in the yoga canon. The section on "Digital *prāṇāyāma* and the Art of Placing the Fingers on the Nose" takes up a full twenty pages in the final publication. And, as we will see below, the subtlety Iyengar developed in this area was difficult to communicate. *Light on Prāṇāyāma* required a complex process of collaboration and dialogue before the eventual finalisation of the published work.

Rather than being directly rooted in an idealistic dyadic *guru-śiṣya paramparā*, Iyengar's development of *prāṇāyāma* technique came from his commitment to observation, practice, and self-reflection.

## Teaching *Prāṇāyāma*: Dialogic Reception

Having successfully brought *Light on Yoga* to publication with the publisher Allen & Unwin through the editorial support of Gerald Yorke (1901–1983) (see Newcombe 2019, 28–35), Iyengar again turned to Yorke in the hopes of securing publication of this new manuscript. Iyengar was confident that it would surpass *Light on Yoga* in its importance.

But upon receiving the first few draft chapters of *Light on Prāṇāyāma*, Yorke was much less confident. It was not easy to articulate in writing the intense introspective attention Iyengar gave to developing his own *prāṇāyāma* practice. Yorke wrote Iyengar in reply:

> It is quite impossible to publish the book in its present form at a profit [...]. It [*Light on Yoga*] was successful because you were able to describe what one has to do in correct sequence, but here you are dealing with extreme subtleties such as sensing and then altering the flow of breath through the nostrils by using the pressure of the thumb and 2 fingers. This sort of thing only makes sense to a trained instructor who can demonstrate to the pupil and explain but it means nothing to the reader who is trying to practice on his own. This is the public who buys your Light on Yoga in quantities. Then you write what to me is nonsense about separating the skin from the nerves and muscles and so on.
>
> (Carbon copy of letter dated February 13, 1978, from Gerald Yorke to B.K.S. Iyengar, Gerald Yorke Collection)

Despite Yorke's concern about the sale's potential for *Light on Prāṇāyāma,* he trusted Iyengar as an exceptional practitioner. The editorial process of bringing *Light on Yoga* to publication took several years and many revisions. Yorke was willing to invest time and energy into bringing the little-known practices of *prāṇāyāma* into wider circulation. He wrote to Iyengar: "Anyway I will write more fully when discussing it with someone who has practiced and whom I respect. I am still worrying about it. I am so sorry" (carbon copy of letter dated February 13, 1978, from Gerald Yorke to B.K.S. Iyengar, Gerald Yorke Collection).

## Gender, Hidden Labor, and the Creation of *Light on Prāṇāyāma*

Recent years have seen considerable interest in exploring themes of gender in both contemporary ascetic and historical yogic traditions within India. Therefore, it is worth highlighting the hidden labor of women in the creation of *Light on Prāṇāyāma.* Most Sanskrit texts were written and sponsored by men. Yet the absence of evidence regarding female practitioners in much of the yoga tradition is not necessarily evidence of their absence. Recreating a narrative of female yoga practice on scant evidence is difficult and fraught with dangers of reading contemporary assumptions into earlier different social contexts. *Light on Prāṇāyāma* could easily be read as being written by a man and edited by a man, even if the majority of yoga practitioners and teachers who were the assumed consumers of this book were women.[6]

6. I have explored the reasons for the predominance of female teachers and practitioners of yoga in Britain during the twentieth century elsewhere (Newcombe 2007; 2019, 109–133).

However, in the case of *Light on Prāṇāyāma*, we have evidence of the role of female practitioners which could easily be obscured from the historical record without this reconstruction from primary sources. When Gerald Yorke wanted the book to be tested by a practitioner to ensure clarity before publication, he wrote to Beatrice (Wendy) Harthan, a woman who shared Yorke's interest in the Buddhist Society activities. She was the first to hand Yorke a draft manuscript of Iyengar's *Light on Yoga*.

At this time, Harthan was the Chair of the Iyengar Yoga Institute in London and her life partner Angela Marris was the Secretary and Treasurer of the association. Both were originally introduced to Iyengar by Yehudi Menuhin as members of his Asian Music Circle and Marris typed the original manuscript of *Light on Yoga* while in Gstaad, Switzerland with the two men (personal interview with Angela Marris, June 30, 2005). Although Harthan and Yorke were obviously acquainted before the publication of *Light on Yoga* because of a shared interest in Buddhism, through the correspondence one can see an increasing intimacy as she moves from being called Beatrice to Wendy. A reading of the correspondence around the publication of both of Iyengar's books with Allen & Unwin, reveals that Harthan had a large role in managing Iyengar's relations to other people in Britain during the 1960s and 1970s; she helped find him accommodation during his visits to London and corresponded in Iyengar's interests with various professional bodies.

Yorke trusted Harthan's opinion and as an intermediary in some communications with Iyengar. To help revise the manuscript, Harthan suggested a "sane and practical" London-based woman who had been taught extensively by Iyengar in Pune, Mary Stewart (letter from Beatrice Harthan to B.K.S. Iyengar, March 29, 1978, Gerald Yorke Collection).[7] On February 26, 1978, Yorke wrote again to Iyengar:

> As you see I was close to throwing my hand in. But I have had a session first with Wendy [Beatrice] Harthan and then with Mary ~~Fletcher~~ Stewart with (the later) whom I have lefy [sic] the chapters I have, both to check what I have rewritten and where I have marked a passage and to make any clarifying suggestions that occur to her. Also to point out redundancies—

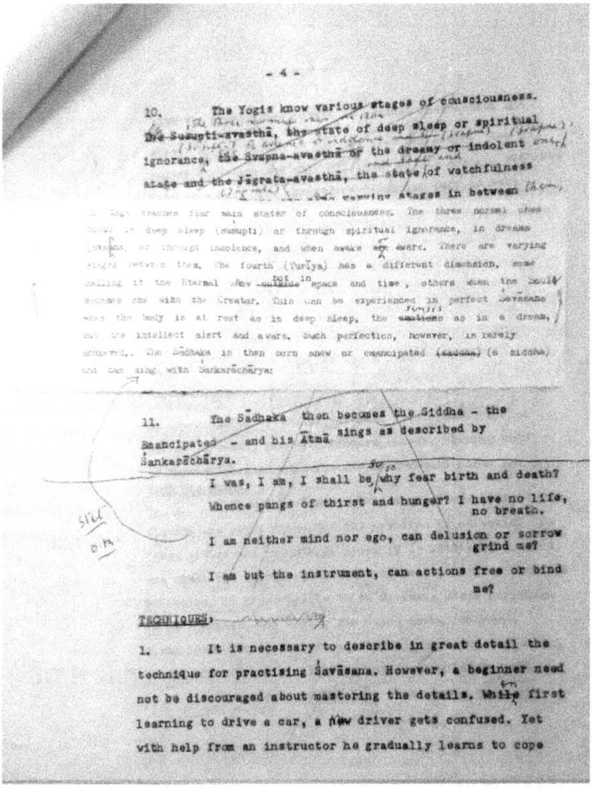

- 4 -

10. The Yogis know various stages of consciousness. The Susupti-avasthā, the state of deep sleep or spiritual ignorance, the Svapna-avasthā or the dreamy or indolent state and the Jāgrata-avasthā, the state of watchfulness ... varying stages in between

... teaches four main states of consciousness. The three normal ones occur in deep sleep (susupti) or through spiritual ignorance, in dreams (svapna) or through indolence, and when awake or aware. There are varying stages between them. The fourth (Turīya) has a different dimension, some calling it the Eternal not in space and time, others when the Soul becomes one with the Creator. This can be experienced in perfect Śavāsana when the body is at rest as in deep sleep, the senses as in a dream, but the intellect alert and aware. Such perfection, however, is rarely achieved. The Sādhaka is then born anew or emancipated (a siddha) and can sing with Śankarāchārya:

11. The Sādhaka then becomes the Siddha - the Emancipated - and his Ātmā sings as described by Śankarāchārya.

I was, I am, I shall be, why fear birth and death?
Whence pangs of thirst and hunger? I have no life, no breath.
I am neither mind nor ego, can delusion or sorrow grind me?
I am but the instrument, can actions free or bind me?

TECHNIQUES:

1. It is necessary to describe in great detail the technique for practising Śavāsana. However, a beginner need not be discouraged about mastering the details. While first learning to drive a car, a new driver gets confused. Yet with help from an instructor he gradually learns to cope

**Figure 4.** Annotated page of the draft manuscript of *Light on Prāṇāyāma*; this page corresponds with page 233 in the final published version. Gerald Yorke Files.

> for instance the Rechaka Puraka successive chapters you devote in each several sentences on the mother and child analogy.
>
> (Gerald Yorke to B.K.S. Iyengar, February 26, 1978, Gerald Yorke Collection)[8]

Yorke then suggests that Mary Stewart continue to work through the manuscript as Iyengar sends the chapters in succession. Stewart agreed to help with this process after writing directly to Iyengar to get his approval of her involvement. She involved her daughter by asking her to type out a new copy of the manuscript for her to annotate and asked a "medical member of the family" (likely her son) to check out the anatomical details of the manuscript. Stewart's comments went back to Yorke, who then integrated them with his own comments and passed them back on a single document to Iyengar for the final decision.

In the preface to *Light on Prāṇāyāma,* as well as in letters to Yorke, Iyengar expresses profuse gratitude to Yorke for his editorial guidance. Iyengar wrote to Gerald Yorke near the end of the revision process: "With your help it is refined and through me you have rendered a greater service to humanity in these two books of mine than my own efforts and practices" (Iyengar to Yorke, April 22, 1978, Gerald Yorke Collection).

However, the contributions of Harthan and Stewart are not acknowledged in the final publication or by Iyengar to Yorke in correspondence. To achieve clarity and coherence in the published work, Iyengar was reliant upon contributions by his editor and his editor's dialogue with his student-practitioner and her associates. Considering the gender mores of the 1970s, it is unsurprising that this female labor remained hidden and unacknowledged in any published documents. However, there is evidence that the contributions and reflections on the likely reception and interpretation of the writings which these women undertook were essential in bringing the manuscript of *Light on Prāṇāyāma* to eventual publication and its status as a canonical text.

## Further Transmission/Reception of *Prāṇāyāma* Practices

Despite Iyengar's own dedication to the practice of *prāṇāyāma*, it was not adopted to the same extent by his pupils as the practice of *āsana*. By Iyengar's own admission *Light on Prāṇāyāma* is "a very difficult book as it contains a lot of subtle points" as well as "a most practical book" (Iyengar to Yorke, February 22, 1978, Gerald Yorke Collection). To some extent relative lack of engagement might be due to the relatively high levels of interoception, self-observation, and concentration required for the application of the more subtle techniques of *prāṇāyāma* in comparison to *āsana* (Ciołkosz 2018).

Another element leading to the relative restraint in teaching *prāṇāyāma* by Iyengar-trained teachers is Iyengar's caution against causing injury or mental disturbance through *prāṇāyāma* practice. Since the publication of *Light on Prāṇāyāma* (1981), much of the Iyengar work focused on making *āsana* more accessible, particularly in therapeutic applications. Books and guides for self-practice in the Iyengar tradition published from the mid-1980s onwards tend to place *prāṇāyāma* within a "restorative" sequence of postures, and at the end of an *āsana* practice (e.g., Mehta 1990; Iyengar 2014). Mary Stewart (the test reader of *Light on Prāṇāyāma)* and Maxine Tobias's book *Stretch & Relax* (1984) is positioned firmly within the Iyengar tradition yet does not even introduce *prāṇāyāma*.

In Iyengar's final illustrated guide to *āsana* practice, *Light on Holistic Health* (2014), the only *prāṇāyāma* exercises are *ujjāyī* and *viloma* 2 done in a supported *śavāsana* (a lying down position with the chest and head raised); these two exercises cover only four pages of a 416-page book. On one of these pages, a small box gives "The Guru's Advice":

> Remember that faulty practice can strain the lungs and diaphragm. Set aside 40–60 minutes at a fixed time of day for pranayama. Never practice just after a meal or immediately after an energetic session of asana.
>
> (Iyengar 2014, 231)

This book is aimed at people with specific physical complaints and one can see how this advice might make it difficult for busy people to contemplate starting *prāṇāyāma*. The reader is warned that not only can faulty practice cause injury, but also a long period of time is suggested at a fixed time each day in addition to the recommended postures. While these injunctions are a common part of the yoga literature, they don't make *prāṇāyāma* practice easy to integrate into a daily routine.

Iyengar yoga retains a considerable degree of coherence throughout the globe, through (1) the exceptionally clear principles articulated by Iyengar in his books, (2) the early (1970s) establishment of an independent teacher-training program, and (3) incentives for more experienced teachers to regularly return to the "home" institute in Pune, India.[9] While there is great uniformity in the principles and techniques through which *āsana* and *prāṇāyāma* are taught by Iyengar yoga teachers, there is also a conservatism deferring to the traditional authority of the Iyengar family in matters of teaching and interpretation. After Iyengar's death, this role fell to his daughter Geeta Iyengar (1944–2018), his son Prashant (b. 1949) and now is largely held by his granddaughter Abhijata Sridhar (b. 1962). Several significant individuals whose main training was by B.K.S. Iyengar later left the constrictions of being part of the Iyengar certification system, including Vanda Scaravelli and Mary Stewart.

Typically, stand-alone *prāṇāyāma* classes by Iyengar yoga teachers have been relatively rare; it is usually taught once a month as part of a "recuperative sequence" of "restorative" postures. These sequences often emphasize "chest opening" and "head quieting" positions, often with the use of supportive props; *prāṇāyāma* is often taught through observing how breathing patterns and thoughts respond to the positioning of the body in *āsana*. A few minutes of more extended exhalation or inhalation (possibly with pauses) might come before the final *śavāsana* (the "corpse posture" which ends a typical Iyengar yoga class)

9. For more detail on this see Ciołkosz (2018, 214–216).

(De Michelis 2004, 257–260). In other words, the intense sequence of *prāṇāyāma*-focused practice suggested in *Light on Prāṇāyāma* is rarely followed as a model for class teaching; it is very likely only practiced regularly by a minority of teachers as well. However recent reformations to the teacher-training syllabus have been made to try to get teachers to include more *prāṇāyāma* in their teaching and practice to establish it as it is an integral part of the tradition.

## Conclusion: Iyengar's Dialogic Ideomotor Exploration

Despite the relative lack of mass practice of *prāṇāyāma* among dedicated Iyengar yoga teachers and practitioners (at least compared to *āsana* practice), *Light on Prāṇāyāma* has become an established part of Iyengar's "Modern Yoga trilogy." In future when scholars and historians look at transformations of yoga practice in the twentieth century, Iyengar's text is likely to be highlighted for its exceptional detail and clarity.

This exploration of the process of how *Light on Prāṇāyāma* was published throws new light on the process of how the yoga tradition develops and continues. While Iyengar positions himself firmly within a *guru-śiṣya paramparā* with J. Krishnamācārya, he also describes how minimal the personal instructions on *prāṇāyāma* were from his guru. Iyengar emphasizes in interviews and autobiographical writings that his development of *prāṇāyāma* came primarily as a process of intense observation and self-study—with important insights coming from some of his contact with J. Krishnamurti and Yehudi Menuhin. He tested the ideas he learned from listening, watching, and observing against his own sensory, interoceptive experiences. In this way Iyengar developed a refined and subtle practice of *prāṇāyāma* which has become a canonical manual of yoga in the modern period.

However, a close examination of the process in which *Light on Prāṇāyāma* came into existence also challenges standard assumptions about the nature of a dyadic *guru-śiṣya paramparā*. Significantly, *Light on Prāṇāyāma* was created through a dialogic process. It was published only after testing his articulations against others' experiences and a process of clarifying how his written instructions were interpreted by experienced practitioners as well as non-practitioners and experts in other fields.

Iyengar's development of *prāṇāyāma* closely parallels Krishnamurti's teaching that "Truth is a Pathless Land." Krishnamurti reflected:

> If you desire to understand yourself, you cannot go to any expert, to any book, because you are your own master and pupil. If you go to another, he can only help you to specialize; but if you are desirous of understanding yourself, that understanding comes only from moment to moment when there is no accumulation of yesterday, no accumulation of a previous moment; and when the mind understands itself and its activities completely, fully, only then is there reality.
>
> (Krishnamurti 1948b)

This comes very close to some of Iyengar's reflections on experience of *prāṇāyāma*. In a 1988 interview Iyengar reflected: "The effect of *prāṇāyāma* is dependent on one's individual practices ..." He goes on to explain in detail:

> Subjectively, each practitioner has to study each inbreath and outbreath, moment to moment, to keep a steady flow. It triggers the life force to be active in the body. A feeling of pleasantness and presentness [sic] is felt. One's mind does not waver between the past and the future.
>
> (Iyengar 2005 [1988], 109)

Despite acknowledging the inspiration of both Menuhin and Krishnamurti in progressing his understanding of *prāṇāyāma*, Iyengar's exploration was an ideomotor process of intense self-study and of cultivating a quiet awareness of the present moment. Although Iyengar has sought to provide a guide for future practitioners in his book, his own development of *prāṇāyāma* was based on his interoceptive experience of each moment while exploring a variety of controlled breathing exercises. He offers *Light on Prāṇāyāma* as a roadmap for the reader's inner ideomotor explorations, an intense and psychologically demanding interoceptive process.

The evidence from this case study suggests that embodied traditions should be understood as dialogical processes in *both* creation and transmission. Of course, we cannot uncritically extrapolate these circumstances when considering the creation of other texts or traditions. However, explicating the dynamics at play in the creation of one of Iyengar's canonical works enriches our understanding of how embodied practices are developed and transmitted. The creation of *Light on Prāṇāyāma* suggests that exemplary ideomotor exploration as well as dialogic pedagogical testing were both essential in the transmission of this embodied tradition across cultures.

## Acknowledgments

The letters which are quoted in this chapter were consulted while the material was in the possession of the Yorke family prior to their acquisition by the University of Reading. I am very grateful to Gerald Yorke's sons for allowing me access to these archives and reminiscing with me about their father in the autumn of 2018.

**Suzanne Newcombe** is a senior lecturer in religious studies at the Open University and director of the educational charity Inform based at King's College London. She recently published the *Routledge Handbook of Yoga and Meditation Studies* (2021), co-edited with Karen O'Brien-Kop and *Yoga in Britain: Stretching Spirituality and Educating Yogis* (Equinox 2019).

## References

Barois, Christèle. 2020. "The Dharmaputrikā Saṃhitā: Preliminary Notes on an Early Text on Yoga." *Journal of Yoga Studies* 3: 5–76. https://journalofyogastudies.org/index.php/JoYS/article/view/2020.V3.BAROIS.DhPS.

Ciołkosz, Matylda. 2018. "Proprioception over Dogma: Sources of Authority and Standards of Orthopraxy in Iyengar Yoga." *Religions of South Asia* 11(2–3): 207–230.

De Michelis, Elizabeth. 2004. *A History of Modern Yoga: Patañjali and Western Esotericism.* London: Continuum.

Hong, Gwi-Souk. 2020. "Iyengar Yoga, Colonization, and Collective Trauma." *Medium*, October 13. Retrieved from https://honggwiseok.medium.com/is-the-guru-the-problem-cd014e81bb16.

Iyengar, B.K.S. n.d. Untitled Autobiographical Reflections. This typed manuscript describes Iyengar's early life up to 1954. Typed manuscript in the archives of Iyengar Yoga Maida Vale (London).

——. 1966. *Light on Yoga.* London: Allen & Unwin.

——. 1978. "Childhood and Education." In *Body Thy Shrine, Yoga Thy Light,* edited by B.K.S. Iyengar 60th Birthday Celebration Committee, 3–12. Bombay: B. I. Taraporewala.

——. 1981. *Light on Prāṇāyāma.* London: Allen & Unwin.

——. 1988. "My Yogic Journey: A Talk Given by Guruji on His 70th Birthday on 14.12.1988 at Tilak Smarak Madīr (Pune)." Typed manuscript in the archives of Iyengar Yoga Maida Vale (London).

——. 1993. *Light on the Yoga Sūtras of Patañjali.* London: Aquarian.

——. 2000 "My Yogic Journey." In *Aṣtadaḷa Yogamālā* 1: 22–50. New Delhi: Allied Publishers Limited.

——. 2000 [1985]. "How I Learnt *Prāṇāyāma.*" In *Aṣtadaḷa Yogamālā* 1: 62–65. New Delhi: Allied Publishers Limited.

——. 2001. "*Prāṇāyāma.*" In *Aṣtadaḷa Yogamālā* 2: 97–104. New Delhi: Allied Publishers Limited.

——. 2004a [1979]. "Yoga–The Power for Turning Imagination into Fact." In *Aṣtadaḷa Yogamālā* 4: 52–64.

——. 2004b [1982]. "Tune Yourself to the Music of Yoga." In *Aṣtadaḷa Yogamālā* 4: 97–107. New Delhi: Allied Publishers.

——. 2004c [1982]. "Paths are Many, But the Goal is One and the Same." In *Aṣtadaḷa Yogamālā* 4: 108–132. New Delhi: Allied Publishers.

——. 2005. *Light on Life: The Yoga Journey to Wholeness, Inner Peace, and Ultimate Freedom.* With Douglas Abrams and John J. Evans. Emmaus, PA: Rodale.

——. 2012 [1993]. *Light on the Yoga Sūtras of Patañjali.* London: Thorsons.

——. 2014. *Yoga, the Path to Holistic Health: The Definitive Step-by-Step Guide.* London: Dorling Kindersley.

Jayakar, Pupal. 1986. "Krishnamurti in India 1847–1949." In *J. Krishnamurti: A Biography,* 95–179. New York: Penguin.

Krishnamurti, Jiddu. n.d. "Series I—Chapter 41—'Awareness.'" Retrieved from https://jkrishnamurti.org/content/series-i-chapter-41-%E2%80%98awareness%E2%80%99.

——. 1929. "Truth is a Pathless Land." Talk at Ommen, The Netherlands, August 3. Retrieved from https://jkrishnamurti.org/about-dissolution-speech.

——. 1948a. "Madras 2nd Group Discussion 13th April, 1948." Retrieved from https://jkrishnamurti.org/content/madras-2nd-group-discussion-13th-april-1948/%22passive%20alertness%22.

——. 1948b. "Poona 7th Public Talk 10 October 1948." Retrieved from https://jkrishnamurti.org/content/poona-india-7th-public-talk-10th-october-1948.

Lutyens, Mary. 2003. *The Life and Death of Krishnamurti.* Eastbourne: John Murray.

Mallinson, James and Mark Singleton. 2017. *Roots of Yoga.* London: Penguin Classics.

Mehta, Sylvia, Mira Mehta and Shyam Mehta. 1990. *Yoga the Iyengar Way.* London: Dorling Kindersley.

Newcombe, Suzanne. 2007. “Stretching for Health and Well-Being: Yoga and Women in Britain, 1960–1980.” *Asian Medicine* 3(1): 37–63.

——. 2019. *Yoga in Britain: Stretching Spirituality and Educating Yogis.* Sheffield: Equinox.

Palkhivala, Rashmi. 2017. *The Biography of B.K.S. Iyengar: A Life of Light.* New Delhi: Harper Element.

Remski, Matthew. 2019. *Practice and All is Coming: Abuse, Cult Dynamics and Healing in Yoga and Beyond.* Christchurch: Embodied Wisdom Publishing.

Shaw, Eric. 2016. “Seizing the Whip: B.K.S. Iyengar and the Making of Modern Yoga.” Self Published PDF. October. Retrieved from www.academia.edu/21443879/Portal_Pages_to_Seizing_the_Whip_B_K_S_Iyengar_and_the_Making_of_Modern_Yoga.

Singleton, Mark. 2008. “The Classical Reveries of Modern Yoga: Patañjali and Constructive Orientalism.” In *Yoga in the Modern World: Contemporary Perspectives*, edited by Mark Singleton and Jane Byrne, 89–111. London: Routledge.

Singleton, Mark and Ellen Goldberg, eds. 2014. *Gurus of Modern Yoga.* New York: Oxford University Press.

Smith, Fredrick M. and Joan White. 2014. “Becoming an Icon: B.K.S. Iyengar.” In *Gurus of Modern Yoga,* edited by Mark Singleton and Ellen Goldberg, 122–146. New York: Oxford University Press.

Tobias, Maxine and Mary Stewart. 1985. *Stretch & Relax: A Day by Day Workout and Relaxation Programme.* London: Dorling Kindersley.

Tuft, N. 1971. “Standing on Her Head to Face the Day.” *Daily Telegraph*, December 31, 1971.

White, David Gordon. 2014. *The Yoga Sutra of Patañjali: A Biography.* Princeton, NJ: Princeton University Press.

– 8 –

# Between Patañjali and Psychology

## Acem's "Classical, Meditative Yoga"

MARGRETHE LØØV

This chapter examines Acem's philosophy and practice of yoga as taught by Acem School of Yoga (Norsk Yoga-skole). Acem was founded as a part of Maharishi Mahesh Yogi's Transcendental Meditation (TM) movement in 1966, but disagreements led to an organizational rupture in 1972. Acem's discursive framing has changed significantly since the rupture with the TM movement. Maharishi was inspired by Advaita Vedānta philosophy and referred to the Vedas for legitimation; Acem promotes its activities as secular and scientifically based. This chapter argues that Acem represents a selective understanding of yoga that is typical of bodily practices on the move from their original context to a Western setting. Acem claims to transmit a "classical" version of yoga in line with Patañjali's *Yogasūtra*, but free from the religious frames of reference found in the Indian tradition. At the same time, the organization implicitly builds upon other forms of modern postural yoga. There is a strong emphasis on personal growth and existential acknowledgment in Acem, which can be traced back to the existential philosophy and humanistic psychology of the 1970s, and which reflects "the therapeutic culture" that permeates contemporary Western societies. The result is an invented tradition labelled as "classical, meditative yoga," which can be used as a point of departure for a secularized and individual-oriented spirituality.

Keywords: Acem, Norsk Yoga-skole, Transcendental Meditation, yoga, meditation, therapeutic culture

## Introduction

> People lie scattered on the floor. They are kicking and turning, shaking and breathing. The instructor repeats: "Go on, give everything you've got." Suddenly it stops. The energetic bodies sink together like wet rags. A sense of quiet and calm engulfs the room. Rest. Relaxation. Then it starts again. "Give in to your urge to move, let yourselves go, breathe." Again, the class turns into wild chaos, almost a form of bodily ecstasy. Arms and legs are in the air, there is panting and grunting.
>
> (Hobbel 2011, 14)[1]

Acem is Norway's largest meditation organization, and only major exporter of meditation to other countries; the organization is currently present in thirteen countries. The organization is best known for its meditation courses. Less known and researched are Acem's other methods for personal growth.[2] The observation report above stems from a sequence of "impulsive exercises" in one of Acem's yoga classes. Alongside postural yoga, breathing exercises and "impulsive dance," impulsive exercises are part of a curriculum of physical exercises at Acem School of Yoga (Norsk Yoga-skole).

The present chapter examines the history and profile of Acem School of Yoga. How is yoga practiced and understood in Acem? Which sources and interpretative frames have influenced the development of Acem's yoga? It will be argued that Acem can be seen in the context of "the therapeutic turn" in Western culture, and that Acem represents a "psychologization" of the phenomenon and practice of yoga. Yoga practice is a form of embodied reception that leaves room for individual meaning-making. At the same time, the individual practice and interpretation are influenced by the larger social setting that the reflexive subject is part of—from the microenvironment of a yoga class to contemporary Western societies at large. The chapter draws on both recent material and older sources that have been relatively little explored in earlier research. The chapter will particularly focus on Acem's interpretation of yoga, as presented

1. The text is translated into English from Norwegian by the author. The same goes for all the direct citations from Norwegian source material in this chapter.
2. I have earlier studied the historical development of Acem meditation (see Løøv 2015 for a general overview). My previous research has particularly emphasized the incorporation of a modern scientific framework (Løøv 2019) and also includes interviews with practitioners of Acem meditation (Løøv 2010). Inga Bårdsen Tøllefsen has produced a useful overview of Hindu-Inspired Meditation Movements in Norway (Tøllefsen 2017). However, Acem's activities when it comes to physical yoga have hitherto not been studied systematically.

in Acem's journals, Acem's books on yoga and as it is presented on the Norwegian and international website of Acem School of Yoga.

## Acem and Acem School of Yoga: A Historical Outline

The course of historical events is often the result both of the structural preconditions in society and culture, and the acts and dispositions of individuals. The year 1945 marks a definitive beginning for our history. This was the year that the Second World War ended, and the "post-war period" began. The surge of interest in Eastern spirituality in the 1960s and 70s is often interpreted as a generational phenomenon related to the "baby boomers"—the generation born during the first years after the war. By the 1960s, the babies had become young people who formed a mass movement of opposition against the religion, politics, and lifestyle of the parent generation (Doggett 2007). Alternative spirituality was subject to a wave of popularity. Seemingly exotic, edgy, and easy—yoga and meditation opened the door to a new worldview and had the potential for a symbolic act of protest against the establishment.

1945 was also the year of birth of Are Holen, who founded the organization today known as Acem. Holen was central in establishing the forerunner to Acem in 1966 and has been leading the organization up until the present. Although Acem has been a joint feature that involves many people, Holen has had a pivotal role in shaping the organization. Holen started practicing yoga at the age of 16. Holen described his early encounter with yoga as an autodidactic experiment; he initially learned from the book *Yoga and Health* by Selvarajan Yesudian and Elisabeth Haich (1953), which he had found in his older brother's bookshelf. The exercises provided a new and agreeable way of getting physical exercise. After some time, yoga also opened up for intense spiritual experiences where he "perceived a connection between what was near and what was far, the infinite of time and space" and "an existential closeness to something far greater than myself." In the aftermath of these experiences, Holen became "determined to explore these aspects of existence," which he now "knew were real" (Holen 2018, 6). In the autumn of 1962, he attended a lecture by Maharishi Mahesh Yogi and signed up for a course in Deep Meditation (later renamed Transcendental Meditation/TM) in the winter of 1963.

Holen soon became an active member of Maharishi's Spiritual Regeneration Movement (later known as the TM movement) and an active proponent of yoga and meditation. In 1963 he began instructing yoga classes at courses arranged by the TM movement. In 1964 Guri

Mehallis, a fellow practitioner of deep meditation and an early pioneer of yoga in Norway, took the initiative to form a yoga school in Oslo. The first yoga courses were rather informal and took place on the premises of a dance studio run by another fellow practitioner of TM. While Holen was an autodidact inspired by books and, subsequently, involved with yoga as it was practiced in the TM movement, Mehallis had learned yoga while living in the US and later became active in the TM movement. The inspiration for Norway's first yoga school thus came from both the TM movement and from other forms of modern postural yoga and exemplifies a widespread tendency towards syncretism and bricolage in modern yoga (cf. De Michelis 2004; Singleton 2010; Williamson 2010).

Maharishi's teachings were grounded in the classical Advaita Vedānta school of Indian philosophy, and he referred to the Vedas for legitimacy and support. At the same time, he wanted to give TM a more scientific and modern profile, and systematic efforts were made to recruit students and academics. In 1965 a group of meditating students was gathered in Germany. At this meeting a new subdivision of Maharishi's Spiritual Regeneration Movement was established: The Academic Meditation Society (AMS). Participants at the meeting were encouraged to establish local branches of the AMS at their respective universities. Are Holen, who participated in the meeting in Germany, went home to Norway and established a Norwegian branch of AMS together with fellow TM practitioners at the University of Oslo in the winter of 1966. This would be the forerunner to the organization today known as Acem (Løøv 2015).

In 1967 Are Holen went on a study tour to India with Maharishi that lasted six months. According to Holen, the tour inspired a more systematic approach to teaching yoga. In 1968 Norsk Yoga-skole (literally "Norwegian School of Yoga," later known as "Acem School of Yoga" in English) was formally established (Holen 2018, 10–11). Nevertheless, Holen claims that he had become increasingly skeptical of TM and Maharishi during his 1967 study tour, especially of Maharishi's role as a guru, and his increasingly eccentric and utopian ideas about the possible outcomes of TM. Holen was critical of the idea that meditation could engender supernatural abilities like "yogic flying," telepathy, clairvoyance, and that world peace would be obtained if a critical mass of people would meditate (Holen and Grøndahl 2015; Are Holen, e-mail to Margrethe Løøv, March 1, 2010). Conflicts over teachings, practice, and leadership caused Maharishi's original AMS to crack and created an eventual fissure between Acem and the TM movement in 1972.

The subsequent history of Acem can be summarized as a process of disenchantment, where scientific modes of explanation on how meditation works have replaced Maharishi's religious frame of reference.

The basic meditation technique remains unchanged, but the terminology and existential framework is changed. "Mantra" is replaced by the more religiously neutral "method sound." Acem's current leadership includes professional medical doctors, psychologists, and academics, who have drawn upon their scientific resources to achieve a more scientifically based understanding of how meditation influences mind and body (see e.g., Davanger *et al.* 2008). Acem meditation is promoted as a scientifically based practice developed by professionals in medicine and psychology. Acem explicitly and repeatedly states that it is a religiously neutral organization. On its international website Acem is presented as a "simple meditation technique for relaxation, more energy, health and personal growth—based on modern psychology and scientific research" (Acem 2021). On its Norwegian website Acem School of Yoga states that "[o]ur teaching has a high educational level and is devoid of phantasm and reverie" (Norsk Yoga-skole 2021). Acem's history thus appears to be a textbook case of organizational secularization (cf. Dobbelaere 2002), where the original religious framework has been replaced by secular psychology and science. However, and as will be discussed at some length later, yoga and meditation may also have an existential significance that resembles that of religion.

Acem School of Yoga offers courses at different levels, workshops, and yoga retreats. The organization has its main seat in Norway, but yoga is also taught in other countries due to the work of Acem International.[3] Some of the longer retreats are also aimed at an international audience. Acem owns two retreat centers: Halvorsbøle in Norway and Lundsholm in Sweden (Holen and Hobbel 2012, 162–163). Acem moreover has its own teacher training, which is open to dedicated students of Acem yoga.

## Yoga as a Concept and Practice in Acem

The term "yoga" has a range of different meanings. In India, the term has been used to denote a certain type of religious discipline such as jñāna yoga, karma yoga, and bhakti yoga. Yoga is also the name of one of the six orthodox schools of Hindu philosophy. The foundational scripture of this school, the *Yogasūtra*, is attributed to Patañjali, and was written around 250 BCE (dating uncertain). In the Western world, yoga is associated with

3. Acem is present in thirteen countries: Norway, Denmark, Sweden, Germany, United Kingdom, Netherlands, France, Switzerland, Spain, Singapore, Taiwan, India, and the USA. As of May 2022 yoga courses are listed on the websites of Acem in Norway, Sweden, and Germany.

a diverse range of bodily and mental disciplines. Any attempt at defining "yoga" encounters issues related to different interpretations of the term across different time periods, languages, practices and goals (Newcombe and O'Brien-Kop 2021). Thus, although individuals and social groups can and do create essentialist definitions for particular purposes, overarching essentialist definitions of the term are impossible (Newcombe 2018).

"Yoga" as used in Acem refers to a series of different exercises that involve the body, the breath, and the mind. The exercises involved in Acem yoga are referred to as "yoga asanas," "impulsive exercises," and "breathing exercises." Although the practice involves different types of exercises, the different components form part of an integrated system. Yoga āsanas constitute the most central part of Acem yoga. The repertoire consists of individual āsanas that may roughly be divided into eight main categories:[4]

1. Inversion postures. Includes low shoulderstand (*viparītakaraṇī*), shoulderstand (*sarvāṅgāsana*), headstand (*śīrṣāsana*).
2. Backward bends. Includes cobra pose (*bhujaṅgāsana*), bow pose (*dhanurāsana*), bridge pose (*setu bandhāsana*), fish pose (*matsyāsana*), camel pose (*uṣṭrāsana*), upward bow (*ūrdhvadhanurāsana*).
3. Forward bends. Includes seated forward bend (*paścimottānāsana*), plough pose (*halāsana*), downward dog (*adhomukhaśvanāsana*).
4. Twists. Includes triangle (*trikonāsana*), spinal twist (*vakrāsana*), half Matsyendra's pose (*ardha matsyendrāsana*).
5. Balance postures. Includes tree pose (*vrikshāsana*) and dancing pose (*naṭarājāsana*).
6. Combined postures. Includes forward-bending thunderbolt pose (*vajrāsana*), sun salutation (*sūryanamaskāra*).
7. Other postures. Includes shoulder roll, head practices, eye practices (*bhrumadhya drishti*), stomach waves, abdominal lock (*uḍḍīyāna bandha*).
8. Resting postures. Includes corpse pose (*śavāsana*), prone pose (*makarāsana*).

A yoga program starts with breathing exercises. These are followed by postures taken from the first four and main groups: inversion postures, backward bends, forward bends and twists. In addition, one could supplement with other types of postures like balance postures, sun salutation, eye practices, locks (*bandhas*), impulsive exercises, and/or sitting

4. The list provides some examples but is not an exhaustive list of all the āsanas that are practiced in Acem.

postures. All programs should end with the corpse pose and should ideally be followed by some kind of meditation (see Holen and Hobbel 2012, 142–143).

There are some foundational principles for how the postures should be practiced. The movements are to be performed slowly and evenly, with meditative awareness. One enters a posture from a starting pose, which is the positioning of the body before entering the actual āsana. After finishing a posture, the practitioner may remain in a starting pose, or lie down for a short while. This rest between the individual postures is considered to be the most meditative phase of yoga practice. During the rest, one should let go of all residues or tensions caused by doing the posture and observe how one feels with a free mental attitude (Holen and Hobbel 2012, 47–50).

One should not apply force, stretch, or strain so much that the body feels uncomfortable. The free flow of breath serves as an indicator that one does not overstrain oneself. The āsana is correctly performed when the breath flows freely and calmly (Ellingsen 1975). The movements should be well coordinated with the breath. The yoga postures should be performed with deep, calm, and regular breathing. Full yoga breathing is frequently used: One consciously inhales air so that it fills the lungs from bottom to top and lets the air out passively in a calm and continuous exhale. The movements should be synchronized with the breath so that one moves on an exhale or inhale, and brings the movements to their peak or end at the end of a full breath (Holen and Hobbel 2012, 27, 124).

In addition to conscious breathing during the performance of postures, Acem yoga includes some exercises that focus primarily on breathing. Some practices are known as classical prāṇāyāma techniques, such as inhaling and exhaling through alternate nostrils (*sukha purvaka prāṇāyāma*) or breathing in while the tongue is shaped like a tube and exhaling through one nostril (*śītalī prāṇāyāma*). Other breathing practices include "pump breathing," where one breathes deeply while lying on the floor and holding one leg, and "cat breathing," where the breathing follows the movement of the cat-cow stretch (see Holen and Hobbel 2012, 128–129). The latter exercises appear to be newer inventions that are also practiced in other forms of modern postural yoga.

As one becomes a more experienced yoga practitioner, one will increasingly be able to tap into a meditative mode while performing the physical exercises.[5] While doing the exercises it is considered important

5. To emphasize the meditative focus of yoga as it is practiced in Acem, the authors of Acem's "yoga bible" *Yogaboken/Meditative yoga* deliberately avoid using the word "exercise" for the yoga āsanas. They view this word as closely associated

to tune inwards and notice how one feels: "Not just doing, but being. Not just perform, but notice. No achievement, but accepting self-care. Look inwards" (Glosimot 2018). When one has learned to master the postures, they may be performed with eyes closed or half-closed, which reinforces the meditative mode. Like in Acem meditation, one should apply a "free mental attitude," where the attention should be free floating and undirected. The awareness flows relatively freely but nevertheless centers around the performance of the exercises. This will allow the awareness to move from the external world to more subtle, inner areas of one's consciousness (Holen 2018, 28–29).

## Impulsive Exercises and Impulsive Dance

"Impulsive exercises" refers to movements that are performed chaotically, intensively, and rapidly. The impulsive exercises are said to be inspired by parts of the tantric traditions, more specifically kuṇḍalinī and laya yoga (*Dyade* 4/1975, 4). They are not regarded as classical or meditative yoga but are considered useful because of their potential to enhance the practitioner's contact with unresolved psychological issues that may be cultivated further by classical yoga and meditation (Holen and Hobbel 2012, 21).

Any part of the body can be chosen as the starting point for the impulsive practice: the legs, hands, tongue, hips, or any other body part. The first stage of the practice is to let these body parts loose and shake them. The next stage is to involve more body parts until the entire body is engaged in the shaking movements. The speed and intensity are gradually increased until one shakes as fast as possible. The final stage is to make the breathing impulsive as well as the body. One should breathe fast and intensively, and the whole body should be involved in rapid movements. This is considered a very challenging practice which may lead to hyperventilation and discomfort, in which case one should stop, breathe slowly, and hold the breath for 10–20 heartbeats between each breath until the discomfort subsides. At the end of the exercise, one lies down on the back to rest (Holen and Hobbel 2012, 110).

Apart from these guiding principles, the impulsive exercises leave room for individual adaptations. The point of departure is one's feelings—bodily or mental. Impulsive exercises have been described as "spontaneous yoga," where the practitioner can act out psychological

with gymnastics and sports, which thereby signifies something remote from the meditative qualities of yoga that they want to underscore (Holen and Hobbel 2012).

and bodily tensions (Hobbel 2011, 13). There is no right or wrong, the ideal is to surrender to one's spontaneous, bodily impulses. The point of departure is the individual practitioner. In a personal account one practitioner describes how he tries to "find the feeling that binds [the body] and let it be expressed through movement," in order to "shake the tensions off" (Ellingsen 1975, 20). The movements that ensue may be slow and calm, or wild and powerful (Hobbel 2011, 17).

Impulsive dance is a relatively new addition to Acem's activities. It is inspired by impulsive exercises in yoga, modern dance, and theatre improvisation. A session begins with a series of instructed movements. The performers may for instance be instructed to stand in a circle with eyes closed and move their heads in as many ways as possible, accompanied by soft music. Then the shoulders are engaged, then the arms, then the back, the hips, the legs, and the feet. After this initial phase the music is changed, and the practitioners are asked to move about freely in the room with eyes closed. The only instruction that is given is to move about freely, guided by one's own impulses—be in one's "personal space" with eyes half closed so that one does not bump into others. The pace of the music changes to an increasingly rapid beat. At the end of the session, the lights are switched off, the music fades, and practitioners are asked to lie down. After some minutes of relaxation the light is lit again, the practitioners sit up and share their individual experiences from the session (Thomte 2018b, 47–48).

The movements in impulsive dance do not necessarily have to be movements that we usually associate with dance; the actual practice can also include movements like crawling, shaking, running, and jumping (Thomte 2018b, 48). "The point of impulsive dance is to feel what moves in us in that very movement. It is like opening something into oneself, enter that room and let whatever is there manifest through movement. It is like listening to something we cannot hear, see or feel." (Thomte 2018b, 51). When one lets the impulses out, internal tensions may loosen and leave the practitioner calmer, both physically and mentally. The practice is supposed to bring the practitioner more in touch with their inner world. One can thus become more aware of internal blockages, feelings, and thoughts, and this may contribute to personal growth. The three main pillars of personal growth in Acem—meditation, yoga, and communication—are all elements of impulsive dance. The meditative aspect is present in the awareness and free mental attitude in the practice (Thomte 2018b, 48).

## Inventing Tradition

The "classical" aspects of its yoga practice are repeatedly stressed in Acem's publications and marketing. On its website, Acem School of Yoga claims to teach "simple, classical meditative yoga." In Acem's "yoga bible," *Meditative Yoga: Integrating Body, Breath and Mind* (Holen and Hobbel 2012), the origins of Acem yoga are explained in further detail. The authors state that Acem sees its yoga practice in continuation with *haṭha yoga* in the Indian tradition. In their presentation of the etymology and semantic meaning of the word yoga, the authors emphasize that the word yoga is derived from the root of the Sanskrit verb *yuj*, which means to "join together," "assemble into a whole," or "make ready, become unified." The "original" meaning of the word "yoga" is seen in conjunction with Patañjali's *Yogasūtra*, which presents the aim of yoga as *chitta vritti nirodhah*—bringing the fluctuations of the mind to silence. The integration of body, breath, and mind is considered to be the original aim of yoga practices:

> In this perspective, yoga aims at helping the individual to become a more complete person through working on one's consciousness. In our opinion, this perspective is the most original and primary aspect of yoga; it covers the classical meaning, i.e., the move towards integration and apprehending the nature of things from within. Integration includes body, breath and mind.
>
> (Holen and Hobbel 2012, 16)

Acem thus claims to represent an original and classical interpretation of yoga. Acem claims Patañjali's *Yogasūtra* as its main source of influence and sees a continuous line of tradition between yoga as it has been practiced in India and the type of yoga that is taught by Acem School of Yoga. The aims of yoga relate first and foremost to the practitioner's inner life, although the whole body is involved. The *Yogasūtra* is presented as an authoritative source that outlines some foundational principles for the practice of yoga.

Acem's understanding of its yoga practice as classical haṭha yoga is less straightforward than it might seem at first. By emphasizing Patañjali as an authoritative source for what haṭha yoga *really* is, Acem has chosen a perspective that is challenged by more critical analyses of the origins and development of haṭha yoga. The original meaning of the word *haṭha* is "forceful" or "violent," and the compound *haṭhayoga* connotes a yoga that involves forceful methods. In the *Yogācāra* literature from the fourth century AD, haṭha yoga is described as a "forceful" process, although its method is not outlined. In the medieval *Haṭhapradīpikā* (*c.*1450), haṭha yoga is described as a technique that involves the use of force but encompasses a specific set of techniques (Singleton 2021, 121–122). In Western twenty-first century uses, hatha yoga is used in such diverse ways that it is difficult to know what a particular hatha yoga class will be like. In most cases, it will be relatively gentle and slow, with an emphasis on holding the poses for some time (Newcombe and O'Brien-Kop 2021, 6, 10). Acem's references to Patañjali and definition of yoga thus need to be seen as a particular interpretation of a concept and a technique that carries a spectrum of meanings.

Acem's account of the origin of the impulsive exercises also demonstrates a selective reading of Indian sources. Acem states laya and kuṇḍalinī yoga as sources of inspiration for the impulsive exercises, but Acem does not consider them to be part of the classical yoga tradition. This is at odds with Indian textual sources, where laya is closely associated with haṭha yoga. For instance, laya occurs in the Haṭhapradīpikā, where it is treated as a synonym of samādhi, which in turn refers to the union of self and mind that arises when *prāṇa* stops and the mind dissolves (Singleton 2021, 125). Raising kuṇḍalinī is described as one of the central aims of yoga practices in early haṭha texts that derive from tantric sources, as well as in later syntheses such as the Haṭhapradīpikā (Singleton 2021, 122). The reason why Acem states that impulsive exercises do not build upon classical yoga might be a lack of knowledge. In any case, the selective understanding of what haṭha yoga *really is* enables Acem to position itself in relation to other forms of yoga.

Acem's official stance towards many modern forms of yoga is critical. The skepticism towards "yoga gymnastics" is presented both on Acem's website, in Acem's journals and books on yoga. On Acem's website we may for instance read that "Yoga today is embraced and modified by a number of trendy body disciplines that are quite at odds with its deeper goals" (Acem School of Yoga 2021). *Meditative Yoga* states that "much of what is taught in yoga schools, health spas and health studios nowadays is quite far removed from classical and meditative yoga" (Holen and Hobbel 2012, 7). The criticism of other forms of yoga mainly relates to two aspects: (lack of) (a) authenticity and (b) effect. We have already seen how Acem relates its practice to Indian sources. In contrast, other forms of yoga are presented as modern inventions. In *Meditative Yoga*, "yoga gymnastics," exemplified by Iyengar yoga and ashtanga yoga, is presented as a synthesis between Indian yoga, English calisthenics, and martial arts. Although such forms of yoga are effective physical training, they do not enable the practitioners to tap into a meditative mode, according to the authors:

> Such training revolves around intense exercises that increase the heart rate, circulation and breathing in ways that are incompatible with meditation, silence and insight. This form of yoga characterizes much of what is presently taught, in India as well as in the rest of the world. Our exposition covers an entirely different orientation.
>
> (Holen and Hobbel 2012, 19–20)

Although they strengthen the body, physically demanding practices will not help the practitioner explore the inner aspects of their being. They therefore have a limited effect when it comes to what Acem presents as the ultimate aim of yoga and meditation.

In an article on the development of yoga in the West, Acem meditation teacher Torbjørn Hobbel also criticizes some forms of modern yoga that make spiritual claims using religious paraphernalia and popularized Indian philosophy:

> Of course, there are still people who do yoga who have a serious and lasting interest in meditation, but the purely physical aspect is most prominent. The "spiritual" aspects of yoga may be represented as outer symbolism, incense, popularized Indian philosophy and religion, mood-enhancing music, chanting of mantras, singing bowls etc. [...] In this way, yoga has become harmless and unable to provoke.
>
> (Hobbel 2018, 61)

The same article features a photo of an athletic young woman doing a handstand and leg flip. The photo carries the text: "It is amazing to watch. But is it yoga?" (Hobbel 2018, 61). Acem holds an essentialist view of what yoga ultimately is. Acem presents its yoga practice as more authentic and closer to its origins in the Indian tradition than other forms of modern yoga.

Any interpretation of yoga as a tradition or practice rests upon a selection of sources—and a selective reading of these sources. As De Michelis (2004) and Singleton (2010) have convincingly argued, the very idea of yoga as a unified Indian tradition is in itself a modern construct. Modern postural yoga emerged in the nineteenth and twentieth centuries through a combination of gymnastics and imagined ideas of old traditions. Patañjali's *Yogasūtra* is one among many Indian texts on yoga and may not necessarily be *the* authoritative source for Indian yoga traditions. Despite the scarcity of information regarding the practice of āsanas in the *sūtras*, the text is commonly referred to as the authoritative text for modern postural yoga. Its status is largely due to the influence of European scholarship and early promoters of practical yoga, like Vivekananda and Helena Blavatsky (Singleton 2010, 26–27). It is probable that other, more recent sources have influenced Acem's view on yoga, as commentaries on and interpretations of Patañjali. At this point it is useful to recall that Are Holen's first encounter with yoga literature was *Yoga and Health* by Selvarajan Yesudian and Elisabeth Haich (1953). From the 1950s to the 1970s several influential interpretations of "Indian" yoga were issued, such as *Hatha Yoga: The Report of a Personal Experience* by Theos Bernard (1950) and B.K.S. Iyengar's *Light on Yoga* (1966) (De Michelis 2004, 190–191). Although this is not explicitly stated in Acem, it is probable that more recent sources constitute "missing links" that bridge the gap in time, geography, and language between Acem's contemporary interpretation of yoga and Patañjali's *Yogasūtra.*

Other sources of influence for Acem have been existentialist philosophy and humanistic psychology. These cultural currents were popular in the 1970s, when Acem established itself as independent from the TM movement. Acem's journal *Dyade* had several thematic issues on psychology and philosophy in the 1970s, where meditation teachers discussed the nature of man and society in light of existentialist philosophers like Søren Kierkegaard, Gabriel Marcel, and Jean-Paul Sartre (see *Dyade* 1 and 5/1976). Humanistic psychology has strong affinities with existentialist philosophy. It is centered around the experiences and values of the individual and is preoccupied with how the individual can liberate itself from destructive patterns of thought and action (Hanegraaff 1998, 48–55). Among Acem's intellectual heritage and sources of influence we find humanist thinkers and psychologists like Erich Fromm, Eric Berne, Carl Rogers, Abraham Maslow, and Carl Gustav Jung (see *Dyade* 2/1974 and 5/1976). Acem's philosophy and practice are clearly inspired by the existentialist idea and ideal of the free, autonomous individual. Acem claims to build upon a "positive" view of the human being and to promote the resources and freedom of the individual so that they can realize their human potential (Acem 2022).

## The Aims of Acem Yoga

Acem sees yoga as a method that integrates the body, the breath, and the mind, and the aims of Acem yoga relate to all three aspects. In an article on the effects of yoga on health written by three meditation teachers in Acem, yoga is presented as an effective form of psychosomatic training (Ekker Solberg *et al.* 2011). Yoga has many physical benefits: It increases muscular strength and flexibility, improves balance, reduces chronic pain, improves sleep, and has a general and positive effect on practitioners' self-reported well-being and quality of life. The psychosomatic effects of yoga can to a large extent be attributed to its stress-reducing capacities. Although the authors do not distinguish between different forms of yoga in this review article, they assume that non-directed[6] forms of yoga and meditation, such as Acem, reduce stress more effectively than other techniques (Ekker Solberg *et al.* 2011, 14).

Many contemporary practices aimed at personal growth and well-being are grounded on the premise that the individual suffers from psychological problems in the form of "blockages," "traumas," or "stress" that inhibit him/her to develop his/her full potential. "Stress" has emerged as a central and negatively charged concept that forms the point of departure for many practices aimed at self-help and well-being. This trend is also apparent in Acem, where the stress on stress is—among other things—reflected in the titles of two publications issued by Acem's publishing house Dyade. *Fighting Stress: Reviews of Meditation Research* (Davanger *et al.* 2008) and *Stress—Work—Love: Acem Meditation in Perspective* (Holen 1998). The idea that stress and tensions may be reduced or eliminated by means of yoga, meditation, mindfulness, or other therapeutic practices is common within the Human Potential Movement,[7] which has strong affinities with Acem. In the context of yoga, therapy becomes embodied, as the body is considered both a repository for our emotional baggage and a gateway to let it out of our lives.

Acem's understanding of how yoga "works" builds upon the idea that there is some kind of unconscious correspondence between the mind and the body: "We can speak about our 'biological memory.' Our body 'stores' the experiences we do not master. Our mind may have forgotten about the situation, but a residue remains in the body, a 'memory' which is unfinished" (Hobbel 2011, 25). Psychological tensions may be reduced simply by stretching and moving the body. Physical movements facilitate the connection between mind and body and enable the practitioner to connect with their inner selves:

> In classical, meditative yoga you meditate on your body. The body is the gateway to your inner life. Body and soul are often understood as two different worlds, but to me in this context it is a unity. If you want to work

6. Acem distinguishes between directed and non-directed forms of meditation. In directed forms of meditation, focus is directed towards an object, thought, or mantra, with an aim to concentrate fully on the object of meditation. Non-directed techniques may also involve a mental focal point, one is encouraged to have an open mental attitude and enable other ideas, thoughts, and sensations to pass freely.
7. The Human Potential Movement grew out of the alternative milieu in the 1970s. It is influenced by modern psychology and existentialist philosophy, and centers around the idea that the individual person can and should realize his/her potential in terms of health, career, material wealth, and psychological well-being.

> on your inner qualities, you can also work on your body. Every opportunity within us needs to have a chance to be realized in our lives. To be able to accept and cultivate this, we need to be able to "listen" inwards with our bodies and our minds.
>
> (Thomte 2018a, 36)

In impulsive dance and impulsive exercises, feelings and memories are given shape and acted out as bodily movements. The implicit becomes explicit, and the subconscious becomes conscious. This provides an opportunity to deal with unresolved issues and to develop as a person (Holen 2018, 30). The practitioners of Acem meditation that I interviewed who had meditated for a longer period generally saw personal growth as their main motivation. The lasting appeal of yoga and meditation was the deeper effects the practice had on their view of themselves, their surroundings, and the world. Many claimed that yoga and meditation had helped them to get to know themselves better. Some emphasized the increased ability to express themselves, others emphasized better abilities to connect with others (Løøv 2010).

In the TM movement the utmost goal of yoga and meditation was to reach full unity with a united divine field called "Pure Being." Without any reference to a transcendent, divine reality, this goal no longer applies to practitioners of Acem meditation and yoga. Nevertheless, yoga is said to enable practitioners to transcend the mundane experience of the world and themselves. According to Acem, yoga and meditation have the potential to "stimulate a deeper understanding of our existence" (Norsk Yoga-skole 2021). The official accounts of what this existential acknowledgment entails tend to be rather vague. In Acem's publications it is presented as something internal, existential, and personal, but a clear and detailed description is conspicuously absent. Consider for instance the following passage:

> If you do classical meditative yoga over some time, the exercises may hit a longing and a feeling that there is a lot to be found here. For some people it will be experienced as an opportunity to connect with a silence deep within. The yoga practice becomes important as a "spiritual" opportunity. A kind of enthusiasm and new direction begins which can introduce a very liberating and satisfying period in life.
>
> (Hobbel 2018, 66)

Here yoga is said to enable the practitioners to connect with a "silence" deep within themselves. Yoga is presented as an opportunity for "spiritual" exploration. The indeterminacy when it comes to the actual content of existential meaning-making can on one level of interpretation be seen in conjunction with Acem's individualism and anti-dogmatism.

Individualism is a core value in Acem, and finite answers are seen as detrimental to existential exploration.

## Existential Meaning-Making in the Therapeutic Culture

Somewhat paradoxically, the existential outcomes of yoga and meditation are stated to be highly individualized—at the same time as there is a shared discourse about these aims in Acem's courses and publications. As Thomas J. Csordas notes, there is a dialectic between perceptual consciousness and collective practice (1993). Any form of meaning-making is embodied because the reflexive subject necessarily has a body. As an embodied practice, yoga is a subjective practice that is at the same time influenced by socially transmitted norms for how yoga is practiced and for how the individual experiences of yoga should be interpreted: "Somatic modes of attention are culturally elaborated ways of attending to and with one's body in surroundings that include the embodied presence of others" (Csordas 1993, 138). In the social context of a society, an organization, or a yoga class, there arises both a collective *habitus* (cf. Bourdieu 2013)—certain shared modes of movement, perception, and interpretation—and a subjective interpretation of experience.

As an embodied practice, yoga is at the same time subjective and collective. Acem's indeterminacy when it comes to the actual outcomes of existential acknowledgment is both prescriptive and open to individual reception. While stating that yoga and meditation can lead to existential acknowledgment, and that the outcome of these practices can be "spiritual" for the serious practitioner, Acem remains accommodating to individual adaptation and reflexivity. By remaining open to the content of the subjective actualization, Acem does not pre-ordain a specific salvific outcome other than the general label of "self-realization" and "existential acknowledgment."

Through the practice of yoga, practitioners are said to connect with their innermost selves and develop opportunities and qualities that lie latent within themselves. A similar understanding of the body has been seen among other Western yoga practitioners (Olsson 2018). Modern postural yoga may be understood in the context of traditional religious concepts, or a more recent understanding of "spirituality" as awareness of and attunement to the inner, essential, and deeper dimensions of oneself and the universe. A session of modern postural yoga can thus be seen as a ritual "which affords various levels of access to the sacred, starting from a "safe," mundane, tangible foundation of body-based practice" (De Michelis 2004, 250–251). The literal embodiment of existential issues can be seen in conjunction with a larger material turn and emphasis on personal experience in contemporary spirituality.

By using psychological concepts and theories, and emphasizing self-development, Acem reflects what Ole Jacob Madsen has described as "the therapeutic culture." In the therapeutic culture, psychology has become a dominant frame for making sense of one's life, not unlike the position that Christianity has traditionally held in Western culture. Psychology as a science and a profession exerts its influence on contemporary culture and society to such a degree that individuals come to make sense of their lives through the lenses of psychology (Madsen 2011). Psychology is also adopted and adapted in new settings. In Acem, psychological terms and theories are used as parts of an explanatory framework for the practice and outcome of yoga and meditation. Acem's "psychologization" of yoga provides an opportunity for existential meaning-making through a secularized, embodied practice. Salvation is brought down to earth: the meaning of life is to be found in the betterment of the individual through the embodied practices of yoga and meditation.

## Conclusion

The idea that you need to "work on yourself" to achieve a sense of identity and meaning is widespread in a highly individualized Western culture. Acem yoga has been adopted and cultivated in conditions of secularization, privatization, and relativization of religion. Acem's selective reading of the Indian tradition and modern psychology as an explanatory framework has resulted in a relatively fixed understanding of what classical, meditative yoga is, and how it should be performed. At the same time, Acem leaves a large room for individual interpretation when it comes to the outcome of the practice. It may be understood in the context of "spirituality" as awareness of and attunement to the inner, essential, and deeper dimensions of the self. Yoga is a do-it-yourself form of spiritual practice where there is room for the practitioner to decide whether to experience the practice as "spiritual"—however that may be defined—or as altogether secular, focusing on the utilitarian and mundane effects of the practice. Thus, yoga can be seen as a practice that has been adopted and acculturated as a "healing ritual of secular religion" (De Michelis 2004, 260) which empowers the individual to meet the demands of contemporary developed societies.

**Margrethe Løøv** is Associate Professor in Religious Studies at NLA University College, Oslo. Her main areas of research are New Age religion, New Religious Movements, the history of missions among the Sami, and the adaptation of Hindu/Buddhist yoga and meditation in the West.

## References

Acem. 2021. "Nordic Meditation. Easy & Effective." Retrieved May 27, 2021, from https://acem.com/.

——. 2022. "Acems visjon." Retrieved May 23, 2022, from https://acem.no/acem_sites/acem_no/om_acem/acems_visjon.

Acem School of Yoga. 2021. "Meditative Yoga." Retrieved July 18, 2021, from www.yoga.no/en/.

Bourdieu, Pierre. 2013. *Outline of a Theory of Practice*. Translated by Richard Nice. Cambridge: Cambridge University Press, 2013.

Csordas, Thomas J. 1993. "Somatic Modes of Attention." *Cultural Anthropology* 8(2): 135–156.

Davanger, Svend, Halvor Eifring and Anne Grete Hersoug. 2008. *Fighting Stress: Reviews of Meditation Research*. Oslo: Acem Publishing.

De Michelis, Elizabeth. 2004. *A History of Modern Yoga: Patañjali and Western Esotericism*. London: Continuum.

Dobbelaere, Karel. 2002. *Secularization: An Analysis at Three Levels*. Brussels: Peter Lang.

Doggett, Peter. 2007. *There's a Riot Going On: Revolutionaries, Rock Stars and the Rise and Fall of '60s Counter-Culture*. Edinburgh: Canongate Books.

Ekker Solberg, Erik, Halvor Eifring and Are Holen. 2011. "Yoga og helse: Hva sier forskningen?" *Dyade* 43(3): 5–15.

Ellingsen, Øyvind. 1975. "Dagen og yoga-programmet." *Dyade* 7(4): 20.

Glosimot, Borghild. 2018. "Ikke bare gjøre, men være." *Dyade* 50(3): 53–56.

——. 2022. "Kan yoga bidra til å bearbeide traumer?" *Acem-magasinet* 49(1): 19–20.

Hanegraaff, Wouter. 1998. *New Age Religion and Western Culture: Esotericism in the Mirror of Secular Thought*. New York: State University of New York Press.

Hobbel, Torbjørn. 2011. *Impulsøvelser: Yoga i fri flyt*. Oslo: Dyade.

——. 2018. "Motstand mot yoga." *Dyade* 50(3): 60–67.

Holen, Are. 1998. *Stress—arbeid—kjærlighet*. Oslo: Dyade.

——. 2018. "Duften av syriner en tidlig morgen i mai: Yoga, kropp og erkjennelse. Are Holen intervjuet av Torbjørn Hobbel." *Dyade* 50(3): 5–32.

Holen, Are and Carl Henrik Grøndahl. 2015. "Erkjennelse og forsoning." *Dyade* (2): 5–50.

Holen, Are and Torbjørn Hobbel. 2012. *Meditative Yoga: Integrating Body, Breath and Mind.* Oslo: Dyade Press.

Løøv, Margrethe. 2010. "Fra Veda til Vitenskap: En kulturanalytisk studie av meditasjonsorganisasjonen Acems historie." Master thesis, IKOS, University of Oslo.

——. 2015. "Acem: Disenchanted Meditation." In *Nordic New Religions*, edited by James R. Lewis and Inga Bårdsen Tøllefsen, 255–268. Leiden: Brill.

——. 2019. "Between Religion and Science: Shifting Views on Knowledge in Acem and the Transcendental Meditation Movement." *Alternative Spirituality and Religion Review* 10(1): 25–47.

Madsen, Ole Jacob. 2011. "The Unfolding of the Therapeutic: The Cultural Influence of Psychology in Contemporary Society." PhD thesis, University of Bergen.

Newcombe, Suzanne. 2018. "Spaces of Yoga: Towards a Non-Essentialist Understanding of Yoga." In *Yoga in Transformation: Historical and Contemporary Perspectives*, edited by Karl Baier, Philipp A. Maas and Karin Preisendanz, 549–574. Göttingen: Vanderhoeck & Ruprecht.

Newcombe, Suzanne and Karen O'Brien-Kop. 2021. "Reframing Yoga and Meditation Studies." In *Routledge Handbook of Yoga and Meditation Studies*, edited by Suzanne Newcombe and Karen O'Brien-Kop, 3–12. London: Routledge.

Norsk Yoga-skole. 2021. "Norsk Yoga-skole." Retrieved March 31, 2021, from www.yoga.no/norsk-yoga-skole/.

Olsson, Tova. 2018. "Genom kroppen: En intervjustudie med tre yogalärare om religion, spiritualitet och fysisk utövning." *Aura: Tidsskrift for akademiske studier av nyreligiositet* 10: 37–62.

Singleton, Mark. 2010. *Yoga Body: The Origins of Modern Posture Practice.* Oxford: Oxford University Press.

——. 2021. "Early Haṭhayoga." In *Routledge Handbook of Yoga and Meditation Studies*, edited by Suzanne Newcombe and Karen O'Brien-Kop, 120–129. London: Routledge.

Thomte, Anne. 2018a. "Kjærlighetserklæring." *Dyade* 50(3): 35–37.

——. 2018b. "Kropp og sinn i bevegelse." *Dyade* 50(3): 47–52.

Tøllefsen, Inga Bårdsen. 2017. "Hindu-Inspired Meditation Movements in Norway: TM, Acem and the Art of Living Foundation." In *New Age in Norway*, edited by Ingvild Sælid Gilhus, Siv Ellen Kraft and James R. Lewis, 217–240. Sheffield: Equinox.

Williamson, Lola. 2010. *Transcendent in America: Hindu-Inspired Meditation Movements as New Religion.* New York: New York University Press.

– 9 –

# *Kaḷarippayaṟṟ˘* in Performance

## Adoptions and Adaptations of a South Indian Martial Art

LUCY MAY CONSTANTINI

*Kaḷarippayaṟṟ˘* is a martial art with an allied medical system that originated in South India in what is now the modern state of Kerala. Its long and complex history includes a revival from near-extinction in the early twentieth century, whose features parallel the creation of modern yoga in the same period. While still a niche activity, *kaḷarippayaṟṟ˘*'s visibility has increased in recent years. I argue that an important factor in the dissemination of *kaḷarippayaṟṟ˘* beyond Kerala and its historical quasi-temple environment is its adoption by contemporary dancers in India in the last half of the twentieth century, both in their training and in performance. This chapter examines the imbrications between *kaḷarippayaṟṟ˘*'s home context of the *kaḷari*-temple and the fertile ground of the Indian contemporary dance scene. My research focuses on the CVN lineage, part of "northern style" or "Malabar" *kaḷaris*, so-called because they originate in the Malabar region of northern Kerala. I draw on my relationship with CVN Kalari Sangham in Thiruvananthapuram which began in 2002, and has, since 2010, included eight extended periods of intensive study and training. My first encounter with this *kaḷari* was among dance artists at an international choreographic laboratory in Bengaluru, and so this chapter contains autoethnographic as well as more conventional ethnographic elements.

Keywords: *kaḷarippayaṟṟ˘*, *kaḷari*, martial arts, postmodern dance, performance, Indian dance

For better or for worse, contemporary understanding of *kaḷarippayaṟṟ̆*[1] is intrinsically influenced by performance, both in the martial art's revival in the early years of the twentieth century and in its dissemination into the wider popular and cultural imagination in India and beyond. Based on my relationship since 2002 with the CVN lineage of *kaḷarippayaṟṟ̆*[2] and contemporary Indian dance artists, I draw on ethnographic interviews, performance and movement analysis, as well as more conventional historical and textual research, to analyze the commonalities that brought *kaḷarippayaṟṟ̆* and performing arts together, and the differences that create tension. Prior to finding a more academic framework, my investigation and training in *kaḷarippayaṟṟ̆* occurred in the context of my dance practice and making,[3] and while not specifically autoethnographic, my own embodied experience underpins my intellectual understanding. I first briefly overview the context from which *kaḷarippayaṟṟ̆* emerged and interrogate the role of performance in this, with particular reference to its articulation within the CVN lineage. I go on to describe how *kaḷarippayaṟṟ̆* was taken up by contemporary Indian dancers and how the values and foci of postmodern dance contributed to this imbrication of the two forms. I then consider the implication for *kaḷarippayaṟṟ̆*'s reception and ongoing transmission, and the possible opacity arising from a perceived conflation of soteriologies, with *kaḷarippayaṟṟ̆*'s roots in a temple environment whose primary deity is the fierce manifestation of

---

1. For Malayalam, I follow ISO 15919 transliteration of Devanagari and related Indic scripts into Latin characters, with the exception that I retain the *candrakala* ( ̆ ), a symbol denoting the half *u* according to its originator, Hermann Gundert (1872, xi), or the schwa vowel /ə/ according to Ophira Gamliel (2020, 7). The Malayalam phoneme *ṟa* is pronounced similarly to an English hard *t* when doubled, which accounts for the confusing multiplicity of *kaḷarippayaṟṟ̆*'s spellings in Roman script. Where words are generally familiar from Sanskrit, I retain their Sanskrit orthography following the conventions of IAST. In Tamil, I follow Roman Sieler (2015).
2. My relationship with CVN Kalari Sangham in Thiruvananthapuram began in January 2002 and has since 2010 included several extended periods of intensive study and training, including initiation into *kaḷarippayaṟṟ*'s healing system in 2012. These were made possible through a combination of a training grant from the Arts Council of Wales (2012), a research and development award from Wales Arts International (2016), and self-funding. My current doctoral research is funded by the UK Arts and Humanities Research Council Open-Oxford-Cambridge Doctoral Training Partnership.
3. Perhaps most visible in *Rituals of Faith and Imagination*, which emerged from a training period at CVN Kalari Sangham Thiruvananthapuram supported by the Arts Council of Wales and which production was supported by Theatrau Sir Gâr (Carmarthenshire Theatres). Extracts can be seen at https://vimeo.com/83771810 (accessed August 13, 2020).

the goddess, while many dancers consider their dance-practice to have effect beyond the materiality of the body. This investigation supports Anne Koch's argument elsewhere in this volume that an aesthetic dimension to embodied spiritualities perhaps increases their likelihood of travelling (this volume, pages 27–28), and it provides one possible answer to the question Henriette Hanky poses in her introduction: "What data do we produce when we consider our own bodies as instruments?" (this volume, page 13).

## *Kaḷarippayaṟṟ˘*: History and Performance

*Kaḷarippayaṟṟ˘* is a martial art with an allied healing system that originated in southwest India. Its multiple forms and lineages reflect the diversity of medical systems (*āyurveda* and *siddha*) and languages (Malayalam, Tamil, and Tulu) of the region. My ethnography to date has focused on the CVN lineage which belongs to the northern style of *kaḷarippayaṟṟ˘*, so named because until the mid-twentieth century its practice was confined to the northern area of Kerala, bounded to the west by the Arabian Sea, to the north and east by mountains, and to the south by the Korapuzha, a river flowing through Kozhikode district (interview with G. Sathyanarayanan Nair, 7 December 2012). Broadly, "northern style" or Malabar *kaḷarippayaṟṟ˘*'s language is Malayalam, its medical practice āyurvedic, and its origin is attributed to Paraśurāma, the axe-bearing incarnation of the god Viṣṇu. With *kaḷarippayaṟṟ˘*'s revival in the first half of the twentieth century, its geographic specificities loosened and styles spread. The term *kaḷari* is polyvalent in Malayalam, one of its meanings being the temple-training space in which northern style *kaḷarippayaṟṟ˘* is practised. To date, my focus of practice and research has been overseen by *gurukkaḷ* (lineage-holder) G. Sathyanarayanan Nair[4] at CVN Kalari Sangham in Thiruvananthapuram, a city in the heartlands of the southern style (more properly, *varmakkalai*).[5] This *kaḷari* was founded soon after the creation of the modern state of Kerala in 1956, when the Travancore royal family invited Sathyan *gurukkaḷ*'s teacher and father, C.V. Govindankutty Nair, son of the original CVN, to establish the present *kaḷari* at East Fort so that the new state capital might house a representative of this northern Keralan art.

4. As Nair is a widespread family and caste name in Kerala and a number of people at the *kaḷari* share it, I hereafter refer to him as Sathyan *gurukkaḷ*.
5. On the geography of *varmakkalai* see Sieler (2015, 10–16); for an overview of *varmakkalai*'s martial and medical systems, see Sieler (2015, 98–132).

Probably the richest historical textual evidence of *kaḷarippayaṟṟ˘* is to be found in the *Vaṭakkan Pāṭṭukaḷ* (*Northern Ballads*), a non-literate tradition of tales from northern Kerala sung by agricultural workers to accompany their labor, as well as by families after their dinner (Mathew 1979, 14–15). K.S. Mathew makes a convincing case that of these, the heroic accounts of a possibly exaggerated golden age of *kaḷarippayaṟṟ˘* date from between the fifteenth and seventeenth centuries CE (1979, 26), and while it is likely that *kaḷarippayaṟṟ˘* is older than this, evidence is scant. The ballads describe a society where multiple chieftains ruled small political entities often in conflict, where martial prowess or economic acuity transcended otherwise rigid religious, ritual and social limitations imposed by caste distinctions (1979, 46). *Kaḷari*s were intrinsic to religious, social, and educational life, and the ballads celebrate the prowess and heroism of female practitioners of *kaḷarippayaṟṟ˘* (1979, 55–56), the matrilineal system they describe allowing women unusual freedom, for example in choosing and discarding their partners (1979, 63). Small chiefdoms were absorbed into larger kingdoms in the eighteenth century, and various invasions, political upheavals (Tarabout 1986, 12) and the changing nature of warfare contributed to *kaḷarippayaṟṟ*'s decline from this time onwards (Silvestri 2023), accelerated by British colonial acts banning the manufacture and ownership of weapons among local people (Logan 1879, 108 v1, 227, 232–233, 237 v2). As a result, by the late nineteenth century, *kaḷarippayaṟṟ˘* was virtually extinguished and only two lineages survived. Chambadan Veedu Narayanan Nair (CVN, 1905–1944) and his teacher Kottackal Kanaran Gurukkal (1850–1935) were two of the chief proponents of its twentieth-century revival, when the knowledge that remained was gathered and new methods developed (interview with G. Sathyanarayanan Nair, December 10, 2012). As with the modern resurgence of yoga in India, performance was a key tool in the revival and popularization of *kaḷarippayaṟṟ˘*, coinciding with the turn towards Indian independence where a new articulation of a valorous Indian body was sought to counter demeaning colonial stereotypes (see Singleton 2010, 98–111).

While certain classes were historically favored, *kaḷari*s have always existed across Kerala's diversity of religious and social groups. A *kaḷari* in which practice takes place is essentially a temple, complete with installed deities, where CVN Kalari follows the tantric Śaiva-Śākta articulation of its Kerala tantric lineage (Constantini, forthcoming). The *kaḷari* is conceived to support practice, set below ground "like a cocoon" (interview with G. Sathyanarayanan Nair, December 20, 2012), the circulation of air designed to keep it relatively cool while avoiding the unwholesome exposure of sweating bodies to direct wind. The *kaḷari* is also designed to nurture qualities of humility, devotion, and focus in the practitioner.

The use of performance in a form with an implicit religious or spiritual body–mind bent has not always been met with approval, despite its necessity as a tool for *kaḷarippayaṟṟ˘*'s survival. Some practitioners, their own celebrated engagement in performance notwithstanding, object to any description of *kaḷarippayaṟṟ˘* as a performing art (John 2011, x), and P.K. Sasidharan maintains that important aspects were lost in the focus on performance during *kaḷarippayaṟṟ˘*'s revival, arguing that this led to a diminished role for *meypayaṟṟ˘* (the body practice) in favor of more showy weapons work, with the danger of reducing *kaḷarippayaṟṟ˘* to a "'cultural relic,' a spectacular and astonishing event for audiences, created through weapons and gimmicks and quite separate from creating finesse of body and mind" (2006, 180). Girija K.P. notes that *kaḷarippayaṟṟ˘*'s performative aspects came to stand for *kaḷarippayaṟṟ˘* as a whole, describing a process where practices within the tradition which conformed to "modern conventions of rationality" (2015) were foregrounded, while others were marginalized, resulting in simplification, flattening, and fragmentation.

From within the CVN lineage, Sathyan *gurukkaḷ* describes (interview with G. Sathyanarayanan Nair, July 26, 2021) the evolution of a form once confined to the inside of *kaḷari*s with no more than two opportunities per year for outsiders to observe it, the number of viewers restricted by the dimensions of the *kaḷari*. Believing him to be inspired by Kīlēri Kuññikkaṇṇan Master, a *kaḷarippayaṟṟ˘* practitioner from northern Kerala who trained in circus in England before returning to become the acclaimed "father of Kerala circus," he explains how CVN set about modifying *kaḷarippayaṟṟ˘* from a purely practicing tradition into the performance of a practicing tradition. Some costumes were introduced, including a very circus-like leopard skin, and the resulting stage show, attempting to showcase all elements of *kaḷarippayaṟṟ˘*, emerged from the temple environment of the *kaḷari* to tour in time the length and breadth of India, then internationally. On the one hand, this led to some fairly straightforward modifications to take into account the interests of an audience, such as changing the facing of salutations which would originally have been directed towards the *pūttaṟa* (flower platform), where the *kaḷari*'s presiding deity is installed, and reconfiguring the number of people performing *meyppayaṟṟ˘* and their spatial arrangements, so that, for example, *vīt˘kāl*, the circling leg exercise which is usually practiced in open space, might be performed facing another person to add an element of spectacle. Jumps were emphasized. The ball which now hangs from the *kaḷari*'s ceiling at East Fort is a legacy of this time, although in those days it was a bunch of plantains hung from the rafters which CVN would scatter with his foot during his famed leaps. On the other hand, this led to movement choices which were to impact the transmission of *kaḷarippayaṟṟ˘* itself. Sathyan *gurukkaḷ* believes the weapons forms were little changed, speedy, precise, and spectacular as they already were, but he suspects more compact body movements, martially practical in certain instances but hard for an audience to read, were enlarged somewhat or discarded altogether, while visually interesting elements were given new prominence. Because of this, he contends that "what we have here now as a repertoire of our training may not be a complete system" (interview with G. Sathyanarayanan Nair, July 26, 2021).

Quite apart from its genesis, this CVN Kalari (there are now several branches of this lineage) has a long and fruitful relationship with performance and performers, collaborating over the years with local and international artists ranging from Peter Brook to Jackie Chan. Sathyan *gurukkaḷ* has featured in both Indian and international films, images of his spectacular leaps taken from a Japanese commercial in the 1980s adorning one of the walls of the *kaḷari* clinic. His family, all of whom also trained at the *kaḷari*, includes dancers, both contemporary and Indian classical. In the 1980s, Sathyan *gurukkaḷ* spent three years adapting and teaching a twice-daily *kaḷarippayaṟṟ˘* program for students of the National School of Drama in New Delhi, going on to do similar for the new course at the School of Drama in Thrissur in Kerala, and has taught on internationally renowned performing arts trainings, such as the International Workshop Festival in London and the Grotowski Institute in Wrocław. My own first encounter with him and with *kaḷarippayaṟṟ˘* was at Facets 2002, an international choreographic laboratory organized by Attakkalari Centre for Movement Arts (henceforth Attakkalari) in Bengaluru, which includes a dance company and various training and movement research programs, and the most frequent non-local visitors to the *kaḷari*, both from other parts of India and abroad, are dancers, other performing artists, and the occasional yoga practitioner. Phillip B. Zarrilli, who wrote the first academic study of *kaḷarippayaṟṟ˘* in English, came to it through his research on the dance-theatre form kathakali, explicit that it was *kaḷarippayaṟṟ˘*'s usefulness to performers that attracted him (Zarrilli 1998, 18). My own first funding to train and research at the *kaḷari* was provided by the Arts Council of Wales in service of my dance practice, and so it is safe to say that the relationship between this *kaḷari* and performing artists is deeply embedded.

Sathyan *gurukkaḷ* describes three aspects of *kaḷarippayaṟṟ˘*'s relationship to performance. The first is the use of it by CVN in its recreation and popularization in order to retrieve it from obscurity. A second aspect is the historical use of *kaḷarippayaṟṟ˘* as a fundamental strand of training in traditional Kerala performing arts, such as kathakali. He understands the circularity of forearm movements, their relationship to the movement of the spine, and the general length of the spine, as a legacy of *kaḷarippayaṟṟ˘* practice in kathakali, along with the low movement through the hips and endurance cultivated to enable performers to maintain depth of stance and activation of feet while wearing heavy costumes in performances that might last through the night. Sathyan *gurukkaḷ* differentiates some modern movement practices which transpose the shapes of *kaḷarippayaṟṟ˘* without fully understanding its fundamental movement principles from this "body training, actually like preparing the clay rather than using the forms [...] because the performance aspect [of kathakali] has got its own character" (interview with G. Sathyanarayanan Nair, July 26, 2021) with no need to borrow shapes or aesthetics from elsewhere. A third aspect of the relationship between *kaḷarippayaṟṟ˘* and performance occurs with the renewed focus on the body that characterized postmodern dance's emergence in the latter half of the twentieth century, where elements and principles of *kaḷarippayaṟṟ˘* held much appeal for practitioners of a dance form in which borrowing, bricolage, and rigorous somatic investigation were inherent (interview with G. Sathyanarayanan Nair, July 26, 2021). It is this aspect I shall now consider in greater detail.

## Postmodern Dance, Western and Indian

The emergence of postmodern dance is generally attributed to the composition classes taught by Robert Dunn at Merce Cunningham's New York dance studios in the mid-twentieth century. The focus of these were the theories and experiments of the composer John Cage, which laid the ground from which postmodern dance arose (Banes 1987, xvi). When a member of this group, Yvonne Rainer, adopted the term "postmodern" to describe their work, Sally Banes notes that she meant it primarily in its chronological sense, in that theirs was the generation following modern dance, itself a term previously inclusive of any theatre dance that was not ballet or popular entertainment (1987, xiii). This generation of dancers did, however, share characteristics with more theoretical understandings of postmodernism, including skepticism *vis-à-vis* what Jean-François Lyotard referred to as *métarécits* (grand narratives), and a fragmentation that embraced plural perspectives (McNay 1992, 118), which, pertinent to this study, enabled enormous innovation in dance technique, because any movement was now potentially "dance," its composition rather than any intrinsic qualities classifying it as choreography. There was a tendency towards minimalism, both in sound and in the cultivation of a more ordinary, supposedly neutral, style of moving, with costumes often reflecting workaday practice clothes, and a general rejection of the spectacle which had thus far characterized theatrical performance. These postmodernists, while diverse in their aesthetic proclivities, were united by a radical urge to re-envision the very essence of dance and choreography (Banes 1987, xiv), and "[t]he body itself became the subject of the dance, rather than serving as an instrument for expressive metaphors" (1987, xviii). This led to the evolution of a slew of dance techniques rooted in rigorous somatic exploration that rejected the emphasis on external shape that had characterized Western dance to date. Instead, new techniques explored ways to investigate interior pathways and alignments, often drawing on imagery of internal physical, and sometimes subtle, anatomy to forge deeper somatic connections and a tangible relationship between internal experience and external (as well as internal) expression. These techniques emphasized virtuosity attained through efficiency rather than excessive effort, softening the muscular tone of the dancer's body (1987, xxii) in what generally came to be classed under the umbrella term of Release Technique. The first postmodern dancers and those that followed were eclectic in their movement influences, drawing on a variety of non-Western forms, which included the martial arts tai chi and aikido, various strands of Buddhism, and, in Rainer's case, inspiration from the epics and mythology of India (Banes 1987, xx). Their incorporation played an important role in the attempt to dismantle Eurocentric and patriarchal hegemony in the arts, however blind this may have been to the experience of people whose ethnicities reflected the global majority (Dixon-Gottschild 1996; Monroe 2011; Chaleff 2018; Ashley 2024).

Based in Chennai, Chandralekha (1928–2006) was one of the most influential innovators of South India's late twentieth-century dance scene. After training in bharatanatyam she gave up dancing in the 1960s, not returning to it until the 1980s, troubled by what she perceived as its "dollification," preoccupation with divinization, and lack of engagement with the social and political reality of contemporary India (Mitra 2014, 7). Uttara Coorlawala remarks that while she consistently denied non-Indian influences in her work, Chandralekha nonetheless collaborated with Western artists such as John Cage (1999, 10–11). Coorlawala argues that "[p]ostcolonial Indians educated in and speaking the English language cannot but be influenced by Western thought structures and knowledge systems. Chandralekha has travelled the world and avidly explores the art and ideas of the cultures she visits" (1999, 12), while Ananya Chatterjea places her challenge to tradition within a larger cultural project of "resistive postmodernism" (1998, 29). Chandralekha's paring down and reduction of excess, in counter to what she saw as the external superficiality of Indian classical dance, entailed a parallel reactionary aesthetic to Indian classical dance traditions as Western postmodern dance-makers had to European ones when they challenged the tendency to "treat Western dance, ballet particularly, as if it was the one great divinely ordained apogee of the performing arts" (Kealiinohomoku 1970, 536). Chandralekha's female dancers performed in the simple practice sari of Indian classical dancers (Basavarajaiah 2016, 48), and a marked feature of the only one of her choreographies still easily accessible, her last work, *Sharira*,[6] is music performed by the Gundecha Brothers, its dhrupad style suffused simultaneously with a postmodern minimalism and a historical sense of transcendent spirituality, magnified by the nature of the text sung and the modern sacred associations of dhrupad (Sanyal and Widdess 2004, 7; Widdess 2010, 119, 134). Most relevant to my argument here was Chandralekha's forging of an explicitly Indian contemporary dance language by deconstructing the "grammar" of bharatanatyam to free it from its classical content and religious narratives (Chettur 2016, 157; Aranyani 2020), while also drawing on yoga and *kaḷarippayaṟṟ˘* in the somatic dismantling and bricolage which is a hallmark of postmodern dance. This innovation can be seen as part of a wider transnational phenomenon of culturally specific practices evolving into modern forms that "are recognisably indigenous and contemporary" (Harvey 2020, 30).

## The Influence of Dance on the Reception of *Kaḷarippayaṟṟ˘*

The effect of this on the wider reception of *kaḷarippayaṟṟ˘* has, I think, yet to be fully appreciated. The visual effect and virtuosity of Chandralekha's performers were striking, and while her methodology tended to keep movement strands separate,[7] it is worth noting that each of these, bharatanatyam, yoga and *kaḷarippayaṟṟ˘*, has its own relationship to a sense of the sacred, or simply access to something beyond the materiality of the body. Inevitably, in the audience's minds, if not in the creator's

6. An early performance of *Sharira*, performed by Tishani Doshi and Shaji K. John with the Gundecha Brothers, can be viewed in full at www.youtube.com/watch?v=OXCc1OlBkIw (accessed August 10, 2021).
7. Both Shaji K. John, the male performer in *Sharira*, also of the CVN lineage, although a different branch, and Sathyan *gurukkaḷ* describe John's performance as 'pure *kaḷarippayaṟṟ˘*,' not dance (personal correspondence, Shaji K. John, July 24, 2021; interview with G. Sathyanarayanan Nair, July 26, 2021).

or performers', the soteriologies of these separate forms, complex and context-dependent even before their juxtaposition in dance-making, conflate and lose their specificity when comingled in this way. In the case of *kaḷarippayaṟṟ˘*, I would argue that it exacerbates a tendency to unmoor it from its base in specifically Kerala tantra and situates it instead in a more generalized, post-Independence, pan-Indian notion of spirituality, ethics, and piety, influenced by neo-Vedanta and modern interpretations of Pātañjala yoga and tantra.

## Flows of Movement Practices and Principles

For Jayachandran Palazhy, founder of Attakkalari (see www.attakkalari.org), Chandralekha's juxtaposition of *kaḷarippayaṟṟ˘* with other movement practices "was not going far enough [...]. I was really interested in developing a contemporary language, because the content of Indian classical dance was a little bit outside of my living experience. It was not my cup of tea. And I wanted to have something to do with my life and my imagination" (interview with Jayachandran Palazhy, August 2, 2021). As well as a more general interest in film, theatre, and philosophy, Palazhy had seriously investigated several Indian movement practices by the time he joined the cast of *Angika*, which according to Shaji K. John was the first choreography in which Chandralekha introduced the martial sequences of *kaḷarippayaṟṟ˘* (personal correspondence with Shaji K. John, July 24, 2021). Although puzzled by its abstraction, Palazhy was inspired by a performance of Merce Cunningham's company in Chennai to consider, "Maybe there is already a wheel existing and I don't have to re-invent the wheel" (interview with Jayachandran Palazhy, August 2, 2021), and before *Angika* opened, he left for London to perform, and to study at London Contemporary Dance School. In 1992 he set up Attakkalari, establishing its Diploma in Movement Arts and Mixed Media in Bengaluru in 2001. Palazhy estimates this has averaged 25 students a year, for whom *kaḷarippayaṟṟ˘* has been a core strand of daily training, along with various traditional Indian and Western contemporary movement forms. Approximately 500 graduates of the diploma have gone on to work throughout India and internationally as dance-makers, performers, and educators in dance and other art forms, as well as in the allied somatic practices in which they trained (such as yoga), with some particularly emphasizing the role of Indian martial arts in their work. Whether overtly stated or quietly absorbed during the transformative process of full-time dance training, principles and practices of *kaḷarippayaṟṟ˘* infuse their aesthetics, movement vocabularies, and somatic understandings, which then diffuse into their other areas of practice.

Rather than juxtaposing *kaḷarippayaṟṟ˘* with other forms, Palazhy's interest was to work with its principles.

> A lot of the time, I felt in India a lot of people wanting to create contemporary expression, were still using traditional language without actually fully processing it. That was one of the difficulties I faced, because my own view, after many years of working and researching on this, is actually, if you look at any of these forms, bharatanatyam, kathakali, *kaḷari*, all of these, they are manifestations of a kinaesthetic idea or a semiotic wisdom in a particular time, in a particular place. So as contemporary artists, our job is to find artistic ideas, not the outer form. And then we have to manifest today. That means you have to deconstruct these forms with a creative mind, and then choose what inherited wisdom you wish to take into your own practice.
>
> (Interview with Jayachandran Palazhy, August 2, 2021)

After working with artists from across the world's cultures, Palazhy concluded that it is not sufficient to "superficially put on some movement on somebody" (interview with Jayachandran Palazhy, August 2, 2021) and what he and Sathyan *gurukkaḷ* call the neurocentric principles of *kaḷarippayaṟṟ˘* must be investigated. These stem from the energetic understanding of *kaḷarippayaṟṟ˘*, where movement is propelled by *vāyu*, an inner wind generated between the activity of the feet and the *nābhimūla*, a point low in the body from which all *kaḷarippayaṟṟ˘* movement should originate and through which it circulates (Constantini, forthcoming). While historical yoga texts place the *nābhimūla* at the navel, Palazhy works with its *kaḷarippayaṟṟ˘* location lower in the body, between the genital root and anus (Constantini forthcoming), from which

> This energy is then transmitted through the nervous system (*Naadi Vyuha*) and goes to the limbs and the entire body. Most of the Asian martial arts share this notion of a center and core where the vital energy is stored. This "neuro-centric" notion of movement is diametrically different from the Cartesian idea of biomechanical movement. In Kalarippayattu, every movement has an imaginary circular trajectory, and even the seemingly straight lines are indeed conceived as part of larger circles. The movements originate in the lower abdominal area (*Naabhi Moola*) and pass through the back and to the limbs only to return to the center and get revitalized so that it can initiate and engage with the next series of movements. [...] Limbs are treated as extension of the back, and their movements are in fact the indicators of how the spine moves. (Palazhy 2020, 7–8)

Unencumbered by the aesthetic trappings of the various Indian dance traditions, he sees *kaḷarippayar̠r̠˘* as "much more of an embodiment of certain ideas [...]. It's much more in terms of movement and body shapes and intention, working with gravity, the sinuous quality, leaps, all of that, how the circularity continues" (interview with Jayachandran Palazhy, August 2, 2021). This coheres with Sathyan *gurukkaḷ*'s view that "*kaḷari* has potential to become a root practice for any performer who uses his body" (interview with G. Sathyanarayanan Nair, July 26, 2021) because its work through the spine and *vāyu*, both as subtle wind and diaphragmatic breath, creates a centering, availability, and focus in the practitioner that go beyond the skills conferred by biomechanical muscular practices (interview with G. Sathyanarayanan Nair, July 26, 2021). Padmini Chettur, who danced with Chandralekha from 1990 to 2000, describes a similar process "that enabled one to receive energy through the feet and harness it in the spine" (2016, 157) in her bharatanatyam training, observing that Chandralekha brought the practices of bharatanatyam, yoga, and *kaḷarippayar̠r̠˘* together because of the inherent similarity of physical qualities she perceived in them, inspired in particular "by the ability of a Kalaripayattu practitioner to stand grounded, while at the same time remaining alive in the body" (2016, 159). Chandralekha herself observed that in *kaḷarippayar̠r̠˘* "the verticality of the body was broken to a more compact and relaxing circularity" where "[t]he idea was to infuse the body not only with the potential for extensions and contractions, but also to convert every movement to an energising exercise" (Chandralekha 2018). Thus the subtle, internal qualities conferred by training in *kaḷarippayar̠r̠˘* have been at least as interesting to performing artists as any external physical virtuosity the martial art confers.

## Transmission and Legacy

Transmitting these subtler inner and outer principles, however, is no quick task, with traditional practitioners often taking years or even decades to embody them. Tamara Ashley, in her work integrating somatic and traditional modalities into the dance programs at the University of Bedfordshire in the UK, finds the process problematic because of the time available for assimilation of these and feels the university trainings at best offer useful encounters for students to choose their own specialisms on which to focus as they later mature into their practices (interview with Tamara Ashley, June 9, 2021). Sathyan *gurukkaḷ* has long considered how best to transmit the core principles of *kaḷarippayar̠r̠˘* in a changing social framework whose values are at odds with the harshness of earlier pedagogies, quite apart from the inappropriateness of such methods for already-formed adult bodies expressing varying degrees of facility, rather than the children who were the traditional beginner students of *kaḷarippayar̲r̲˘* (interview with G. Sathyanarayanan Nair, July 26, 2021). Palazhy widens this observation to encompass the contemporary imaginative landscape:

> If you look at a kathakali artist, earlier time, he probably was mostly confined to his district, if not his village. The imagination is primarily propelled by all the epics and all the traditional texts and the life they deal with, so they have a different internal landscape. That shaped the [movement] language. Then when you transplant the language [...] people are talking about mobile phone, Facebook, WhatsApp, and Instagram and all of that, there is a disjunction unless you spend huge number of hours and a lot of energy to really internalise all of those things. So that's why one has to find a new authenticity. [...] And people can't also spend that much time on one thing. Lives are much more broader and other influences are there and all. It's not necessarily a bad thing but I'm just saying there is definitely a change.
>
> (Interview with Jayachandran Palazhy, August 2, 2021)

Seeking a new way to record the movement principles and concepts embedded in these traditions while harnessing Palazhy's long-standing interest in the integration of technology into movement arts, Attakkalari embarked on an interactive digital research project, *Nagarika* (see http://nagarika.attakkalari.org), which drew on a variety of expert consultants, Sathyan *gurukkaḷ* included. Research into new methods of transmission is multi-faceted, experimental, and ongoing, with Sathyan *gurukkaḷ* also suggesting the creation of a modified, more accessible curriculum of *kaḷarippayar̲r̲˘*, with only particularly able students going on to complete more traditional-style training (interview with G. Sathyanarayanan Nair, July 26, 2021).

## Soteriologies of Practice

One reason for the blurring of distinctions between separate forms gathered under the umbrella of a contemporary movement investigation or choreographic exploration is that dance itself is often understood by its practitioners to be in some way soteriological. Ashley argues that certain postmodern dance practices encompass an explicitly spiritual dimension. Examples include Nancy Stark Smith's *Underscore*, which contains statements of intention, a ritualized framework, the building of a community of practice, and deeply somatic enquiries that "really invite reflection on the present state of the body–mind and what's arising from that" (interview with Tamara Ashley, June 9, 2021), or her work in the final decade or so of her life on "States of Grace," the term the dance-artist Simone Forti gave to Stark Smith's investigations into intangible qualities, including attuned physical, energetic, and listening states, and the embodied presence that lend skill, surprise, and virtuosity to groups of improvisers (notes from Stark Smith's Earthdance intensive, January 5, 2009). While in India practitioners of contemporary forms may be wary of the religious trappings of classical dance, many nonetheless also express their practice as encompassing more than the materiality of the body. Palazhy emphasizes the importance of "developing the ability to inhabit spaces beyond the physical contours of the body" (2020, 24), asserting that skills and conceptual understanding gleaned from traditional knowledges can anchor an evolving contemporary movement language in a sense of identity and belonging associated with a historical lineage (2020, 25). Chandralekha "experienced dance as an essential freedom" (Chandralekha 2017), the language of liberation a clear echo of the emancipatory ontologies of the tantric and *sāṃkhya* philosophies from which she drew the power of the feminine principle (Ganesh 2015), especially visible in *Sharira*. Her understanding of *bindu* (seed) as the centeredness of body-as-*maṇḍala* are a personal evolution of her studies of tantra, implying that mysticism was intrinsic to her dance, where the universe and its forces mapped onto the moving body (Coorlawala 1999, 9). Similarly, Palazhy argues that a *kaḷari* "is an abstract representation of both time and space in which the human body of the practitioner is placed [...] imagined as a microcosm" where "linking every molecule of oneself to the larger universal ideas of space and time helps in achieving a very special focus and quality to Kalarippayattu movements" (2020, 6). His interpretation of the more esoteric dimensions of the *kaḷari* space and body reflect a very postmodern artistic sensibility: "Basically my feeling is anything which works with the inner body or subtle bodies are image-based. It primarily comes from your imagination. So my own theory is it all resides in the imagination and the body is trained to grow into that imagination" (interview with Jayachandran Palazhy, August 2, 2021). The fleeting, time-based nature of dance leads some practitioners and viewers to experience transcendent qualities through it, and it is not uncommon for it to be described as facilitating access to the supra-ordinary (Palazhy 2020, 28–29).

When dance and *kaḷarippayaṟṟ˘*, which emerged from a religious tradition that venerates the fierce form of the goddess, meet in a rehearsal studio, it is unsurprising that a new and blended ontology emerges from what they were separately. *Vāyu*, both subtle inner wind and more prosaic breath, is said to generate the movement and flow of a skilled *kaḷarippayaṟṟ˘* practitioner. While the effect and presence of *vāyu* in the physical body are visible to a trained eye, it is also a subtle energy carefully cultivated by the ritualized nature and layout of the *kaḷari*, and by the mental, some might say spiritual, attributes the space and practice are conceived to nurture (Constantini, forthcoming). Sathyan *gurukkaḷ* asserts that training in *kaḷarippayaṟṟ˘* principles enables performers to access their spines, and through the spine to connect to the breath. "When you are connected to the breath, your performance changes" (interview with G. Sathyanarayanan Nair, July 26, 2021). This change on the one hand is evidenced as skillful movement of the physical body, but it is also understood to be the result of subtle inner forces, *vāyu*, linked to an esoteric articulation of the tantric body and its function in an interconnected cosmos.

## Concluding Remarks

I have sought to show here the key role played by performance in the revival of *kaḷarippayaṟṟ˘*, its dissemination by various artists into a wider popular and cultural framework, and the role of dance artists in contributing to the analysis and transmission of its core principles in an evolving modern context in which traditional modes of transmission are increasingly difficult to maintain and elements of the practice are in danger of being lost. This is complex, because a fundament of postmodern dance is experimentation and bricolage, where forms frequently lose their specificities and cultural referents, although key principles transmit through the artists' work, according to their interests. While crediting sources is considered good practice, the system for this in a dance studio is not formalized and relies on artists' personal and variable understandings of the histories of their practices in a creative ecosystem which prizes individual interpretation and innovation over accuracy. In contrast to Western practitioners where this has not always been the case, Chandralekha and Palazhy both credit their sources, reflective perhaps of the strong attachment to lineage in Indian art forms. However, here too this acknowledgment of source is reliant on the understanding of the artists involved, who, depending on their own rigor and the amalgamations of forms they experienced in dance practice and training, may or may not have a clear understanding of the specificities of *kaḷarippayaṟṟ˘*. Thus the performing arts in general and dance in particular have a peculiar and sometimes contradictory role in the evolution of *kaḷarippayaṟṟ˘*, at once popularizing and disseminating it, while simultaneously implicit in its dilution and change, and yet also, through projects like *Nagarika*, contributing to its transmission and preservation in new forms for contemporary society.

## Acknowledgments

I am grateful to this volume's other contributors for their generous feedback and comments during an online workshop organized via the University of Bergen. I also thank Ruth Westoby for commenting on an early draft of this chapter. I extend special thanks to my interviewees, for their time and generosity in sharing their thoughts with me.

**Lucy May Constantini**'s doctoral research at the Open University (UK) explores the relationship between practice and textual traditions in *kaḷarippayaṟṟ˘*, funded by the UK Arts and Humanities Research Council's Open-Oxford-Cambridge Doctoral Training Partnership. Lucy's background is in dance, where her work investigates the confluence of her practices of postmodern dance, martial arts, and yoga.

## References

Aranyani. 2020. "Chandralekha's Experiments with the Dancing Body." *The Hindu*, December 10. Retrieved from www.thehindu.com/entertainment/dance/chandralekhas-experiments-with-the-dancing-body/article33299839.ece.

Ashley, Tamara. 2024. "Steps Towards Decolonising Contact Improvisation in the University." In *Ethical Agility in Dance: Rethinking Technique in British Contemporary Dance*, edited by Noyale Colin, Catherine Seago and Kathryn Stamp. London: Routledge. https://doi.org/10.4324/9781003111146

Banes, Sally. 1987. *Terpsichore in Sneakers: Post-Modern Dance*. Hanover: Wesleyan University Press.

Basavarajaiah, Veena. 2016. "Chandralekha Mahakal." In *Tiltpauseshift: Dance Ecologies in India*, edited by Anita E. Cherian and Gati Dance Forum (India), 46–55. New Delhi: Tulika Books.

Chaleff, Rebecca. 2018. "Activating Whiteness: Racializing the Ordinary in US American Postmodern Dance." *Dance Research Journal* 50(3): 71–84.

Chandralekha. 2017. "'Probe Deeper into Your Art': Chandralekha on the Duty of the Indian Classical Dancer." Scroll.In, October 29. Retrieved from https://scroll.in/magazine/855678/probe-deeper-into-your-art-chandralekha-on-the-duty-of-the-indian-classical-dancer.

——. 2018. "The Militant Origins of Indian Dance." *The Wire*, December 9. Retrieved from https://thewire.in/the-arts/the-militant-origins-of-indian-dance.

Chatterjea, Ananya. 1998. "Chandralekha: Negotiating the Female Body and Movement in Cultural/Political Signification." *Dance Research Journal* 30(1): 25–33. https://doi.org/10.2307/1477892.

Chettur, Padmini. 2016. "The Body Laboratory." In *Tiltpauseshift: Dance Ecologies in India*, edited by Anita E. Cherian and Gati Dance Forum (India), 155–168. New Delhi: Tulika Books.

Constantini, Lucy May. 2023. "Firm Feet and Inner Wind: Introducing Posture in the South Indian Martial Art Kaḷarippayaṟṟ˘." In *Yoga and the Traditional Physical Practices of India: Influence, Entanglement and Confrontation*, edited by Daniela Bevilacqua and Mark Singleton. *Journal of Yoga Studies* 4: 347–371.

Coorlawala, Uttara. 1999. "Ananya and Chandralekha: A Response to 'Chandralekha: Negotiating the Female Body and Movement in Cultural/Political Signification.'" *Dance Research Journal* 31(1): 7–12. https://doi.org/10.2307/1478306.

Dixon-Gottschild, Brenda. 1996. *Digging the Africanist Presence in American Performance: Dance and Other Contexts*. Westport, CT: Praeger.

Gamliel, Ophira. 2020. *A Linguistic Survey of the Malayalam Language in Its Own Terms*. Wiesbaden: Harrassowitz.

Ganesh, Kamala. 2015. "Remembering Chandralekha—Artist, Choreographer, Feminist." *The Wire*, December 30. Retrieved from https://thewire.in/culture/remembering-chandralekha-artist-choreographer-feminist.

Girija, K.P. 2015. "Attiring Local Tradition for the Global Market." *Economic and Political Weekly*, June: 7–8.

Gundert, Hermann. 1872. *A Malayalam and English Dictionary*. Mangalore: Stolz, Basel Mission Book & Tract Depository. Retrieved from http://idb.ub.uni-tuebingen.de/opendigi/CiXIV68#p=1.

Harvey, Graham. 2020. "Indigenous Rituals Remake the Larger-than-Human Community." In *Reassembling Democracy: Ritual as Cultural Resource*, edited by Graham Harvey, Michael Houseman, Sarah M. Pike and Jone Salomonsen, 69–85. London: Bloomsbury. https://doi.org/10.5040/9781350123045.

John, Shaji K. 2011. *Kalarippayattu: The Martial and Healing Art of Kerala*. Kottayam: Shaji K. John.

Kealiinohomoku, Joann. 1970. "An Anthropologist Looks at Ballet as a Form of Ethnic Dance." In *What Is Dance? Readings in Theory and Criticism (1983)*, edited by Roger Copeland and Marshall Cohen, 533–549. Oxford: Oxford University Press.

Logan, William. 1879. *A Collection of Treaties, Engagements and Other Papers of Importance Relating to British Affairs in Malabar.* 2 vols. in 1 bk. Calicut: A. Manuel.

Mathew, K.S. 1979. *Society in Medieval Malabar: A Study Based on Vadakkaṅ Pāṭṭukaḷ.* Kottayam: Jaffe Books.

McNay, Lois. 1992. *Foucault and Feminism: Power, Gender and the Self.* Oxford: Polity Press.

Mitra, Royona. 2014. "The Parting Pelvis: Temporality, Sexuality, and Indian Womanhood in Chandralekha's Sharira (2001)." *Dance Research Journal* 46(2): 5–19. https://doi.org/10.1017/S0149767714000254.

Monroe, Raquel L. 2011. "'I Don't Want to Do African ... What About My Technique?': Transforming Dancing Places into Spaces in the Academy." *Journal of Pan African Studies* 4(6): 38–55.

Palazhy, Jayachandran. 2020. "Contemporary Movement Arts Practices and Traditional Somatic Education." In *Handbook of Education Systems in South Asia*, edited by Padma M. Sarangapani and Rekha Pappu, 1–29. Singapore: Springer. https://doi.org/10.1007/978-981-13-3309-5_3-1.

Sanyal, Ritwik and Richard Widdess. 2004. *Dhrupad: Tradition and Performance in Indian Music*. Aldershot: Ashgate.

Sasidharan, P.K. 2006. "Kalarippayatt: Performance Paradigm as Aesthetics and Politics of Invisibility." In *Performers and Their Arts: Folk, Popular, and Classic Genres in a Changing India*, edited by Simon Charsley and Laxmi Narayan Kadekar, 164–182. London: Routledge.

Sieler, Roman. 2015. *Lethal Spots, Vital Secrets: Medicine and Martial Arts in South India*. Oxford: Oxford University Press.

Silvestri, Laura. 2023. "Managing Wind and Fire: Some Remarks from a Case Study on Kaḷarippayaṟṟu." In *Yoga and the Traditional Physical Practices of India: Influence, Entanglement and Confrontation*, edited by Daniela Bevilacqua and Mark Singleton. *Journal of Yoga Studies* 4: 331–346.

Singleton, Mark. 2010. *Yoga Body: The Origins of Modern Posture Practice*. Oxford: Oxford University Press.

Tarabout, Gilles. 1986. *Sacrifier et Donner à Voir En Pays Malabar: Les Fêtes de Temple Au Kerala (Inde Du Sud): Étude Anthropologique*. Publications de l'Ecole Française d'Extrême-Orient, vol. 147. Paris: Ecole française d'Extrême-Orient.

Widdess, Richard. 2010. "The Emergence of Dhrupad." In *Hindustani Music, Thirteenth to Twentieth Centuries*, edited by Joep Bor, Françoise "Nalini" Delvoye, Jane Harvey and Emmie te Nijenhuis, 117–140. New Delhi: Manohar Publishers & Distributors.

Zarrilli, Phillip B. 1998. *When the Body Becomes All Eyes: Paradigms, Discourses, and Practices of Power in Kalarippayattu, a South Indian Martial Art*. Delhi: Oxford University Press.

# Part IV

# EMBODIED MEANING-MAKING

– 10 –

# Osho in a Nutshell? Dynamic Meditation and the Relationship between Bodily Performance and Meaning-Making

HENRIETTE HANKY

This chapter discusses how contemporary performances of mind–body techniques relate to the authoritative figures and institutions that lay claim to them. The case under investigation is OSHO Dynamic Meditation, the most famous meditation technique created by the controversial guru Osho (Bhagwan Shree Rajneesh) that has been practiced from the early days of the Neo-Sannyas Movement in the 1970s until today. Dynamic Meditation has five characteristic stages leading meditators from chaotic breathing, cathartic explosion, and complete exhaustion to stillness and celebration. Both sannyasins and scholars have referred to the technique as a "microcosm" of Osho's teaching and method. Based on ethnographic observations and interviews from Osho-related meditation centers in Scandinavia, Germany, and India, the chapter scrutinizes this claim and enquires in what ways performing Dynamic Meditation can be understood as an embodied reception of Osho's work. A stable communicative form in an otherwise dispersed and diverse field, Dynamic Meditation has a specific affective dramaturgy tailored to induce experiences in need of interpretation. How meditators make sense of their experience varies according to contextual factors and can be detached from Osho's authority. Still, the communities under investigation share discourses around therapy and meditation that are reproduced and legitimized through bodily techniques (such as Dynamic Meditation) that again socialize newcomers into the communicative milieu of the Sannyas scene.

Keywords: Osho, Dynamic Meditation, mind–body techniques, experience, meaning-making, authority, communicative form

## Introduction

Many mind–body techniques that gained popularity in twentieth-century counterculture have outlived their composers and spread into new contexts. Examples reach from Maharishi Mahesh Yogi's *Transcendental Meditation* over Arthur Janov's *Primal Scream Therapy* to Gabrielle Roth's *5Rhythms*. With increasing historical distance to their original contexts, it is worthwhile to investigate how stable these techniques are both in terms of how they are performed and how they are made sense of by contemporary practitioners (see Prohl 2017). In yoga cultures, for example, there are great variations regarding gurus' authority and lineage logics as well as questions of orthopraxy (Ciołkosz 2017; Wildcroft 2020). In this chapter, I look at *OSHO Dynamic Meditation* to investigate how contemporary performances of the technique relate to the controversial guru Osho (Bhagwan Shree Rajneesh, 1931–1990) and his teachings.[1]

Dynamic Meditation is Osho's most famous technique and has been practiced since the early days of the Neo-Sannyas Movement[2] in the 1970s. Today, it is still a common denominator binding the scattered Sannyas scene together. Dynamic Meditation has five characteristic stages leading meditators from chaotic breathing, cathartic explosion and complete exhaustion to stillness and celebration. This is a case of a technique that was "explicitly designed to shock us out of our habitual patterns of thought and behaviour" (Urban 2015, 59) and claimed to have an intrinsic effect on body and mind. Understanding these claims as legitimization strategies while at the same time taking seriously the bodily effects of the practice, makes the question of how the discursive and the bodily interlink in contemporary performances particularly intriguing.

Both sannyasins and scholars have referred to the technique as a "microcosm" of Osho's teaching and method (Urban 2015, 59)—a kind

1. Osho has been controversial due to problematic experimentations with violence and sex in the Indian ashram of the 1970s, as well as his fleet of Rolls Royces and criminal activities in the USA in the 1980s (Urban 2015, 25–26, 76–77, 130–136). Recently, encouraged by the #MeToo movement, (former) sannyasins have made public sexual abuse and abuse of power cases, including child abuse, accusing prominent figures of the scene as well as Osho himself. While many sannyasins assert that they have not been affected, sexual abuse has been a systemic problem in the Sannyas movement (for a recent report of a survivor see Dunn 2022; for the topic of abuse in guru movements and Osho in particular see Lucia 2018, forthcoming).
2. Playing with the Hindu concept of *saṃnyās* that denotes initiation into becoming a renunciate (*saṃnyāsin*), Osho called his saffron-clad followers, whose lifestyle was quite opposed to Hindu renunciates, (neo-)sannyasins.

of "Osho in a nutshell." My chapter scrutinizes this claim and enquires in what ways performing Dynamic Meditation can be understood as an embodied reception of Osho's work. In the absence of the late guru, to what extent is Osho's symbolic cosmos inscribed into the form of the meditation—rather than merely attributed to it (or not)? How does the meditation become meaningful to its screaming, jumping, and dancing practitioners today?

These questions speak to a classic debate in the study of religion, namely how experiences become meaningful as *religious* experiences (Taves 2009, 2010; Stausberg 2010). A well-established way to approach the problem, often glossed as constructivist, is by analyzing how actors acquire the vocabulary to interpret their experiences by way of socialization into their religious communities and their discursive repertoires (S. T. Katz 2020). Recently, sociologists of religion have sought to expand this attributional approach by studying how the bodily and material aspects of practices shape how and why actors consider them "special" (Pagis 2010; Winchester and Pagis 2022). This perspective resonates with the growing field of aesthetics of religion which calls for an "analysis of sensory practices *within* religious traditions (for instance, how a religious body is created, how distinctions and norms are persuasively imagined, implemented and embodied, or experiences of 'other worlds' are trained by specific engagements of the senses)" (Grieser and Johnston 2017, 15).

Combining social constructivist and embodiment theories, I approach Dynamic Meditation from a sociological perspective as a "communicative form" (Knoblauch 2020a, 2020b). The concept of the "communicative form" has been developed by sociologist Hubert Knoblauch to designate fixed and institutionalized sequences of action that structure social reality. In this line of thinking, which integrates impulses from ethnomethodology, social form and cultural content are intimately connected. Social reality is created by *how* actions are performed. Building on earlier social constructivist work, notably Thomas Luckmann's work on "communicative genres" like sermons in the realm of religion (Luckmann 2013; Günthner and Knoblauch 1995), Knoblauch's notion of communicative forms goes beyond language and includes corporeal and material aspects of communication. It is therefore suited to analyze how non-verbal bodily forms of institutionalized (inter)action such as meditation or dance "make sense," i.e., generate meaning through their form. While studying situational performance with all its variations, approaching Dynamic Meditation as a communicative form allows me to address the features of the fixed form that stabilize the social reality of the post-Osho milieus under investigation.

In the first part of the chapter, I will show how Dynamic Meditation, itself an eclectic collage combining elements from yoga, tantric "Crazy Wisdom" and Sufism with impulses from Reichian and primal therapy, became Osho's hallmark meditation that still serves to legitimize his guruhood. After Osho's death, the canonization of the technique was reinforced by the OSHO International Foundation's branding and copyrighting efforts. In the second part of the chapter, I will investigate how Dynamic Meditation is performed and understood at contemporary Osho centers based on my ethnographic research in India, Germany, and Scandinavia. By contrasting empirical cases, I will analyze how structures at different Osho centers, the situational performance of the communicative form, and individual meaning-making relate.

## OSHO Dynamic Meditation: A Canonized Form in a Contested Field

Today, Dynamic Meditation is performed in its canonical form throughout the loosely connected scene that the Sannyas movement has developed into. It is a common denominator in a diverse field with a confusing array of events, groups, small communities, centers, and individual therapists. While the OSHO International Foundation (OIF) runs the former main ashram in Pune and is the legal owner of Osho's intellectual property—books, recordings, and other media, as well as meditation and therapy techniques—many sannyasins are critical of their politics and form attachments to local communities rather than to the OIF. Attitudes toward Osho also vary with participants ranging from devoted Osho sannyasins to self-explorers without further interest in the late guru.

There are several reasons for the techniques rather than the guru forming the glue for the contemporary scene. After the collapse of the Oregon commune, Osho's imprisonment, and the sannyasins' exodus from the US and back to India—all of which have recently been covered by the Netflix documentary *Wild Wild Country*—the movement reinvented itself. Bhagwan Shree Rajneesh declared the religion of "Rajneeshism" dead and eventually changed his name to Osho, conveniently distancing himself from the bad press on Bhagwan, the "sex guru" or "guru of the rich." The former ashram in Pune turned into the OSHO International Meditation Resort, marketed for wealthier and less counterculturally inclined audiences (Urban 2015). Marion Goldman attributes the survival of the Osho movement to these efforts that the OSHO International Foundation has intensified after Osho's death. Rather than trying to remain a guru movement or become an institutionalized religion, she argues, they redirected their focus to becoming a "global cultural influence" (Goldman 2014, 191). Throughout these upheavals and (de-) institutionalization periods, Dynamic Meditation as well as other core meditation techniques such as Kundalini Meditation remained stable.

The OIF's branding and copyrighting strategies also contributed to stabilizing the meditation techniques in their fixed form. The OIF section *OSHO Global Connections* oversees the Osho centers around the world to ensure that they do not infringe copyright and follow their guidelines. The OSHO Global Connections guidelines state: "The OSHO Meditations should be done exactly as Osho created them, as they are scientifically designed" (OSHO Global Connections 2021) and advise facilitators to stick to the exact wording of the standard instructions when guiding meditations.

While the copyright issue has become a major conflict—and court case—between the OIF and other Osho centers and initiatives, it evolves mainly around questions of ownership and rightful heritage. I have met many sannyasins who are highly critical of the OIF and visited centers that resist or at least bend their rules. However, I have yet to come across an Osho center that changed the instructions for Dynamic Meditation. The idea that the technique is efficient in itself, independent of organizational politics or guru devotion, is widespread. When I interviewed Preethi, a meditator and facilitator at *Osho UTA* in Cologne, she explained: "I don't have to think about anything, whether it's right or wrong, because I do it according to this structure, and if I do it in this structure, everything is already right" (interview with Preethi, 2022).[3]

This charismatization of techniques rather than individuals corresponds to the preferences of a milieu that privileges their own experiences over external authorities. While this might seem counter-intuitive for a guru movement, experience-oriented self-spirituality (Heelas 1996) was at the core of Osho's teachings, even if made to fit with the social form of the master-disciple relationship. For this reason, the downplaying of Osho's importance that characterizes parts of the contemporary scene is often legitimized with Osho's own teachings reminding sannyasins that they should focus on themselves, not on him.

As is the case with other gurus and their signature techniques (see Newcombe, this volume), fashioning Osho as the author and creator of Dynamic Meditation serves the legitimization of his authority and safeguards the OSHO International Foundation's institutional power. From a historical point of view, Osho was not the source but himself part of

3. All names are changed. Interview quotes that are not English in the original are translated by the author.

larger processes of transmission and reception. However, the form in which Dynamic Meditation has been consolidated is the result of an intentional and reflexive composition. While the question about the relation between intention and effect remains to be empirically answered, the first step is to look at the reasoning behind how the technique is built up.

## Reflexive Eclecticism Molded into Five Stages

In the canonized instructions, Dynamic Meditation is introduced as follows:

> Dynamic Meditation is a fast, intense and thorough way to break old, ingrained patterns in the bodymind that keep one imprisoned in the past, and to experience the freedom, the witnessing, silence and peace that are hidden behind those prison walls.
>
> (OSHO 2013, 80)

As pointed out by the OIF (OSHO Global Connections 2021), this is not a spontaneous statement but a condensation of Osho's talks on Dynamic Meditation. It is informative of the discourses and cultural-historical influences that continue to shape the technique.

First, the basic assumption that Osho put into practice in Dynamic Meditation is that therapy is a precondition for meditation. Inherent in this assumption is the diagnosis that "modern man" is corrupted by society's destructive conditioning. Troubled not least by repressed sexual drives, modern man, according to Osho, cannot simply sit down, meditate, and become enlightened. Psychotherapeutic groundwork in the form of catharsis is necessary to find peace: "Unless the repressions in your mind are released, you cannot proceed further" (OSHO International Foundation 2012, 4). This causal as well as temporal order is implemented in the sequential process of Dynamic Meditation.[4]

Second, Osho's understanding of therapy is highly influenced by post-Freudian psychoanalysts, particularly Wilhelm Reich, and Humanistic Psychology as it was developed by Abraham Maslow and colleagues and the many therapeutic approaches developed around the Esalen Institute in California from the 1960s onward.[5] The term

4. Cult critics have portrayed Dynamic Meditation and similar techniques as gateways to manipulation through psychological destabilization (see e.g., Remski 2018).
5. In the 1970s, therapists flocked to Poona, and a multitude of groups, from Encounter to Primal therapy, gave the ashram the reputation of an "Esalen of the East" (Urban 2015, 44).

"bodymind" expresses the assertion that there is a nexus between the physical and the psychological, the mind and the body. Drawing on Wilhelm Reich's idea of the "body armor" (*Körperpanzer*), Osho asserted that trauma and destructive behavioral patterns manifest in the body and can likewise be overcome through the body. Dynamic Meditation is understood to be a "jet method" (OSHO International Foundation 2012, 83–85), a radical and fast method for catharsis and transformation. Osho's teachings share several characteristic traits with the wider Human Potential Movement. One is the assertion that individuals can unlock and realize their full potential through certain self-techniques. Another trait that Dynamic Meditation shares with techniques such as contact improvisation, 5Rhythms, or family constellation, is a performative and affective staging of emotions. The instructions state: "A little acting often helps to get you started" (OSHO 2013, 81). By performatively expressing emotions, "real" emotions are supposed to be tapped into and thus released.

How are these assumptions put into the instructions for Dynamic Meditation? In its canonical form, Dynamic Meditation lasts one hour and is performed in the morning before breakfast. The standard instructions stress that the meditation is an "individual experience" and ask participants to "remain oblivious of others around you." To this end, meditators are instructed to keep their eyes closed throughout the meditation or wear a blindfold. Furthermore, meditators are advised to "be continuously alert, conscious, aware, whatsoever you do. Remain a witness" (OSHO International Foundation 2021).

The meditation is accompanied by music, composed by sannyasin and New Age musician Georg Deuter (Swami Chaitanya Hari), which changes in mood and instrumentation, indicating the beginning of each new stage. In the *first stage* (10 minutes), meditators breathe "chaotically" through the nose, "intense, deep, fast, without rhythm, with no pattern," while using "natural body movements to help you to build up your energy." This energy is supposed to be released in the *second stage* (10 minutes) where meditators "EXPLODE" and "[c]onsciously go mad" by expressing "whatever is there." Meditators "[s]cream, shout, cry, jump, kick, shake, dance, sing, laugh." In the *third stage* (10 minutes), meditators are instructed to "exhaust yourself completely" by jumping up and down with arms raised shouting the mantra "Hoo! Hoo! Hoo!," while letting the sound "hammer deep into the sex center" when landing on the flats of the feet. A shouted "Stop!" in the recording initiates the *fourth stage* (15 minutes) and orders meditators to "[f]reeze wherever you are" and remain completely still: "A cough, a movement, anything, will dissipate the energy flow and the effort will be lost. Be a witness to everything that

**Figure 5.** Illustration of Dynamic Meditation's five stages. Doodle by the author.

is happening to you." In the *fifth stage* (15 minutes), participants start moving again and "[c]elebrate" by dancing to uplifting music (OSHO International Foundation 2021).

The one-hour meditation is thus a miniature of the larger envisioned process from therapy to meditation, from madness to bliss. It follows a dramaturgy that is supposed to lead meditators through a curated experience.

For assembling the five stages, Osho blended elements of existing techniques ranging from yogic *prāṇāyāma* and psychotherapeutic breathwork methods, Primal Scream Therapy, Sufi *dhikr*, Crazy Wisdom methods, and Gurdjieff Movements (Urban 2015, 63). Urban attributes the eclectic meditation also to its "late capitalist global context, in which ideas from 'East' and 'West' are increasingly melding together and often intersecting in the physical body itself" (Urban 2015, 62). For Osho and his followers, this eclecticism was no sign of unoriginality but rather of Osho's knowledgeability in mind–body techniques from both "East" and "West." The narrative in Osho's accounts on Dynamic Meditation is that he tested and combined the most efficacious techniques available for self-realization. Like countercultural experimenters such as Abraham Maslow, who investigated religious "peak experiences" and aimed at intentionally inducing them, Osho also claimed a "scientific" approach to spiritual experience:

> My method is more scientific and less religious. It gives you a religious experience, but the method itself is more scientific than religious, more psychological than spiritual. The modern mind only accepts the body and the mind; the spiritual realm is taken as a romantic fallacy. So you cannot begin anything from the spiritual. At the most, you can start from the psychological.
>
> (OSHO International Foundation 2012, 4)

This narrative concerning Osho's geniality and the virtue of existing contemplative and psychotherapeutic techniques legitimizes Dynamic Meditation's efficacy up until today.

Looking at the cultural-historical formation that Dynamic Meditation is a part of, it becomes clear that discourses around embodiment do not only inform a scholarly etic perspective. There was plenty of contact as well as overlap between spiritual and therapeutic practitioners and academics in the 1960/70s counterculture (Stuckrad 2003; Kripal 2007). Actors such as Osho reflexively utilized psychological and physiological knowledge to work on practitioners' bodies and cognition. For sannyasins, many of them academics themselves, Osho's academic background as well as the reflexivity and referentiality of his techniques are important.

For analyzing the bodily effects of the technique, the fact that it was intentionally designed to induce certain states must be considered. On the other hand, how the technique affects practitioners and how experiences are made sense of, needs to be investigated empirically. In the following ethnographic part of the chapter, I, therefore, look at both the discursive and the performative, corporeal aspects of practitioners' experiences: I will isolate some corporeal aspects of Dynamic Meditation as a communicative form and look at how these inform practitioners' meaning-making. But I will also show that the mentioned discourses around the technique's efficacy shape how practitioners evaluate their experiences.

## Doing Ethnography While Wearing a Blindfold: Methodological Remarks

The observational and interview data concerning Dynamic Meditation I draw on in the following have been generated over several research periods. I first participated in Dynamic Meditation in 2017 during an exploratory study on the Berlin Sannyas scene. For my doctoral research, I conducted a focused ethnography of meditation retreats and centers associated with Osho in Scandinavia, Germany, and India (2019–2023). During fieldwork, I participated in Dynamic Meditation at OSHO Studio in Berlin, Osho UTA in Cologne (Germany), OSHO Risk in Brædstrup (Denmark), Dharma Mountain in Hedalen (Norway), Oshodham in Delhi, and the OSHO International Meditation Resort in Pune (India).

The most important source for investigating how Dynamic Meditation is performed is observing it in action. However, there are several challenges in doing this. Observing others while doing Dynamic Meditation is generally frowned upon in the field, not only because of the intimacy of emotional expression but also because meditators' attention should be on themselves, not on others. Consequently, videography, which would be the most rewarding method for studying performance, is not appropriate in this intimate setting. However, the "collective solitude" (Pagis 2019b) of a meditation class is still a social situation where actors are aware of other bodies around them and tacitly coordinate their movements with them. From many conversations I had, I know that people do peek at each other, particularly newcomers trying to figure out how to "do it right."

However, participants do not even have to break the rules and peek to notice how others perform Dynamic Meditation, the other senses are informative as well. They hear people breathing hard, screaming, or smashing pillows to the ground, shouting "Hoo" and turning silent, they feel the vibrations of the floor when people jump, and they might even perceive the room turning damp and people around them sweaty. For me as an ethnographer, this solved a dilemma. I could observe the situation without staring and thus, as I was not observing individual persons, my observations were mostly de-identified from the start.

The interview material I draw on to show how participants make sense of their bodily experiences has been collected at or around the mentioned research sites. However, the experiences that my conversation partners talk about are not fresh impressions but sometimes memories from several years ago. This means that these accounts are already narratively processed. It is therefore difficult to reconstruct any "actual" (whatever this may mean in the first place) experiences from these accounts. Nevertheless, their reports show which parts of the bodily experience they find relevant and what frameworks they turn to for making sense of them.

## Performing Dynamic Meditation in the Contemporary Post-Osho Field

### Contexts and Frames

Dynamic Meditation is practiced in different settings and event formats that again coincide with varying organizational structures and groups of participants. For how meditators experience Dynamic Meditation, it matters if it happens in a resort setting, a meditation retreat assembled by an "enlightened," or an urban meditation challenge. A tourist trying out something weird and exotic will make a different experience than someone committed to a therapeutic process of self-discovery. Institutional structures, event formats, socio-spatial factors, and previous stocks of knowledge shape how participants understand what they are doing when they do Dynamic Meditation. Furthermore, it is in interactions with others, authority figures as well as co-participants, that meditators verbalize their experiences of Dynamic, pick up others' understandings or reject them.

I will give three examples of how these interpretive communities vary. In the OSHO International Meditation Resort in Pune—the former main ashram run by the OIF—old sannyasins, spiritual wanderers, and curious tourists intermingle. Given the size of the resort and the fluctuation of visitors, it is fully possible to remain anonymous. While the local therapists cannot address each individual guest in person, the resort still provides plenty of material for scaffolding their guests' experiences. Not only do visitors receive leaflets with information on each of the provided meditations, but video instructions with the canonical wording are also played on a big screen at the beginning of each session and are available on touchscreens outside. In addition, Osho's former physician Swami Amrito (George Meredith aka John Andrews) gives a weekly evening talk on Dynamic Meditation where he explains the "science" behind the technique and illustrates typical mistakes that according to him corrupt the whole process.[6] Amrito's talk is clear in stating that if Dynamic Meditation is not done exactly as Osho prescribed it, all efforts are in vain. All this illustrates the OIF's effort to preserve Dynamic Meditation in its fixed, branded form and to claim exegetical monopoly.

A second example are the Dynamic Meditation sessions I joined at the Danish countryside community OSHO Risk. At Risk, community ideals and flat hierarchies have led to a diverse, but cordial set of permanent residents and temporary guests with varying degrees of commitment to Osho. The group I meditated with in spring 2022 consisted of a handful of sannyasins and non-sannyasins in their 20s and 30s. While responsibility for preparing the room and turning on the music rotated, they usually dispensed with the formal instruction sequence and just wished each other a good meditation. This easy-going approach to meditation also translated into their performance. There was much more variation in how the meditators filled the stages than in more regulated settings. While there was no consensus about Osho, the meditators shared a common understanding that individual self-expression trumped orthopraxy. The daily screened Osho video discourses as well as personal conversations provided sufficient available frames for interpreting experiences, but there was no central authority invested in explaining meditators' experiences to them.

6. The talk is available on YouTube: see www.youtube.com/watch?v=0HUrWofjyVs&t=28s (accessed February 3, 2023).

A last example of another different type of frame and interpretive community is the Norwegian retreat center Dharma Mountain built around "enlightened" Vasant Swaha, a Norwegian Osho sannyasin who now initiates sannyasins of his own. Here, I joined Dynamic Meditation as an obligatory part of a three-week summer retreat claimed to have been specifically designed by Swaha. This notably echoes Osho's narrative of the enlightened master assembling efficacious methods for spiritual transformation:

> That's how I have designed these retreats: first you can [...] empty yourself out in many different ways. You start feeling instead of thinking. [...] If you are restless, sad, angry—with all these things that you normally carry with you ... who wants to be in silence? [...] First all this has to go. That is my recipe.
>
> (Vasant Swaha 2021)

The structure of the whole retreat mirrored the dramaturgy of Dynamic Meditation, from catharsis to stillness. Swaha's retreats thus not only integrate Osho meditations into the program but reproduce Osho's method of intentionally combining techniques in a therapeutic process design. Different from Risk's focus on individuality, Swaha's retreats encourage "surrender" and trust in the process that Swaha has conceived. The main authority that participants turn to for making sense of their experiences is Swaha himself who answers his followers' letters during Satsang. In addition, Swaha's closest disciples function as "caretakers" that participants can address their questions and concerns to. While meditators share experiences with each other as well, the social form of the master-disciple relationship with its possibilities for sanctioning deviations leaves no doubt that it is Swaha who has the final interpretive authority.

In addition, at all these centers, guests find a selection of Osho books. At some of the centers, these are laid out in the space where meditators have tea after meditation. Particularly in more anonymous settings, I have often observed that people sit down and browse through an Osho book after meditation rather than talking to other people. Here, the Osho books provide prompts for making sense of an experience just made.

The social, organizational, and material variations of the described contexts clearly provide different frames for how meditators understand their Dynamic Meditation practice. However, there are also aspects of framing that were stable across settings and thus belong to the consolidated communicative form.

In all settings, meditators entered the already prepared space of a meditation hall. They found tissue boxes (for cleaning the nose for chaotic breathing), cushions (for hitting during the catharsis stage), and blindfolds. Before the start of the meditation, I observed participants perform an almost choreographed preparation routine of getting themselves and their personal meditation space ready. Beyond practical reasons, these preparations frame Dynamic Meditation as a special experiential time and space demarcated from everyday life. Particularly putting on blindfolds which materially shut off the visual sense performs the turn inward and away from the outside world. The blindfolds nudge participants into a perceptive shift, as they make focusing on intero- and proprioception (sensing the body from the inside and outside) easier. These pre-sequences that meditators perform even before the gong signals the start of the first stage, frame the experience of the following hour as an intimate journey inward.

## Performance and Experience

As laid out above, the idea of Dynamic Meditation as a therapeutic cleansing process to make space for experiencing silence is embedded into countercultural and spiritual discourses. However, meditators also perform actions with their bodies in the five stages of Dynamic Meditation that produce experiences that are particularly easily interpretable in these terms. Moving through the stages, particularly the emotional expression in the second stage, is affective and makes the performance a personal, subjective experience. In her work on Christian events, sociologist of religion Meike Haken coined the term "affective dramaturgy" to describe the affective dynamics related to the "temporal unfolding of the event" (Haken 2020, 117). This fits particularly well for the communicative form of Dynamic Meditation with its five-stage build-up that guides meditators through different bodily and emotional states.

In the catharsis stage, meditators are instructed to release old tensions and suppressed emotions. As noted above, this presupposes an idea of an "inner space" where suppressed emotions and past trauma are stored and from where they can be released. This shared knowledge is not only transmitted and received discursively, but also embodied. Through Dynamic Meditation (and other embodied self-exploration techniques) this interiority is created and trained performatively.

In the instructions for the catharsis, the affectivity of emotional expression, even if theatrical, is acknowledged: "A little acting can help you get started" (OSHO International Foundation 2021). While the goal is for emotions to be "real," their release starts from a script. As among others sociologist Jack Katz has shown, sensually perceiving the bodily effects of emotional display is so affective that even fake laughing or fake crying can become overwhelming (J. Katz 1999; Knoblauch 2020a, 95–98). Rather than replicating the field understanding of "emotions coming up," we can understand the experiences that people have in the catharsis stage as effects of the communicative form that they perform with their bodies. As participants feel themselves feeling and make the expressed emotions become their own, connected to their own stories, their experience becomes subjective.

When Bhavya, a meditator I met in Cologne, told me what she liked about active meditations and bodywork, she said:

> I noticed that this bodywork, these dynamic meditations, are taking me into myself, you know? And not just like Zen, sitting there quietly and uh no idea, you know? But this dynamic ... bodywork, that really got me in touch with my issues.
>
> (Interview with Bhavya, 2022)

That Bhavya stresses a feeling of intimacy—she feels in touch with herself and works through her issues by using her body—points to the affectivity of the communicative form. She understands Dynamic Meditation and similar techniques as utterly personal experiences that she makes sense of in a therapeutic language.

Dynamic Meditation is a group interaction, and the other bodies around are important for the individual meditator. They help not only to coordinate one's own movements, but also enhance the individual experience. However, the social norms that shape everyday interaction, are partly set aside. This pertains mainly to the "feeling rules" (Hochschild 1979) that prescribe that you should not scream and "go mad" in front of other people. The experience of being allowed to express feelings is among the most common descriptions of what participants appreciate about Dynamic Meditation.

Preethi, for whom Dynamic Meditation was an entry point to becoming a sannyasin, reports:

> I found it incredibly liberating for me to allow these emotions in this structure. [...] And that was simply good for me [...] to have a fixed framework where I knew that once a day, I would feel myself and let everything out.
>
> (Interview with Preethi, 2022)

In both Bhavya's and Preethi's accounts, the idea of an inner true self is apparent that is usually constrained by everyday life, but which can and should be expressed. While this idea is widespread in contemporary therapy and self-help culture (Illouz 2008; Madsen 2018), Bhavya and Preethi share Osho-typical assumptions around the bodymind and appreciate the unrestrained bodily expression.

While both talked about their experiences as life-changing, their frame of reference is more therapeutic than spiritual. Other practitioners embed their experiences into more spiritual frameworks. In the following quote, Prem Govind, a meditator from Berlin, recalls experiences he had during Dynamic Meditation about ten years ago:

> [In Dynamic], I suddenly discovered kind of something new for me every day. From the first moment, chaotic breathing, everything goes haywire, the whole life flies apart. Then the catharsis, where I [...] experienced everything from almost feeling nothing to completely freaking out and experienced states where I didn't know ... what it was all about. Where I then was brought back to my own roots. And in the "Hoo," which I could not have held out for even a minute at the beginning, later I jumped through and thought: What was that? I stood dripping like a waterfall and jumped for ten minutes as if nothing had happened. And there I stood in a kind of ... *baf* ... "Stop." It just said "Stop," I was standing, it was dripping, and it was a completely different moment ... *Silence happened* ... [English in original, H.H.] That was the turning point for me, where I thought, what happened now? At that time, I still hadn't read Osho. "Stop."
>
> (Interview with Prem Govind, 2017)

Prem Govind reports an experience of transcendence, "a completely different moment," and in going through the stages, is reflexive about the processual nature of his experience. He interprets it in Osho's language as "Silence happened." However, he only partly theorizes the experience. Instead, the narration remains close to the bodily sensations and even resorts to onomatopoeia—"*baf*"—conveying a non-discursive surplus of the experience, something that the mind can only be puzzled by. By portraying it as unaffected by reading Osho, Govind presents his experience as a result of the technique, not of preconceptions.

In Govind's narrative, he symbolically performs Osho's vision of a journey from madness to meditative bliss. Can this be accounted for by the bodily effects of the technique? Looking at these stages from a strictly bodily perspective, half an hour of extremely strenuous movement (chaotic breathing, cathartic explosion, jumping) culminates in 15 minutes of complete motionlessness—which is also physically demanding—before ending with 15 minutes of effortless dancing.

In her work in the sociology of meditation, Michal Pagis describes the shift from "doing meditation" to "being done by meditation" as a core phenomenological characteristic of meditators' experiences (Pagis 2019a, 63–65). She stresses that a common goal for meditators is to experience a flip where meditating no longer feels like doing but like something is happening *to* them. For that to happen, meditators train to shift their attention from the outside, the social sphere, to their "inner lining" (described as a "somatic inversion" by Winchester and Pagis 2022). This is already prepared by putting on the blindfolds as discussed above. Although very different from the Vipassana meditation that Pagis studied, this meditative turn inward characterizes Dynamic Meditation as well.

Dynamic Meditation is, in fact, so physical that meditators are forced to attend to their bodies. The transition from high-intensity jumping to complete stillness produces a state where participants are very aware of their bodily sensations. Meditators feel their heart pounding and sweat running, they are out of breath, their mouth is dry, and their muscles are tight. But instead of tending to these sensations by drinking, stretching, or resting, they remain frozen for 15 minutes which creates a heightened awareness of these uncomfortable sensations. Different from the somatic inversions in Vipassana where meditators learn to keep their attention focused on the breath instead of their thoughts, Dynamic Meditation's form produces such intense bodily sensations that they push to the fore and demand meditators' attention.[7]

In their study of Christian fasting and Buddhist meditation, Winchester and Pagis show how these practices trigger meaning-making processes by

> directing actors' attentions to dimensions of corporeal experience that would otherwise remain hidden and disrupting their everyday sense-making routines, social roles, and identities. These kind of novel experiential disruptions, in turn, "call out" for interpretation as they throw actors into a search after explanations.
>
> (Winchester and Pagis 2022, 14)

Reading Osho and interpreting experiences through the lens of Osho's teachings, as Prem Govind eventually did, is common. But the technique itself does not determine a specific relationship to Osho. Particularly in contexts where the guru is of little importance, people find other frames of reference. The Norwegian Dharma Mountain, the center built around the former Osho disciple and spiritual master Vasant Swaha, can serve as an example of this dependency on context. The following quote from Dharma Mountain's website about Dynamic Meditation shows that Swaha's disciples can relate the practice to their guru: "Only with the help of Dynamic can I be open and able to receive the beauty and love that Swaha has to give" (Dharma Mountain 2021). Dynamic Meditation

7. To be clear, participants regularly fail to put the script into practice. Exercising the stages as instructed requires training and discipline, even for young, able-bodied practitioners. As the technique presupposes a certain physical condition, it excludes groups of practitioners.

thus becomes not only a necessary cleansing to be able to meditate but also to be receptive to the master. Meditators link back their experiences to the context in which they were made and reinforce the social roles that structure them.

## Conclusion

I set out to examine the idea that Dynamic Meditation is a "microcosm" of Osho's teaching and method and asked whether this makes performing the meditation an embodied Osho reception. I showed that Dynamic Meditation is the most popular of a canon of practices that bind the heterogeneous and fragmented post-Osho field together. It is safeguarded by the OSHO International Foundation through branding and copyrighting. While these efforts are contested, most sannyasins still share the idea that Dynamic Meditation is a perfect technique not to be tinkered with. Its efficacy is attributed to Osho's insight into the psyche of modern man, knowledge of the Eastern and Western methods and finally the idea of his "scientific" experimentation. From its formation, Dynamic Meditation has been conceptualized and legitimized as a technique for exploring and expressing the self and for inducing specific states.

However, if Dynamic Meditation is understood by practitioners as "Osho in a nutshell," depends on the knowledge performers acquire. The centers that I visited for my ethnographic research vary in terms of social structure, event formats, and relationship to Osho, making them different interpretive communities. However, they are still prominently shaped by sannyasins who have spent a long time in the Osho movement. Discourses around therapy and meditation pervade the settings and are transmitted by the facilitators to the meditators as a repertoire for interpreting their experiences. While in field language Dynamic Meditation is an opportunity for expressing the self, I argue that it brings about embodied processes of subjectivation which vary in different settings and can be linked up to different forms of community and authority relations. In some settings, Dynamic Meditation creates a community of practitioners, in others it also reinforces a master-disciple relationship.

While institutionalized interpretations can be rejected, a specific affective dramaturgy is inherent to the form of Dynamic Meditation. With its extremely physical and affective sequences, it is hard to be unmoved even for people unfamiliar with Osho. The communicative form of Dynamic Meditation performatively constructs a therapeutic self-relation and an imagined "inner space" from where suppressed emotions can be released. In addition, the dramaturgy from intense movement to complete stillness produces sensations that are notably different from everyday experience and thus lend themselves to religious meaning-making.

This echoes Grieser and Johnston's perspective that "perceiving and meaning-making is influenced *by* religious cultivation and judgment of the senses, independent of whether people see themselves as adherents or not" (Grieser and Johnston 2017, 15). Many of the therapeutic discourses that make up the symbolic order of the Osho field have meanwhile become diffused into mainstream culture. This means that also participants without specific knowledge of Osho, often share assumptions of the field about the "bodymind" and the need for the release of tensions in today's stressful world.

Dynamic Meditation functions as a stable institution holding the dispersed field together as meditators validate field discourses through their own subjective embodied experiences (see Pagis 2010). At the same time, their experiences are shaped by the contexts of the retreats, centers, and communities that provide frames for interpretation that are infused by these same discourses.

Dynamic Meditation shares many of the described traits with other forms of self-exploration and expression techniques that push participants out of their comfort zone for transformational purposes. Examples range from contact improvisation over neo-tantric bodywork and hyperventilation techniques, to substance-related rituals like Ayahuasca journeys (see Lucia 2020, 120–126). These techniques are not empty containers that are easily filled with new meaning as they depart from their cultural origins. While their meaning is not determined by their form, the unusual—and potentially destabilizing—physical and psychological experiences that they induce, make them less detachable from discursive frameworks than more "portable practices" such as unmarked forms of modern postural yoga (Csordas 2009). As puzzlement and search for meaning are part of the form, they are less likely to float completely free of institutional control. Therefore, practitioners often partake in chains of embodied transmission and reception that link their bodily practice back to certain therapeutic and spiritual discourses—even if they are not aware of it.

**Henriette Hanky** is a doctoral candidate and university lecturer in the Study of Religions at the University of Bergen, Norway. Her doctoral research focused on contemporary forms of the Osho/Sannyas movement in Europe and India. She has published articles on Osho-related meditation retreats, new religious movements and mediatization as well as on religion and embodiment.

## References


Ciołkosz, Matylda. 2017. "Proprioception over Dogma: Sources of Authority and Standards of Orthopraxy in Iyengar Yoga." *Religions of South Asia* 11(2–3): 207–230.

Csordas, Thomas J. 2009. "Introduction: Modalities of Transnational Transcendence." In *Transnational Transcendence*, edited by Thomas J. Csordas, 1–30. Berkeley, CA: University of California Press.

Dharma Mountain. 2021. "Dynamic Saves My Life." Retrieved May 12, 2021, from http://dharmamountain.com/dynamic-saves-my-life/.

Dunn, Lily. 2022. *Sins of My Father: A Daughter, a Cult, a Wild Unravelling*. London: Weidenfeld and Nicolson.

Goldman, Marion S. 2014. "Controversy, Cultural Influence, and the Osho/Rajneesh Movement." In *Controversial New Religions*, edited by James R. Lewis and Jesper Aagaard Petersen, 176–194. New York: Oxford University Press.

Grieser, Alexandra and Jay Johnston. 2017. "What Is an Aesthetics of Religion? From the Senses to Meaning—and Back Again." In *Aesthetics of Religion: A Connective Concept*, edited by Alexandra Grieser and Jay Johnston, 1–50. Berlin: De Gruyter.

Günthner, Susanne and Hubert Knoblauch. 1995. "Culturally Patterned Speaking Practices: The Analysis of Communicative Genres." *Pragmatics* 5(1): 1–32.

Haken, Meike. 2020. "Religious Emotions in Christian Events." In *Affect and Emotion in Multi-Religious Secular Societies*, edited by Christian von Scheve, Anna Berg, Meike Haken and Nur Ural, 114–131. New York: Routledge.

Heelas, Paul. 1996. *The New Age Movement: The Celebration of the Self and the Sacralization of Modernity*. Oxford: Blackwell.

Hochschild, Arlie Russel. 1979. "Emotion Work, Feeling Rules, and Social Structure." *American Journal of Sociology* 85(3): 551–575.

Illouz, Eva. 2008. *Saving the Modern Soul: Therapy, Emotions, and the Culture of Self-Help*. Berkeley, CA: University of California Press.

Katz, Jack. 1999. *How Emotions Work*. Chicago, IL: University of Chicago Press.

Katz, Steven T. 2020. "Exploring the Nature of Mystical Experience." In *The Cambridge Companion to Religious Experience*, edited by Paul K. Moser and Chad Meister, 239–260. Cambridge: Cambridge University Press.

Knoblauch, Hubert. 2020a. *The Communicative Construction of Reality*. London: Routledge.

——. 2020b. "Von kommunikativen Gattungen zu kommunikativen Formen: Konsequenzen des kommunikativen Konstruktivismus." In *Verfestigungen in der Interaktion. Konstruktionen, sequenzielle Muster, kommunikative Gattungen*, edited by Beate Weidner, Katharina König, Wolfgang Imo and Lars Wegner, 19–38. Berlin: De Gruyter.

Kripal, Jeffrey J. 2007. *Esalen: America and the Religion of No Religion.* Chicago, IL: University of Chicago Press.

Lucia, Amanda. 2018. "Guru Sex: Charisma, Proxemic Desire, and the Haptic Logics of the Guru-Disciple Relationship." *Journal of the American Academy of Religion* 86(4): 953–988.

——. 2020. *White Utopias: The Religious Exoticism of Transformational Festivals.* Oakland, CA: University of California Press.

——. Forthcoming. "The Guru and His 'Invading Army': Nativist Constructions of Osho's Rajneeshpuram in 'Wild Wild Country.'" In *Mythologizing and South Asian Religions, Literatures and Films*, edited by Diana Dimitrova.

Luckmann, Thomas. 2013. "Predigten, Moralpredigten und Moral predigen." In *Kommunikative Konstruktion von Moral*, edited by Jörg R. Bergmann and Thomas Luckmann, 80–111. Mannheim: Verlag für Gesprächsforschung.

Madsen, Ole Jacob. 2018. *The Psychologisation of Society: On the Unfolding of the Therapeutic in Norway*. London: Routledge.

OSHO. 2013. *Meditation: The First and Last Freedom. A Practical Guide to OSHO Meditations.* Pune: Osho Media International.

OSHO Global Connections. 2021. "Orientation Information for OSHO Centers." Retrieved March 26, 2021, from www.osho.com/static-informative-pages/orientation-information-osho-centers#Sannyas.

OSHO International Foundation, ed. 2012. *A Compendium on OSHO Dynamic Meditation.* Pune: Osho Media International.

——. 2021. *OSHO Dynamic Meditation.* Retrieved August 20, 2021, from www.osho.com/meditation/osho- active-meditations/osho-dynamic-meditation.

Pagis, Michal. 2010. "From Abstract Concepts to Experiential Knowledge: Embodying Enlightenment in a Meditation Center." *Qualitative Sociology* 33(4): 469–489.

——. 2019a. *Inward: Vipassana Meditation and the Embodiment of the Self.* Chicago, IL: University of Chicago Press.

——. 2019b. "The Sociology of Meditation." In *The Oxford Handbook of Meditation*, edited by Miguel Farias, David Brazier and Mansur Lalljee, 570–589. Oxford: Oxford University Press.

Prohl, Inken. 2017. "Same Forms, Same Sensations? The Practice of Sitting Still in Traditional Japanese and Contemporary Urban Settings." In *Eastspirit: Transnational Spirituality and Religious Circulation in East and West*, edited by Jørn Borup and Marianne Qvortrup Fibiger, 100–119. Leiden: Brill.

Remski, Matthew. 2018. "What That Rajneesh Documentary Leaves Out." Retrieved June 10, 2021, from http://matthewremski.com/wordpress/what-that-rajneesh-documentary-leaves-out/.

Stausberg, Michael. 2010. "From 1799 to 2009: Religious Experience Reconsidered—Background, Argument, Responses." *Religion* 40(4): 279–285.

Stuckrad, Kocku von. 2003. *Schamanismus und Esoterik: Kultur- und wissenschaftsgeschichtliche Betrachtungen*. Leuven: Peeters.

Taves, Ann. 2009. *Religious Experience Reconsidered: A Building-Block Approach to the Study of Religion and Other Special Things*. Princeton, NJ: Princeton University Press.

——. 2010. "Experience as Site of Contested Meaning and Value: The Attributional Dog and Its Special Tail." *Religion* 40(4): 317–323.

Urban, Hugh B. 2015. *Zorba the Buddha: Sex, Spirituality, and Capitalism in the Global Osho Movement*. Oakland, CA: University of California Press.

Vasant Swaha. 2021. "The Retreat Experience." Retrieved May 27, 2021, from http://vasantswaha.net/the-retreat-experience.

Wildcroft, Theodora. 2020. *Post-Lineage Yoga: From Guru to #MeToo*. Sheffield: Equinox.

Winchester, Daniel and Michal Pagis. 2022. "Sensing the Sacred: Religious Experience, Somatic Inversions, and the Religious Education of Attention." *Sociology of Religion* 83(1): 12–35.

-11-

# "Being Here Fully"

## Autoethnographic Approaches to Mindfulness-Based Stress Reduction as an Embodied Group Interaction of an Authentic Self

ALAN SCHINK

Alongside modern yoga, mindfulness meditation is considered to be a driving force for "revolutionizing" body–mind practices in Western societies. The Mindfulness-Based Stress Reduction (MBSR) program, developed in the late 1970s by the MIT-educated scientist Jon Kabat-Zinn, is of great importance here. MBSR positions itself predominantly within scientific and therapeutic discourses, while at the same time universalizing the method of mindfulness meditation. This chapter investigates what it means to be present in modern mindfulness and MBSR. Focus is laid upon the group setting and interaction in which mindfulness as an *embodied practice of being present* is enacted and cultivated. It is shown how discourses of authenticity are linked to embodied performances of "being here fully." The chapter is based on (auto-)ethnographic accounts, produced by the author as a practitioner and trained teacher of MBSR/mindfulness and sociologist in one person.

Keywords: mindfulness, MBSR, modern Buddhism, intercorporeality, authenticity

## Introduction

In this chapter I will describe autoethnographically what it means to be present in modern mindfulness, and particularly in the setting of

Mindfulness-Based Stress Reduction (MBSR). MBSR is a progressional 8-week intervention program to help the participants cope with stress, pain, and other forms of suffering through methods of mindfulness meditation. Special to MBSR is, as I will argue, the group setting and dynamic in which mindfulness as an *embodied practice of being present* is enacted and cultivated. While a large quantity of the mindfulness practice during the 8-week course consists of formal and informal exercises at home and in the daily routines of the individuals concerned, the mindful self is formed by embodied interaction with the social and spatial environment of which this self makes sense.

Although it is a "secular" program, MBSR is part of the so-called modern "meditation" or "contemplative movement" (Kucinskas 2018). Modern mindfulness and MBSR in this respect are crucially influenced by practices of "Western" Buddhism as well as by concepts of natural science (McMahan 2008), therapeutic and stress discourses (Cook 2017), and capitalistic and consumer demands (Purser 2019). As Sun (2014, 403) has demonstrated in a historical discourse analysis, since the mid-1970s there has been a trend of the "de-Buddhicisation of mindfulness," which "enabled the concept to enter the mainstream." Braun (2017) states that the innovator of MBSR and an important leader of the contemplative movement, Jon Kabat-Zinn, played a crucial role in "enchanting" the everyday experience of pain and stress within the language of modern mindfulness. This language is itself located within "romantic" and "naturalistic" discourses of "authenticity," particularly the semantics of "fullness" as carved out in various works by Charles Taylor (2007). In his bestseller *Full Catastrophe Living: Using the Wisdom of Our Body and Mind to Face Stress, Pain, and Illness* for example, Kabat-Zinn writes about the "*practice*" of meditation that "[w]e practice mindfulness by remembering to be present in all our waking moments" and that "[w]e are not trying to get somewhere else, only working at being where we already are and being here fully" (Kabat-Zinn 2005, 29–30). This often criticized so-called "present momentism" (Purser 2019, 90) is hence to be seen as a typical sort of language in modern mindfulness discourse. But it is more than that. It is also a manifestation of the modern concept of an autonomous self, developed in Europe and Northern America as part of an "ethics of authenticity" from the eighteenth century onwards. Within this discourse "the inner voice" instead of "external" moral sources such as God or the state "is important because it tells us what is the right thing to do. Being in touch with our moral feelings would matter here, as a means to the end of acting rightly" (Taylor 1991, 26). In a "secular world," Taylor writes:

> we all see our lives, and/or the space wherein we live our lives, as having a certain moral/spiritual shape. Somewhere, in some activity or condition, lies a fullness, a richness; that is in that place (activity or condition), life is fuller, richer, deeper, more worth while [*sic*], more admirable, more what it should be. [...] Perhaps this sense of fullness is something we just catch glimpse of from afar off; we have the powerful intuition of what fullness would be, were we to be in this condition, e.g., of peace and wholeness; or able to act on that level, of integrity or generosity or abandonment or self-forgetfulness. But sometimes there will be moments of experienced fullness, of joy and fulfillment, where we feel ourselves there.
>
> (Taylor 2007, 5)

By being "willing to pay attention in the moment and remember that we have only moments to live" (Kabat-Zinn 2005, 30), mindfulness, in the framework of MBSR, therefore gives a secular and capitalist world of "disenchanted" routines and everyday activities "a sense of depth and value" (Braun 2017, 175).

In the following sections, I will examine what it means to be here "fully" in mindfulness as an embodied practice. More specifically, I will elaborate on the connection between embodied mindfulness practices and the aforementioned "ethics of authenticity" within the setting of MBSR. I look at MBSR as a group enactment and will show how various interactions and practices like yoga postures and bodily movements or the use of voice, support the subjectification process to form an "authentic self."

Meditation is often seen as a merely subjective or "internal" practice. Hence, in the investigation of the social performance of MBSR it becomes evident how mindfulness meditation is always also a form of "interactive introspection" (Ellis 1991). As I will show, the group setting enhances the individual practice of mindfulness in several ways: First, it can *motivate* the practitioners in their personal practice if they share their experiences with peers. Second, the mindful group interaction gives (deeper) *meaning* to the practice, which is in itself a factor of motivation. Third, the group setting *solves a functional paradox* of mindfulness: that mindfulness is somehow *required* to become or "stay" mindful. The practical challenge therefore lies within the tension of wanting to keep awareness in the present moment when at the same time the mind is so distracted by thoughts, feelings, or other stimuli that the practitioner forgets to remain "here and now." So, when the practitioner notices his or her absentness, the absence has already been overcome. This moment of recollection could be called a *waking moment* but is in itself an *instant of mindfulness* as an embodied practice. In this way, mindfulness is on the one hand an active, intentional and sometimes instrumental practice, a *doing*, and on the other hand a passive, receptive and "open," and hence embodied, mode of *being*. Both aspects are inherently interconnected. Renowned scholar and Buddhist monk Bhikkhu Anālayo describes this double aspect of *sati*, the Pali word for mindfulness, as follows:

> A closer examination [...] reveals that *sati* is not really defined as memory, but as that which facilitates and enables memory. What this definition of *sati* points to is that, if *sati* is present, memory will be able to function well. (Anālayo 2006, 46–47)

It is in this double aspect of mindfulness in which the power of the group interaction unfolds. In the social organization of mindfulness, the individual body becomes part of a social body, meaning its capability of "being here fully" unfolds within a transpersonal sphere of interacting embodied subjects. In this sense, as I will show, the individual can partake in the active part (recollection) while the group can practically embody or function as the passive part (memory).

To show what I mean by that, I will first briefly give some autobiographical annotations on MBSR from a personal viewpoint and reflect on my position as researcher and practitioner. I will also give a concise overview of my research method. Next, in addition to an operational definition of mindfulness, three core practices of MBSR are described from a first- and third-person perspective: the body scan, breathing meditation and mindful hatha yoga. Together with the cultivation of the right voice, which is especially relevant for teachers and instructors, those practices help to balance mindfulness as a practice of an authentic self. While the aforementioned exercises can and should be practiced daily at home, the individual experience in MBSR is complemented by the weekly group meetings. I will describe the structured and interactive setting as a specificity of the MBSR program. In the weekly sessions, exercises cannot just be practiced in a safe, trusted and exploratory environment but also get a deeper sense and meaning within group inquiries and discussions. The group enactment does not just *motivate* and *deepen the experience* within modern discourses of an authentic self but is very often the *condition for the emergence* of mindfulness as a social practice. I will show this with the example of two case vignettes which are especially relevant in the context of the experience of shared silence. Finally, I will summarize my empirical findings and link them to more theoretical discussions. I show here how, apart from discursive differences, on an embodied and phenomenological level, MBSR and Buddhist practice are not mutually exclusive.

## Autoethnographic Accounts on "Being Present"

My own path led me from being a stressed-out doctoral student to MBSR part-time teacher training in the spring of 2016. Three years before, when I wrote my master thesis, I took part in the program myself. During this time, I was plagued by alternating bouts of depression and anxiety. I found it very difficult to stay in touch with my body and feelings since I got distracted very easily. When I finished the 8-week-program, I was happy it was over. I could not manage to do the exercises as regularly as I had planned to during my daily routines which had hurt my ambition. My view on the MBSR program changed when I realized that what I had learned practically during the eight weeks was not something I could keep and take away, but something I had to build upon. Since then, I made several attempts to anchor meditation in everyday life. The MBSR teacher training was an important step on the path of developing my individual mindfulness meditation practice.

The following paragraphs refer mainly to observations of my own MBSR classes made in the role of course instructor. The data that were analyzed for this purpose originate from the period from April 2016 to March 2022 and comprise just under 300 handwritten pages along with material from the official MBSR curriculum. During that period, I conducted my teacher's training, gave seven MBSR 8-week classes, as well as some similar or more in-depth course formats on mindfulness meditation. The events took place in Austria and Germany and included a group size of four to twelve participants. Two of the courses were held at the university as part of a preventive health program for students. Here, central parts of the course were held online. The handwritten notes consist primarily of personal course diaries and reflections. They were fabricated casually without a special intention or research focus (cf. Goffman 1996, 268). The quality of the data differs. Some of that material is very detailed reflections, some are just shorthand notes and sketches. In working with these data, simple coding (such as "bodily experience," "voice," "silence," "structure") was used to sort the material.[1] Within the context of the aforementioned discourses, I will refer to some of the relevant literature in the field to give proper meaning and context

1. It is important to note that these categories have a provisional character in the sense of "conceptual categories" (Glaser and Strauss 1967, 23) which have not gone through the process of deductive- or comparative-recursive verification or even *saturation*. The categories were primarily used to organize the material and raise awareness of certain interrelationships (Bowen 2006). They form the basis for a possible systematic elaboration in the future.

to the descriptions of observed situations. My focus is on the situated construction of meaning and interaction. I therefore also draw on my experience as an embodied researcher, by which I refer to a perspective on the body as "an integral part of the perceiving subject" (Csordas 1990, 30; cf. Wacquant 2015).

## Embodying Mindfulness in MBSR

Technically mindfulness in MBSR is defined as "paying attention, on purpose, in the present moment, non-judgmentally" (Santorelli *et al.* 2017, 9; Kabat-Zinn 2005). In the context of stress reduction, this is realized through different body–mind practices, ranging from eating a raisin mindfully to mindful walking, hatha yoga, and sitting on a cushion motionless for about an hour. One key method is the so-called moment-to-moment awareness. The participants of the 8-week program are instructed to observe the body–mind continuum wakefully, disturbances are to be ignored. In the words of Jon Kabat-Zinn, you "are actively tuning in to each moment in an effort to remain awake and aware from one moment to the next" (Kabat-Zinn 2005, 20). If practitioners do this correctly and persistently, they should be able to detect and overcome "unwholesome" conditions in body and mind, especially stress and similar forms of psychosomatic defects or complaints.

Within this operational definition of mindfulness, which highlights mindfulness as an *activity*, there are other factors and facets which are less obvious at first glance but become practically important during the progression of cultivating mindfulness. For example, the aspects of *non-reaction*, of *self-care* and *acceptance*, or at least the above-mentioned double aspect of *recollection* and *memory*. As mentioned, this latter aspect, which is sometimes seen as a kind of paradoxical tension, reveals itself at various points in the practice of mindfulness. It can be found in the rules of conduct in the form of "trust" and "openness to experience" on the one hand and discipline with a focus to practice on the other (cf. Santorelli *et al.* 2017, 3, 16). In this respect, there is a tension between *purposeful* action and *non-judgmental* responsivity. Mindfulness would represent the middle way, the right balance and compound of the two.

### Exploring the Body: The Body Scan

While the intellectual *concept* of mindfulness just mentioned is introduced in the second course session at the earliest, the very first *experience* of mindfulness comes through the so-called body scan. In the 45-to-60-minute practice, the participant learns to connect with the body, sensing and feeling it. This can lead to intense experiences. In the process of subjectification, these experiences can become emotional pinnacles and as such leave traces in the memory of the practitioner, motivating further engagement. For example, I vividly remember an event that happened about ten to eleven years ago during one of my first body scans: I felt the body pulsating from the inside out, it seemed as if I was moving through thousands of inner blood vessels and being revitalized from the inside out. It was very energizing and awakening. The recollection of this experience brings me into a warm and light mood and inspires the practice—it is worth noting here that this recollection is more often a passive event than an active effort.

In the beginning of the eight-week course, I guide the practitioners' attention through different parts of the body with my voice. Step by step the participants learn to do this on their own. At home, they practice with an audio guide, recorded by me. The participants are instructed to stay awake and to consciously direct their attention to the addressed areas of the body. Here, I often remind them that "sensing is not thinking." The verbal guidance is often provided by metaphors or concepts helping the practitioner to *let go* of bodily tensions or even pain and to get more and more relaxed without falling asleep. The quality of "letting go" is one of the core principles of embodied mindfulness. In guiding the participants, I try to associate with *their* feelings and imaginations by keeping in touch with *my* body awareness and concepts. In this way, my tension or relaxation resonates (e.g., by voice) with theirs. Conversely, in hearing them or seeing their bodies lying on the ground, I try to put myself in their place. This connection is an empathetic as well as an imaginative act that is difficult to put into words. According to the feedback I have received, many practitioners get inspiration and motivation from sound and images. Nevertheless, others fall asleep, stray into thoughts, or are very awake and conscious of their bodily sensations.

In the second class of an 8-week course, for example, one participant fell asleep and snored during the body scan. Later he recounted that by the end of the meditation, he was "very aware." He described it as an interesting experience of being *in* the body and *out* of it at the same time, experiencing it as an object as well as subjectively. Another participant in the same situation was relaxed and calm and then began to shake—something, he said, that happens frequently when he lets go. Meanwhile, a third participant had problems with sensing the body as a whole. She wondered how her feet could be so "separate" from her even though she "goes through life" with them. She also had many thoughts and said she had been pondering on problems of her working life during the guided meditation.

## Mindful Breathing

In the second session of the course, breathing meditation is introduced. The attention in this practice is on the breath, respectively on the body areas where the para-autonomous activity of breathing is sensed. The breath functions as an "anchor": when the mind is distracted by thoughts or other stimuli, the practitioner has to remember to be mindful and therefore bring attention back to breathing. The objective of this basic practice is to improve moment-to-moment awareness with the side effect of calming the mind. One participant focused on the breathing coming in and out around the nostrils or the pressed sound it made during the breathing meditation.[2] The sound helped this person to stay "awake" during long periods of sitting meditation. Another participant in the same class could "enjoy" experiencing her breath deep in the abdominal cavity. The constant focus on breathing helped her to get deeper inside herself. Her feedback on the 8-week course was that she liked "the experience that I can become calm through [...] meditation." Another participant in that class could not manage to practice the breathing meditation every day for the scheduled period of about 45 minutes but was happy that she could enjoy conscious moments of silence again and again during a demanding daily routine.

## The Body in Motion: Mindful Yoga

While this same participant enjoyed breathing meditation, she had difficulties with the yoga postures and movements. The biggest obstacles for her were her operated knee and her general limited physical ability to move. Mindful yoga, as I tell the participants regularly, is supposed to help us get in touch with the body and to experience but not cross its boundaries. The postures that are exercised here are relatively simple postures (*āsanas*) of modern hatha yoga but introduced in a non-religious and "secular" manner. The practitioners are encouraged to stay aware of the different movements and postures. While the moving (and resting) body and not the breath is the object of attention in this exercise, being present at every moment while the postures are being performed is elementary here as well. One participant who disliked the body scan said

2. The participant wore a face mask due to health concerns.

that for him yoga was "totally good" because in contrast to the body scan or breathing meditation there was some "action" there and it was "not boring." Another participant in the same class recalled that she had consciously observed how the boundaries of her mobility had shifted during the progression of a stretching exercise. This seemed not to happen often to her. Occasionally, I remind the participants to relax certain areas of the body where tension often sets in, such as the forehead, eye sockets, jaw, shoulder, and neck area. At this point, subtle "aha-moments" sometimes occur. Similar "waking" experiences often happen during yoga, when practitioners consciously feel the moved body areas after a movement or exertion during the rest and relaxation phase. In the teacher training, we called this *sensing* (German: *Nachspüren*). Sensing is an essential part of the *āsana* practice in the program. While sensing marks the main activity of the mind during the relaxation phase of the exercise, it is important that focus and moment-to-moment awareness is trained during each stage of the yoga practice, be it in tension or relaxation. Being aware of the changes in bodily perceptions while relaxing after a movement phase is often enjoyable. Regularly participants express their surprise at how small consciously perceived movements or sensual receptions make a big difference in overall bodily awareness.

## Embodying an Authentic Self: The Voice

One of these supposedly small differences concerns the voice. When listening to audio meditation guides of MBSR teachers, a typical sound will be noticed. The mood is usually gentle but bold. The words are deliberately chosen and are not too intrusive or overloaded, but concise and clear. The tone is motivating but not pushy; not too monotone but also not too vital or even vigorous. Longer periods of silence stretch between the words. The voice of the teacher is a helpful tool and medium for the practitioner to calm and concentrate the mind. When meditating in silence or immersed in an *āsana*, the voice is the first and the last or only thing to be perceived by sensory awareness. Anatomically the voice is a product of the right use of the vocal fold and the vocal tract in modulating sound. It is embodied as we can utilize it physically, but we cannot utilize and objectify it as we do with an external object, like a hammer for example. We *use* our voice, but at the same time, as talking creatures, we *are* our voice in the realm of verbal expression. In this sense, the voice expresses our emotional body and at the same time, the capability of intentionally transforming the voice can transform the mood of the audience, including the speaker.

For me as a course instructor, finding the right tone in the guidance of a meditation group was a great challenge, beginning in the MBSR teacher's training. A reflection and feedback note of my training, where we learned to guide the body scan in a small group, reads: "Timing: somewhat longer introduction?," followed by "Ambition in voice → play a little more with the voice: a little less monotone." Finally, the feedback of my peers was: "coherent overall concept: authentic." Today these notes remind me on the one hand of the early difficulties of finding the right velocity and words, which were settled by practice over the months and years. On the other hand, this short note shows the importance of the voice, which is not just an audible instrument, but a kind of medium of subjectification as well as a benchmark of one's own emotional and mindful state. In this manner, the voice corresponds to the inner mood of the speaker, which in turn very often reflects or expresses the social or spatial atmosphere, since it often unwittingly adapts to the actual situation. The voice expresses the speaker's inner emotional and bodily vibe and can give the audience (including him or herself) implicit knowledge of his or her subjective being—especially if the person is not trained and used to instruct and teach meditation or speak to others in a mindful manner.[3]

In tracing back the development of my teacher's voice within notebooks and journals, the correspondence between "inner" mood and "outer" vocal expression becomes visible. In an entry about an advanced meditation course, I recollected that I "felt [...] not well prepared." It was my first session of this type of course as a teacher, starting with just three out of four participants, because one of them had excused herself only five to ten minutes before the beginning of the class. The situation for me was "chaotic" and I felt "insecurity." Accordingly, I noted, "my voice was not very confident, [and I felt] inner unrest." Gradually the inner turmoil dissolved. Notably, when I "improvised" and spoke of "my own experience" the performance felt more authentic than when I tried to stick to my original plan and course structure: "in the last phase of the session I became more eased and could also accept the situation better than in the beginning." For another session of this same course, I noticed, in clear contrast to the first session, that "everything" was "more eased," because I "had enough time to prepare [the room], prepare a tea," sat down and had a little chat with the early course participants. Following later notations of "voice" in my records, it appears that the more I learned to become "myself" in practicing and teaching, the more

3. Erving Goffman discriminates those embodied and implicit signs as "cues given off" from intentional and explicit "cues given" (Kotarba and Fontana 1984, 31).

balanced my communication was. This was not so much an effect of active vocal exercise but rather resulted indirectly from the development of an authentic practice—including my own time and stress management—which in my case meant not presenting or pretending anything that I could not account for myself in that situation.

## Modern Mindfulness as a Group Enactment

In the following paragraphs, I will describe the aspect of embodiment based on the above-mentioned practices from a more processual perspective and especially with a focus on group dynamics. Embodiment is never a mere individual and instrumental but first and foremost an interactive and habitual process. This process in MBSR is structured by certain rules and agreements. The structure of rules limits the practice to a specific order and selected actions and empowers the participants to stick to a certain discipline. In this context of group settings, I will also explore the practices of shared silence in the description of two case vignettes. The cases illustrate the embodiment of "being here fully" in two different practitioner types. It is significant to emphasize here once again that everything I describe derives, in accordance with the approach of Ellis (1991), from my observation of (and interaction with) the participants as well as from self-observation (introspection).

### Rules of Conduct and Participant Selection

The group work in MBSR is based on mindful interaction with verbal and nonverbal communication. From the beginning of a course, this interaction is bound to *rules of conduct*. These are made explicit even before the start of a course in personal preliminary discussions as well as in the group setting. First, the course rules represent a pre-selection of possible participants. Beyond that, they clarify the qualities to be internalized if one continues to practice mindfulness. It is the embodiment of those rules that also lays the foundation for an authentic practice of mindfulness:

- The participants are *willing to "trust"* (Kabat-Zinn 2005, 36) the program, the teacher, and the group; they are *open to the experience* and "non-judging" (Kabat-Zinn 2005, 33).
- They *commit themselves to try their best* to become more mindful during course time but also while practicing in everyday life (cf. Santorelli *et al.* 2017).

- They are "*fully present*" at the course: physically as well as mentally; they try to take part in every session if possible and focus on the contents for the time of the 8-week program.
- They *participate* in the course *voluntarily* and can leave at any time; they do not have to do any of the exercises, especially if it is felt that they cross one's personal boundary.
- They *pay respect* to one another; they respect their bodies and boundaries (Santorelli *et al.* 2017, 104), do not interrupt each other, do not give advice, if not asked for, and *speak only for themselves.*

Besides those rules, it is made clear to the potential participant that MBSR is a non-religious program, free from specific worldviews and ideologies.[4] If the rules are broken, the group enactment may suffer badly. Therefore pre-talks are provided. Besides the casual talk, there is a fixed set of questions to be answered by the applicants, such as: "What is your motivation for this course?," "Are there any real or possible hindrances?," "What is your current situation and stress level?" Applicants who are seriously physically or mentally ill may not take part in the course. Although there are clear indicators of participation, these may conflict with organizational or financial requirements. Together with the course fee, the pre-talk is the first selection factor of MBSR. Since the program works as a group enactment, the presence/absence and the mood and manner of every single participant play an important role and shape the atmosphere and thus the intersubjective experience of the shared practice.

The course rules structure the performance of being present and discipline the ability to attend "here and now," while at the same time, they also limit the aforementioned capability of openness and "letting go." In the group interaction, the participants learn to balance and embody both qualities. I want to illustrate this process with the comparison of two case vignettes.

## Endurance and Focus: The Case of Dietrich

Dietrich,[5] a graduate engineer, told me that he was under a lot of pressure at his workplace. He had practiced Zen meditation in a group setting once a week for some years in the past which he had to stop due

4. From a critical sociological perspective, this can of course be disputed to the extent that the concept of MBSR and its proliferation follow, for example, "Western" and neoliberal ideas.
5. All names are fictional to protect the participants' identities.

to time constraints. He also had tinnitus and told me that he wanted to see if he could get rid of it through MBSR. Dietrich talked about this illness pragmatically as if it was a technical problem to solve. He said for him participation in the class was a "little test," but that he had no great expectations. He was a sporty, punctual, and communicative character and repeatedly participated in group inquiries. At some point in the first part of the course, he informed the group about his tinnitus and that he sometimes grinds his teeth at night. If you knew it, you could see it in his face. His facial features often looked tense, sometimes petrified. He was a very ambitious practitioner, bringing his own little meditation bench with him every week, but at the same time, he seemed permanently busy and active outside the course. His job was a recurring topic of discussion. In class six, Dietrich appeared strikingly different, looking very relaxed. He did not sit so stiffly, and his facial features looked softer. He told us that he had had a relaxed weekend. Interestingly, he was aware of his changed external appearance. However, the change was not permanent. In the last session's discussion, Dietrich admitted he was glad to have Tuesday evenings for himself again after the course would end. Concurrently, he was sure that he would maintain his meditation practice. Dietrich was pragmatically optimistic since his tinnitus had gotten better in the meantime.

Within the group interaction, Dietrich stood out from the rest with his clear language, his analytical ability, and his meditation experience. In this regard, he often gave other participants advice, even if they had not asked for it. However, Dietrich was not pushy, he had learned to take a step back, listen and, if necessary, wait for the right moment to contribute to discussions. I perceived him as extremely attentive, and his gaze behavior showed me that he participated very well in the respective interactions of the group even if he held back with verbal expressions. When he did not talk, Dietrich's glances told me where his attention was—albeit not in every single interaction. When he spoke, he looked directly at his communication partner and usually appeared very serious. Sometimes I felt this was almost encroaching. At the same time, Dietrich did not seem to want to attract "negative" attention, in the sense of seeming undisciplined or not respecting the rules.

One specific situation illustrates this behavior. It was "silent retreat" day and the participants arrived one by one while I was preparing the room for the beginning of the silence for the next five to seven hours. The day before I had promised another participant, Stefan, that he could leave after the lunch break to attend another appointment. When Dietrich overheard me confirming to Stefan that he could leave earlier, Dietrich spoke up and wanted to leave this option open for him, too. This brought unrest and uncertainty to the situation and seemed to undermine group discipline. In my personal reflections on this situation, I wrote:

> Stefan and also Dietrich threatened to break the mold with their announcements to possibly leave earlier, at noon → I should have excluded this option from the beginning—either one comes, or one stays away; very important for the future; [...] Nevertheless, I managed to open the frame and I could let go of my inner anger about the "laissez-faire" of Stefan and Dietrich: I left them the option ["everyone is free ..."], but also urged them that it is part of the program to also sometimes withstand bad moods.

In the end, to my surprise, none of them had left earlier. In the afternoon discussion after a seemingly hard but also beneficial day in silence, Stefan told me that he had liked the atmosphere but that he had enjoyed the morning part more. Dietrich recalled that in the morning his presence and focus were strong, while in the afternoon staying awake was exhausting and a "fight" for him—especially when digesting after lunch. He would have preferred to be outside. In the room, the air was "thick," he said. He tried to frame his decisions positively and confirmed that it had been okay to stay, adding that "when I start something, I finish it."

## The Power of Group Silence

In my interpretation of the situation, this case reveals some important aspects of mindfulness within the setting of a practice group. Communicating a possible exit from the course before the end of the session made a big difference to the group dynamics that followed. When Dietrich heard about this option, his motivation seemed to fade. However, in this event, *he and the other person stayed*, even though I had explicitly given them the option to leave earlier. Could my gentle remark that also "bad moods" are bearable, have at least motivated Dietrich, perhaps even challenged him to stay? I am sure, this little remark had an effect in that direction. Also the dynamic of social expectation played a crucial role here: From the logic of the situation, it was not easy for Dietrich to leave as long as Stefan did not go either—vice versa Stefan was presumably also motivated by Dietrich's "endurance."

But there is another important aspect. According to my notebook, three of the other four participants said they enjoyed the silence, and I wrote that, besides some minutes of calm breathing meditation in the beginning, the following "yoga was very beneficial—It felt also good for myself." I remember to this day, how—even though I had to stick to my structure while the participants could just "let go"—I felt deep inner peace, which happens regularly during such silent retreats. Gradually, the shared silence developed a strength that was wholesome and meant that most of the attendees did not feel the need to speak or to leave. They just could *be* here "fully." While in mindfulness discourse it seems obvious that silence deploys a healing power, I want to contrast this perspective with the case of Dietrich. My data point to the interpretation that when other participants stayed and enjoyed the silence, for Dietrich it was overall a hard time and a tough decision to stay. His "fighting" statement ("when I start something, I finish it") therefore has to be seen, at least partially, as "rationalization." However, his behavior suggests that if some small factors would have been different, he possibly could have left. One factor that kept him in the room till the end was surely the shared power of silence. But in his case, it seemed to be the power of silence in exactly the reverse way as for the others. In deep silence, every slightest movement is perceived like a storm. As I knew Dietrich, I am sure that he did not want to disturb the others or the performance as such nor did he want to break the rules, which in effect would be the same in this situation. After a silent day of another course, I jotted down the following sentences:

> I noticed—in myself and others—how difficult it was or how needless it was to say something; the silence had *unfolded a power*—one could not escape it so easily; I myself also enjoyed just being *there*, not having to say anything, not having to do anything. I became aware: sometimes it is difficult for us to be silent—sometimes it is difficult to break the silence!

### Gratitude and Openness: The Case of Erika

As we have defined earlier, embodying mindfulness means not just the "*doing*" of a good performance but *being aware* of every action and performance within the present moment. Both represent the active and passive quality of the practice. In this complementary sense to be aware—to stay "here and now"—a certain amount of endurance as well as focus is necessary. Dietrich doubtlessly incorporated the latter two qualities. Yet he seemed to lack some of the qualities of receptivity, as he was not capable to be *fully* there in some situations, illustrated by his discomfort in the last stage of the "silent retreat" day.

In the following, I will argue that what Dietrich was lacking is the capability of "letting go" and thus the aspect of "openness" and "acceptance." To illustrate this, I want to contrast Dietrich with the case of Erika. She was in her early 60s and told me about histories of sickness in her family, her role as a caregiver, and her search for alternative healing practices in the face of her own illness. She assured me, she had been "highly sensitive." Erika's objective to partake in the 8-week program was to find other people to share things like meditation with and to find her way back into her own meditation practice. When I signed her up for the course, she was visibly grateful. It was almost the norm for her to thank me or the others in the group at the beginning and at the end of a session. Her eyes were often moist in these situations and when she spoke, she used to look into space or to the ground. While existential and spiritual topics arose in her comments and questions regularly, she often searched for the right and fitting words. Nonetheless, Erika visibly felt at home in the course. Almost without exception, she was the first to arrive at the door on time and the last to leave the room before me or together with me. From the first session onwards, Erika regularly talked about how great the meditation experiences were for her. She enjoyed the body scan very much, as well as all other methods of mindfulness we practiced. In correspondence to her being the most experienced meditator of her course, she expressed gladly how familiar it feels to get in touch with her body again or how beneficial breathing meditation is.

So, how is the quality of openness embodied in Erika's mindfulness practice? First, Erika was *quite communicative* during breaks, before the beginning or after the end of a session and in the group discussions. This she had in common with Dietrich. But secondly, in conversations, by the glance of her eyes, she was usually as often *in touch "with herself" as she was with her counterpart*. During the meditation, she was always very focused on herself. Her eyes were closed, she sat upright, seemed in good ground contact and her *facial features looked soft and relaxed*. Judging by her leisurely pace through the room, she *felt comfortable* in almost any situation. Erika usually appeared peaceful and introverted by her facial features. In contrast, Dietrich's facial expression and body tension was different. While he also sat upright and inverted in the sitting meditation phases and could be very reserved, he seemed tense and inwardly restless in other situations. This physical impression was underlined by statements like the one in the last session when Dietrich said he was "happy" that the course is over so that he then would have time for other activities. This is not to say that there were no obvious periods of time and situations where Dietrich was fully present. But obviously, he had not *fully* "arrived" in the same way as Erika. Another facet that expressed her openness in different situations and in sharp contrast to Dietrich was her *gratitude*. I interpret this gratitude as an expression of the group's appreciation. While Erika *accepted* the group in all her expressions and felt at home in it, Dietrich had rather *endured* the group setting in most situations and was facilitated when the time was over. Meditation for him seemed sometimes individual and *hard work*, while Erika felt at least in every situation of the group meetings comfortable and visibly *enjoyed* it. So comfortable, in fact, that she not only talked very freely about rather private topics but at the same time emphasized how good it was to be in community. Since Erika was capable of being with herself and with the other participants at the same time, she incorporated mindfulness in a "fuller" way, which with Taylor (2007, 481) could be called "mutual presence."

## Conclusion and Discussion

In Mindfulness-Based Stress Reduction, stress and similar sufferings are encountered using body–mind practices. Embodying these practices means not just using them intentionally and technically correctly but incorporating and internalizing them in a balanced way. The embodiment of this "right mindfulness" (Pali: *sammā sati*) does not take place in a solitary space but within social interaction. Voice and silence are good examples of that. While the use of voice in guided meditation seems primarily an "outer" communicative process, the voice of the teacher is also internalized by practice so that the practitioners can guide themselves. The same applies to silence. The silence "within" (body and mind) is interconnected to the silence "outside" (in the group and social space). This shared silence has a greater "power" than just the individual silence and therefore it can support and carry the individual mindfulness practice. Such ethnographic observation can also be grasped phenomenologically and understood theoretically by the concept of "intercorporeality" (Fuchs 2016). When the group cultivates silence together, each member is part and object as well as subject of that process. The same reciprocal structure can also be found between formal meditations during course sessions and informal mindful practice in everyday life. The habitual process of internalization and thus the embodiment of mindfulness then is functionally the same as cultivating "the inner voice" of an authentic self (Taylor 1991, 26).

The initially mentioned paradox of mindfulness as a *requirement* as well as an *outcome* of the practice corresponds to, as we have argued with Bhikkhu Anālayo, the double aspect of recollection/memory as an active as well as a passive factor of mindfulness. It also corresponds to the poles of "narrow" and "wide" that phenomenologically characterize "bodily understanding" (Gugutzer 2006). In terms of mindfulness as an embodied practice, this tension interferes with the process of habitualization: "Whereas explicit recollection is directed to the past, implicit or body memory re-enacts the past through the body's present performance;

in other words, it may be regarded as our 'lived past'" (Fuchs 2016, 11). "Being here fully" is not just an instrumental issue we can achieve by willpower and technique but a kind of habit, an embodied and therefore a "holistic" matter. It is technical as well as ethical and aesthetical as it involves both our actual expression and our (self-)perception within a dynamic social environment. If somebody can sit calmly and peacefully for 45 minutes but is full of unrest, discontent, and anger shortly afterwards, this would not be an "authentic" enactment of mindfulness—be it for him or herself or for the social others to which mindfulness is displayed. This kind of mindful enactment would rather be conflicting and exhausting, the ease would be missing. In cases where the practice is more exhausting than nourishing and joyful, the state of "being here fully" is not reached. At this point, an authentic practice and the embodiment of mindfulness are mutually dependent. Mindfulness is in this respect always "situated knowledge" (Eisenmann and Oberzaucher 2019). It is not just the *ability* of "paying attention, on purpose, in the present moment, non-judgmentally" but entails the situated *capability* of "acceptance" and "let go" (Kabat-Zinn 2005, 38–40) as well as a kind of compassion and "empathy" for ourselves and our environment (Kabat-Zinn 2005, 182–184) as a condition of "being here fully."

The embodiment of an authentic self in the practice of modern mindfulness can but need not be a contradiction to Buddhist mindfulness (cf. Bodhi 2011, 36). Although the claim of MBSR and other mindfulness-based prevention programs is the conscious *empowering of the self* (cf. Anderssen-Reuster 2011), this does not mean that this self is not let go again with increasing practice and insight, in the sense of the non-self (Pali: *anattā*) doctrine. As Anālayo (2006, 74) shows, the "Path to Realization" does not deny the "self" in the sense of "oneself" or "the subjective sense of continuity or the influence of karma." The Buddhist self-concept is primarily a "conditional" one, that goes first against the extremes of "selfishness" or "dissociation" which both lead to *dukkha* (Pali: suffering). In this case, the embodiment and cultivation of an authentic self in MBSR would *not be a contradiction* to the non-self in Buddhism, but a *prerequisite* for serious spiritual practice—just like the concept of *anattā* "does not make us dysfunctional" as Anālayo writes:

> On the contrary, to the extent to which we are able to let go of the burden of ego and self-reference, to that extent we become more functional and better at doing what we have to do. In this way, cultivating insight into emptiness is quite different from a tendency to dissociate and become disconnected. It is the precise opposite of that. [...] Due to the emphasis given throughout the practice to an embodied form of mindfulness as the central reference point, helpful groundwork has been established to

> counter any tendency to dissociation. If such a tendency should manifest, then this calls for increased emphasis on embodied presence of the mind. This will ensure that the type of emptiness cultivated is a genuine one.
> (Anālayo 2006, 76)

**Alan Schink**, PhD, is a sociologist with a focus on the sociology of culture, religion, and the body. His dissertation was an ethnography on conspiracy culture in Germany. He works in a research project on the stigma of mental disorders at the University of Ulm in Germany and teaches qualitative research methods at a private university in Austria. Alongside, Alan works as a freelance stress reduction and mindfulness trainer.

## References

Anālayo. 2006 [2003]. *Satipaṭṭhāna. The Direct Path to Realization.* Cambridge: Windhorse Publications.

Anderssen-Reuster, Ulrike. 2011 [2007]. "Ich-Stärkung oder Ich-Überwindung?" In *Achtsamkeit in Psychotherapie und Psychosomatik. Haltung und Methode*, edited by Ulrike Anderssen-Reuster, 91–107. Stuttgart: Schattauer.

Bodhi, Bhikkhu. 2011. "What Does Mindfulness Really Mean? A Canonical Perspective." *Contemporary Buddhism: An Interdisciplinary Journal* 12(1): 19–39.

Bowen, Glenn A. 2006. "Grounded Theory and Sensitizing Concepts." *International Journal of Qualitative Methods* 5(3): 12–23.

Braun, Erik. 2017. "Mindful but not religious. Mindfulness and Enchantment in the Work of Kabat-Zinn." In *Meditation, Buddhism, and Science*, edited by David McMahan and Eric Braun, 173–197. Oxford: Oxford University Press.

Cook, Joanna. 2017. "'Mind the Gap': Appearance and Reality in Mindfulness-Based Cognitive Therapy." In *Meditation, Buddhism, and Science*, edited by David McMahan and Eric Braun, 114–132. Oxford: Oxford University Press.

Csordas, Thomas J. 1990. "Embodiment as a Paradigm for Anthropology." *Ethos* 18(1): 5–47.

Eisenmann, Clemens and Frank Oberzaucher. 2019. "Das Selbst kultivieren: Praktiken der Achtsamkeit in spirituellen und psychotherapeutischen Handlungsfeldern" *Psychosozial* 42(158): 31–48.

Ellis, Carolyn. 1991. "Sociological Introspection and Emotional Experience." *Symbolic Interaction* 14(I): 23–50.

Fuchs, Thomas. 2016. "Intercorporeality and Interaffectivity." In I*ntercorporeality. Emerging Socialities in Interaction*, edited by Christian Meyer, Jürgen Streeck and J. Scott Jordan, 3–23. Oxford: Oxford University Press.

Glaser, Barney and Anselm Strauss. 1967. *The Discovery of Grounded Theory: Strategies for Qualitative Research*. New York: Aldine Publishing Company.

Goffman, Erving. 1996 [1974]. "Über Feldforschung." In *Kommunikative Lebenswelten. Zur Ethnographie einer geschwätzigen Gesellschaft*, edited by Hubert Knoblauch, 261–269. Konstanz: UVK.

Gugutzer, Robert. 2006. "Leibliches Verstehen. Zur sozialen Relevanz des Spürens." In *Soziale Ungleichheit, kulturelle Unterschiede. Verhandlungen des 32. Kongresses der Deutschen Gesellschaft für Soziologie in München 2004*, edited by Karl-Siegbert Rehberg, 4536–4546. Frankfurt a. M.: Campus.

Kabat-Zinn, Jon. 2005 [1990]. *Full Catastrophe Living: Using the Wisdom of Your Body and Mind to Face Stress, Pain, and Illness*. New York: Delta.

Kotarba, Joseph A. and Andrea Fontana. 1984. *The Existential Self in Society*. Chicago, IL: University of Chicago Press.

Kucinskas, Jaime. 2018. *The Mindful Elite. Mobilizing from the Inside Out*. Oxford: Oxford University Press.

McMahan, David L. 2008. *The Making of Buddhist Modernism*. Oxford: Oxford University Press.

Purser, Ronald. 2019. *McMindfulness. How Mindfulness Became the New Capitalist Spirituality*. London: Repeater.

Santorelli, Saki F., Florence Meleo-Meyer and Lynn Koerbel, eds. 2017. *Mindfulness-Based Stress Reduction (MBSR). Authorized Curriculum Guide*. Worcester, MA: Center for Mindfulness/University of Massachusetts Medical School.

Sun, Jessie. 2014. "Mindfulness in Context: A Historical Discourse Analysis." *Contemporary Buddhism* 15(2): 394–415.

Taylor, Charles. 1991. *The Ethics of Authenticity*. Cambridge, MA: Harvard University Press.

——. 2007. *A Secular Age*. Cambridge, MA: Harvard University Press.

Wacquant, Loïc. 2015. "For a Sociology of Flesh and Blood: Questions to Loïc Wacquant." In *Revealing Tacit Knowledge: Embodiment and Explication*, edited by Frank Adloff, Katharina Gerund and David Kaldewey, 185–194. Bielefeld: transcript.

– 12 –

# Moving Beyond the Mind through "Listening by Heart"

## The Role of Experience in Modern Advaitic Satsangs

ELIN THORSÉN

Modernized forms of the philosophical system *Advaita* ("nondual") *Vedānta*, usually referred to as Neo-Advaita or Modern Advaita, constitute an integral part of the range of South Asian spiritualities that are being taught and practiced globally today. This chapter explores the embodied dimensions of Modern Advaitic *satsangs*, a form of dialogical lectures in which Modern Advaitic teachings are being disseminated. Based on ethnographic material from satsangs held in Rishikesh, a northern Indian pilgrimage town and center for international spiritual tourism, the chapter discusses the importance ascribed to the process of turning abstract concepts of the nondual Self into experiential, and hence embodied knowledge in these contexts. This was a process that not only involved discourses but equally much the presence of the guru and other fellow satsang participants. A focus on experience, I suggest, provides valuable insights into the embodied reception of Advaita in partly new social, cultural, spatial, and temporal contexts. The emphasis put on personal experience in Modern Advaitic satsangs serves as an illustration of the adaptations of these types of events, as it reflects a synthesis of Advaitic tenets and a form of subjective "self-spirituality."

Keywords: Modern Advaita, satsang, experiential knowledge, nondual discourses

Between 2017 and 2019 I was conducting ethnographic fieldwork for a PhD project in Rishikesh, a small town in northern India.[1] Besides being

1. This chapter is based on a part of my doctoral thesis (Thorsén 2022).

part of a larger circuit of Hindu pilgrimage places in the Himalayan region, since around the end of the 1960s, Rishikesh has also been a popular destination for international spiritual tourism (Norman 2013; Strauss 2005, 29). Today the vast offer of yoga and meditation courses, as well as numerous other miscellaneous spiritual teachings and practices, attract people from around the world.

My research interest was focused on the many satsangs held during February and March, a time of the year when Rishikesh attracts many foreign tourists. Satsang ("meeting in truth") in this context is a form of gathering where a teacher presents discourses to an audience. Oftentimes, participants are invited to ask questions and the discourses take the form of dialogues.

The informal "satsang scene" appearing in Rishikesh was a transnational phenomenon, as both gurus and participants came from various parts of the world to join in these activities. While some gurus had a connection to Rishikesh through being part of a *guru paramparā* established in the area, far from all had such a local affiliation. Rather, Rishikesh's satsang scene could be seen as a part of an ambulating network of teachers who tend to appear at the same places at the same time, including at spiritual centers and festivals in Europe and North America (see Frisk 2002).

The size of the satsangs in Rishikesh varied from small gatherings of ten people to large events with thousands of participants. While some of the teachers encouraged inquiries of a purely spiritual character, others received a more varied type of questions, ranging from working life to personal relations. The verbal communication was oftentimes interspersed with the singing of *bhajans* and short periods of meditation.

Although there were variations in the style and approach of different teachers, a common denominator for the discourses offered in these satsangs was that they all represented modernized versions of the Indian philosophical system *Advaita* ("nondual") *Vedānta*. Advaita represents a form of nondualism, where the Self (*ātman*) is seen as being a form of nondual awareness, identical with absolute reality (*brahman*).[2] Satsang has been identified as one of the main methods of transmitting teachings within the transnational scene of Modern Advaita (see Davis 2011, 58; Frisk 2002; Lucas 2014, 23–25).

Modernized forms of Advaita, referred to in academic terms as Neo-Advaita (Gleig 2013; Lucas 2013) or Modern Advaita (Lucas 2014) have, to varying degrees, moved away from the emphasis put on scriptural

2. To distinguish the Advaitic concept of the nondual Self (*ātman*) from other usages of the term self, it is here referred to with a capital S.

knowledge and requirements of eligibility of students that characterize more traditional forms of Advaita, and in many ways represent a rather different approach. One defining characteristic of non-traditional forms of Advaita is that what is referred to as "awakening" to a nondual understanding of the Self is seen as being possible here and now without the requirements of years of spiritual preparation in the form of *sādhanā*, or any particular religious affiliation.[3]

During the initial stages of this project, I was grappling with a fundamental contradiction: although verbal communication appeared to lie at the heart of satsang, participants at these events would adamantly claim that words, in fact, only made up a small part of what they valued with attending satsang. They would furthermore often express wonder at my choice of research topic, as they thought nonduality to be something impossible to grasp intellectually.

The focus of attention, therefore, gradually came to shift from the *discourses* presented in satsangs to the ways in which these were "realized" and *embodied*, and with that, the role played by *personal experience*. Inspired by Michal Pagis's (2010) work on vipassana meditation retreats as producing a form of situated knowledge where abstract concepts are turned into experiential knowledge, I will here argue that satsangs mirror a similar process. It will also be suggested that a focus on experience is a fruitful approach for understanding the adaptations following the embodied reception of Advaita in partly new social, cultural, spatial, and temporal contexts as the ways in which participants and teachers justified, explained, and interpreted the need of personal experience reflected not only the philosophy of Advaita, but also a form of subjective self-spirituality (Heelas 1996).

In the remaining part of this chapter, satsang will be analyzed as an embodied practice by mapping out how the process of turning abstract concepts of the nondual Self into experiential knowledge looked in these settings—settings dominated by talk rather than by silent meditation. This process involved not only a specific function of dialogues and discourses but also the bodily presence of teachers and participants.

The material used for the analysis consists of observations at satsangs held in Rishikesh during altogether five months between 2017 and 2019.

3. For presentations of the defining features of classical and modern forms of Advaita, see Davis (2011) and Forsthoefel (2005, 2018). For discussions on the points of disagreement between more traditional and non-traditional forms of Advaita, see Lucas (2014). In relation to Lucas's (2014) categorization, the satsangs in Rishikesh mainly (although not exclusively) included what he calls Non-Traditional Modern Advaitic teachers, but for the sake of readability, I only use the term Modern Advaita here.

This included satsangs with twelve different teachers, although the main part of observations was conducted at satsangs with four of these, belonging to two different traditions: Mooji, a student of H. W. L. Poonja (1910–1997) who in turn was a disciple of Ramana Maharshi (1879–1950), and ShantiMayi, Prem Baba, and Om Baba, all disciples of Hans Raj Maharajji (1922–2011) of the Sacha lineage. The material also includes interviews with twenty-five satsang participants, of whom the majority were living in Western parts of the world, mainly in Europe.[4]

## The Importance of Experiential Knowledge

A good place to begin the analysis of the emphasis put on experiential knowledge in satsang is to present the arguments put forward by teachers and practitioners to explain and justify this sentiment.

Pagis notes that achieving Buddhist knowing "requires both bodily experience and intellectual reflection" (2010, 472). Meditation retreats provide environments where Buddhist tenets can be infused with embodied meaning. Besides analyzing the process of turning abstract concepts into experiential knowledge in vipassana meditation retreats, Pagis also offers a more general framework for studying the relations between conceptual and embodied dimensions of different types of knowledge: *Relativity* "helps us to determine the comparative importance of each dimension of knowledge in a specific process of knowing"; *directionality* "reveals the temporal dynamic of processes of knowing"; and last, "a variation exists in the *mutual influence* that the embodied and conceptual dimensions of knowledge exercise over each other" (Pagis 2010, 487).

While Advaitic satsang represents a different kind of tradition and setting than a vipassana meditation retreat, Pagis's framework is helpful for analyzing the relations between conceptual and experiential knowledge in this particular context.

Taking relativity as starting point, it was clear that the experiential dimension of teachings was seen as superior to that of intellectual knowledge in the process of making sense of nondual tenets. The importance of "realizing"—rather than intellectually grasping—the nondual nature of the Self was a frequently occurring theme both in satsangs and in interviews with satsang participants.

There was a particular logic and set of arguments applied for explaining the emphasis on experiential knowledge that appeared to be widely

4. For a further presentation of the fieldwork process, sampling, and material, see Thorsén (2022).

shared among both teachers and those who were being interviewed. Victor, who had regularly been attending satsangs with his guru for about seven years at the time we met, aptly illustrated these arguments in his reflection on the nature of nondual teachings:

> That we are many is more like an illusion, and that the reality is that we are somehow ... under a spell, you could say to express it simply. This is a very well-known thought, but this is not like ... this is what is behind the teachings. Not to make people believe that, because there is no value in believing that more than in believing ... a sea monster that is God, or, you know, a guy sitting in the clouds judging you, whatever belief you can have about God. Or that there is no God. It's all beliefs, these are the same. So, for [Guruji] and for enlightened masters this is more like a reality, this is what they are living.
>
> (Interview with "Victor," March 2018)[5]

Three crucial things about the importance of experientially understanding nonduality come to the fore in Victor's narrative. The first of these is that the essence of nonduality lies *behind* the teachings and discourses, implying that nonduality cannot really be encapsulated in language. Secondly, *believing* in nondual teachings is not different from any other system of belief, be it a theist or an atheist position. Thirdly, what distinguishes gurus and "enlightened masters" from other beings is that they have a *living* understanding of nonduality, that is, it has become their mode of perception.

This emphasis put on experiential knowledge can partly be traced back to the philosophical foundations of Advaita, where this position is encapsulated in concepts such as *anubhava*, referring to a form of unmediated experience of absolute reality gained independent of the day-to-day faculties of sensory perception and inference (see Davis 2011, 34–35; Forsthoefel 2018, 44–53; Halbfass 1990, 387–393; Long 2019, 11–13), and *jīvanmukta*, a state of liberation while alive (King 1999, 182; Sharma 1999).

But there were also other, rather different types of arguments raised for valuing personal experience higher than intellectual knowledge. These were connected to questions of personal authenticity and integrity: Accepting the views of others without "inner resonance" was seen as potentially harmful to one's spiritual development, as it was thought to suppress one's personal authenticity, and hence could be equal to "faking."

---

5. In order to reduce the possibilities of identifying interlocutors, I have, besides altering their names, further removed the details of the particular guru they were following in quotations from interviews and replaced it with "Guruji." "He" or "she," when the guru is referred to, is written out as "s/he."

John, one of those interlocutors who expressed such concerns by stating his distrust of external authority, interpreted this sentiment as an outcome of his cultural background:

> And so, you try things, you have to see if they resonate with you. Don't believe what other people tell you, don't accept faith based on faith. In other words, I don't accept a belief system which I can't—this is the Western aspect of my background—that I can't... either test myself or see tested in the real world.
>
> (Interview with "John," February 2018)

John connected his reluctance to follow teachings without validating them by personal experience with the anti-authoritarian ideology which had been prevailing during his years as a student at the end of the 1960s. Inspired by counter-cultural icons such as Alan Watts (1915–1973) and Ram Dass (1931–2019), he had taken to heart ideals of trusting his own feeling rather than submitting to authorities. John's narrative reveals that the reasons for emphasizing personal experience were not only the result of a nondual logic but also had their roots in a form of anti-authoritarian and anti-dogmatic outlook reminiscent of that commonly found in the "spiritual but not religious" category today (see Heelas and Woodhead 2005; Huss 2014; Parsons 2018).

The relativity between intellectual and experiential knowledge in the satsang scene was thus one which heavily favored experience. Partly, this was an outcome of the nondual logic itself, as the stated aim of nondual discourses, to "awaken" to one's true, nondual nature, was thought to be made possible only by experiential means. The importance of experiential knowledge was further justified by ideas of personal authenticity and integrity.

The question that remains to be answered now is how such an emphasis on personal experience and discernment could be cultivated and expressed in satsang—events which, at least on the surface, were based on verbal discourses delivered by an authority. As will be suggested in the following sections, the dialogues between teachers and participants in satsang could be understood as a form of experience-facilitators. Moreover, the setting and the bodies of those present were other significant factors in facilitating certain experiences. This partly involved the communitas of fellow satsang participants, but above all, it seemed, the guru.

## The Guru's Embodiment of an Awakened State

While gurus have been called "multifarious" due to their multiple and often shifting roles (Copeman and Ikegame 2014), in the satsang scene, the most central role of a guru was first and foremost that of someone having the ability to guide others in spiritual matters. The ability to teach and transmit nondual knowledge was furthermore closely related to a teacher's experiential understanding of an "awakened" state. As Victor put it, for "enlightened masters" nonduality was something *lived* rather than a merely intellectual concept. This kind of embodiment of what was variously referred to as awakening or enlightenment brought with it that the corporeal presence of the guru was thought of as being a vital part of satsang.

Even for someone not accustomed to the particularities of satsang, it would probably be clear that the teacher, or guru, had a somewhat elevated position in these events already before the actual teachings began. The standard procedure would be that teachers only entered the satsang hall when the audience had been seated in silence for some minutes, and, upon their arrival, the audience would oftentimes stand up and fold their hands and/or slightly bow down their heads. This procedure would be accompanied by evocative bhajans, either played from recordings or performed live, and when seated, the teacher would sit either on a chair or platform slightly elevated above the rest of the audience.[6]

As Frisk noted in her study of the Satsang network (Frisk 2002, 72), it was rare that teachers received direct questions regarding whether they were awakened or not in satsang. But by the way adherents discussed the merits of different teachers and satsangs, it was clear that the skill to transmit nondual teachings was thought to be based on experiential, and hence embodied knowledge.[7] Soma, a long-term practitioner of Advaita, expressed this sentiment in a characteristically nondual manner:

---

6. There were some noticeable differences in the ways teachers related to their status as a guru. While some seemed to accept this status, others were more reluctant to be seen as set apart from the ordinary and hence downplayed any acts of reverence towards them.
7. These assumptions usually came together with expectations of gurus behaving according to their elevated status—and this was, in some cases, a point associated with controversy and differing opinions. After the main part of my fieldwork in Rishikesh had ended, articles critically examining and questioning the behavior of Prem Baba (Bergamo 2018) and Mooji (Scofield 2019) in their roles as gurus were published. For the responses of the gurus and their sanghas to this, see Prem Baba (n.d.) and Mooji (n.d., 2019).

> A friend recently said, she expressed it as you just know that they [the gurus] know. And maybe a more sort of specific way of saying it is that it's really clear that it's nobody there. You know, it's not somebody inside micromanaging or nobody inside with desires or... it's just like the eyes are empty. So the presence is just obvious.
>
> (Interview with "Soma," 2017)

According to Soma, the absence of a sense of (dual) personhood in a teacher made a form of (nondual) presence obvious. From this perspective, the elevation to the status of guruhood was hence dependent on some form of recognition of spiritual maturity in the form of having "awakened" to a nondual state. And while part of such recognition could come from appeals to tradition (Hammer 2004; Lewis 2003) in the sense of being affiliated with an established guru *paramparā*, it mainly appeared to be derived from personal experience, and more represented a sort of charismatic authority (Lewis 2003, 13–14; Weber 1964).

This form of charismatic authority stemming from personal experience and embodiment of nonduality was reflected in the ways in which interlocutors talked about the importance of being in the physical presence of a guru. While the concept of *darśan* (see Eck 2007) was occasionally used, a more common expression was that of "energy," as comes to the fore in Matt's narrative about the experience of being in the presence of a teacher in satsang:

> Yeah, the personal presence is really quite relevant. There is an energy there that ... that it's really for me hard to define what it is, but I know that there's something there, energetically. And I just know that the moment s/he kind of enters the room, you know, I just sometimes feel a lot of emotion inside. And especially, you know, how s/he looks around in the room, and it's almost like in this stare, there just seems to be a connection there that is really ... you're not going to find anywhere else.
>
> (Interview with "Matt," February 2018)

Other interlocutors referred to energy in a similar way when explaining why they preferred satsangs with some teachers more than with others. Different satsangs were thought to have different energies, they meant, and people therefore "resonated" more or less with different teachers and their satsangs.

With the view of the guru as an embodiment of the state of awakening, we can begin to understand parts of the non-verbal communication in satsang. Not only the words but also the "energy" emanating from the guru was seen as a contributing factor beneficial for experiencing nondual tenets by interviewed satsang participants.

## Communitas and Existential Oneness

If the presence of the guru represented one factor which made satsangs into environments particularly suitable for attaining knowledge about the nature of the Self, then the sense of community with other people was pointed out as another such factor. Writer and psychoanalyst Sudhir Kakar (2002) captures the sense of intimacy resulting from being squeezed together with large numbers of unknown people in his vivid description of attending a Radha Soami satsang. Recalling the initial unease arising from the fierce press of other bodies, he reports how "[d] istances and differences—of status, age and sex—disappear in an exhilarating feeling (temporary to be sure) that individual boundaries can indeed be transcended and were perhaps illusory in the first place" (Kakar 2002, 130).

While Kakar's (2002, 128) observation reportedly was made at a satsang with a crowd far larger than any of the events I attended during fieldwork, there could often be a sense of involuntary physical closeness at the satsangs in Rishikesh too. One might have to step over someone's crossed legs in order to reach an empty spot in front, and while seated, sit knee to knee or elbow to elbow and hear the breathing, shifting of position, and occasional laughter or cry of one's neighbors.

That satsangs could offer a sense of closeness to others unlike that found in most everyday situations, as Kakar's description implies, was highlighted by interlocutors as well. Some pointed out that the sense of sharing they could experience in a satsang was not necessarily of the same kind as "ordinary" friendships. One participant, for instance, explained that sharing spirituality with others was one aspect of satsang she appreciated, but added that it was not so much the friendship relations or being part of a group that were important. Rather, it was more about sharing the experience of the moment with someone (interview with "Emilia," March 2018).

A similar sentiment came to the fore in Katja's narrative, as she spoke of how listening to the life stories of unknown people could affect her deeply, since she could relate to them by often having been in similar situations and circumstances (interview with "Katja," February 2018).

What Emilia and Katja described, a sense of communion with unknown people arising in a particular setting can, in Victor Turner's (1969) words, be interpreted as communitas. More specifically, it can be seen as what Turner calls existential or spontaneous communitas which "is not the pleasurable and effortless comradeship that can arise between friends, coworkers, or professional colleagues any day," but rather represents "a transformative experience that goes to the root of each person's being and finds in that root something profoundly communal and shared" (1969, 138).

Referring to van Gennep's work on rites of passage (1960), Turner states that all rites of passage are marked by the phases of separation, margin, and aggregation (1969, 94). Communitas is intimately linked with liminality, a marginal state where otherwise hegemonic social structures are put out of place. The ritualized behavior imposed on participants when entering the satsang hall—the requirements of dressing in a particular way (not too exposing), staying silent, turning off mobile phones, greeting the guru, listening to music and/or singing, effectively acted to demarcate the space of the hall from the outside world and thus represented a form of separation act. For the duration of the satsang, a liminal state pervaded, in the sense that "normal" social structures were no longer dominating.

Turner notes that there are certain modalities which are characteristic of a liminal state. Participants often display attributes such as sexlessness and anonymity as well as submissiveness and silence (Turner 1969, 102–103). Contrasting with those status systems which normally characterize society, liminality represents totality, homogeneity, equality, humility, and so on (Turner 1969, 106). In satsangs, the code of conduct and social status participants usually displayed in other situations was put out of place, and another form of regulated behavior and hierarchy was implemented. Inside the satsang hall, the guru held the position of authority, while other participants, due to their inferior position in relation to the guru, attained the status of neophytes.

The most crucial implication of the liminal state pervading during a satsang could be seen in the efforts of questioning one's habitual identification with thoughts and a sense of separate personhood; that is to say, that this was meant to be a situation where "normal" conceptions of the person were critically scrutinized in favor of the adoption of a different kind of perception of the Self.

Turner further notes that in certain types of communitas arising from a liminal state, fear or danger is importantly present (1969, 154). While satsangs did not in any direct way contain elements of danger or threat, they could include confrontations with feelings such as grief, despair, pain, or a general sense of unease, as many interlocutors pointed out that starting to question taken-for-granted ideas around one's sense of self-identity could bring up unpleasant or suppressed emotions to the surface. While the confrontation with intense emotional states did not represent danger or threat in any immediate sense, it does not appear far-fetched to claim that intense display of emotions such as crying or talking about intimate details of one's life in the presence of strangers would be considered out of place—and possibly even socially threatening—in many other situations. Thus, an important part of the liminal state in satsangs stemmed from the altered view of what was possible to share with others. Intimate, personal details could be disclosed in a way which would normally not be considered appropriate.

The sort of emotional intimacy that could arise in satsang was illustrated by interlocutors' descriptions of it as a "safe place" with a "welcoming and supportive" atmosphere, where one did not run the risk of being criticized for what one believed in. Some interlocutors would take their interpretation one step further by talking about their sense of community in satsang in terms of "oneness." Katja, for instance, connected her experiences of satsang with a oneness feeling conducive to removing a sense of separation:

> It's like inspiration [to be in satsang], but also to get into this energy. I can recognize it. In satsangs for instance, to take part of this, as they say, oneness feeling. That it's not just words, but that you really feel that you are in this state, as a part of everything. And that has been very abstract, that has only been like words to me before. Now I feel I get to partake in this feeling, and I think that's really important. Just to remove this feeling of separation.
>
> (Interview with "Katja," February 2018)

Of course, visiting a satsang did not automatically lead to becoming absorbed in a feeling of oneness and communion. For someone not accustomed to these settings, the whole thing might very well appear as one big spectacle, as alienating rather than giving rise to a sense of togetherness. One could also argue that the hierarchical structures dominating outside of satsangs were not so much disappearing as they were being altered, with participants' experience and relation to the guru forming a new, subtle form of hierarchy.

What seemed to be needed in order to partake in this sort of existential communitas was some sort of pre-existing familiarity and sympathy with the basic tenets of Modern Advaita. For people who had such a sympathetic attitude, satsangs offered situations where it was possible to experience those states discussed by teachers, such as being "a part of everything" by having a "oneness feeling," and by that, moving away from a sense of existential separation. The experiences that Katja described serve as an apt example of abstract tenets such as nonduality and oneness having—at least temporarily—been turned into embodied knowledge, aided by the particular context of the satsang hall, including the communitas with other participants.

## Discourses as Experience-Facilitators

While the physical presence of the guru and other satsang participants played a vital part in satsang, this did not mean that the verbal discourses that gurus presented were thought of as being without value or function. As Pagis notes, salvation religions or soteriological philosophies "require a conceptual dimension that gives their practitioners structure and a goal but that cannot become fully meaningful without verification through embodiment" (2010, 487). Conceptual knowledge did play an important role in providing an interpretive framework in satsang.

But more exactly how influential conceptual knowledge was in the experiences of satsang participants was not always easy to determine, as conceptual and experiential knowledge was often found to be intertwined. Tulasi, for instance, found it difficult to describe her guru's teachings, since

> the guru teaches you to be with what is. And, um, well, to worship God inside you and then ... you are the reflection of the other. Or, the other is the mirror of you. And s/he teaches you to be neutral, in this space where we are all the same. And that's what s/he says the whole time, when you are in the quiet space, which is a big mystery, non-comprehensible, non-dividable, non-deniable, it is always there. And whatever you meet in life, how big the challenge is, you can always rely on that part inside yourself. And it sounds so simple and it is so difficult in real life.
>
> (Interview with "Tulasi," March 2018)

Although this narrative provides a number of examples of conceptual knowledge, such as the tenets that God is to be worshipped within, that "you are the reflection of the other," and that we are all the same, aspects such as the guru teaching you "to be with what is" appears to linger on the border between conceptual and experiential knowledge, as it is a statement open for personal interpretation that arguably needs to be experienced to make sense. The directionality in the sense of the temporal dynamic in processes of knowing (that is, what comes first—conceptual or embodied knowledge), and the mutual influence that the embodied and conceptual dimensions of knowledge exercise over each other (Pagis 2010, 487) was therefore often difficult to establish.

More generally, just how much influence conceptual factors have in the process of experiencing spiritual tenets—what we might call "mystical experiences"—is a debated question. In many classical Asian traditions of spirituality, the possibility of unmediated and unconstructed awareness is accepted, expressed in the "acknowledgment of the possibility of transcending one's own personal and cultural particularity and the attainment of some final state of ultimate understanding" (King 1999, 182). In Western academia, on the other hand, social constructivist perspectives pointing to the inevitability of social and cultural factors in the process of experience have come to predominate (King 1999, 169).

As King points out, this "constitutes a major point of disagreement between mainstream Western intellectual thought and classical Asian traditions of spirituality," and furthermore one with significant implications, since "to accept neo-Kantian versions of constructivism is to reject the possibility of such [culturally transcending] enlightenment and therefore to subvert the central tenet of these traditions" (1999, 182).

No matter which position one takes in this question (and here King suggests the adoption of partial constructivism as an option; King 1999, 184), it is important to keep in mind that the possibility of having a direct and unmediated experience of absolute reality should better be understood as the *culmination* of an Advaitic path rather than as something which rules out the importance of conceptual knowledge altogether.

In classical Advaita as formulated by Śaṅkara, strict demands, including the knowledge of scriptures, were put on the adept wishing to reach insight into absolute reality (Forsthoefel 2018, 56–71). Even if lack of emphasis on scriptures is one point of criticism directed against non-traditional forms of Advaita from their more traditionalist counterparts (Lucas 2014), there definitely exists a conceptual dimension in non-traditional Advaita as well.

How, then, might we make sense of the relation between conceptual and experiential, embodied knowledge in the dialogues and discourses in satsangs? A useful way of thinking of the role and purpose of discourses and dialogues in satsangs, I suggest, is as experience-facilitators.

While some of the dialogues in satsangs were more reminiscent of question-and-answer sessions, there was a specific, almost ritualistic mode of dialogue where experience was at the center that was highly characteristic of these events. This type of dialogue would usually come into action when a participant from the audience came forward with a more open-ended question related to the nature of the Self. The following extract from a dialogue with the American teacher ShantiMayi illustrates such a conversation:

> *I have fears around letting go.*
> What are you afraid to let go of?
> *My thoughts.*
> What will happen if you let go of your fears and your thoughts?
> *I'm not there anymore.*
> Do you think you are your thoughts and your fears?
> *Yes.*

> Oh, I doubt that you actually think that. You couldn't even speak this way if you did not understand clearly that you are not the fears that you think you are. You know you're not your thoughts.
>
> (ShantiMayi 2007, 21)

As pointed out by Leesa S. Davis, the master-student dialogues and teaching strategies of Advaita are "rhetorically structured and semantically geared for maximum experiential impact" (2011, 12). This is achieved by the adoption of a *deconstructive* mode of teaching leading to a form of "experiential undoing" (Davis 2011, 160–169), where taken-for-granted notions of the empirical self are questioned by their gradual deconstruction, as seen in the dialogue above. Hence, rather than providing ready-made answers, teachers would on these occasions invite participants to experientially investigate what lay behind their habitually perceived sense of self.

The deconstructive mode of teaching aiming to facilitate experiences further put requirements on participants to adopt a particular kind of listening. My interlocutor Lalita explained this as the ability to "listen by heart": "serious devotees," she explained, were those who had the ability to "listen by heart" in satsang. Those who merely listened with their intellect, whom she called the "students," would soon get bored, as the messages put forward in satsangs could be quite repetitive (Interview with "Lalita," February 2018).

The relation between conceptual and experiential knowledge in such deconstructive dialogues can fruitfully be analyzed by the adoption of what Hammer (2004, 347–348) calls a sociocognitive model. According to such a model, experiences are produced through the interplay of social and cognitive factors, as "the experiencer will tend to adopt the culturally accepted definition of the experience if the person or group who proffers this definition is seen as authoritative" (Hammer 2004, 347). A sociocognitive model thus emphasizes the cognitive impact on the construction of experience through the selective workings of recollected memories of past and present experiences (Hammer 2004, 348–349), as well as the social aspects in the form of the influence of significant authoritative others.

In short, the experientially based words of an authority offer a model of cognition which can be used for constructing and interpreting experience, and hence offer a model for cognition (Hammer 2004, 419). From such a perspective, dialogues like the one above serve to cue a person into having experiences according to a certain conceptual perspective. The ability to "listen by heart," as Lalita expressed it, could from such a perspective be translated as a form of experiential responsiveness, or willingness to adopt a certain form of cognition.

The specific deconstructive mode of transmitting nondual tenets further brought with it that the words of the guru appeared less dogmatic and more as pointing to the obvious "truth," possible to verify by personal experience, hence reconciling the inherent contradiction in trusting one's inner authority while simultaneously accepting the words of a teacher.

## Concluding Reflections: Locating Satsang amid Subjective-Expressive Individualism and Advaita

I have argued that in order to understand the perceived spiritual value of Modern Advaitic satsang among those who participate in such activities, we need to move beyond verbal discourses and pay attention to the role of experience and the embodiment of nondual discourses. Aided by the presence of the guru, seen as an embodiment of a state of "awakening," as well as the communitas among fellow participants, abstract concepts such as the ultimately nondual state of the Self could temporarily transform into an embodied reality, possible to experience, if only for a brief moment. This did not mean that the verbal discourses presented in satsang were of no perceived spiritual value at all—they were—but their main function was rather to facilitate experiences than explain nondual tenets conceptually. This, in turn, required that participants had the ability to "listen by heart," as one interlocutor put it, implying a different type of listening involving not only intellectual faculties but also a form of experiential responsiveness.

Concluding this exposé of the importance of experiential knowledge in the Modern Advaitic satsang scene, I suggest that the focus on embodiment through experiential knowledge in this context can be seen as an expression of the "confluence" between two major "flows" (Tweed 2006) of the satsang scene, namely Advaita and the subjective-expressive individualism characteristic of New Age "self-spirituality" (Heelas 1996).

The satsang scene in Rishikesh, both by its location and by the philosophical foundation of the teachings put forward, clearly reflects a Vedāntic, and particularly Advaitic, orientation. Parts of the local monastic milieu of Rishikesh have been described as representing a form of cosmopolitanism, as tenets such as a philosophical orientation toward detachment, positive value on displacement, the cultivation of emotional aloofness, and openness to bodily practice make them generally open for foreign visitors to joining in activities (Khandelwal 2014, 209–214). This form of universalist outlook was accentuated from around the nineteenth century by the attempts of Indian thinkers such as Rammohan

Roy (1772–1833) and Swami Vivekananda (1863–1902) to "reform" Hinduism in response to colonial power by presenting it as a universalist form of Neo-Vedānta (De Michelis 2004; Halbfass 1990; Paranjape 2012). Partly as a result of this Neo-Vedāntic cosmopolitanism, many of those involved in the satsang scene, both teachers and satsang participants, come to Rishikesh from parts of the world such as Europe and North America and bring with them different forms of *habitus* influenced by the cultural climate of their home countries.

According to Olav Hammer (2004), experience is, along with appeals to tradition and science, a common strategy of epistemological legitimation particular for religion in the late modern West. Today, the "emphasis on inner spirituality has become part of a common sense impression of the nature of 'religion'" (Hammer 2004, 338), and this revalorization of experience can be seen as "a sign of the general cultural climate of late modernity" (Hammer 2004, 339). Arguably, this tendency is particularly evident within the field characterized by Heelas as "self-spirituality" (1996, 18–28), a "New Age" form of spirituality where a subjective-expressive focus on the individual lies at the center. Common expressions among interviewed satsang participants such as "resonating with" a teacher or teaching, sensing the "energy" of a setting, or finding out what was "true for oneself" are more akin to such subjective-expressive sentiments than to Advaita, since they presuppose personal preferences to be a valid source of judgment.

At the same time, the emphasis put upon unmediated awareness as a prerequisite to truly experience and embody a nondual state has its roots in Advaitic philosophy. "Realizing" the nondual nature of the Self, according to such a perspective, cannot be done by conceptual means alone, as it requires transcendence of the habitual and conditioned sense of being a separate individual, as well as of intellectual faculties.

In that sense, personal experience was, somewhat contradictory, used in the satsang scene as a legitimating factor for (while following the logic of Advaita) *negating* the habitual identification as a separate, individual self, as well as (while following the logic of individualism) *affirming* the value of subjectivity by appeals to what "feels right."

Although Advaita, at first sight, might appear as a rather abstract and intellectual system, embodied dimensions played an essential role, as manifested by the emphasis put on experiencing rather than intellectually grasping nonduality in satsang. And as I have suggested here, a focus on embodiment provides valuable insights into the reception of Advaita in partly new social, cultural, spatial, and temporal contexts, as it illustrates how Advaitic teachings in their lived form were being synthesized with a form of self-spirituality.

**Elin Thorsén** completed a PhD in religious studies at the University of Gothenburg in 2022. Her thesis revolves around the international scene of Modern Advaitic satsang in Rishikesh. Thorsén's research areas are Modern Advaita and Hindu-inspired meditation movements, with a focus on lived religion.

## References

Bergamo, Mônica. 2018. "Spiritual Leader Prem Baba Accused of Sexual Abuse." *Folha De S.Paulo* (English version), 30 August 2018. Retrieved April 27, 2021, from www1.folha.uol.com.br/internacional/en/world/2018/08/spiritual-leader-prem-baba-accused-of-sexual-abuse.shtml.

Copeman, Jacob and Aya Ikegame. 2014. "The Multifarious Guru: An Introduction." In *The Guru in South Asia: New Interdisciplinary Perspectives*, edited by Jacob Copeman and Aya Ikegame, 1–45. London: Routledge.

Davis, Leesa S. 2011. *Advaita Vedānta and Zen Buddhism: Deconstructive Modes of Spiritual Inquiry*. London: Continuum.

De Michelis, Elizabeth. 2005. *A History of Modern Yoga: Patañjali and Western Esotericism*. London: Continuum.

Eck, Diana. 2007. *Darśan: Seeing the Divine Image in India*. Delhi: Motilal Banarsidass.

Forsthoefel, Thomas A. 2005. "Weaving the Inward Thread to Awakening: The Perennial Appeal of Ramana Maharshi." In *Gurus in America*, edited by Thomas A. Forsthoefel and Cynthia Ann Humes, 37–53. Albany, NY: State University of New York Press.

——. 2018. *Knowing Beyond Knowledge: Epistemologies of Religious Experience in Classical and Modern Advaita*. London: Routledge.

Frisk, Liselotte. 2002. "The Satsang Network: A Growing Post-Osho Phenomenon." *Nova Religio: The Journal of Alternative and Emergent Religions* 6(1): 64–85.

Gleig, Ann. 2013. "From Being to Becoming, Transcending to Transforming: Andrew Cohen and the Evolution of Enlightenment." In *Homegrown Gurus: From Hinduism in America to American Hinduism*, edited by Ann Gleig and Lola Williamson, 189–214. Albany, NY: State University of New York Press.

Halbfass, Wilhelm. 1990. *India and Europe: An Essay in Philosophical Understanding*. Delhi: Motilal Banarsidass.

Hammer, Olav. 2004. *Claiming Knowledge: Strategies of Epistemology from Theosophy to the New Age*. Leiden: Brill.

Heelas, Paul. 1996. *The New Age Movement: The Celebration of the Self and the Sacralization of Modernity*. Oxford: Blackwell.

Heelas, Paul and Linda Woodhead. 2005. *The Spiritual Revolution: Why Religion is Giving Way to Spirituality*. Malden, MA: Blackwell.

Huss, Boaz. 2014. "Spirituality: The Emergence of a New Cultural Category and Its Challenge to the Religious and the Secular." *Journal of Contemporary Religion* 29(1): 47–60.

Kakar, Sudhir. 2002. *Shamans, Mystics and Doctors: A Psychological Inquiry into India and its Healing Traditions*. New Delhi: Oxford University Press.

Khandelwal, Meena. 2014. "The Cosmopolitan Guru: Spiritual Tourism and Ashrams in Rishikesh." In *The Guru in South Asia*, edited by Jacob Copeman and Aya Ikegame, 202–221. London: Routledge.

King, Richard. 1999. *Orientalism and Religion: Postcolonial Theory, India and "The Mystic East."* London: Routledge.

Lewis, James R. 2003. *Legitimating New Religions*. New Brunswick, NJ: Rutgers University Press.

Long, Jeffrey D. 2019. "Religious Experience, Hindu Pluralism, and Hope: *Anubhava* in the Tradition of Sri Ramakrishna." In *Religious Experience in the Hindu Tradition*, edited by June McDaniel, 7–23. Basel: MDPI.

Lucas, Phillip Charles. 2011. "When a Movement Is Not a Movement: Ramana Maharshi and Neo-Advaita in North America." In *Nova Religio* 15(2): 93–114.

——. 2013. "Neo-Advaita in America: Three Representative Teachers." In *Home-grown Gurus: From Hinduism in America to American Hinduism*, edited by Ann Gleig and Lola Williamson, 163–187. Albany, NY: State University of New York Press.

——. 2014. "Non-Traditional Modern Advaita Gurus in the West and Their Traditional Modern Advaita Critics." In *Nova Religio* 17(3):6–37.

Mooji. n.d. "Letter from Monte Sahaja: Response to Rumours and Allegations about Mooji, the Sangha and Monte Sahaja in Portugal." Retrieved November 23, 2020, from https://mooji.org/monte-sahaja-response-to-allegations-of-abusive-cult

——. 2019. "Mooji statement." Facebook, January 31. Retrieved January 12, 2021, from www.facebook.com/moojiji/videos/mooji-statement/389955211579819/.

Norman, Alex. 2013. *Spiritual Tourism: Travel and Religious Practice in Western Society*. London: Bloomsbury.

Pagis, Michal. 2010. "From Abstract Concepts to Experiential Knowledge: Embodying Enlightenment in a Meditation Center." *Qualitative Sociology* 33: 469–489.

Paranjape, Makarand R. 2012: *Making India: Colonialism, National Culture, and the Afterlife of Indian English Authority*. Heidelberg: Springer.

Parsons, William B., ed. 2018. *Being Spiritual but Not Religious: Past, Present, Future(s)*. London: Routledge.

Prem Baba. n.d. "Testimonials." Retrieved October 14, 2021, from https://ensriprembabaorg.webflow.io/testimonials.

Scofield, Be. 2019. "Becoming God: Inside Mooji's Portugal Cult." *The Guru Magazine*, March 4. Retrieved from https://gurumag.com/becoming-god-inside-moojis-portugal-cult/.

ShantiMayi. 2007. *In Our Hearts We Know*. Rishikesh: N Season Books.

Sharma, Arvind. 1999. "*Jivanmukti* in Neo-Hinduism: The Case of Ramana Maharshi." In *Asian Philosophy* 9(2): 93–105.

Strauss, Sarah. 2005. *Positioning Yoga: Balancing Acts Across Cultures*. Oxford: Berg.

Thorsén, Elin. 2022. *In Search of the Self: A Study of the International Scene of Modern Advaitic Satsang in Present-Day Rishikesh*. Dissertation, Department of Religious Studies, University of Gothenburg.

Turner, Victor. 1969. *The Ritual Process: Structure and Anti-Structure*. London: Routledge & Kegan Paul.

Tweed, Thomas. 2006. *Crossing and Dwelling: A Theory of Religion*. Cambridge, MA: Harvard University Press.

Van Gennep, Arnold. 1960. *The Rites of Passage*. Translated by Monika B. Vizedom and Gabrielle L. Caffee. London: Routledge and Kegan Paul.

Weber, Max. 1964. *The Theory of Social and Economic Organization*. Translated by A. M. Henderson and Talcott Parsons, with an introduction by Talcott Parsons. New York: The Free Press.

– 13 –

# Aligning the Good and the Beautiful

## Yogic Aesthetics in a Globalized World

AMANDA LUCIA

This chapter argues that modern postural yoga—and the spiritual wellness industry more broadly—often exhibits an ideal formulation of the body wherein beauty and morality are co-constituted, each providing an index of the other. Beautiful people, that is to say, people who are deemed beautiful, are celebrated for their presumed moral elevation and spiritual advancement. The demand to present as perfected-wellness-embodied has significant ramifications for wellness influencers (including yogis), not the least of which are financial. This chapter argues that there are South Asian antecedents to this type of indexing of beauty and morality in South Asian religious forms, and provides evidence by looking to the bodily descriptions of religious virtuosi in religious and yogic texts, and in the presumptions of Ayurvedic remedies. However, it also shows how the contemporary global yoga industry colludes with the beauty industry creating an "embodied reception" that is also a moral hierarchy based in unequal access to economic and social capital.

Keywords: yoga, ethics, aesthetics, body, dharma, South Asian religions

> Beauty is in the eye of the beholder.
>
> —Margaret Wolfe Hungerford, "The Duchess" in *Molly Bawm*, 1878

> *Satyam Śivam Sundaram.*
>
> —Hindu *mantra*

The practice of *haṭha* yoga in the West is often iterated as a practice that helps cultivate physical strength, beauty, and longevity. Postural yoga has developed in tandem with the expansion of the wellness industry. This includes the banal ideal of attaining a "yoga booty" to aspirations for bodily health, mental clarity, and emotional and physical wellness. While the mid-twentieth century figure of the yogi—even in the West—was likely an elderly South Asian man, since then the ideal yoga practitioner in the West has changed skin tones, gender, and attire. After 1998, perhaps marking the year that yoga became "pop culture" (Jain 2014), *Yoga Journal* covers exhibited a sharp decline in representations of men and people of color (Strings *et al.* 2019, 334). Today, the contemporary yoga practitioner in the West increasingly embodies the bodily stereotypes of Hollywood film stars and supermodels—thin, lithe, beautiful, female, and white.[1] In interrogating "embodied reception," one must ask: which bodies?

Multiple studies have shown that in the contemporary yoga industry, the idyllic yogic body has become particularly classed, gendered, and sexualized to conform to normative and dominant beauty standards (Singleton 2010, 174; Newcombe 2019; Lucia 2020; Shaw and Kaytaz 2021). Globally, yoga is often advertised as an elixir for youth and beauty and celebrated as a practice with "beauty benefits." Whether *Glamour* magazine or *Hindustan Times* and *India Today*, the titles of articles are remarkably consistent: "5 Yoga Poses that Come with Serious Beauty Benefits" (Erickson 2016); "9 Yoga Poses that Promise Beautiful and Glowing Skin" (Chopra 2015); "Yoga Should Be Part of Your Beauty Routine, Here's Why" (*Hindustan Times* 2018). Yoga is a disciplinary strategy, one of many technologies of femininity (Bartky 1998) through which women conform to the ideal of the feminine and "prove themselves to be proper, upstanding, members of bourgeois society" (Strings *et al.* 2019, 334).

Primed and practiced yoga bodies are aspirational bodies that serve as exemplars of the "perfectible self" (Singleton 2010, 174). The exemplary yogic body is powerful in its physical presence, but it is perhaps even more powerful in its digital form as an ethereal, unattainable, yet perfectible ideal of self. On the internet and particularly on social media, the perfected yoga body is advertised as a lifestyle aesthetic, which novices are encouraged to emulate. Their desirability is not only based in the notion that the representations of yogic bodies are perceived as beautiful, but rather that their beauty is an index of their value. They are beautiful because they are good, and good because they are beautiful: their beauty signifies ethical, yogic actions, "right" dietary choices, and holistic, spiritual lifestyles. As a result, they represent aspirational capitalism,

1. Joan C. Chrisler and Ingrid Johnston-Robledo (2018, 38) write definitively, "Today's Western beauty ideal is tall, with long legs, a very thin body, small hips and waists, large breasts, well-toned muscles, no obvious body fat, wrinkle- and blemish-free skin, and European hair and facial features."

and in Suzanne Mrozik's terms: "virtuous bodies" (Mrozik 2007). Digital media platforms become critical sites where virtuous yoga aesthetics are shared, circulated, and reinforced (Korpelainen 2019, 47).

Of course, the false equivalence between beauty and virtue is a significant feature in a variety of different cultures, not only in contemporary yoga aesthetics. One might recall the physiognomy of ancient Greece (Porter 2004, 245), medieval Slavic fairytales (Vargas and Zych 2020), Leonardo Da Vinci's "Vitruvian man" of the Renaissance period, colonial-era anti-Blackness and bestialization (Jackson 2020), or even contemporary American Disney princesses. But this chapter aims to show that in contemporary transnational yoga, the current conversation around beauty and virtue is undertheorized, and often misunderstood.

Take for example the following event. In 2015, *Yoga Magazine* published an article which instructed its readers on the yogic practice called "the Tiger" (*vyaghra kriya*), a practice which demanded tickling the uvula with the fingers and then inserting the fingers deeper into the esophagus in order to induce vomiting. "The Tiger," the article suggested was a good strategy to help remove any excess food that had been consumed, to "shape the abdomen and hips," to bring strength to the sexual organs and back, and to improve posture and stamina (Wilkinson-Priest and Davies 2015). As *Yoga Magazine* editors might have predicted, outrage ensued from concerned readers who saw the article as promoting eating disorders, such as bulimia, and further exacerbating an already vicious beauty standard for women that demands that grown women exhibit thin bodies—along the lines of adolescents and anorexics—and maintain empty stomachs. Body positive yogis found in this one more reason to deride popular yoga publications, like *Yoga Magazine* and *Yoga Journal*, for their projection of an unrealizable standard of beauty for women. For many readers, this step-by-step instruction on "yogic" purging was damning evidence that the narrow, racialized, yogic beauty standards were violent means of disciplining women.

At the time of publication, body positive activist yogis opposed the presumed industry equivocation that only "beautiful" yogis, according to Anglo-European standards, were "good" yogis. Many demanded that the yoga industry "decolonize" yoga,[2] by recognizing that all bodies can practice yoga. But "decolonizing" was an inaccurate terminology, because voluntary vomiting *is* actually a South Asian yogic practice, as is prolonged fasting (Balakrishnan *et al.* 2018). And in South Asian

2. Diversity and inclusivity are often equated with decolonization; see, for example, https://www.thepharm.love/post/resources-for-a-more-inclusive-diverse-and-decolonized-yoga-practice (accessed August 9, 2021).

religious, medical, and yogic contexts, there is a strong correlation between the beautiful and the good, wherein "the good" signifies the spiritually advanced, the morally virtuous, and the divine (Holt 2023, 227; Flood 1996, 63; Mahony 1997, 227). Instead of "The Tiger" signifying the Hollywoodification, corruption, or colonization of yoga, the emphasis on physical beauty as evidence of the effects of yogic prowess and spiritual advancement is in fact an elaboration of a predominant South Asian theme.

This chapter interrogates this correlation between beauty and goodness as a "technology of femininity" wherein women are disciplined in the embodied reception of transnational yoga. First, I show how the beautiful and the good become mutually signified in yogic rhetoric, practice, and representation. In this section I draw evidence from my ethnographic research among yogis in transformational festivals (Lucia 2020, 229–238), but also through netnographic research (Kozinets 2020) that traces those participants into online and social media forums. Second, I show how these ideals operate in concert with broader trends in Jain, Buddhist, and Hindu traditions, wherein goodness and beauty are often equated to signify one's positive karmic endowment, proximity to divinity, or divine favor. There too, just as in contemporary postural yoga, physical beauty functions as a proselytizing tool that represents the efficacy and positive effects of a spiritual lifestyle for aspirants.

## Embodiment in the Ethnographic Field

Throughout my field research in yoga spaces in transformational festivals, which spanned nearly a decade (2011–2019) (see Lucia 2020), I was routinely made aware of the intersections of yoga, white femininity, and Anglo-European beauty standards. Although body positive yoga was gaining momentum at that time, the yogis in my field sites exhibited an aesthetical ideal of the bohemian chic, slender and toned, white, heterosexual woman. Ideotypically, this ideal feminine yogi was also high-classed and manicured, with minimalist, yet moneyed taste, displayed through delicate and unique artisan jewelry, manicured yet subtle nails, premium yogic athleisure wear, and radiant and flawless skin. Her aesthetic symbolized the affluence and intention to curate the self through organic and sustainable locally sourced products and foods, self-care beauty regimens, artisan-handcrafted fashion, and unique and unusual, beautiful, and special everyday objects. The aesthetic and ethical yogic values represented in these fields invoked the leisure of boutique, expensive, understated but affluent taste, manicured and attentive, with the luxury of time dedicated to self-care, personal growth, and health consciousness.

Throughout my ethnographic field research, I interacted uncomfortably and often in tension with this narrow conception of idyllic beauty. I understood it as an expression and an exclusionary practice of white femininity, but also felt viscerally how it also serves to regulate—and discipline—white femininity. In some ways, as a white and (relatively) affluent female, I was able to "pass" easily in these environments. But in other ways, as a slightly overweight single mother with unhealthy addictions and credit card debt, I did not. In my own psyche, this topic was so taboo that I confronted my own body dysmorphia only once, when I narrated my own "ugliness" upon arrival at Wanderlust Great Taupo with a sty. At the time, I understood myself in stark contrast to the "pure-living, beautiful yogis of New Zealand, who looked like they just walked off of a commercial for a beach" (Lucia 2020, 140). In my field notes, I wrote that I felt that my unsightly sty was a result of my "bad behaviors," as a result of which I felt "broken," "dirty," "self-conscious," "furtive," "disfigured," and "ashamed" (Lucia 2020, 141). Clearly at the time of writing, I, too, had adopted the communally held belief that physical beauty is evidence of health, morality, and goodness.

## Aligning Beauty, Health, and Morality in Contemporary American Yogic Discourses

The bodily aesthetics of contemporary yoga aficionados serve as mimetic models for aspiring yogis. In yoga class environments, students are instructed to manipulate their bodies to mimetically form the instructor's yoga posture. Yoga classes discipline bodies through these repeated patterns of expectations and mimesis. As teachers control students' bodily comportment in both overt and subtle ways, the yoga class can easily cultivate a toxic environment of "somatic dominance" (Remski 2020). Online—particularly on social media—these memetic conventions have created the phenomenon of "Instagram yogis," or yoga influencers who model yoga poses, attire, and lifestyles for aspirants' consumption and replication.

Instagram yogis encourage mimesis not only of *āsana* (yoga postures) but also of a yogic lifestyle. In so doing, they are "lifestreaming," a relatively recent but commonplace digital sociality practice of being "always on" and sharing personal information of quotidian life to a networked audience (Kumar 2021, 158). Yoga influencers curate an aesthetic, which often operates in dialogue with major brands, including skin care, essential oils, and yoga accoutrements. Emily Hund explains that "this apparent feedback loop of looks—where an aesthetic is initiated, shared, and imitated by users, before being repackaged, reproduced, and recirculated by major brands—is predicated on and perpetuated by the primary role that social media metrics have assumed in recent years" (Hund 2017, 1). Lifestreaming is a common avenue for yoga influencers, who use digital platforms to engage with their followers, by encouraging aspirational capitalism. They aim to create traction around their brand and new product offerings, by cultivating mimetic desires in their followers.

However, as Sangeet Kumar rightly notes, lifestreaming has a disciplining effect on influencers as "mechanisms that placed the subject under a pervasive gaze represented an iron inversion of technologies of freedom metamorphosing into structures of discipline and control" (Kumar 2021, 158). The controlling structures that encompass the influencer yogi are on constant display as teachers' social media content is critiqued by the yoga community, "followed" and "unfollowed," "liked" and disregarded. The pressures to constantly create content are also visible as yoga influencers make regular (often daily) posts of their idealized bodies and lifestyles, despite inevitable periods of injury, illness, and fatigue (Remski 2015).

In its contemporary branding, beauty is frequently invoked as a positive effect of yoga, as evidenced by the names of influential yoga brands and products, such as Radiant Body Yoga, Buti Yoga, Hottie Yoga Wear, "Healthy Beautiful Sexy Kundalini Yoga" DVD, and hundreds of websites of "sexy" women in yoga poses—from pornography sites to Facebook groups. In 2008, Kathryn Budig made her entry into the yoga scene by posing nude in yoga poses for Toesocks. In 2014, *Yoga Journal* failed in its attempt to respond to body positive critics who sought to diversify beauty standards in contemporary yoga, when its editors put the lithe, young, white Budig on the cover of the magazine for "the body issue" in an attempt at body inclusivity (Miller 2016). Though Budig opened up about her body insecurities about her "curves" in her article in the issue, *Yoga Journal's* reproduction of yet another thin, white, youthful, healthy, conventionally beautiful, and "sexy" yogi on its cover was identifiably unsympathetic to community demands.

Beauty is also idealized as a character trait; attention spent on self-care, mindfulness, healthy living, and gratitude results in a yogic evolution that gives rise to physical beauty. An Instagram post by Elena Brower, extracted from her forthcoming book, *Softening Time*, reads, "Allow yourself to evolve. You are a creature of distinct beauty, daily discovering what it is to be human, to be close to yourself, to stake your claim on your own happiness" (March 25, 2022). Other yogi influencers produce yogic content where physical beauty indexes the beauty of nature, and inner beauty of consciousness and personal development (e.g., @bohobeautifullife, @ashleygalvinyoga, @kinoyoga, @chelseasyoga).

Yogic beauty ideals suggest that the ideal that physical beauty is not a result of genetics, leisure, or affluence, but rather it is a result of yogic accomplishment. Physical beauty represents the physical, emotional, spiritual, and mental effects of a refined yoga practice.

> In this worldview, the external is a direct result of the internal. By extension, there is the commonplace presumption that beautiful people are also spiritually—and yogically—advanced. This presumption pressures those who would like to be regarded with the positive attributes of being spiritually advanced, yogic, or conscious to discipline themselves through ascetic practice in order to cultivate both internal and external beauty.
> (Lucia 2020, 140)

Today, seventy-five percent of yoga practitioners in the United States believe that "yoga is good for you" (Yoga Alliance 2016). Furthermore, there is presumed bodily evidence that yoga is indeed good for you; accomplished yogis are healthy, fit, and thin—with clear skin and clear eyes. In the context of wellness work, community members were constantly evaluating both themselves and others for evidence of good health, which was equated with physical beauty and spiritual evolution.

In festival yoga classes, yoga teachers routinely capitalized on this by articulating the power of yoga to "detox" and correct health challenges, such as drugs, alcohol, smoking, and indulging in unhealthy foods and habits. Students were told that they could cultivate the necessary discipline to avoid chocolate, carbohydrates, alcohol, and caffeine. Yoga teachers promised that yoga could also help practitioners overcome seemingly unsurmountable health troubles. Taking Bhava Ram's yoga classes at Bhakti Fest, I learned of how his regular yoga practice cured him of an addiction to opioids, chronic back pain, and throat cancer; I also had the opportunity to purchase his autobiography, *Warrior Pose* (Willis 2013). At Wanderlust, I took classes with Ana Forrest, who writes of her own overcoming of childhood abuse and trauma through her spiritual yoga practice in her autobiography, *Fierce Medicine* (2012). Many famous yoga teachers publish books celebrating the positive health outcomes that they attribute to postural yoga.[3] The result of this repeated yogic wisdom is that healthy, beautiful people are celebrated in these communities for their yogic acuity, spiritual advancement, and for their adherence to the "good" diets and habits. In this way, beauty becomes indexed with "goodness" in relation to health, and also moral virtue.

In yoga classes and the media (both print and social media), the healthy body of the yoga teacher represents evidence of advanced—and especially spiritually advanced—yoga practice. Slender bodies with considerable muscular strength display their good health through prolonged holds in advanced poses (such as inversions and body suspensions). The beautiful yoga body becomes an aspirational ideal, emblematic of not only skill and proficiency in yoga, but also evidence that the practitioner has engaged in a regulated practice of habituated "right" choices—choosing to eat the right foods, to cultivate the right mentality, and above all, to enact the discipline to adhere to a regular (and rigorous) yoga practice.

This neoliberal conception of morality suggests that making good individual choices results in positive outcomes, and the individual is ascribed with moral value based in the accumulated value of those choices. Numerous scholars have highlighted the detriments of such a worldview (Godrej 2017; Jain 2020; Brown 2006). To mention only the most banal: it assumes that everyone has access to the same opportunities to achieve positive health outcomes and it assumes that society is comprised of autonomous, individuals, who are solely responsible for maintaining their health independently.

## But Is This New?

There is a lot of emphasis on physical beauty in contemporary yoga cultures, which actively controls and disciplines yoga practitioners, the majority of whom (in the West, and perhaps even globally) are white or 'light' thin females. This bodily disciplining enacts exclusivity, as was made explicitly clear in Chip Wilson's public gaffe in 2013, when the then CEO of Lululemon commented that Lululemon's yoga pants simply "don't work for some women's bodies," (referring particularly to women whose thighs touch). For many, such a view was evidence of the corruption or Hollywoodification of yoga, the superimposition of film industry beauty standards onto a spiritual South Asian practice. Henry Stevenson articulated this perspective during his yoga class at Lightning in a Bottle:

> Iyengar went on to popularize yoga in America as some kind of gymnastic effort, and then Lululemon got hold of it and turned it into fashion and body dysmorphia—you know, people hating their bodies and working out—and it just played into the whole fitness, fashion, cosmetic, body dysmorphic illness of America, and this is not what yoga is.[4]

4. Henry Stevenson [pseud.], yoga class, audio recording, Lightning in a Bottle, Bradley, CA, May 27, 2016.

In fact, contemporary commercialized yoga culture in the West is often derided in just this way, with arguments that the equation between beauty, morality, and the aspirational, perfectible body is a product of yoga repurposed as neoliberalism (Godrej 2017; Jain 2020). After all, weren't the wandering ascetics of India practicing yoga in pursuit of religious liberation, and not in pursuit of an arched hollow between their thighs?

In South Asian religious traditions beauty is a vibrant character, and beauty and physical attractiveness are often equated not only with the good, but with purity, spiritual prowess, and even with divinity. As Beatrix Hauser explains:

> there are several specific [South Asian] terms that cover the nexus of beauty, splendour, and well-being, for instance, the noun *śobhā* (Hindi, from the root *śubh*, literally "auspiciousness"). Furthermore, the word *śrī* refers to both beauty and prosperity. Moreover, the goddess Lakṣmī is known by the same name. She is regarded as the embodiment of beauty and perfection, and worshipped as the goddess of wealth.
>
> (Hauser 2012, 211)

In Hindu traditions, this is particularly evident in Vaishnavism (in which Lakshmi is Vishnu's consort), and also especially in Gaudiya Vaishnavism, wherein Krishna is celebrated for his beauty, and his attractiveness to all beings signifies his divinity, and vice versa. In guru traditions, the beauty of the guru is often celebrated as one of the many significations of his (or her) divinity. Classical texts in the canon of Ayurvedic literature promise not only good health, but physical beauty and, importantly, they understand both to be evidence of moral virtue. A wide variety of Buddhist scriptures also celebrate the beauty of the Shakyamuni Buddha as evidence for his exemplary character and as evidence of his divinity. And as this chapter will show, in Jain traditions, the beauty of Mahavira is intentionally described as a self-conscious means of proselytization.

## Beauty and Health

According to Sanskritist Jim Mallinson (2021), the promised and desirable effects of practicing yoga shifted sometime around the turn of the first millennium. Prior to that point, the term yoga—and the practice thereof—signified a world-rejecting and predominantly body-rejecting asceticism. References to yoga signified breathing, seated meditation, and strict austerities, such as standing suspended on only one leg, raising one arm above the head, fasting, and remaining awake—all for extended periods of time. These disciplined, body-denying, and even body-mortifying ascetical practices can be understood as an evocation of ancient forms of South Asian yoga, and importantly, ones that influenced, and continue to influence, Buddhist, Hindu, and Jain asceticism.

During the colonial period, these forms of yogic asceticism became notorious because of their visibility, sensationalism, and exoticism. Some of the first travelogues that circulated in Europe included multiple representations of the "extreme" practices of India's ascetics (Tavernier 1677). British East India Company paintings, and later ethnographic photography, were also used as a tool for surveillance and control of India's itinerant ascetic population (Diamond 2008, 238). Circulating photographs of ascetical practices of yogis catalyzed demand for the nineteenth and twentieth century performative arenas for yogic displays in circuses, exhibits, World's Fairs, and magic and Vaudeville shows around the globe (Diamond 2008, 258–263; Zubrzycki 2018; Siegel 1991). Today, practices of yogic asceticism (*tapasya*) that radically discipline, deny, and injure the body are practiced by *naga sādhus* (naked renunciates), and rigorous yogic asceticism and world-denying bodily practices are experiencing a revival among some sects (Bevilacqua 2022).

But in the medieval period (thirteenth–eighteenth centuries), yoga texts begin to include complex balancing *āsanas* and breathing methods (*prāṇayāma*), as dynamic methods of manipulating the vital energies. Here, yoga was presented as a body-cleansing technique that secures longevity, youthfulness, and good health. In the *Dattātreyayogaśāstra*, a text attributed to the thirteenth century, yoga is described as *kālājīt*, in that it is the conqueror of time/death. Through practice of yoga, "grey hair disappears," "wrinkles disappear," and one conquers death. In the *Haṭhapradīpikā*, a yogic text dated to approximately the fifteenth century, yoga *āsana* grants steadiness, good health, and lightness of limb. It also grants "thinness, clear complexion, clear eyes, good health, and kindling of digestive fire" (*Haṭhapradīpikā* 2.78). In the *Haṭhatattvakaumudī*, a text ascribed to the eighteenth century, the text states that through the practice of yoga, "he [the yogi] loses weight, his lifespan increases and he overcomes untimely death" (Mallinson 2021).

These texts suggest a continuity with the more mainstream yogic developments in the nineteenth and twentieth centuries, wherein figures like Pattabhi Jois, B.K.S. Iyengar, Shivananda, and Yogendra (Manibhai Haribhai Desai), among others, popularized yoga globally as a "scientific" practice that was promised to foster good health, longevity, and a strong, muscular physique. Early twentieth-century yoga advocates, such as Shri Yogendra, Swami Kuvalayananda, and Shivananda tended to medicalize the practice, by claiming that "yoga is primarily a set of techniques for realizing and maintaining good health" (White 2019, 185). Mark Singleton's

*Yoga Body* (2010) detailed how the early twentieth-century popularization of yoga in Mysore developed in tandem with a nationalistic desire to cultivate strong and healthy citizenry. In these yogic systems, which would form the foundations of modern postural yoga, they also incorporated the fitness practices of European gymnastics. Anya Foxen has also traced Anglo-European ideals of harmonialism and its contributions to postural yoga, including the correlation between mind–body–spirit and breath (Foxen 2020). As yoga spread globally in the twentieth century, its promotion as "scientific" and good for health became a primary justification for the universalization of the practice, beyond the context of South Asian religiosity.

## Beauty and Morality

Crafting a holistic view of bodily and mental wellness, South Asian Āyurvedic texts supply an interwoven conception of lifestyle and morality, both of which impact medical conditions, including the diagnosis of illness. Early medical texts addressing the nature of the body, mind, self and its relation to illness articulate what South Asianist Ram-Prasad Chakravarthi calls "the compositional nature of the human being" (2018, 35). In his analysis of one of the oldest Āyurvedic texts, the *Caraka Saṃhitā* (a medical compendium dating to the first few centuries CE), Chakravarthi shows how "'life-style'—and not just impeccable moral guidelines—is folded into the conception of wellness, so that continual attention to the whole of our subjectivity is espoused as the model of the well life by Caraka" (2018, 52). In this holistic approach to wellness, behaviors and life-circumstances are understood to be just as influential as genetics and diet, and suggested medical treatments address those factors as much as they do the physical body. The *Caraka Saṃhitā* equates good health with the fulfillment of a virtuous life. Particularly, the text demands the suppression a variety of negative "urges," such as "impetuous and dishonourable deeds," "greed, grief, fear, fury, pride, shamelessness, envy, and excessive passion, as well as covetousness," and the desire to "speak extremely harshly, critically, falsely, or inappropriately." One must also suppress "urges that involve causing bodily harm to another person, such as rape, robbery or injury" (Chakravarthi 2018, 53). In this view, good health is a result of proper self-care, diet, and preconditioned circumstance (genetics and karma), but also it is the evidence of the cumulative result of honorable deeds and virtuous action.

South Asian thought and practice often exhibit strong connections between beauty and morality, and this correlation is well known and widely discussed in the scholarly field.[5] This manner of thinking can also be understood as an adaptation of karmic theory, which poses a resonant understanding that life-circumstances are a "karmic effect" of individual action, value, and morality (Mrozik 2007, 62). According to karma theory, the circumstances of our current existence are the product of our actions in previous lifetimes; and accordingly, the circumstances of our existence in future lifetimes will be the product of our actions in this lifetime. Unpleasant or difficult experiences in this lifetime are the result of previous actions—whether one acted to accrue negative karmic merit in this lifetime or previously. In this sense, disenfranchised people—whether poor, unhealthy, disabled, unbecoming, or unsuccessful—suffer as a result of their negative karmic endowments.

In Buddhist contexts, this ideal exhibits an explicit connection between physical beauty, good health, favorable circumstances, and virtue. In his discussion of "extraordinary physical endowments" of the historical Buddha, John Powers cites the *Legend of Miserly Nanda*, which asserts that "the form of a man, possessing the pleasant beauty of a bunch of flowers, which attracts...the eyes of men and women, unwavering in energy and strength and perfect in its proportions, is the reward of virtue." In contrast, he notes passages where the Buddha attributes karmic endowments at birth as the cause for those who are "ugly, unsightly, deformed, chronically ill, have deficient vision or maimed hands, are lame or paralyzed" (Powers 2009, 5) In Suzanne Mrozik's explanation:

> Buddhist traditions admit no easy or absolute separation between the physical and moral dimensions of living beings. Body and morality are inextricably linked. Thus Buddhist literature is replete with descriptions of living beings who literally stink with sin, are disfigured by vices, and conversely, are perfumed or adorned with merit and virtues. The close relationship Buddhists posit between body and morality means that the formation of ethical persons is conceived of as a process of both physical and moral transformation, affecting the entire complex of body, feelings, and thoughts.
>
> (Mrozik 2007, 4)

This propensity to view physical beauty as an index of morality, Mrozik names "physiomorality," which she carefully parses as being both the effect of karmic endowments and as the potential predictor of future moral action. That is to say that the body is both a reflection of karmic

5. Suzanne Mrozik lists E. Valentine Daniel, Ronald Inden, Ralph W. Nicholas, and McKim Marriott as key contributors to this subfield in South Asian studies (Mrozik 2007, 62), though of course an updated list would include John Powers (cited above), Mrozik herself, Phyllis Granoff (cited below), among many others.

positionality, and the body sets the parameters for future karmic agency. Simply put: "All bodies, not just those of extraordinary beings, are the karmic effects of past deeds" (Mrozik 2007, 63). Mrozik writes, "bodies are also cast as the *very conditions* for morality. The kind of body a person has can actually enable or disable particular kinds of moral agency" (Mrozik 2007, 63; emphasis in the original). Among a litany of examples drawn from Buddhist texts, Mrozik gives the example of eating meat and its dire consequences for future births. Citing the *Compendium of Training*, she writes that meat-eaters will be "reborn into families of beasts of prey (literally, "eaters of raw flesh," *kravyāda*) or into the low-caste families of *caṇḍālas*, *pukkasas*, and *ḍomvas*; they will be reborn with a foul smell (*durgandha*) ..." Those who are born into such environments will have less prohibitions or inhibitions about eating meat in future births, and thus "unfortunate rebirths" also "create the conditions for further unfortunate rebirths" (Mrozik 2007, 73).

However, as an important caveat, negative karmic endowments create the body's current ugliness, or "stink of sin," but the negative karmic action that created that unfortunate condition may not have occurred in this lifetime and in this physical body. The result is that the disenfranchised person is simultaneously morally culpable for their previous negative actions and morally absolved because they are outside of their control. In Victoria Kain's discussion of the karmic implications of "babies born dying" (babies born who will die within the first year of life), she recognizes that some interpretations suggest that karma is the "sole causal factor for one's present condition," while others "assert that physiological factors, accidents, and changes of the season could also be responsible for one's present predicament." In some interpretations of karma, these latter factors are often invoked in order to prevent Buddhists from blaming individuals for their misfortune, which would be considered "non-Buddhist" (Kain 2014, 1755).

As is well known, South Asian religions offer distinctive strategies to overcome the impact of negative karma (the idea of karma is common to Buddhism, Jainism, Hinduism, and Sikhism). However, individual capacity to transcend karmic limitations is curtailed by the fact that karmic endowments determine the circumstances of future births, which then set the boundaries for possible moral actions, and so the cycle continues *ad infinitum*. In this way, South Asian philosophical systems can be deployed to justify existing social hierarchies. Simultaneously, they advocate for the importance of moral action, including the obligation to care for the karmically afflicted and the karmic merit derived from such ethical care.

## Beauty and Divinity

A variety of South Asian religious traditions also articulate a correlation between the beautiful and the good and the inverse, between the ugly and the bad. Beauty, and even the ability to perceive beauty, is the result of karmic merit, which is in turn the result of right action and spiritual practices and austerities. Importantly, the bodies of divine persons are also especially marked with beauty and signs of divinity. In the aforementioned *Compendium of Training*, the Buddha is marked with divinity by thirty-two major and eighty minor marks of divinity, and he is praised for the "beauty of his golden-colored skin; the softness of his hair and nails; the magnificence of his turbanlike head; the brilliance of the tuft of hair between his eyebrows; the beauty of his lotus like eyes; the length, shape, and hue of his tongue; the whiteness and evenness of his teeth; the shape of his calves; and the majesty of his gait" (Mrozik 2007, 66). Jain sources also narrate a correlation between beauty and spiritual perfection, as well as the importance of experiencing beauty for the religious aspirant. Medieval Jain monks repeatedly recounted the beauty of the Jina (the founder of Jainism, Mahavira), that the body of the Jina was "flawlessly beautiful" and "just seeing the image of the Jina can produce profound religious awakening and set one on the path to salvation." Physical beauty was a reward for virtuous acts (Granoff 2013). South Asianist and art historian, Phyllis Granoff, argues that Jain commentators, such as the second-century Kundakunda, argued that because the body was perceived to be both different and non-different from the soul, the act of praising the beauty of the body was also an act praising the perfection of the soul. Jains, Buddhists, and Hindus understood physical beauty to be the "natural counterpart" to spiritual perfection (Granoff 2013).

In Hindu depictions of divinity, numerous examples illustrate this correlation between the beautiful, the good, and the divinely favored or even divine. The litany of adjectives used for Hindu gods and goddesses often include elaborate metaphors of their beauty: Sita's eyes are like lotuses, Krishna is beautifully dark like the iridescent night sky, Rama is the strongest and most beautiful son, the Ashvin twins are beautiful, perfect boys, Durga sits stridently picturesque atop her handsome tiger mount, Vishnu is attractive as he lays upon the cosmic ocean, as is his consort, the lovely Lakshmi. South Asianist, Rachel Fell McDermott argues that it is likely Vaishnava influence that beautified the terrifying and once macabre goddess Kali, and that since at least the nineteenth century, depictions of Kali have accentuated her more becoming aspects as opposed to her terrifying ones (McDermott 2001, 184). In the twentieth century, both Kali and Rama became increasingly depicted as idealized gendered beautifications of their forms: Kali has become more buxom and Rama more muscular.

In the epics, ugliness and disability are often associated with evil, while beauty is associated with goodness and divinity. For example, in the Rāmāyaṇa, it is Manthura, described variously as ugly, a dwarf, or a hunchback slave, who convinces Kaikeyi to cheat Rama out of his throne. Surpanaka is depicted as hideous (and made even more so by Rama's sword) as she convinces Ravana to steal Sita and wage war with Rama. In contrast to Surpanaka, Sita is depicted to be as virtuous as she is beautiful. And similarly, in extended version (*uttarakanda*) so too are her two sons, Lava and Kusha, who are described to be as virtuous, skilled, and as strikingly handsome as their father, Rama. In the Māhabhārata, Draupadi's beauty and virtue are celebrated in tandem. When the Kauravas win her in the dice game and attempt to violate her virtue, they are depicted as lecherous and ugly in their immoral act (a point visualized in the television serial). Marking the contrast, at this moment, the beautiful and virtuous Draupadi calls on the beautiful lord Krishna, who heroically saves her from ruination. In Gaudiya Vaishnavism, Krishna is directly equated with both truth and beauty, which are understood to be synonymous (Tripurari 2011, 21). In the Bhagavatām, even the alluring *gopīs* (cowherdesses) who are granted special access to Krishna are understood to have practiced spiritual austerities in previous lives or in this one in order to have been granted that special privilege (10.44.14).[6] Swami Tripurari, a Gaudiya Vaishnvava theologian, writes that when Krishna gathers with the *gopīs*, "Indeed, all of the beauty within the phenomenal world appeared to rest in him alone, for it is ultimately his *parā-śakti* that is responsible for the beauty of the world. This *parā-śakti* also rests in him in eternity, making him ever more beautiful" (Tripurari 2011, 138).

In the Guru Gītā, the guru is celebrated as one who has auspicious form, long feet, lotus-like hands, and a pleasing face and eyes. Different contemporary guru traditions also create additional prayers highlighting the beauty of the guru, as in the 1000 names of Mata Amritanandamayi, many of which enumerate her physical beauty. Other gurus, most notably Swami Vivekananda, Anandamayi Ma, and Paramhansa Yogananda, were greatly celebrated for their beauty, which also signified their divinity (Hallström 2008, 30, 33, 184; Neumann 2019). In a 2018 television serial, the famed nationalistic guru Baba Ramdev's "crooked smile" had to first be explained away by the narrators before he could be considered

6. See https://btg.krishna.com/the-reservoir-of-all-beauties.

a spiritual exemplar (Jhaveri 2018). In their memoirs, devotees routinely describe their attraction to the beauty of their guru, including their admiration of, and beloved attention to, his or her physical form.

## Conclusion

In a fifth-century Jain Śvētāmbara text on monastic rules, it is asked explicitly, "why should it matter if the body of the Jina is beautiful?" and it is answered: "beauty comes from the merit of practicing the Jain teachings. Even those who are good-looking practice the Jain teachings, the handsome person is listened to, and so we praise the beauty of the Jina." The later twelfth-century Sanskrit commentary explains that "when people hear that physical beauty is the result of practicing the Jain teachings, they too want to follow the Jain way. Furthermore, if they see good-looking people practicing the *dharma*, they are motivated to do so themselves. And there is also the factor that people pay closer attention to what a good-looking person says" (Granoff 2013). No doubt the Buddha's physical beauty was also intended to make Buddhist doctrine appear attractive so as to allure followers. Similarly, Rama's newfound handsome and muscular physique and the goddess Kali's buxom beauty are endemic aspects of an aggressive and expansive Hindu nationalism.

This notion of beauty as proselytizing tool is not so dissimilar to the idea that thin, manicured, beautiful, white women are more effective marketers for yoga products, classes, retreats, and lifestyle. Then as now, the physical body of the spiritual adept represents the aspirations of religious practitioners. It advertises and recruits through its bodily representation. Yogic beauty and health demonstrate the efficacy of yogic practice while providing evidence for the moral virtue acquired through yogic austerities.

It is possible then that in indigenous South Asian views, the beautiful, healthy, and wealthy Instagram yogis are endowed with such gifts because of their positive karmic endowments. Further, Ayurvedic understandings of holistic health, as discussed in the *Caraka Saṃhitā* would suggest that their good health and overall yogic wellness are also the result of virtuous actions, moral restraint, and honorable deeds. Such a view differs slightly from the neoliberal understanding that their health, beauty, and wealth are the direct result of their individual choices, because it considers the holistic social context in which the person exists (and existed previously in past lifetimes). In this view, there are no autonomous individuals making choices, but rather interconnected webs of beings acting out their karmic circumstances in tandem.

**Amanda Lucia** is Professor of Religious Studies at the University of California-Riverside. Her research engages the global exportation, appropriation, and circulation of Hinduism. She is author of *White Utopias: The Religious Exoticism of Transformational Festivals* (2020), *Reflections of Amma: Devotees in a Global Embrace* (2014), and numerous articles.

## References

Balakrishnan, Ragavendrasamy, Ramesh Mavathur Nanjundaiah and Nandi Krishnamurthy Manjunath. 2018. "Voluntarily Induced Vomiting: A Yoga Technique to Enhance Pulmonary Functions in Healthy Humans." *Journal of Āyurveda and Integrative Medicine* 9(3): 213–216.

Bartky, Sandra Lee. 1998. "Foucault, Femininity, and the Modernization of Patriarchal Power." In *The Politics of Women's Bodies: Sexuality, Appearance, and Behavior*, edited by Rose Weitz, 25–45. New York: Oxford University Press.

Bevilacqua, Daniela. 2022. "Towards a Nath Re-Appropriation of Hatha-Yoga." In *The Power of the Nāth Yogīs: Yogic Charisma, Political Influence, and Social Authority*, edited by Daniela Bevilacqua and Eloisa Stuparich, 281–306. Amsterdam: Amsterdam University Press.

Brown, Wendy. 2006. "American Nightmare: Neoliberalism, Neoconservativism, and De-Democratization." *Political Theory* 34(6): 690–714.

Chakravarthi, Ram-Prasad. 2018. *Human Being, Bodily Being.* New York: Oxford University Press.

Chopra, Neena. 2015. "9 Yoga Poses that Promise Beautiful and Glowing Skin." *India Times,* 13 November. Retrieved March 25, 2022, from www.indiatimes.com/health/healthyliving/5-yoga-poses-that-promises-beautiful-skin-and-glowing-skin-240220.html.

Chrisler, Joan C. and Ingrid Johnston-Robledo. 2018. *Woman's Embodied Self: Feminist Perspectives on Identity and Image.* Washington, DC: American Psychological Association.

Corn, Seane. 2019. *Revolution of the Soul: Awaken to Love through Raw Truth, Radical Healing, and Conscious Action.* Louisville, KY: Sounds True Publishing.

Diamond, Debra. 2008. *Yoga: The Art of Transformation.* Washington, DC: Arthur M. Sackler Gallery, Smithsonian Institution.

Erickson, Katheryn. 2016. "5 Yoga Poses That Come with Serious Beauty Benefits." Retrieved March 25, 2022, from www.glamour.com/story/sky-ting-yoga-poses-that-you-can-do-at-home.

Flood, Gavin. 1996. *An Introduction to Hinduism*. London: Cambridge University Press.

Forrest, Ana T. 2012. *Fierce Medicine: Breakthrough Practices to Heal the Body and Ignite the Spirit*. New York: HarperOne.

Foxen, Anya. 2020. *Inhaling Spirit: Harmonialism, Orientalism, and the Western Roots of Modern Yoga*. New York: Oxford University Press.

Godrej, Farah. 2017. "The Neoliberal Yogi and the Politics of Yoga." *Political Theory* 45(6): 772–800.

Granoff, Phyllis. 2013. "Beauty and Enlightenment: Looking at Jain Art." Keynote lecture at The San Diego Museum of Art, June 10. Retrieved August 4, 2021, from https://youtu.be/RYSkN8Sw0k8.

Hallström, Lisa Lassell. 2008. *Mother of Bliss: Ānandamayī Mā (1896–1982)*. New York: Oxford University Press.

Hauser, Beatrix. 2012. "Purity, Beauty and Luxury as Performative Categories in Hindu Rituals and Beyond." In *How Purity Is Made*, edited by Petra Rösch and Udo Simon, 195–215. Wiesbaden: Harrassowitz.

*Hindustan Times*. 2018. "Yoga Should Be Part of Your Beauty Routine, Here's Why." June 18. Retrieved March 25, 2022, from www.hindustantimes.com/fashion-and-trends/yoga-should-be-part-of-your-beauty-routine-here-s-why/story-RtopCiM4tuFWVvWboVjNjO.html.

Holt, Amy-Ruth. 2023. "The Visual Multiplicity and Materiality of Guru Nityānanda's Portraits." In *Devotional Visualities: Seeing Bhakti in Indic Material Cultures*, edited by Karen Pechilis and Amy-Ruth Holt, 210–234. London: Bloomsbury.

Hund, Emily. 2017. "Measured Beauty: Exploring the Aesthetics of Instagram's Fashion Influencers." *#SMSociety17: Proceedings of the 8th International Conference on Social Media & Society*, 1–5.

Jackson, Zakiyyah Iman. 2020. *Becoming Human: Matter and Meaning in an Antiblack World*. New York: New York University Press.

Jain, Andrea. 2014. *Selling Yoga: From Counterculture to Pop Culture*. New York: Oxford University Press.

——. 2020. *Peace, Love, Yoga: The Politics of Global Spirituality*. New York: Oxford University Press.

Jhaveri, Kushal, dir. 2018. *Swami Baba Ramdev: The Untold Story* [Hindi: *Swami Ramdev: Ek Sangharsh*]. Ajay Devgn FFilm Productions and Watergate Productions.

Kain, Victoria J. 2014. "Babies Born Dying: Just Bad Karma? A Discussion Paper." *Journal of Religion and Health* 53(6): 1753–1758.

Korpelainen, Noora-Helena. 2019. "Sparks of Yoga: Reconsidering the Aesthetic in Modern Postural Yoga." *The Journal of Somaesthetics* 5(1): 46–60.

Kozinets, Robert. 2020. *Netnography: The Essential Guide to Qualitative Social Media Research.* London: Sage.

Kumar, Sangeet. 2021. *The Digital Frontier: Infrastructures of Control on the Global Web.* Bloomington, IN: Indiana University Press.

Lucia, Amanda. 2020. *White Utopias: The Religious Exoticism of Transformational Festivals.* Oakland, CA: University of California Press.

Mahony, William K. 1997. "The Guru-Disciple Relationship: The Context for Transformation." In *Meditation Revolution: A History and Theology of the Siddha Yoga Tradition*, by Douglas Renfrew Brooks, Swami Durgananda, Paul E. Muller-Ortega, William K. Mahony, Constantina Rhodes Bailly and S. P. Sabharathnam, 223–276. New York: Agama Press.

Mallinson, Jim. 2021. "A History of the Role of the Body in Yoga: From Subjugation to Cultivation." Keynote lecture at Karwaan—The Heritage Exploration Initiative, June 21. Retrieved August 4, 2021, from https://youtu.be/3A1wI8N-_4U.

McDermott, Rachel Fell. 2001. *Mother of My Heart, Daughter of My Dreams: Kālī and Umā in the Devotional Poetry of Bengal.* New York: Oxford University Press.

Miller, Amara. 2016. "Eating the Other Yogi: Kathryn Budig, the Yoga Industrial Complex, and Appropriation of Body Positivity." *Race and Yoga Journal* 1(1): 1–22.

Mrozik, Suzanne. 2007. *Virtuous Bodies: The Physical Dimensions of Morality in Buddhist Ethics.* New York: Oxford University Press.

Neumann, David J. 2019. *Finding God through Yoga: Paramahansa Yogananda and Modern American Religion in a Global Age.* Chapel Hill, NC: University of North Carolina Press.

Newcombe, Suzanne. 2019. *Yoga in Britain: Stretching Spirituality and Educating Yogis.* London: Equinox.

Porter, Roy. 2004. *Flesh in the Age of Reason.* New York: W.W. Norton & Company.

Powers, John. 2009. *A Bull of a Man: Images of Masculinity, Sex, and the Body in Indian Buddhism.* Cambridge, MA: Harvard University Press.

Rea, Shiva. 2014. *Tending the Heart Fire: Living in Flow with the Pulse of Life.* Louisville, KY: Sounds True Publishing.

Remski, Matthew. 2015. "Kino's Hip: Reflections on Extreme Practice and Injury in Asana." *Matthew Remski* (blog), July 12. Retrieved from https://matthewremski.com/wordpress/kinos-hip/.

——. 2020. "Somatic Dominance: Climate Collapse & the Spectre of Cultic Yearnings. Convo with Patrick Farnsworth." Retrieved March 26, 2022, from https://matthewremski.com/wordpress/tag/somatic-dominance.

Shaw, Alison and Esra S. Kaytaz. 2021. "Yoga Bodies, Yoga Minds: Contextualizing the Health Discourses and Practices of Modern Postural Yoga." *Anthropology & Medicine* 28(3): 279–296.

Siegel, Lee. 1991. *Net of Magic: Wonders and Deceptions in India.* Chicago, IL: University of Chicago.

Singleton, Mark. 2010. *Yoga Body: The Origins of Modern Posture Practice.* Oxford: Oxford University Press.

Strings, Sabrina, Irene Headen and Breauna Spencer. 2019. "Yoga as a Technology of Femininity: Disciplining White Women, Disappearing People of Color in *Yoga Journal*." *Fat Studies* 8(3): 334–348.

Tavernier, John Baptista. 1677. *The Six Voyages of John Baptista Tavernier.* London.

Tripurari, Swami B.V. 2011. *Aesthetic Vedanta: The Sacred Path of Passionate Love.* N.p.: Sri Caitanya Sangha.

Vargas, Witold and Paweł Zych. 2020. *Bestiariusz słowiański: Część pierwsza i druga [The Slavic Bestiary: Part One and Two].* Lesko: Bosz.

White, David Gordon. 2019. *The Yoga Sutras of Patañjali: A Biography*. Princeton, NJ: Princeton University Press.

Whitwell, Mark. 2004. *Yoga of Heart: The Healing Power of Intimate Connection.* New York: Lantern Books.

Wilkinson-Priest, Genny and Madlen Davies. 2015. "Does YOGA Encourage Eating Disorders? Leading Magazine Is Slammed for Advising Readers How to Throw Up to Get a Flatter Stomach." *Daily Mail*, May 11. Retrieved August 7, 2021, from www.dailymail.co.uk/health/article-3073616/Does-YOGA-encourage-eating-disorders-Leading-magazine-slammed-advising-readers-throw-flatter-stomach.html.

Willis, Brad, aka Bhava Ram. 2013. *Warrior Pose: How Yoga (Literally) Saved My Life.* Dallas, TX: BenBella Books.

Yoga Alliance. 2016. "2016 Yoga in America Study conducted by Yoga Journal & Yoga Alliance." Retrieved August 9, 2021, from www.yogaalliance.org/2016YogaInAmericaStudy.

Zubrzycki, John. 2018. *Empire of Enchantment: The Story of Indian Magic*. New York: Oxford University Press.

# Index

#MeToo, 11, 108, 202n
5Rhythms, 41–42, 202

Abhinavagupta, 14, 72n, 73n, 73–74, 86, 88n
abuse, 11, 43, 54, 108–110, 202n, 267
  abuse of power, 202n
  child abuse, 202n, 267
  sexual abuse, 11, 202n
Academic Meditation Society (AMS), 164
*ācārya*, 123–125, 127–131, 134–135
Acem, 16, 161–177
  Acem School of Yoga *see* yoga and meditation centers
Advaita Vedānta, 81, 99, 161, 164, 242–244, 244n, 246, 248, 254–257
  Modern Advaita, 17, 242–244, 244n, 252
aesthetics of religion, 2, 5, 8, 12, 12n, 14, 15, 27, 28n, 29, 33–34, 39, 95, 97, 101, 101n, 102n, 108, 203
aestheticscape, 40–41
affect, 36
  affect economy, 40–41
  affect theory, 3
  affective dramaturgy *see* dramaturgy
  affectivity, 2, 12–13, 32, 42–43, 201, 207, 213–214, 217
aikido, 188
aisthesis, 12
alertness, 207
  passive alertness, 148–149
Alexander, Gerda, 112n, 113
Almora, 82
Anagarika Govinda, 82
Anandamayi Ma, 275
anatomy, 16, 110, 154, 188, 230
anthropology, 4, 5n, 31, 44, 50, 55, 90, 106
  anthropology of religion, 102
  anthropology of the senses, 102n
  cognitive anthropology, 32
  neuroanthropology, 32
*anubhava*, 246
Anuttara, 74
Aparā, 73
*āsana*, 8, 15, 74, 98, 103–104, 109–113, 119, 121–122, 122n, 124, 128, 134n, 135, 142, 145, 147, 148, 154–156, 166–167, 166n, 167n, 172, 229–230, 270,
  *padmāsana*, 122n, 124, 130–131, 134–135, 147
  *śavāsana*, 145, 147, 155–156, 166
asceticism, 76, 81, 270
Ashvin twins, 274
astrology, 82
*ātman*, 243, 243n
Attakkalari, 186, 190, 193
attention, 31, 34, 102n, 107, 168, 176, 209, 215–216, 224, 227–229, 234, 239
  focused attention, 107
  passive attention, 149
  somatic attention, 34, 103
Austria, 38–39, 226
authenticity, 17, 37, 62, 171–172, 193, 222–25, 230–232, 238–239, 246–247
authority, 11, 49, 120, 201–202, 205, 211- 212, 217–247, 249, 251, 255–256
  anti-authoritarianism, 247

charismatic authority, 249
traditional authority, 155
authorship, 3, 10–11, 15
awakening, 244, 248–249, 256, 274
awareness, 13, 28, 36, 62, 84, 107, 131, 157, 167–169, 176–177, 216, 224, 230, 253, 257
bodily awareness *see* somatic awareness
moment-to-moment awareness, 227, 229–230
nondual awareness, 243
self-awareness, 103, 108
somatic awareness, 103, 110, 228, 230, 242
Ayahuasca, 218
ayurveda/*āyurveda*, 10, 82, 183

baby boomers, 163
ballet, 119, 187, 189
*bandha*, 103, 109, 144, 166
Bayesian inference, 36, 36n
beauty, 9, 18, 78, 261–277, 262n
belief, 27, 37–38, 96, 246–247, 265
Bengal, 15, 120, 122, 124, 134
Bengali (language/script), 15, 120–121, 125, 130, 134
Bengaluru, 181, 186, 190
Berlin, 209, 215
Berne, Eric, 173
Besant, Annie, 148
Bhagavad Gītā, 99
Bhagavatām, 275
Bhagwan Shree Rajneesh *see* Osho
Bhairava, 73–74, 74n, 76n, 78, 86
*bhajan*, 130, 243, 248
*bhakti*, 7, 18, 165
Bhakti Fest, 267
bharatanatyam, 188–189, 191–192
Bharatiya Janata Party (BJP), 10
Bhāskara, 124, 127, 134
Bheraghat, 71–72, 77–80, 90
Bhikkhu Anālayo, 225, 238
Bhubaneswar, 78, 80
Bihar, 120
biomedicine, 15–16, 95–97, 102–103, 113
Blavatsky, Helena, 174, 196
blockage, 146
body
academic body, 50
bodily fluids, 83
body armor, 207
body dysmorphia, 265, 269
body ideal, 17–18, 261
body image, 34, 41, 106, 108
body positivity, 18, 263–264, 266
body scan, 225, 227–231, 237
body scheme, 14, 34–35, 38, 40, 102–103, 106–107
body style, 28
body turn, 4
bodybuilding, 119
bodymind/body-mind, 194, 206–207, 214, 218
body-mind practices, 15, 97, 222, 227, 238
bodywork, 43, 112, 214, 218
divine body, 7
researcher's body, 7, 53, 63
subtle body, 7–8, 13, 16, 35, 43, 194
yoga body, 9, 15, 63, 96, 262, 268
Bourdieu, Pierre, 31, 42, 102n, 176
*brahman*, 243
Brahman, 90, 101, 101n, 120
branding, 4, 10, 204–205, 217, 266
breath/breathing, 28, 29, 42, 49, 62, 88, 102, 104–105, 111–112, 128, 142–144, 146, 149, 151, 156–157, 162, 166–168, 170, 172–173, 192, 195, 210, 216, 225, 229, 250, 270–271
breathwork, 208
chaotic breathing, 201–202, 207, 212–213, 215
hyperventilation, 168, 218
mindful breathing, 229
*prāṇa*, 120, 144, 171
*prāṇāyāma*, 11, 141–151, 154–158, 167, 208, 270

*nāḍi śodhana*, 147
*ujjāyī* breath, 109, 147, 155
bricolage, 164, 187, 189, 195
Brook, Peter, 186
Buddha, 121, 269, 272, 274, 276
Buddhism, 7, 18, 29, 121, 152, 188, 216, 223, 225, 239, 245, 264, 269–270, 272–274, 276
modern Buddhism, 222

calisthenics, 171
Candomblé, 38
canon, 33, 103, 142, 150, 154, 156, 157, 204, 207, 211, 217, 269
canonization, 10, 204, 206
capital
economic capital, 261
social capital, 261
capitalism, 10–11, 223–224
aspirational capitalism, 262, 266
late capitalism, 208
*Caraka Saṃhitā*, 271, 276
Cartesianism, 7, 191
caste, 120, 124, 183n, 184, 273
catharsis, 206–207, 212–215
celebration, 201–202
Chan, Jackie, 186
Chandralekha, 188, 190, 192, 194–195
chanting, 100, 100n, 131, 134, 172
charisma, 29, 31, 59
charismatization, 205
Chennai, 188
Christianity, 40–43, 177, 213, 216
Charismatic Christianity, 40, 43
Christian Science, 120
evangelical Christianity, 40
Pentecostal Christianity, 40
circus, 185, 270
class, 6, 262, 264
cognition, 31–34, 36, 38, 41, 101, 102n, 209, 255
embodied cognition, 12, 14, 30–31, 34, 43, 101
cognitive studies, 2, 12, 12n, 31–32
Cologne, 205, 209, 214
colonialism, 8, 10, 29, 145n, 184, 257, 263, 270
decolonization, 18, 263, 263n
commodification, 10
communication, 17, 28, 36, 56, 60–61, 169, 203, 232, 234, 238
non-verbal communication, 60, 232, 249
verbal communication, 232, 243–244
communicative form, 201, 203–204, 209, 212–214, 217
communicative milieu, 201
communitas, 17, 247, 250–252, 256
community of practice, 49, 54–55, 193
consciousness, 8, 32, 73, 75, 84–88, 88n, 89n, 131, 133, 150, 168, 170, 176, 267
extraordinary states of consciousness, 102, 107
consecration, 71–72, 74, 77, 77n, 89–90
contact improvisation, 207, 218
contemplation, 8, 17, 79, 84, 125–126, 208
contemplative movement practices, 1, 3, 10–11, 13
contemplative studies, 8
movement-based embodied contemplative practices, 10, 12
contemporary yoga philosophy (CYP), 95–98, 110–112
co-practice, 14, 48, 50, 58, 60–62
copyright, 11, 204–205, 217
corporate law, 11
corporeal turn *see* body turn
cosmopolitanism, 256–257
counterculture *see* culture
covert imitation, 102–103
Crazy Wisdom, 204, 208
Csordas, Thomas J., 4–5, 31, 102n, 176
culture, 4–5, 28–29, 33, 40–41, 43–44, 49–50, 56, 60, 97, 100, 102, 162–163, 177, 185, 188, 195, 205–206, 218, 242, 244, 253–254, 257, 263

counterculture, 16, 202, 204, 208–209, 213, 247
(inter)cultural exchange, 98
cultural heritage, 10
cultural product, 3–4
cultural studies, 15, 30–35, 49, 95–97, 102, 113
cultural transfer, 8, 14, 16, 61, 71, 100, 158
cultural turn, 27, 31
embodied therapeutic culture, 9
fitness culture, 15
(inter)cultural transmission *see* cultural transfer
military culture, 8
popular culture, 262
therapeutic culture, 161, 176–177, 214
Cunningham, Merce, 187, 190
CVN lineage, 181–183, 185, 189n
CVN Kalari Sangham, 181, 182n, 183–184, 186

dance, 14, 16, 39, 41, 164, 169, 181–183, 186–195, 203, 207
dance studies, 48, 62
ecstatic dance, 41
impulsive dance, 162, 168–169, 175
Indian classical dance, 189–190, 192, 194
postmodern dance, 182, 187, 189, 193
*darśan*, 249
*Dattātreyayogaśāstra*, 270
Delfs, Eugenie, 89, 89n
Delsarte, François, 112n
Denmark, 165n, 209
Derrida, Jacques, 4, 44
Deuter, Georg, 207
Devanāgarī/Devanagari, vii, 125, 126, 130, 182n
devotion, 1, 7, 60, 130, 185, 205
*dharma*, 261, 276
Dharma Mountain *see* yoga and meditation centers
Dharmamegha Āraṇya, 124–125, 128, 131
*Dharmaputrikā Saṃhitā*, 144
*dhikr*, 11, 208
*dhyana*, 145
dialogical process, 15, 141, 143, 156–157
digitalization, 9
disability, 61, 272, 275
discipline, 88, 145n, 165, 216n, 227, 232, 235, 266–268, 270
disenchantment, 164, 224
divinity, 60–61, 73, 131, 264, 269, 274–276
Douglas, Mary, 4
dramaturgy, 208, 212, 217
affective dramaturgy, 201, 213, 217
Draupadi, 275
*duḥkha*, 124–125, 127, 133
Dunn, Robert, 187
Durga, 274
Dvivedi, Manilala N., 99, 99n
*Dyade* (journal), 173

ego dissolution, 108
embodiment, 1–2, 4–8, 5n, 12, 14–18, 27–34, 37–38, 41–44, 48–53, 56–58, 62–63, 76n, 95, 101–102, 108–110, 113, 118, 130, 135, 141–143, 147, 149, 157–158, 174, 176–177, 182–183, 192, 194, 201, 203, 209, 213, 217–218, 222–225, 227–228, 230, 231n, 232–233, 236–239, 240, 242, 244–245, 248–249, 253, 256–257, 264, 269
embodied interface, 34
embodied reception *see* reception
embodied skillset, 13, 14, 48–49, 62–63
emic–etic distinction *see* insider-outsider distinction
emotions, 37, 40–41, 43, 84, 86, 103, 105–106, 111, 112n, 144, 174, 207, 209, 213–214, 217, 228, 230–231, 249, 251–252, 256, 262, 267

energy, 35, 41, 43, 82–83, 89, 144, 162, 165, 191–192, 194–195, 207, 249, 252, 257, 270
English (language), 15, 119–120, 122, 124, 145, 186, 188
enlightenment, 206, 210, 212, 246, 248, 254
epistemology, 7–8, 14, 27, 29, 33, 51, 257
Esalen Institute, 41, 206, 206n
esotericism, 8, 28–29, 41, 49, 77, 80–81, 194–195
ethics, 49, 54–55, 57, 85, 99n, 109, 239, 261–262, 264, 272, 274
  ethics of authenticity, 223–224
ethnography, 2, 5–7, 12–14, 16–17, 33–34, 39, 48–63, 97, 102, 108, 181–183, 201, 204, 209–210, 217, 222, 238, 242, 264–265, 270
  autoethnography, 52, 57, 181–182, 222, 226
ethnomethodology, 203
Eurocentrism, 188
eutony, 95, 97, 103, 108, 110, 112–113, 112n
Evans-Wentz, Walter, 83
exegesis, 73, 73n, 95–96, 98, 99n, 112, 211
  biblical exegesis, 3
exercise studies, 36
exhaustion, 37, 201–202, 207, 235, 239
experience, 2–3, 6, 8–9, 11–17, 29, 31, 36–43, 48, 50–63, 72n, 78–79, 81–86, 91, 95, 98, 100–101, 103, 105–107, 109–110, 118, 131, 133, 134n, 141, 143–146, 148–149, 156–157, 163, 169, 173–177, 182, 188, 190, 194, 201, 203, 206–218, 223–234, 237, 242, 244–257, 272, 274
  experience filter, 39
  peak experiences, 208
expert mover, 14, 61–62

family constellation, 207
fascia tissue, 105–106, 108, 113
femininity, 194, 262, 264–265
festivals, 18, 131, 131n, 186, 243, 267
  transformational festivals, 9–10, 17, 264
fieldwork *see* ethnography
film studies, 36n
fitness culture *see* culture
flow state, 40, 103, 107–108
Foucault, Michel, 4, 43
framing, 1, 5, 11–12, 16–17, 40, 99–100, 142, 161–162, 164–165, 177, 193, 210–213, 215, 218, 253
Fromm, Erich, 173

Gaga, 39–40
Gaurī-Śaṅkar, 78–79
Gaya, 120
Gebser, Jean, 85n
Geertz, Clifford, 54
gender, 6, 151–154, 262, 275
Germany, 12, 12n, 14–15, 33, 38–39, 71–72, 79, 82, 89–90, 95, 97, 101n, 164, 165n, 201, 204, 209, 226
Ghosh, Bishnu Charan, 120
Ginsberg, Allen, 81
globalization, 2, 10, 15, 96, 135, 261
god, 73, 109, 129, 132, 223, 246, 253, 274
goddess, 1, 71, 73, 73n, 75–79, 76n, 81n, 83n, 182, 194, 274
goodness, 18, 261–265, 268–269, 274–275
*gopīs*, 275
Great Britain, 28–29, 145n, 151n, 152
Grof, Stanislav, 85n
group interaction, 214, 222, 224–225, 233–234
Gstaad, 152
Gurdjieff Movements, 208
guru, 2, 10–11, 15, 17, 99, 107, 109–110, 131, 141–147, 149, 155–156, 164, 201–205, 216, 242–243, 246–253, 248n, 256, 269, 275–276
  guru movement, 17, 202n, 204–205

guru-disciple relationship, 10, 15, 144–146
*guru-śiṣya paramparā*, 10–11, 141–143, 150, 156, 243
Guru Gītā, 275
*gurukkaḷ*, 183
gymnastics, 8, 112n, 113, 119, 122, 168n, 171–172, 271

habitus, 40–41, 49, 51, 102n, 176, 257
hagiography, 109, 145
Hall, Edward T., 106
Halvorsbøle *see* yoga and meditation centers
Hamburg, 71, 75, 82
Hariharānanda Āraṇya, 15, 118, 120–124, 127–131, 133–135
harmonialism, 28, 271
Harthan, Beatrice, 141, 152, 154
*Haṭhapradīpikā*, 170–171, 270
*Haṭhatattvakaumudī*, 270
healing, 8, 9, 29–31, 35, 41, 97, 109, 177, 236
healing system, 182n, 183
health, 10, 15, 89, 97, 113, 120, 122, 122n, 142, 144–145, 148, 155, 163, 165, 171, 173, 174n, 229n, 262, 265–272, 276
health prevention, 29, 43, 226
Hennigs, Ulrich, 14–15, 72, 75, 79–91
heritage, 10, 173, 205
cultural heritage *see* culture
hermeneutics, 3, 32, 43, 99
Hinduism, 7, 10, 18, 29, 75, 119–120, 124, 130, 162n, 165, 202n, 243, 261, 264, 269–270, 273–274
Hindu reformers, 99, 257
Hirapur, 71–72, 77–79
Hobbel, Torbjørn, 172
Holleman, Donna, 152n
Holen, Are, 163–164, 173
holism, 9, 29, 35, 39, 42, 103, 111, 142, 155, 239, 262, 271, 276–277
homeostasis, 35, 103
Human Potential Movement, 174, 174n, 207
Husserl, Edmund, 5
hyperventilation *see* breath/breathing

identity, 10, 54, 59, 133, 177, 194
ideomotor principle, 36, 141, 143, 149, 156, 157
illness, 145, 223, 234, 236, 266, 271
impulsive exercises, 162, 166, 168–169, 171, 175
India, 2, 10–11, 14–16, 17, 71–72, 72n, 75, 77–82, 87, 90, 95–96, 98–100, 113, 118–123, 130, 134, 142, 144, 148, 151, 155, 161, 164–165, 165n, 170–173, 177, 181–182, 184–192, 194–195, 201–202, 204, 209, 242–243, 256, 269–270
Central India, 72, 77
East India, 9, 77
Indian epics, 188, 275
Indian mythology, 188
North India, 17, 82, 242
South India, 1, 16, 73–74, 77, 82, 97, 181, 183, 188
individualism, 175–176, 256–257
Indology, 81, 96n, 98, 122
influencer, 261, 265–267, 267n
initiation, 38, 77, 90, 128, 142, 144, 182n, 202n, 212
innovation, 8, 11, 49, 53, 187–189, 195, 223
insider-outsider distinction, 48–50, 54–55, 63, 101, 103, 209
Instagram, 9, 18, 193, 265–267
institutionalization, 10, 12, 203–205, 217
intellectual property, 11, 204
Intensive Interaction, 61
intercorporeality, 222, 238
interdisciplinarity, 5, 12, 30, 51, 95, 102
interoception, 15, 41, 48, 51, 62, 104–105, 141, 143, 149–150, 154, 156–157, 213

interpretation, 3, 6, 8, 13, 32, 34, 51, 56, 72–73, 73n, 74n, 86–88, 88n, 89n, 91, 96n, 98–100, 109–113, 119, 121, 123, 141, 143, 154–155, 157, 162, 166, 170–173, 175–177, 190, 194–195, 201, 203, 211–213, 215–218, 244, 247, 252–253, 255, 273
interpretive communities, 17, 211–212, 217
interview, 13–14, 38–39, 51–52, 58–62, 97–98, 98n, 109n, 156, 162n, 182, 201, 209–210, 245
intimacy, 49, 53, 56–61, 107, 209–210, 213–214, 250, 252
introspection, 13, 150, 232
  interactive introspection, 224
Iser, Wolfgang, 3
Iyengar Yoga Institute London *see* yoga and meditation centers
Iyengar, B.K.S., 10–11, 15–16, 141–158, 173, 268, 270
Iyengar, Geeta, 155
Iyengar, Prashant, 155

Jacobson, Edmund, 28
Jainism, 18, 264, 269–270, 273–274, 276
  Śvētāmbara, 276
Janov, Arthur, 202
Jauss, Hans Robert, 3
Jharkhand, 120
Jina *see* Mahavira
*jīvanmukti/jīvanmukta*, 88, 246
joint speech, 35
Jois, Pattabhi, 97, 99–100, 108–110, 270
Jung, Carl Gustav, 173

Kabat-Zinn, Jon, 10, 222–223, 227
Kaikeyi, 275
*kaivalya*, 125, 127–128, 131, 133
*kaḷari*, 181, 183–186, 191–192, 194–195
Kaḷarippayaṟṟ˘, 16, 181–196
Kali, 275–276
Kāpil Mandir, 125, 130
Kāpil Maṭh, vii, 15, 118–135
karma, 133–134, 239, 272–273
*karmāśaya*, 118, 128, 133, 134n
karmayoga, 56, 165
kathakali, 186–187, 191, 193
Kaula, 74, 76
Kerala, 181, 183–187, 190
Kierkegaard, Søren, 173
Kīlēri Kuññikkaṇṇan Master, 185
kinesthetics, 40, 62, 105, 110
kinesthesia, 105
*kīrtan*, 130
knowledge, 1–2, 4–6, 10, 14–15, 30, 33, 36–37, 49–50, 54–55, 58, 62, 108–109, 135, 143, 184, 188, 194, 209–210, 213, 217, 218, 245, 248, 250
  body knowledge, 6–7, 13–16, 27–28, 30, 32–34, 36–37, 39, 43–44, 49, 85, 95, 97, 101–102, 105, 108, 111, 113, 119, 123, 127, 131, 135, 141, 149, 242, 248, 252–254
  conceptual knowledge, 245, 253–255
  embodied knowledge *see* body knowledge
  experiential knowledge, 242, 244–247, 253, 255–256
  history of knowledge, 1, 18, 96
  implicit knowledge, 6, 97, 213
  intellectual knowledge, 245–247
  knowledge transmission, 6, 10, 49
  situated knowledge, 239, 244
  tacit knowledge *see* implicit knowledge
  training knowledge, 14, 27, 30, 36–37, 43
Kolkata, 124
Kottackal Kanaran Gurukkal, 184
Krishna, 269, 274–275
Krishnamacharya, Tirumalai/ Kṛṣṇamācārya, T., 15, 97, 100, 145–146
Krishnamurti, Jiddu, 16, 82, 141, 147–149, 156–157
Kundakunda, 274
*kuṇḍalinī*, 168, 171

labor, 184
hidden labor, 16, 141, 151, 154
Lakṣmī/Lakshmi, 269, 275
Lalitā Tripurasundarī, 74
legitimization, 9–10, 15–16, 161, 164, 201–202, 204–205, 208, 217, 257
Lévi-Strauss, Claude, 4
liberation, 74–75, 86, 88, 91, 127–128, 132–133, 144, 173, 175, 194, 214, 246, 269
*Light on Prāṇāyāma*, vii, 15, 141–158
*Light on Yoga*, 142, 143n, 150–152, 173
liminality, 251–252
lineage, 2, 9–11, 14–15, 49, 51, 54, 56, 100n, 113, 123, 141–142, 181–186, 189n, 194–195, 202, 245
London, 152, 186, 190
longevity, 9, 261, 270–271
Luckmann, Thomas, 203
Lundsholm *see* yoga and meditation centers
Lyotard, Jean-François, 187

Madhupur, vii, 120, 124, 129, 133
Madras *see* Chennai
magic, 29, 31, 76, 84, 87, 270
Maharajji, Hans Raj, 245
Maharishi Mahesh Yogi, 10, 16, 161, 163, 164, 202
Maharshi, Ramana, 81, 245
Mahavira, 269, 274, 276
Malabar, 181, 183
Malayalam (language), 182n, 183
Manthura, 275
mantra, 73–74, 76, 81, 86, 88n, 129, 131, 165, 172, 174n, 207, 261
Marcel, Gabriel, 173
martial arts, 1, 4, 16, 171, 181–196
Maslow, Abraham, 85n, 173, 206, 208
Mata Amritanandamayi, 275
material turn, 4, 177
MBSR *see* Mindfulness-Based Stress Reduction
McGuire, Meredith, 4
meaning-making, 2, 5, 12–13, 17, 33, 51, 54, 96n, 101, 162, 175–177, 199, 201, 204, 209, 216, 218
mediality, 4
mediatization, 9
medical system, 181, 183, 183n
meditation, 1, 4, 8–9, 11, 14–15, 17, 34, 49, 79, 81–82, 86–88, 88n, 91, 100–101, 111, 128, 130–131, 145, 161–165, 167–169, 171–177, 201–218, 223–224, 226, 228–231, 234, 237–238, 243–245
Acem meditation, 162, 165, 168, 172, 174–175
breathing meditation, 225, 229–230, 235, 237
Deep Meditation *see* Transcendental Meditation
guided meditation, 229–230, 238
meditation movement, 16, 162n, 223
mindfulness meditation, 222–224, 226
objectless meditation, 81, 174
OSHO Dynamic Meditation, 11, 16–17, 201–218
OSHO Kundalini Meditation, 205
Osho meditations, 9, 11
Sāṃkhyayoga meditation, 122n, 124n
sitting meditation, 229, 237, 270
Transcendental Meditation, 16, 161, 163–164
Vipassana meditation, 13, 244–245
Zen meditation, 12, 233
Mehallis, Guri, 163–164
memory, 31, 49, 53–54, 133, 174, 225, 227–228, 238
Menuhin, Yehudi, 16, 141, 147, 150, 152, 156–157
Merleau-Ponty, Maurice, 5
Mesmerism, 28, 120
metaphors, 6, 39, 91, 188, 228, 274
method sound, 165
methodological guesthood, 55, 57

military culture *see* culture
mimesis, 6, 11, 52–53, 58, 60–61, 265–266
mind-body dualism, 7
mind-body techniques, 201–202, 208
mindfulness, 1, 17, 43, 99, 174, 222–240, 266
Mindfulness-Based Stress Reduction (MBSR), 17, 222–240
Mishra, Rammurti, 81, 81n
Modern Advaita *see* Advaita Vedānta
Mooji, 245, 248n
morality, 18, 54, 223–224, 261, 264–265, 268–269, 271–276
Morocco, 82
movement, 11, 13, 37, 39–42, 48–50, 53, 61–62, 102–105, 108, 111–112, 112n, 146, 149, 167–169, 174, 175–176, 186–195, 207, 210, 214–215, 218, 224, 229–230, 236
  movement notation, 14
  moving style, 29, 39
  movement analysis, 16, 182
  movement repertoire, 2, 11, 16, 53, 191
*mudrā*, 144
muscle tone, 14, 17, 34, 37, 39, 102, 104–106, 111–113
Müller, J. P., 113
Mysore, 146, 271
  Mysore Palace, 145
  Mysore yogashala, 146

*nābhimūla*, 191
Naharin, Ohad, 39
Nair, C.V. Govindankutty, 183
Nair, Chambadan Veedu Narayanan, 184
Nair, G. Sathyanarayanan, 183
narrative, 14, 31, 51, 81, 98, 100–101, 106, 151, 189, 208, 210, 212, 215, 246–247, 249–250, 253
  grand narrative, 187
nationalism, 271, 276
  Hindu nationalism, 10, 276
Neo-Advaita *see* Modern Advaita
neoliberalism, 11, 39, 42, 233n, 268–269, 276
Neo-Sannyas Movement, 201–202, 204
neo-tantric bodywork, 218
netnography, 18, 264
neurophysiology, 15, 97, 104
neuroscience, 12, 30, 95
  cultural neuroscience, 32
  social neuroscience, 32
New Age, 1, 8, 41, 96, 207, 256–257
New Delhi, 186
new materialism, 3
New Thought, 120
New York, 81n, 187
nociception, 102, 104–106, 108–109, 113
nonduality, 17, 73, 75, 81, 86, 89, 89n, 242–257
non-judgement, 227, 232, 239
Norsk Yoga-skole *see* yoga and meditation centers
North America, 28–29, 100, 119, 243, 257
Norway, 162, 162n, 164–165, 165n, 209

occultism, 105
Om Baba, 245
oneness, 17, 250, 252
ontology, 60, 97, 100, 194
Order of the Star in the East, 148
Oregon, 204
Orientalist scholarship, 122
origin, 2, 9–10, 38, 119, 170–172, 183, 218
Orissa, 76n, 77
Osho (Bhagwan Shree Rajneesh), 10–11, 17, 201–218
OSHO International Foundation (OIF), 11, 204–205, 217
Osho meditations *see* meditation

OSHO Risk *see* yoga and meditation centers
Osho UTA *see* yoga and meditation centers
Oshodham *see* yoga and meditation centers
Oslo, 164

Palazhy, Jayachandran, 190–195
Pali (language), 121, 225, 238–239
Parā, 73
Parākrama *see* Anuttara
*paramparā see guru-śiṣya paramparā*
Parāparā, 73
Paraśurāma, 183
*Parātrīśikā*, 14, 71–76, 72n, 73n, 74n, 84, 86–89, 88n, 91
*Parātrīśikālaghuvṛtti*, 73, 74n
*Parātrīśikāvivaraṇa*, 71, 72n, 73, 88n
Paris, 81
participatory paradigm, 85
Pārvatī, 78, 80, 90
*Pātañjalayogaśāstra*, 15, 96n, 101, 118, 120–122, 125, 127–128, 131, 133–135, 134n
Patañjali, 101, 121–123, 131, 142, 161, 165, 170–171, 173
patriarchy, 188
Payson Call, Annie, 28
Peltzer, Guido, 87–89, 87n, 88n
perception, 5–6, 30, 32n, 33–35, 38, 43–44, 74, 89n, 103–106, 148, 176, 213, 230, 239, 246, 251
  intrapersonal perception, 41
  prosthetic perception, 34, 42, 102, 107
  sensory perception, 12, 107, 246
perennialism, 85
perfection, 7, 18, 60, 74, 76n, 77, 122n, 261–262, 269, 274
  spiritual perfection, 274
performance, 1–8, 11–12, 14, 16–18, 36–37, 40–42, 44, 59–60, 62–63, 69, 72, 74, 78–79, 90, 96, 101, 106, 108, 110, 119, 144–146, 167–169, 177, 181–196, 201–204, 207, 209–211, 213–215, 217, 222, 224, 229, 231, 233, 236, 238, 248, 270
  performance studies, 50, 62
  performativity, 2, 207, 209, 217
peripersonal space, 34–36, 102, 106–107
phenomenology, 4–5, 13, 31, 49, 215, 225, 238
philosophy, 5, 11, 15, 31–32, 72n, 75, 85, 91, 95–96, 98, 100–101, 113, 121–123, 122n, 132, 134n, 135, 147, 161, 164–165, 172–173, 190, 194, 242–244, 246, 253, 256–257, 273
  existential philosophy, 16, 161, 173, 174n
  philosophy of mind, 14, 27, 29–30, 36
physical culture movement, 29, 113, 122n
piety, 40, 190
placebo research, 30
Poona *see* Pune
Poonja, H. W. L., 245
popularization, 9, 172, 184, 186, 195, 268, 270–271
positionality, 14, 48–51, 61, 273
postcolonialism, 8, 10, 29
postmodernism, 16, 181–182, 187–189, 193–195
posture, 32, 34, 37–39, 62, 88, 102–105, 108–109, 111–112, 119–120, 122n, 128, 142, 155, 166–168, 224, 229, 263, 265
post-war period, 163
participant observation, 39, 51, 209
Prabhupada, A. C. Bhaktivedanta, 120
*prakṛti*, 124, 127
*prāṇa see* breath/breathing
*prāṇāyāma see* breath/breathing
praxeology, 31
predictive processing (PP), 14, 30, 32
Prem Baba, 245, 248n

present momentism, 223
proprioception, 28, 102–106, 108–109, 113, 149–150, 213
psychedelic drugs, 81
psychoanalysis, 37, 41, 250
  post-Freudian psychoanalysis, 206
psychology, 15, 28, 33, 38, 75, 84–87, 97, 104, 161, 165, 168, 173–174, 174n, 177, 209
  cognitive psychology, 95
  depth psychology, 86
  humanistic psychology, 16, 161, 173, 206
  medical psychology, 30, 34, 72
  positive psychology, 99
  psychologization, 162, 177
  transpersonal psychology, 41, 84–87, 85n
psychophysiology, 33–34, 38, 100, 102, 104, 110
psychosomatics, 34, 43, 71, 87n, 88, 173, 227
*pūjā*, 60, 90
Pune, 145, 148, 152, 155, 204, 206n, 209, 211
*puruṣa*, 127, 133

Radha Soami, 250
*rāja yoga/raja yoga*, 28, 119–120, 122n
Rajneeshism, 204
Ram Dass, 247
Rama, 274–276
Rāmāyaṇa, 275
reader-response theory, 3
reception, 2–6, 10–12, 27–30, 36, 42–43, 52, 71, 95–96, 96n, 98, 112–113, 141, 150, 154, 176, 182, 189, 206, 257
  cultural reception, 27–29, 37, 41
  embodied reception, 1–2, 3n, 5–7, 14–15, 27, 30, 32, 36–37, 42–43, 141, 162, 201, 203, 217–218, 242, 244, 261–262, 264
  reception history, 3, 3n
  reception theory, 3, 3n, 14, 28, 143
recitation, 11, 15, 38n, 118, 129–131, 134–135
referentiality, 50, 209
reflexivity, 17, 55–57, 162, 176, 206, 209, 215
Reich, Wilhelm, 204, 206–207
relaxation, 28–29, 105, 112, 145, 162, 165, 169, 228, 230
relaxationism, 28, 29
religion
  aestheticization of religion, 1, 8
  contemporary religion, 6, 38, 41, 95
  institutionalized religion, 204
  lived religion, 51
  non-religion, 42
  religious affiliation, 244
  somatization of religion, 1, 8
religious studies *see* study of religions
*Rezeptionsästhetik see* reader-response theory
Rishikesh, 17, 242–244, 244n, 248n, 250, 256–257
rites of passage, 251
ritual, 1, 8, 11, 14, 16, 31–32, 34–36, 38–39, 49–50, 60, 72, 74, 76–77, 76n, 77n, 79, 88n, 90–91, 107, 118, 120, 129, 134–135, 176–177, 182n, 184, 193, 195, 218, 251
Rogers, Carl, 173
romanticism, 84, 122, 208, 223
Roth, Gabriele, 41, 202
Roy, Rammohan, 256–257
rules of conduct, 227, 232

*sādhanā*, 244
Sarasvati, Brahmananda *see* Mishra, Rammurti
Śaivism, 73, 144
  Kashmir Śaivism, 71, 72n, 79
  Tantric Śaivism, 71–72, 73n, 74n, 75–76, 84, 86, 184
  Trika school of Śaivism, 71
Śākta-Śaiva traditions, 73
Śakti, 73–74, 86, 275
*samādhi*, 125, 128–131, 133, 171

Sāṃkhya, 11, 15, 121–123, 131, 133, 135, 194
*Sāṃkhyakārikā*, 121, 124
Sāṃkhyayoga, vii, 1, 9, 11, 15, 118–135
*saṃnyāsin*, 15, 120–122, 129, 133, 202n
Śaṅkara, 81, 254
Sanskrit (language), 15, 73, 75, 76n, 81–82, 88n, 90, 100–101, 101n, 112, 120–121, 125–126, 134–135, 151, 170, 182n, 276
Sartre, Jean-Paul, 173
Sathyan *gurukkaḷ see* Nair, G. Sathyanarayanan
*sati*, 225, 238
satsang, 1, 9, 17, 212, 242–257
  satsang scene, 27, 243, 247–248, 256–257
Scandinavia, 201, 204, 209
Scaravelli, Vanda, 152n, 155
Schloss Aubach yoga school *see* yoga and meditation centers
scholar-practitioner, 12–13
Schütz, Alfred, 5
science, 16, 27, 32–33, 84, 145, 161, 162n, 164–165, 177, 205, 208, 211, 217, 222–223, 257, 270–271
science and technology studies (STS), 32–33
Second World War, 163
secularization, 1, 11, 161, 165, 177
self, 13, 37, 40, 43, 56, 58, 60, 74, 86, 89, 103–104, 106–107, 109–110, 127, 129, 131, 171, 177, 214, 217, 223, 239, 243, 243n, 250–251, 254–255, 257, 262, 264, 271
  authentic self, 17, 222, 224–225, 230, 238–239
  autonomous self, 223
  cosmic self, 42
  nondual Self, 17, 242, 243n, 244–245, 256–257
self-awareness, 103, 108,
self-help, 174, 214
self-observation, 147, 154, 232
self-realization, 176, 208
semiogenesis *see* meaning-making
senses, 5–6, 12–13, 28–29, 30–31, 33, 36, 63, 89n, 101–102, 101n, 102n, 104–105, 107–108, 132, 143, 149, 156, 203, 210, 213, 218, 230
  sensory exploration, 141, 143
  sensorial strategies, 40
*sevā*, 48, 50, 56–57, 63
sexuality, 11, 74, 77, 81–83, 202n, 206
  ritualized sexuality, 14–15, 76
  sexual organs, 74, 263
  sexualization, 262
Shakyamuni Buddha *see* Buddha
ShantiMayi, 245, 254–255
Shivananda, 270–271
Shri Yogendra, 271
Shunyata Baba, 82
*siddha*, 77, 183
*siddhi*, 76–77, 81
Sikhism, 273
simulation, 33, 38
Sita, 274–275
Śiva, 73–74, 78, 80, 90–91, 261
Smith, Jonathan Z., 54
*smṛti*, 133
social constructivism, 6, 102, 203, 254
social field theory, 42
social media, 18, 122, 262, 264–266, 268
social mind, 30
socialization, 13, 28, 41, 201, 203
sociology, 5n, 6, 13, 17, 31–32, 43, 102, 203, 213, 222, 233n
  sociology of meditation, 215
  sociology of knowledge, 2
  sociology of religion, 13, 203, 213
somatic investigation, 16, 187
somatic turn *see* body turn
somatology, 16
soteriology, 16, 182, 190, 193, 253
sound, 35, 41, 82, 103, 146, 187, 207, 228–230
  sound studies, 3n
  soundscape, 40
Spain, 81–82, 165n

spirit incorporation, 14, 38
Spiritual Regeneration Movement *see* TM movement
spirituality, 1, 2, 6–7, 10, 13–14, 17, 29–30, 38, 40–42, 75, 81, 85–88, 96, 102, 104–105, 109–110, 119–120, 123, 130–131, 161, 163, 172, 175–177, 183, 185, 189–190, 193, 195, 208–209, 211–213, 215–216, 218, 224, 237, 239, 242–244, 246, 248–250, 253–254, 256–257, 261–262, 264, 267–269, 274–276
  self-spirituality, 17, 205, 242, 244, 256–257
  spiritual but not religious, 247
sports, 122, 168n
  modern sports movement *see* physical culture movement
  sports sciences, 36–37
Sridhar, Abhijata, 155
Stark Smith, Nancy, 193–194
Steiner, Ronald, 97–98, 101, 111, 112n
Stewart, Mary, 152–155, 152n, 153n
stillness, 62, 201–202, 212, 216, 218
*stotra*, 11, 15, 118, 129–132, 134
stress, 9, 29, 173–174, 218, 222–223, 226–227, 232–233, 238
stretching, 9, 28, 105, 109, 146, 155, 167, 174, 216, 230
STS *see* science and technology studies
study of religions/religion, 4, 6–7, 12–13, 31–33, 48–50, 54, 62, 203
  cognitive study/science of religion, 31–32, 102
subjectivation/subjectification, 13, 217, 224, 228, 231
subjectivity, 13–14, 18, 33, 42–44, 257, 271
suffering, 118, 124, 132–133, 174, 223, 238–239, 272
Sufism, 11, 204, 208
Surpanaka, 275
surrender, 110, 169, 212
Swaha, Vasant, 212, 216
Swami Kuvalayananda, 271
Sweden, 165, 165n
Swedenborgianism, 120
Switzerland, 38, 82, 152, 165n
syncretism, 99, 164
synthesis, 27, 32, 38, 99, 171, 242, 257

tai chi, 188
Tamil (language), 182n, 183
tantra, 1–2, 12, 14–16, 41, 71–91, 168, 171, 184, 190, 194–195, 204, 218
  Kerala tantra, 184, 190
  tantric goddess traditions, 1, 71, 76–77, 81n
  *tantrapīṭha*, 79
tattooing, 34, 102–104, 108, 110, 113
*Tattvavaiśāradī*, 121, 123
teacher, 17–18, 36–37, 39, 50, 52, 54–55, 58–61, 74–75, 81, 89–90, 98, 98n, 100–101, 108, 110–111, 119–121, 142–143, 145n, 147–148, 151, 151n, 152n, 154–156, 172–173, 183–184, 222, 225, 230–232, 238, 243–249, 244n, 248n, 252, 254–257, 265–268
  teacher-student relationship, 52–53, 108, 111, 142, 265
  teacher training, 10, 95, 97, 100, 155–156, 165, 226, 230–231
Terra Sagrada, 38
theatre, 3, 182, 186–187, 190
  theatre improvisation, 169
Theosophical Society, 148
theosophy, 8, 35, 43, 120, 148
therapy, 1, 9, 11, 14, 17, 28, 37, 41, 61, 71–72, 85–89, 97, 105, 109n, 110, 154, 162, 174, 176–177, 201, 204, 206, 206n, 208–215, 217–218, 222–223
  behavioral therapy, 84
  body therapy, 29, 41
  embodied therapeutic culture *see* culture
  Gestalt therapy, 41

primal scream therapy, 11, 202, 208
primal therapy, 204
Reichian therapy, 204
therapeutic culture *see* culture
transpersonal therapy, 15, 71–72, 75, 85–89, 85n, 87n, 88n
Thiruvananthapuram, 181, 182n, 183
Thrissur, 186
Tibet, 87
Tiruvannamalai, 81
TM *see* Transcendental Meditation
touch, 33, 35, 40–41, 95, 97, 103–104, 107–110, 113, 214
deictic touch, 104, 108–110, 113
trademark, 11
trance, 38, 40, 83, 87
transcendence, 40, 54, 75, 85, 175, 189, 194, 215, 257
transformation, 7, 9–10, 17, 37, 39–42, 53, 56, 59, 76n, 77, 82, 84–85, 89, 96, 119, 133, 135, 145, 148, 156, 190, 207, 212, 218, 230, 251, 256, 264, 272
transmission, 2–3, 5–8, 10, 14–18, 49, 52–54, 60–61, 63, 109–110, 141–143, 145n, 146, 154, 157–158, 161, 176, 182, 186, 191–193, 195–196, 206, 213, 217–218, 243, 248, 256
trauma, 43, 174, 207, 213, 276
Trondheim, 90
thermoregulation, 35, 102, 106, 111
transfer, 5–6, 38, 42, 71, 111
cultural transfer *see* culture
Tulu (language), 183
Turner, Victor, 250–251

ugliness, 265, 272–275
United States of America, 119, 122, 165n, 202n, 267
universalism, 10, 37, 50, 222, 256–257, 271
Upaniṣads, 75, 81, 99

Vācaspatimiśra, 121
Vaishnavism, 269, 275
Gaudiya Vaishnavism, 269, 275
Vaital Deul temple, 80
van Gennep, Arnold, 251
Vasan, T. S., 82, 82n
*vāsanā*, 118, 128, 133–135, 134n
Vaṭakkan Pāṭṭukaḷ, 184
*vāyu*, 191–192, 194–195
Vedas, 161, 164
Vedic recitation, 130
vegetarianism, 80
videography, 13–14, 58–59, 209
Vidyāpīṭha, 76
*vinyāsa*, 103–104, 109
*vīra*, 74, 77, 77n
Viṣṇu/Vishnu, 183, 269, 274
Vivekānanda/Vivekananda, Swami, 28, 99, 119–120, 122n, 172, 275
voice, 51, 83, 223–226, 228, 230–231, 238
video analysis, 51, 59
*Vyāsabhāṣya see Yogabhāṣya*

Watts, Alan, 247
weapon, 184–186
well-being, 1, 39, 43, 110, 173–174, 174n, 269
wellness, 109, 261–262, 267, 271, 276
spiritual wellness industry, 261
whiteness, 9–10, 18, 262, 264–266, 268, 274, 276
Wilber, Ken, 85, 85n
Wilson, Margret, 31
women, 76, 101, 108, 141, 151, 154, 184, 262–264, 266, 268, 276
World Parliament of Religions, 28
worldview-building, 15, 96, 102
Wrocław, 186

yoga, 1, 4, 8–18, 28–29, 41n, 48–63, 76, 76n, 78, 81, 84, 87, 95–113, 118–135, 141–158, 161–177, 181, 184, 186, 189–192, 202, 204,

222, 224–225, 229–230, 235, 243, 261–271, 276
Acem's "classical, meditative yoga", 16, 161–177
Ashtanga Yoga, 15, 95–113, 171
bhakti yoga, 165
Bikram Yoga, 106
female yoga practitioners, 16, 76, 151–152, 151n, 262, 268
*haṭhayoga*/hatha yoga, 99, 144, 170–171, 173, 225, 227, 229, 261
Iyengar yoga, 11, 142, 144, 145n, 152, 155–156, 171
jñāna yoga, 165
karma yoga, 165
kuṇḍalinī yoga, 171, 266
laya yoga, 168
mindful yoga, 229–230
modern postural yoga, 1, 10, 51, 96, 120, 122, 161, 164, 167, 172, 176, 218, 261, 271
modern yoga revival, 123, 142
post-lineage yoga, 11, 14, 49, 51, 54, 56
yoga aesthetics, 261, 263
Yoga *darśana*, 121
yoga class, 100, 156, 162–163, 171, 176, 265, 267–268
yoga of cessation, 128–129
yogic flying, 164
yoga and meditation centers
Acem School of Yoga, 16, 161–165, 170
Dharma Mountain, 209, 212, 216
Halvorsbøle, 165
Iyengar Yoga Institute London, 152
Lundsholm, 165
Norsk Yoga-skole *see* Acem School of Yoga
OSHO International Meditation Resort, 204, 209, 211
OSHO Risk, 209, 211
Oshodham, 209
Osho UTA, 205, 209
Schloss Aubach yoga school, 81
yoga studies, 48, 50, 97, 101
modern yoga studies, 8, 28
*Yogabhāṣya*, 96n, 120–121, 123
Yogananda, Paramahansa, 120, 275
*Yogasūtra*, 15–16, 88, 95–96, 96n, 98–100, 98n, 110, 118, 120–125, 127, 131, 161, 165, 170, 172–173
Yogendra (Manibhai Haribhai Desai), 270
Yogeśvara, 128, 131
yogi, 9, 18, 76, 101n, 120, 261–267, 270, 276
*yoginī*, 71–91
*yoginī* temple, 14, 71–72, 75, 79, 90–91
Yorke, Gerald, 16, 141, 143, 150–154
YouTube, 9, 52, 211n

Zen, 99, 214
Zimmer, Heinrich, 81

www.ingramcontent.com/pod-product-compliance
Lightning Source LLC
Chambersburg PA
CBHW062001220426
43662CB00010B/1196